IJMY

D1528434

CHINA'S INDIA WAR

BERTIL LINTNER

CHINA'S INDIA WAR

COLLISION COURSE ON THE ROOF OF THE WORLD

OXFORD
UNIVERSITY PRESS

OXFORD
UNIVERSITY PRESS

Oxford University Press is a department of the University of Oxford.
It furthers the University's objective of excellence in research, scholarship,
and education by publishing worldwide. Oxford is a registered trademark of
Oxford University Press in the UK and in certain other countries.

Published in India by
Oxford University Press
2/11 Ground Floor, Ansari Road, Daryaganj, New Delhi 110 002, India

© Oxford University Press 2018

The moral rights of the author have been asserted.

First Edition published in 2018

ISBN-13: 978-0-19-947555-1
ISBN-10: 0-19-947555-5

Typeset in Arno Pro 10.5/14.5
by Tranistics Data Technologies, New Delhi 110 044
Printed in India by Replika Press Pvt. Ltd

Contents

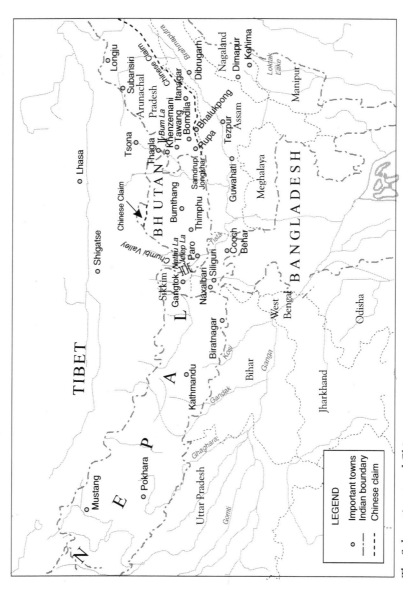

The Subcontinent and China

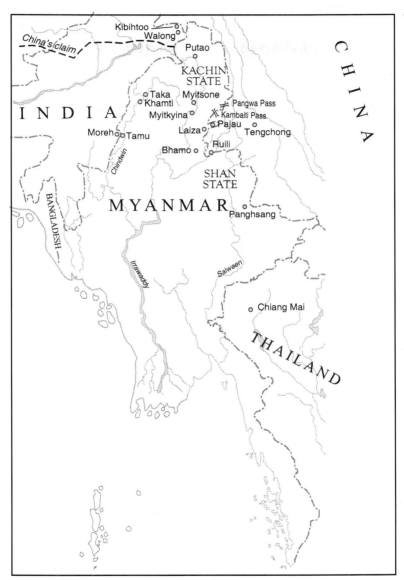

Southeast Asia and China

Introduction and Acknowledgements

My interest in the border conflict in the Himalayas goes back to 1967 when, as a 14-year-old schoolboy in Sweden, I sent a handwritten letter to the Indian embassy in Stockholm asking them for information about the problem. I was very young but already interested in international affairs. I was curious to know about the dispute and why it had led to a short but vicious war in 1962.

I received a box in the mail with a stack of White Papers that contained reproductions of letters, official statements from New Delhi as well as Beijing, and detailed foldout maps of areas claimed by both India and China. I became somewhat familiar with the geography of the region and learned about the basics of the conflict from the Indian point of view: China had launched a massive attack over the Himalayas; India was the victim of Chinese aggression.

The war ended with a devastating defeat for the Indians. But, to the surprise of many, the Chinese did not keep any territory they had captured in the east. After driving the Indian Army out of most of the disputed areas, the Chinese withdrew to the old Line of Actual Control (LAC) along the crest of the Himalayas. Indian administrators and military personnel could move back into those territories, which official Chinese maps even today show as part of the People's Republic of China. It was only in Ladakh in the west that the LAC was altered somewhat in China's favour.

Several years later, in the mid-1970s, I came across a book called *India's China War*. It was written by Neville Maxwell, an Anglo-Australian journalist, who presented a completely different view of the conflict. Maxwell argued that though it may have been China that attacked on 20 October 1962, it was India that had provoked the war. As part of a Forward Policy launched by independent India's first prime minister, Jawaharlal Nehru, Indians had established a string of armed outposts along the LAC, and even beyond it.

Maxwell based his arguments on a classified Indian intelligence report that had been leaked to him, known as the Henderson Brooks–Bhagat Report, and written by two senior Indian Army officers, Lieutenant General T.B. Henderson Brooks and Brigadier Premindra Singh Bhagat. The report supposedly backed up Maxwell's claim that the war was India's fault and China did little more than strike back to reassert its territorial claims along the Sino-Indian border. China was the largely innocent victim of Nehru's hostile policies.

Also, according to Maxwell, India had no case when it came to the actual disputed areas. Those had been included in some, but not all, maps produced unilaterally by the British India Government in the 1930s, and, more consistently in those produced in independent India after 1947. Prior to that, the northern borders of British India as shown on the official maps had essentially been identical to those on the Chinese ones, at the foot of the mountains where the Assam plains begin.

The British, Tibetan, and Chinese delegates had met at Shimla, British India's summer capital in the highlands above the northern plains, in 1913 and 1914 to sort out the status of Tibet and its borders. But the conference, it has been argued by Maxwell, Alastair Lamb, and other Western scholars, ended inconclusively, as the Chinese refused to accept the British and Tibetan proposals.

I found Maxwell's book very persuasive. It was well written, rich in details, and meticulously footnoted. Reading more about the issue, I also discovered that Maxwell's book had had a tremendous impact on studies by many Western and Asian scholars as well as policymakers.

Not surprisingly, China's leaders have heaped praise on Maxwell's book. At an official banquet in Beijing in 1971, China's Premier Zhou Enlai and Pakistan's Prime Minister Zulfikar Ali Bhutto, both rose from the head table and walked over to where the foreign correspondents were seated. Maxwell was there, and Zhou offered him a toast. 'Mister Maxwell,' Zhou said through his interpreter, 'your book has done a service to truth and China has benefited from that.'[1]

Even former US Secretary of State Henry Kissinger was impressed, as shown in his book *On China*, in which he refers to India's Forward Policy in unfavourable terms.[2] Maxwell[3] said in a 2014 interview that Kissinger had read *India's China War* in 1971, when it came out in America, and that

> it changed his thinking on China, and he pressed the book on [President] Nixon—all that's on the record now, in the transcripts of Nixon-Kissinger-Mao [Zedong] talks [1971–2]. While Kissinger was in Beijing, Zhou Enlai sent me a personal message to tell me that Kissinger had said to him, 'reading that book showed me I could do business with you people'.[4]

But the more I read about the conflict, the more I came to realize that Maxwell's version of the events leading up to the 1962 War did not stand up to any serious scrutiny. First of all, Nehru's Forward Policy, which was designed to secure the entire Sino-Indian frontier from Ladakh in the west to the North-East Frontier Agency (NEFA; an administrative unit under the government of Assam and now the Indian state of Arunachal Pradesh) in the east, was decided upon at a meeting in New Delhi on 2 November 1961, less than a year before the war. Nehru chaired the session, which was also attended by Defence Minister Vengalil Krishnan Krishna Menon, head of the Intelligence Bureau, Bhola Nath Mullik, Foreign Secretary M.J. Desai, and the then newly appointed Army Chief of Staff, General Pran Nath Thapar.

It was obviously an important meeting at the highest level. However, rather than being an aggressive measure, the instruction to the army was to 'patrol as far forward [in Aksai Chin, Ladakh] as possible from our present positions. This will be done with a view to establishing our posts which should prevent the Chinese from advancing any further and also dominating any posts which they may have already established in our territory.'[4] The new outposts that were set up in the eastern sector above the plains of Assam were manned by relatively small contingents of poorly equipped personnel, mostly from the paramilitary Assam Rifles.

Rather than India provoking China, it could be argued that it was the new communist leaders of China who had behaved aggressively after they seized power in 1949. In 1950, they sent thousands of troops to invade

Tibet, a de facto independent nation. For the first time in history, India shared a common border with China without Tibet functioning as a buffer between the two civilizations.

In the mid-1950s, the Chinese also built a highway through Aksai Chin, an area claimed by both India and China. But the area was evidently controlled by the Chinese, as it took almost a year for the Indians to discover that there was a highway connecting Xinjiang in China with Tibet, over the heights of Aksai Chin. As Aksai Chin was uninhabited except for nomadic yak herdsmen, the Chinese had been able to build the road without being detected.

But Tibet was another story. Civilians were butchered, and Buddhist monasteries and shrines destroyed. The repression that the Chinese unleashed in Tibet led to a revolt in the capital, Lhasa, in March 1959. It was crushed by the People's Liberation Army (PLA) of China, killing hundreds of monks and civilians, and sending tens of thousands of refugees to safety over the Himalayas to India. Among them was the spiritual head of the Tibetans, the 'god-king' Dalai Lama.

Before—and especially after—the Lhasa revolt, the Chinese had established military outposts all over Tibet, including in areas close to the Indian territory. New roads had also been built down to the Indian border opposite the NEFA in the east. It is not hard to arrive at the conclusion that China's own Forward Policy (although it was not called that) had been much more aggressive and assertive than India's.

Maxwell believes that the likeliest date of decision by the Chinese to attack seems to lie 'in mid-October 1962 because India has established an outpost at a place called Dhola, and escalated tension at the eastern sector of the border, which until then had been "dormant".[5] According to some maps, Dhola is located north of the McMahon Line, the border between India and Tibet, on which the delegates from the British Indian and Tibetan governments had agreed upon at the meetings in Shimla in 1914. The reason why the Chinese representative only initialled and did not sign the agreement was because China did not recognize Tibet as an independent nation—an issue that has lingered since then and has prevented normalization of the situation along the border.

It is uncertain whether Maxwell is deliberately feigning ignorance of the Chinese build-up across and along the McMahon Line, which began shortly after the Lhasa revolt in 1959, or whether he is unaware of it. No serious military analyst could conclude that the decision to go to war with India on such a massive scale as occurred on 20 October 1962—or even the fighting that took place during the days before that—could have been taken only a week or even a couple of weeks before the PLA crossed the McMahon Line in the east as well as the LAC in Ladakh, 3,000 kilometres to the west.

Chinese preparations for the war obviously began long before October 1962—and the November 1961 meeting where Nehru had outlined his Forward Policy. Even if there already were new roads and military camps in the area, tens of thousands of more PLA troops and tons of supplies, including heavy military equipment, had to be moved over some of the most difficult terrain in the world. Mao sent altogether 80,000 Chinese soldiers to Ladakh and the eastern Himalayas to attack India.[6] Supply lines had to be established and secured to the rear bases inside Tibet.

Once across the border, it was also apparent that the Chinese had detailed knowledge of the terrain, where the Indian troops were stationed, and how to best attack them. This was well before China had access to satellite imagery. Aerial surveillance from spotter planes would also have been impossible at that time. China depended entirely on human intelligence collected by its agents in the field, which would have taken time in the NEFA's rough and roadless terrain. But China's agents would also be confined largely to areas where the local population spoke languages and dialects related to Tibetan. It was nearly impossible for the Chinese to penetrate most parts of the NEFA where the local tribal population spoke other, non-Tibetan languages and dialects.

Consequently, the areas where the Chinese launched their attacks were carefully selected, and contrary to what many researchers, including those from India, have assumed, relatively limited. There is a common misperception that the PLA overran most of the NEFA and reached the lowlands at Bhalukpong, which now marks the state border between Arunachal Pradesh and Assam. Bhalukpong was abandoned and the PLA's last encounter with Indian troops was at Chakhu, a small town near Bomdila, south of Rupa. In the east, they did not go much farther than Walong, and the incursions into Subansiri and Siang in the central sector were relatively minor.

All these areas have one thing in common. They are populated by Tibetan-speaking people or people speaking languages and dialects related to Tibetan. These were also areas where human intelligence operations had been possible before the war, and where the Chinese, through their Tibetan interpreters, were able to communicate with the locals who had stayed behind once the PLA crossed into the NEFA. Although the Indian Army had retreated from all its positions in the northeastern mountains, it is significant that the PLA did not venture into areas of the NEFA populated by Mishmis, Apatanis, Nyishis, and other non-Tibetan speaking tribes, because no on-the-ground intelligence had been collected from there before the meticulously planned war. Those tribal groups would have been perceived as alien and therefore potentially hostile.

There were also other preparations that the Chinese had undertaken before the attacks in October 1962. Indian Brigadier John Dalvi, who was captured alive with some of his men on 22 October 1962 and remained a prisoner of war in China until May 1963, recorded the events in his book *Himalayan Blunder: The Angry Truth about India's Most Crushing Military Disaster*. Once captured and taken to the other side, Dalvi was able to observe how meticulously the Chinese had prepared their blitzkrieg against India. He discovered that the Chinese had erected prisoner-of-war camps to hold up to 3,000 men and found out that interpreters for all major Indian languages had been moved to Lhasa between March and May 1962. Not only had tens of thousands of troops been redeployed to the area to be acclimatized to the high altitudes of the border mountains well before the attacks took place, but thousands of Tibetan porters had also been recruited and forward dumps had been established all along the frontier. Even more tellingly, Dalvi noticed that the Chinese had built a road strong enough to hold 7-tonne vehicles all the way up to Marmang near the McMahon Line. All this, Dalvi wrote later, 'was not an accident and was certainly not decided after 8th September 1962. It was coldly and calculatingly planned by the Chinese.'[7]

While it is not inconceivable that the very final order to attack was given a week or so before the PLA swung into action (which would make sense from a tactical military point of view), it is also important to remember that the 1962 War also had nothing to do with the establishment of an Indian Army post in one of the remotest corners of the subcontinent. That could be seen as a pretext, but even then, at best, a rather flimsy one. Even Mao Zedong had told the Nepalese and the Soviet delegations before and after the war that the issue was never the McMahon Line or the border dispute. China thought that India had designs for Tibet, which, in the 1950s, was being integrated into Mao's People's Republic.[8]

At a meeting on 25 March 1959, only three weeks after the outbreak of the Lhasa uprising and as the Dalai Lama was on his way over the mountains to India, Deng Xiaoping, then a political as well as a military leader, made China's position clear: 'When the time comes, we certainly will settle accounts with them [the Indians].'[9] And, according to Bruce Riedel, one of American's leading experts on US security as well as South Asian issues, '[p]robably as early as 1959, Mao decided that he would have to take firm action against Nehru'.[10]

Zhao Weiwen, a South Asian analyst at the Ministry of State Security, China's premier intelligence agency, wrote after the war in 1962 that 'India ardently hoped to continue England's legacy in Tibet' and that Nehru himself 'harboured a sort of dark mentality'. Those factors, Zhao argued, led Nehru to demonstrate an 'irresolute attitude' in 1959. And that 'dark mentality', US-China scholar John Garver quotes him as saying, led Nehru to give free rein to 'anti-China forces' in an attempt to foment unrest in Tibet to 'throw off the jurisdiction of China's central government'.[11]

According to Garver, Mao was also present at the same meeting as Deng in March 1959, and the Chairman said that India 'was doing bad things in Tibet' and therefore had to be dealt with. Mao, however, told the assembled members of the inner circle of the Chinese leadership that China should not condemn India openly for the time being. Instead, India would be given enough rope to hang itself, *quo xingbuyi bi zibii*, literally 'to do evil deeds frequently brings ruin to the evil doer'.[12] China was waiting for the right moment to 'deal' with India. But first, it needed precise and accurate intelligence from across the border.

Findings by Nicholas Eftimiades, an expert on China's intelligence operations, reveals that the Chinese began sending agents into the NEFA and other areas two years before the military offensive. 'The PLA gathered facts on India's order of battle, terrain features, and military strategy through agents planted among road gangs, porters and muleteers working in border areas.' These agents, Eftimiades states, 'later guided PLA forces across the area during offensive operations... junior PLA commanders—disguised as Tibetans—had reconnoitred their future area of operation.'[13]

'Two years before the military offensive' began in October 1962 means at least a year before the Forward Policy was conceived, which makes it hard to argue that India's moves in the area provoked China to attack. Furthermore, the date, 20 October 1962, for the final assault after years of preparations was carefully chosen because it would coincide with the Cuban missile crisis, which the Chinese knew about beforehand through their contacts with the leaders of the Soviet Union. With Soviet missiles on Cuba, the Chinese were convinced that the USA would be too preoccupied to pay much attention to a war in the distant Himalayas.[14]

Given the increasingly hostile relations between China and the Soviet Union at the time, the Soviet leader Nikita Khrushchev did not himself tell Mao that he was sending missiles to Cuba, and, as Riedel, writes in his book: 'Nor did Mao tell Moscow that he was going to war with India until two days before the attack.'[15] However, according to British analyst and writer Roderick MacFarquhar, China's Moscow ambassador, Liu Xiao, reportedly 'informed Beijing in advance about Khrushchev's missile plan although the Chinese probably knew about it anyway, for they had excellent sources of information in Cuba.'[16]

Chinese intelligence gathering in the NEFA may even have begun well before 1959, the year Deng Xiaoping said that 'accounts' would have to be 'settled' with India. According to a 1952 intelligence report, it had then just been detected that Tibetan monks from a dissident sect, not loyal to the Dalai Lama, had been sent into India 'as spies and agitators'. The same sect had, the report also stated, 'acted as their [the Chinese] fifth-column during the [1950] occupation of Tibet.'[17]

It is also clear that China was prepared for a long conflict with India. But after 1962, it would be a proxy war, fought by rebel forces inside India. The seemingly unlikely partner would be the Nagas, a predominantly Christian tribe living in the hills of the easternmost part of India. Led by Angami Zapu Phizo, they had declared their independence on 14 August 1947, a day ahead of India, and had taken up arms against the government in New Delhi. Almost immediately, they received military support from India's arch-rival, Pakistan. Naga rebels were also permitted to set up camps in the eastern part of Pakistan, now Bangladesh, from where they launched raids into India. Phizo himself had continued from East Pakistan via Switzerland to Britain, where, from his exile in Kent, he stayed in touch with his comrades in the Naga Hills.

In June 1962, one of the Naga rebel commanders, Mowu Gwizan, stopped over in Karachi on his way to London to see Phizo. While in Karachi, Mowu's Pakistani hosts introduced him to a 'Chinese friend', who promised the Nagas aid and assistance.[18] As a result of that meeting, the Nagas assembled a force of 132 men who eventually set off from the Naga Hills in October 1966. They trekked for months through the jungles of northern Myanmar and, in January 1967, reached Yunnan, China, where they received political and military training. The first batch of Nagas returned to India at the end of 1967 with modern Chinese-made assault rifles, machine guns, and rocket launchers. During the decade 1967–76, more than 700 Naga rebels went to China for training and returned, heavily armed, to fight the Indian Army. After the Nagas, Mizo rebels, also from the eastern border mountains, trekked to China, where they too received military training and went back to their hills with Chinese weapons. In the 1970s, a group of rebels from Manipur received political and military training by the Chinese in Tibet.

Before the 1962 War, the PLA had gained some useful experience in launching a decisive assault into a neighbouring country. From November 1960 to February 1961, thousands of Chinese troops crossed the border into Myanmar to attack nationalist Chinese Kuomintang (KMT) forces, which, after their defeat in the Chinese Civil War that ended in 1949, had retreated into the remote, northeastern mountains of that country. From those cross-border sanctuaries, they had carried out raids into China. That operation, codenamed the Mekong River Operation in Myanmar, and the Burma [Myanmar] Border Surveying and Security Operation in China, was carried out in co-operation with the Myanmar Army, which also wanted to get rid of the intruders.

But the campaign was only partly successful. Most of the KMT troops managed to escape the onslaught and retreat down to the Thai border, while the PLA's weaknesses were exposed, as they had to fight in an unfamiliar terrain and environment. Although the units that took part in the operation were not the same as those that attacked India in 1962, it is reasonable to assume that China's military strategists learned from their mistakes and, therefore, a year later were able to conduct a more victorious campaign in the Himalayas.[19]

But then, what about the Henderson Brooks–Bhagat Report? It remains classified but I managed to get a copy of it in 2013, passed on to me by a senior Indian journalist. A year later, Maxwell decided to make it public. He posted a copy of the report as a PDF file on the internet, and the Hong Kong daily *South China Morning Post* reported on it under the headline, 'Neville Maxwell discloses document revealing that India provoked China into 1962 border war'. The article went on to make the astonishing assertion that 'Journalist's Snowden-like revelations about 1962 war boost China's claims on peaceful rise'.[20]

One would need to have a lot of imagination to conclude from the Henderson Brooks–Bhagat Report that India was the aggressor and China the aggrieved party in 1962. The question of who attacked whom, or determining who was responsible for the war, was not even within the scope of the enquiry, which had been set up to look into four specific aspects of the war that could explain the Indian defeat: possible shortcomings in training and equipment; the system of command; the physical fitness of the troops; and the capacity of commanders at all levels to influence their subordinates.[21]

In essence, the Henderson Brooks–Bhagat Report states little more than that India was ill prepared for the war and therefore unable to withstand the Chinese assault over the Himalayas. It also points out weaknesses in

India's command structure, and the lack of effective co-operation between the government and the military. It certainly does not say that India was responsible for the war, nor does it question the Forward Policy per se.[22]

After Maxwell made the report public and it became clear that it was not, after all, that exciting, many Indian journalists and researchers began to speculate whether there was also a second report or an appendix to the first which would reveal more. But, to the disappointment of many, there is not as much to the report as Maxwell and others have claimed. Or, as B.G. Verghese, a former assistant editor of *The Times of India*, wrote in 2012, 'The report brings out the political and military naiveté, muddle, contradictions and in-fighting that prevailed and failures of planning and control. There is no military secret to protect in the Henderson Brooks report; only political and military ego and folly to hide.'[23] When I began to scrutinize the footnotes in *India's China War*, I also found discrepancies between what Maxwell wrote and what the sources in the footnotes actually said.

After reading Maxwell, I turned to the writings of the British academic Alastair Lamb, who has written profusely about the border disputes between India and China, and India and Pakistan. While Lamb's books and articles are much more scholarly than Maxwell's writings on the border issue and the 1962 War, there are serious shortcomings and justifiable criticisms to make even there. Leo E. Rose, professor of Political Science at the University of California, Berkeley, wrote in his 1968 review of Lamb's monumental, two-volume work *The McMahon Line: A Study in the Relations Between India, China, and Tibet, 1904 to 1914*, 'The line between scholarly objectivity and special pleading is per-force a narrower one when the subject is a current political controversy, as this study amply indicates'. There is no doubt, Rose wrote, that Lamb's works

constitute a statement of the Chinese position in the current dispute with India over their eastern Himalayan border. This is not unwelcome. The Chinese do have a case, and Mr. Lamb presents it in much clearer and persuasive terms than the Peking [Beijing] Government. The non-specialist reader, unfamiliar with this little-known border area, should be fully aware of the author's particular bias in evaluating his analysis of events and conclusions.[24]

In my view, Lamb's near-obsession with map details and minor issues relating to border demarcation also clouds the broader, geopolitical picture. The more I studied the issue, the clearer it became that it was indeed much more than a border dispute—and that the Chinese never intended to hold on to the territory they captured during the war, areas they claimed as theirs.

The Chinese withdrawal from the occupied areas in 1962 has actually puzzled many military historians and others, who have speculated that it was the approaching winter or the long supply lines from the rear that had halted the advance. Despite those difficulties, the Chinese could actually have pushed down even further, to Assam proper and the Brahmaputra plain, where the weather would not have been a problem and food was in abundance. They could easily have captured Tezpur, a town just south of the mountains with an excellent airport, which the Indian military and the local administration had wholly abandoned.

The development of the Chinese air force began in earnest after the Korean War in the early 1950s, and by the time of the war with India, China had thousands of aircraft, including transport planes. Some were imported from the Soviet Union, while others were copies manufactured under licence in China.[25] Although there is no indication that the Chinese in 1962 had deployed aircraft to Tibet (which, at that time, had only five operational airports), or that the People's Liberation Air Force was suffering from an acute shortage of pilots, US intelligence believed that '[i]f the Chinese Air Force were able to operate from Burma, or were able to seize airfields in the Brahmaputra Valley, its capability would be greatly enhanced'.[26] It would also have been possible to use airfields in China's southwestern provinces, Yunnan and Sichuan, for operations against India, the American report suggested.

But it was never China's intention to conquer and keep territory. That was not part of the plan when the Chinese leadership decided to attack India. Geopolitically, China had made an important point, and that was sufficient. Nehru, in the 1950s a proponent of non-alignment, was humiliated and was no longer a leading voice among the then newly independent nations in Asia and Africa, as he had been since the historic conference in Bandung, Indonesia, in 1955. After the 1962 War, it was China rather than

India, that became the leader of the Third World—an entirely new concept that China's omnipotent Chairman Mao Zedong had introduced to replace the old idea of non-alignment. The leader of the Third World would, of course, be Mao's China.

The timing of the decision by the Chinese leadership to 'settle accounts' with the Indians, to quote Deng, and to make use of all their preparations for war, must also be understood in the context of internal problems in China at the time. In 1958, Mao had initiated the disastrous Great Leap Forward to modernize China. By 1961, anywhere between 17 and 45 million people had died as a result of Mao's policies, which had caused a famine rather than, as intended, any rapid industrialization.

Mao was discredited and, very likely, on his way out. He must have felt he had to regain power—and that the best way to do that would be to unify the nation and especially the armed forces against an outside enemy. India was a 'soft' target because it had, in 1959, granted the Dalai Lama asylum after he had fled there in the wake of the failed uprising against the Chinese occupation of Tibet. The Tibetan god-king had been allowed to set up a government in exile in McLeodganj in northern India. And then there was the issue of a border that China did not recognize.

MacFarquhar writes in his comprehensive history of the origins of China's Cultural Revolution that there is always a close relationship between China's domestic and foreign policy. In Mao's worldview, the Chinese revolution was part of a global series of events, with interaction both ways. However, MacFarquhar states that the connection between Chinese military actions and domestic politics is more obscure. According to him, 'China's involvement in the Korean War, which broke out in 1950, enabled the Chinese Communist Party's leaders to launch a patriotic campaign to solidify the people behind them'.[27]

The Korean War broke out in 1950, the year after Mao's communists had seized power in China, and lasted until 1953. At that time, it was imperative for China's new rulers to consolidate their grip on power and get support for a regime that large segments of the population may not necessarily be in favour of. Now, hundreds of thousands marched in anti-American demonstrations, and it is estimated that in the space of six

xxii   Introduction and Acknowledgements

months, in the wake of the Korean War, 710,000 people, who had been
branded counter-revolutionaries and suspected of links to the old regime,
were executed or driven to suicide.[28]

The situation after the disastrous Great Leap Forward was somewhat
similar. A successful war would be a godsend for Mao and those who still
supported him. Whether or not a direct connection between the war
and his return to power can be positively verified by internal Chinese
documentation, the fact is that he did manage to regain control of the Party
and the state after the 1962 War. Several of his enemies were also purged
while some remained. So, in 1966, Mao launched his Great Proletarian
Cultural Revolution, during which all his political rivals were eliminated
and he was elevated to a god-like status in China.

When taking into account China's regional ambitions and domestic
politics at the time, it should be clear to every serious observer and analyst
that the border dispute was only an excuse for launching the 1962 War.
But, at the same time, it has to be remembered that China's attitude has
consistently been that it is always right, and any attempt to challenge its
claims, whatever they might be, is regarded as a 'provocation'. Treaties that
China for one reason or another does not like are deemed 'unequal', and
therefore not to be honoured.

As a journalist specializing in regional security issues in Asia, it is also
not hard for me to detect parallels between the Sino-Indian border dispute
and territorial disputes in the South China Sea. China may well be more
open and less ideologically rigid today than it was in 1962, but its behaviour towards its neighbours remains the same.

China never controlled or ruled over any of the areas in India's
northeast, which it today claims and includes in its maps, and the situation
in the Spratly Islands in the South China Sea is strikingly similar. China,
with a large U-shape on its maps, lays claim to virtually all of the Spratly
Islands, which today are claimed in whole or in part also by Taiwan, the
Philippines, Vietnam, Malaysia, and Brunei. And, according to Beijing,
those countries, not China, are behaving 'provocatively'.

Chinese spokesmen have asserted that fifteenth and sixteenth century
documents from the Ming Dynasty show that China ruled over the entire
South China Sea. But nothing could be further from the truth. The Ming

emperors paid only scant attention to maritime ventures. During China's brief historical stint as a sea power in the fifteenth century, an explorer called Zheng sailed with his fleet to South and Southeast Asia, the Indian subcontinent, the Arab peninsula, and even as far as the coast of East Africa. The detailed accounts and maps, which were compiled by Zheng's aide Ma Huan, list more than 700 place names in Southeast Asia and the Indian Ocean, including remote islands in the Andamans, the Nicobars, Maldives, and Lakshadweep.[29]

Chinese cartographers were aware of the existence and location of the Spratlys, and Ma Huan mentions them as well, but not in such great detail as other places he documents in his logbooks. The reason is quite simple: the Spratlys are not islands, but treacherous shoals and underwater reefs, which the ancient navies sailed around to avoid being shipwrecked. But that has not prevented China from making its spurious assertions—and, most recently, from constructing artificial islands on top of those shoals and reefs to, literally speaking, cement its claims. Any opposing view would be branded as an interference in China's internal affairs.

In July 2016, the Permanent Court of Arbitration in The Hague, in response to a complaint lodged by the Philippines, found that China has no credible 'historic rights' over the South China Sea in accordance with the UN Convention on the Law of the Sea (UNCLOS). It said that there was no evidence that China ever exercised such rights of an exclusive sovereign nature. The government in Beijing responded angrily, calling the ruling a 'farce' and declared that China's territorial and marine rights in the seas would not be affected by the ruling.[30] A strongly worded editorial in the official newspaper *Renmin Ribao* ('the people's daily') asserted that the tribunal had 'ignored basic truths' and 'trampled' on international laws and therefore 'the Chinese government and the Chinese people firmly [oppose] the ruling and will neither acknowledge it nor accept it'.[31]

There may not be another war in the Himalayas, but China's similarly intransigent attitude and behaviour in the South China Sea could well lead to a more serious regional conflict there than what we are experiencing today. Then, there is the question of China as the world's biggest dam-builder, with rivers flowing from Tibet and Yunnan into other countries downstream—and dams being built without even consulting those countries. There are even plans to divert Tibet's water on a massive scale to China proper.

Tibet, as Maptia, a Western NGO, pointed out,

> is unique in the world as a mass provider of fresh water, via rivers, to China and to a dozen nations downstream. Tibet is the source of major head-waters for the rivers of Asia, and additionally provides key tributaries or feeders for other rivers (such as the Ganges). There is no parallel to this situation anywhere else on the planet. We only have one Tibet: there are no backups, no second chances.[32]

And is the de facto independent island of Taiwan really a part of China, as Beijing claims? Again, China would consider any opinions on these issues other than its own an interference in its internal affairs.

Given this broader perspective of today's geopolitical realities, it makes sense to study further the origin and development of the conflict in the Himalayas as well. China and India remain powerful regional rivals, and the animosity between the two countries began in the Himalayas more than half a century ago.

My research into that border dispute took me to Arunachal Pradesh, Sikkim, and northern West Bengal in India; to Kachin State, Shan State, and Sagaing Division in northern and northeastern Myanmar; China's Yunnan province; Nepal; and Bhutan. I have also spent time at the British Library in London, whose India Office Records are a treasure trove of information. For me, as a journalist, to get to Tibet would have been impossible, but I have studied Chinese documents and maps in detail to find out on what background and historical records Beijing is basing its claims. Numerous people have helped me along the way, but there are just too many to be mentioned, and given the sensitivity of the issue, most of them requested to remain anonymous.

Even so, I would like to thank Dorjee Khandu Thongdok in Rupa, who had to flee when the Chinese attacked his town and later wrote a book about it; two elderly Tibetans I met in Tawang who remembered the Chinese occupation of their town in 1962; a local villager in Walong who told me about events in that area during the war; an elderly Tibetan in Darjeeling

who knows more about conditions along the border than anyone else
I have met; and local officials in Gangtok, Sikkim. In Siliguri, northern
West Bengal, I met Abhijeet Mazumdar, son of the late Naxalite firebrand
Charu Mazumdar, and I have on numerous previous occasions met and
interviewed Naga, Mizo, and Manipuri rebels from India's northeast who
underwent training in China in the 1960s and 1970s. I have also met and
interviewed rebels from the United Liberation Front of Assam, among
them their top leaders Arabinda Rajkhowa and Paresh Barua. In Nepal, I
met veteran journalist and author Kanak Mani Dixit and others from the
local media as well as researchers from international entities who study
violent conflicts in the region. I also visited refugee camps in southern
Nepal, where ethnic Nepalese from Bhutan have been sheltered since the
early 1990s. In Bhutan, I was able to discuss China-related issues with several government officials, who, however, preferred not to be named. Julian
Gearing, an expert on Tibet, helped with the unenviable task of guiding
me through the maze of Tibetan sects, an often bewildering aspect to the
outside observer of the Buddhist world of the Himalayas. I am also thank-
ful to Alastair Lamb, whom I met when I was doing research at the British
Library in January 2016. Although I disagree with his presentations and
conclusions, Lamb proved to be generous with information and even gave
me some of his books. I never tried to contact Neville Maxwell, but apart
from reading *India's China War*, I also read his other, lesser-known book,
China's Borders: Settlements and Conflicts as well as several articles by him
that have appeared over the years in the *Economic and Political Weekly*.[33]

It is, of course, impossible to be completely accurate when it comes
to a heated and controversial issue like the dispute between India and
China, with its many conflicting and contradictory accounts of history
and current events. But I have, to the best of my ability, presented here
a comprehensive and nuanced picture of the conflict; why and how it
began; what it became; and the meaning of it all in the realities of today's
Asia. Any factual errors are entirely my own, for which my sources,
written as well as oral, should not be blamed.

Notes

1. Debasish Roy Chowdhury, 'Neville Maxwell discloses document revealing that India provoked China into 1962 border war', *South China Morning Post*, 31 March 2014, available at http://www.scmp.com/news/asia/article/1461099/neville-maxwells-revelation-reveals-india-was-hiding-nothing-over-its-1962 (accessed on 3 April 2016).

2. Henry Kissinger, *On China* (London: Penguin, 2012), pp. 187–9.

3. Debasish Roy Chowdhury, 'Neville Maxwell: The full transcript', *South China Morning Post*, 31 March 2014, available at http://www.scmp.com/news/china/article/1461102/neville-maxwell-interview-full-transcript (accessed on 3 April 2016).

4. Bruce Riedel, *JFK's Forgotten Crisis: Tibet, the CIA, and the Sino-IndianWar* (New Delhi: HarperCollins India, 2016), p. 88.

5. Neville Maxwell, *India's China War* (Harmondsworth, Middlesex: Penguin, 1972), p. 380.

6. Eric S. Margolis, *War at the Top of the World* (New York: Routledge, 2001), p. 229.

7. John P. Dalvi, *Himalayan Blunder: the Angry Truth About India's Most Crushing Military Disaster* (Dehra Dun: Natraj Publishers, 2010) pp. 152–4.

8. Riedel, *JFK's Forgotten Crisis*, p. 98.

9. Quoted in 'The Politico-Diplomatic Prelude Part-2', P.J.S. Sandhu, Bhavna Tripathi, Ranjit Singh Kalha, Bharat Kumar, G.G. Dwivedi, Vinay Shankar (eds.), *1962: A View from the Other Side of the Hill* (New Delhi: Vij Books India, 2015) p. 24.

10. Riedel, *JFK's Forgotten Crisis*, p. 101.

11. John Garver, 'China's Decision for War with India in 1962', Alastair Iain Johnston and Robert S. Ross (eds.), *New Directions in the Study of China's Foreign Policy* (Stanford: Stanford University Press, 2006), pp. 90–1.

12. For Garver's excellent study of the 1962 War, see his essay 'China's Decision for War with India in 1962', p. 93.

13. Nicholas Eftimiades, *Chinese Intelligence Operations* (Ilford, Essex: Frank Cass, 1994), pp. 90–91.

14. Riedel, *JFK's Forgotten Crisis*, pp. 105–7, 114, 119.

15. Riedel, *JFK's Forgotten Crisis*, p. 107.

16. Roderick MacFarquhar, *The Origins of the Cultural Revolution 3: The Coming of the Cataclysm 1961–1966* (Oxford and New York: Oxford University Press and Columbia University Press, 1997), p. 317.

17. 'A Tibetan Communist Plot', Kenneth de Courcy (ed.) *Intelligence Digest: A Review of World Affairs*, New York, October 1952, p. 4.
18. Author's interview with Mowu Gwizan, Kohima, 18 October 1985.
19. For an account of the Mekong River Operation, and a list of the PLA units that participated in the campaign, see this unusually detailed account in Wikipedia: 'Campaign at the China–Burma border (1960–61)', available at https://en.wikipedia.org/wiki/Campaign_at_the_China%E2%80%93Burma_border (accessed on 15 April 2016).
20. Chowdhury, 'Neville Maxwell discloses document revealing that India provoked China into 1962 border war', 2014.
21. V.K. Singh, *Leadership in the Indian Army: Biographies of Twelve Soldiers* (New Delhi: Sage Publications, 2011), p. 280.
22. See the Henderson Brooks–Bhagat Report, available at http://www.indiandefencereview.com/wp-content/uploads/2014/03/TopSecretdocuments2.pdf (accessed on 15 April 2016). For a reference to the Forward Policy, see p. 8 and p. 10, where it is stated that 'it is obvious that politically the "Forward Policy" was desirable and presumably the eviction of the Chinese from Ladakh must always be the eventual aim'.
23. B.G. Verghese, '50 Years after 1962: A Political Memoir', *South Asia Monitor*, 23 September 2012, available at http://pragati.nationalinterest.in/2012/10/50-years-after-1962/ (accessed on 15 March 2017).
24. Leo E. Rose, 'The McMahon Line: A Study of the Relations Between India, China and Tibet, 1904 to 19145', *Pacific Affairs*, Vol. 41, No 1 (Spring), 1968, pp. 132–3.
25. Li Xiaobing, *A History of the Modern Chinese Army* (Lexington: The University Press of Kentucky, 2007), pp. 109–10, 125.
26. 'The Chinese Air Threat', P.J.S. Sandhu, Bhavna Tripathi, Ranjit Singh Kalha, Bharat Kumar, G.G. Dwivedi, Vinay Shankar (eds.), *1962: A View from the Other Side of the Hill* (New Delhi: Vij Books India, 2015), p. 119.
27. MacFarquhar, *The Origins of the Cultural Revolution 3*, p. 297.
28. Philip Short, *Mao: A Life* (London: Hodder & Stoughton, 1999), pp. 435–6.
29. Ma Huan, *Ying-hai Sheng-lan: The Overall Survey of the Ocean's Shores* (Bangkok: White Lotus, 1997). This is a reprint of a work compiled in 1935 by the Chinese scholar Feng Ch'eng-chun.
30. The ruling can be found at https://www.documentcloud.org/documents/2165479-phl-prc-press-release.html (accessed on 18 September 2016). See also Tom Phillips, Oliver Holmes, and Owen Bowcott, 'Beijing rejects

tribunal's ruling in South China Sea case', *The Guardian*, 12 July 2016, available at https://www.theguardian.com/world/2016/jul/12/philippines-wins-south-china-sea-case-against-china (accessed on 20 July 2016).

31. Phillips et al., 'Beijing rejects tribunal's ruling in South China Sea case'. The response from the Chinese Ministry of Foreign Affairs is available at http://www.fmprc.gov.cn/mfa_eng/zxxx_662805/t1379492.shtml (accessed on 20 July 2016).

32. See https://maptia.com/michaelbuckley/stories/stealing-tibet-s-rivers (accessed on 30 May 2016).

33. These books and articles are listed in the Select Bibliography.

1

The Improbable Border Dispute

The Bumla Pass, high up in the eastern Himalayas and 5,000 metres above sea level, sits on the crest of the craggy mountain ranges that separate the Indian subcontinent from the Tibetan high plateau. Sharp, even taller peaks rise in the distance along the watershed that today forms the LAC between India and China. The air is thin, there are no villages in the vicinity, and the only local people who venture up here are semi-nomadic yak herdsmen. They cross freely between Chinese- and Indian-controlled territory with their beasts during the grazing season, which is in summer when the slopes of the mountains are covered in grass instead of snow.

Other outsiders are not allowed to visit Bumla without special permits issued by Indian authorities. This is a heavily militarized area and nearly all the vehicles on the narrow road that winds its way up to the pass are army trucks and jeeps. On the southern edge of the pass stands a cluster of solid buildings: a meeting hall, observation towers, and guard posts. A sign has been erected to show where the area under Indian control ends. It displays an Indian and a Chinese flag and the text 'Two Old Neighbouring Civilisations. India, China, Partners in Progress'.[1] Bumla is one of the few places along the Sino-Indian boundary where army officers from both countries meet to discuss issues of mutual concern, or to celebrate each other's national days. When that happens, the Chinese put up some tents, which are dismantled as soon as the events are over. There are no solid structures immediately on the other side of the pass, because that would, for the Chinese, be tantamount to recognizing that the crest of the mountains is the official border between the two countries.

This is the McMahon Line, which was named after Henry McMahon, the chief British negotiator at Shimla in 1913–14, and recognized by Britain and Tibet, but not by successive Chinese governments. And it was here at Bumla that one of the most decisive battles was fought during the 1962 War.

Fighting erupted early on the morning of 23 October 1962 as Chinese forces north of the pass unleashed a massive artillery barrage on the Indian side. Explosions lit up the sky and echoed between the mountains. At daybreak, the Chinese had overrun the nearest Indian position, a small outpost manned by 30 soldiers from the paramilitary Assam Rifles; 17 men lay dead, and the 13 survivors were captured alive. A somewhat stronger Sikh regiment, which was based a distance away from the actual pass, put up fierce resistance—until they ran out of ammunition and had to withdraw.[2]

With a total strength of six infantry regiments and an independent battalion, the victorious forces of China's PLA could begin their advance without much hindrance. The Indians had hundreds of troops in the area, but they were poorly equipped and supply lines from the plains of Assam in the south were long and hazardous. Only jeeps and convoys of pack animals could make it all the way to Tawang, the main town in the northwestern corner of what was then called the North-East Frontier Agency (NEFA), an administrative unit under the state government of Assam, and now is the Indian state of Arunachal Pradesh. There was no resistance at Tawang, as the Indian Army had evacuated the town during the night after the attack on Bumla. Tawang fell into the hands of the PLA on 24 October 1962.

The Chinese assault on Indian positions along the frontier had actually begun on 19 October, with the bombardments of Indian army positions northwest of Tawang followed by massive artillery barrages and infantry attacks on 20 October at Thaglaridge, west of Bumla and near the border with Bhutan. On the same day and at the very same time in the morning, other Chinese regiments attacked Indian outposts in Ladakh in the north-western corner of Kashmir at the other end of the Indian subcontinent. Thus, the war was not confined to the NEFA, though the losses were the heaviest on the eastern front. At Thagla, the PLA wiped out almost the entire Indian Seventh Brigade and captured its commander, Brigadier John Dalvi. Unable to withstand the onslaught of the stronger and more heavily armed units of the PLA, India's defences in the western part of NEFA were in disarray.

Getting supplies to their troops was not as big a problem for the Chinese as it was for the Indians because of the roads that had been built years before the attack. Several of those led right down to the LAC, opposite the NEFA in the east. In the west, there was the highway that the Chinese had built through Aksai Chin connecting Xinjiang with Tibet.

After the Indian defences near Thagla and Bumla had been obliterated, the PLA was able to march down to Tawang. At 3,048 metres above sea level, Tawang is still high up in the mountains, but in a relatively fertile valley well below the much higher peaks and passes along the frontier. As soon as Tawang was captured and the surrounding area secured by the PLA, thousands of porters, construction workers—and bulldozers and heavy machinery—poured across Bumla. Working round the clock in three shifts, it took the Chinese only 13 days to construct a road from the pass to Tawang, a distance of nearly 40 kilometres through extremely difficult and mountainous terrain. The PLA trucks now rolled into Tawang, which now became a major supply base for the Chinese. Then they pushed south, and the strategic Sela Pass, 78 kilometres south of Tawang, was in Chinese hands after a fierce battle with Indian troops. On 19 November, the Chinese juggernaut reached the town of Bomdila, 170 kilometres south of Tawang. The Chinese were now only a few days' march from Assam and the fertile plains around the River Brahmaputra.

By that time, the war had spread as Chinese troops had crossed into the far eastern corner of the NEFA. On 22 October, the Chinese launched an attack on an Indian outpost at Kibihtoo, north of the small town of Walong near the border with Myanmar. After a lull in the fighting, the PLA resumed its advance on 13 November, and Walong was overrun three days later. The

PLA units also attacked and captured some villages in what the Indians then called the Subansiri and Siang Frontier Divisions immediately south of the Line of Control (LoC) in the central sector of the NEFA.

There was total panic on the Indian side. Outgunned and overwhelmed by a superior force, India's defences in the NEFA had crumbled and Indian soldiers were in retreat from the entire territory. Many believed that the PLA would march on to capture Assam with its oil fields, tea gardens, jute plantations, and other riches. Even the garrison town of Tezpur in the Brahmaputra Valley was evacuated as the Indians awaited what seemed to be the inevitable outcome of the debacle in the Himalayas.

The attacks were not confined to the Indian positions along the eastern border, between the NEFA and Tibet; a remote Indian Army outpost in Ladakh's Aksai Chin area in the northeastern corner of the state of Jammu and Kashmir was also attacked. Ten minutes later, Chinese ground forces commenced their attack, and that outpost was overrun. According to Indian military sources, the defenders had no artillery pieces or mortars, only small arms and open trenches to fight from.[3] Not a single Indian soldier at that company outpost escaped alive or unhurt. Of the 68 men defending the position, 36 were killed, and the others were wounded or taken prisoner.

Following this initial success in Ladakh, the Chinese advanced, launching multidirectional attacks from the north, south, and east on other Indian positions in the area. Chinese intelligence gathering in the area prior to the attacks had been meticulous. Having spent several years in Tibet, occupying the country, and preparing for a war against India, the Chinese were also acclimatized to the high altitude, and they were evidently trained in how to make breaches in the half-constructed network of Indian defences.[4]

By the end of October, the Chinese had occupied most of the strategic Kailash Range that rises from the eastern flank of the upper Indus Valley, the strategic Kongka Pass, and the area down to Pangong Lake, an endorheic lake with saline water situated at an altitude of more than 4,000 metres. Four battalions of Indian troops had entirely been wiped out and others were in retreat from their positions in the highlands. Then followed a lull in the fighting while the Chinese reorganized their forces, strengthened their defence lines, and brought in more supplies. On 18 November, they were ready to strike again, and multidirectional attacks were used here as elsewhere on the battlefront to encircle and crush the Indian outposts that remained in the area.

But then, on 19 November, the same day as the PLA reached Bomdila, China's Premier Zhou Enlai called Purnendyu Kumar Banerjee, the Indian chargé d'affaires in Beijing, to his residence. Zhou informed him that, on 21 November, the Chinese would declare a ceasefire and begin to withdraw all their troops to positions 20 kilometres north of the LAC. The Chinese stuck to their pledge, and the war was over. Within a couple of weeks, the PLA was back on the Chinese-controlled side of the mountains.

The Indians were stunned, and so were many political and military observers all over the world. What had prompted the Chinese to attack and what had caused such a short but extremely bloody and vicious war? According to Chinese records, Indian casualties stood at 4,897 dead and wounded and 3,968 captured alive. The Ministry of Defence in New Delhi puts India's losses at 1,383 soldiers killed, 1,047 wounded, 1,696 missing in action, and the same number of soldiers captured alive as the Chinese had announced, at 3,968. The PLA casualties were considerably lower, with 722 killed and 1,697 wounded, according to Chinese sources. No Chinese soldier was captured alive, which, as US military historian Larry Wortzel and Chinese scholar Cheng Feng point, out is 'a rarity in the history of warfare'.[5]

But the Chinese attack should not have come as a total surprise. Chinese encroachments into what the Indians considered their territory had begun as early as the mid-1950s. Apart from finding out, in 1957, that the Chinese had built a 179-kilometre road through Aksai Chin in the west, the first skirmishes on the Sino-Indian border occurred as early as 25 August 1959, when a Chinese patrol attacked an Indian position at Longju on the NEFA frontier. Then, on 21 October of the same year, a fire fight broke out at Kongka La in Ladakh. The first incident, at Longju, resulted in two casualties on the Indian side and at Kongka La, 17 Indian soldiers were killed in what China claimed was an act of 'self-defence'. The Indians, on the other hand, said that their troops had been subjected to 'sudden and aggressive firing' from the Chinese side.[6]

The key to understanding the origins of the 1962 War, and the conflict and rivalry between India and China, lies in taking a critical look at the writing on the sign at Bumla. Despite what it says about the 'Old Neighbouring Civilisations', which are supposed to be 'Partners in Progress', it is hard to imagine two cultures that are more different than India and China in terms of history, social structure, and political culture.

The Indian kingdoms and empires, which have waxed and waned in the subcontinent over the centuries, have always been immensely diverse, with a multitude of languages and different religions. And most of these languages have their own alphabets, all different from one another. Even today, 'unity in diversity' is what holds India together. No single religious, linguistic, or political group can claim monopoly on power, and that is why democracy has survived in India.

China, on the other hand, has a long history of imperial rule under one dominant ethnic group, the Han Chinese, which has, over the centuries, subdued and, in some instances, absorbed, other, minor groups of people. It is true that the last imperial dynasty in China, the Qing, was Manchu and that the country was somewhat multicultural in character during its reign (which lasted from 1644 to 1912) than it had been under previous emperors, possibly with the exceptions of the Liao, Jin, and Mongol dynasties, which were also non-Han. But while retaining some of their own ethnic identity, the Manchu elite also acquired all the trappings of traditional Chinese rulers. They spoke standard Chinese and the Manchu language almost died out in China in the nineteenth century. Even so, Dr Sun Yat-sen, one of the founders of the anti-Qing movement, wrote in 1904 that the goal of the struggle was 'to expel the Tatar [i.e., Manchu] barbarians'.[7] In 1912, the Qing Dynasty was overthrown and Dr Sun became the first president of the Republic of China. For decades after that, many families of Manchu descent tried hard to conceal their heritage and to conform to the Han Chinese customs and culture.[8]

Local dialects may differ in China, and several, among them Cantonese, Hakka, and Fujianese, are not mutually intelligible and differ from 'standard' Chinese, but the writing system, based on logograms and not on a phonetic alphabet, remains essentially the same all over the country. As for its political culture, China has long been dominated by authoritarian schools of thought, be it Confucianism or Communism in the past, or today's post-Communist totalitarian capitalism.

This is not to say that Chinese society would necessarily be incompatible with democratic values. Taiwan is a shining example of a country with a Chinese culture that has managed to shake off authoritarianism and become one of Asia's most vibrant democracies. But mainland China during the days of confrontation with India in the 1960s was a brutal dictatorship with a centuries-long history of authoritarian rule, and that has not changed even though a remarkable economic liberalization has taken place since the 'capitalist roader' Deng Xiaoping introduced his free-market reforms in the 1980s. There is a democratic opposition in China today, but it is still small and largely limited to dissident intellectuals.

When India became independent in 1947, it maintained many institutions that had been introduced during British rule such as an elected parliament and a professional judiciary. After the British left, those institutions were developed into fully democratic entities, not dominated by a foreign power. India became a parliamentary democracy with an abundance of political parties. The Indian Army, too, although now commanded exclusively by Indian officers, is steeped in the encrusted regimental traditions of the British era. The command structure remains the same, its ethnically based units have been retained and new ones have been added, and, most importantly, civilian control of the armed forces has been the rule since independence.

The British Indian Army had fought alongside other British forces in Asia and Europe during World War II, while soldiers from independent India took part in the United Nations' peace keeping missions in the Middle East in the mid-1950s and in the Congo in the early 1960s. A paramedical unit was sent to Korea in 1950 and Lieutenant General Kodendera Subayya Thimayya served as the Chairman of the Neutral Nations Repatriation Commission set up by the UN when hostilities there were over. Timmy to his friends and even the general public, he was trained at the British military academy at Sandhurst and was the only Indian to command an infantry brigade in the British Indian Army during World War II. Thimayya was awarded the prestigious Distinguished Service Order by the British Crown and was also mentioned in dispatches for his outstanding record during the war against the Japanese in Asia.

In 1954, India sent an infantry battalion to Indochina—Vietnam, Laos, and Cambodia—and supporting staff for ceasefire monitoring and repatriation of prisoners of war. Never involved in combat, their duty was to supervise the implementation of the 1954 Geneva Accord for peace in Indochina, and the Indians remained there until 1973, working together with personnel from Canada and Poland.[9]

On the home front, the Indian Army fought a bitter war with Pakistan over Kashmir immediately after independence in 1947, and armed security forces were used to integrate some former princely states, which were reluctant to join independent India. In the mid-1950s, the army was sent in to quell a separatist rebellion in the Naga Hills near the eastern border with Myanmar and became involved in a long drawn-out war with tribal guerrillas in the area. In 1961, the army also took over Goa, Daman, and Diu, three Portuguese enclaves on India's western coast. Then came the 1962 conflict with China, and several more wars fought with Pakistan since the first armed confrontation in 1947.

The Indian Army has, by and large, remained a professional force that has stayed clear of involvement in politics. Its main objective has always been to defend the country's frontiers and to safeguard what the elected government considers India's national security interests to be. Even retired army officers prefer to become security analysts for think-tanks rather than seeking careers as politicians.

On the other hand, the role-model for the PLA, after the war, was personified in the fictitious soldier Lei Feng,[10] a humble, apple-cheeked character who would repair his army truck with a wrench in one hand and a book by Chairman Mao in the other—and whose goal, allegedly in his own words, was to 'become a stainless-steel screw for the Party'.[11] The legend—and myth—of Lei Feng may seem comical in today's world, but it has survived decades of political change in China. Even today, 5 March is officially celebrated as Learn from Lei Feng Day.

With or without Lei Feng, the PLA, as the name suggests, had always been an ideologically motivated 'people's army' set up in the late 1920s at the end of the first alliance between the Chinese Communist Party (CCP) and the nationalist Kuomintang (KMT). Led by Zhou Enlai, He Long, and Zhu De, some of the KMT troops had rebelled against the government during an uprising at Nanchang. The uprising was crushed, but a Communist armed force, first called the Chinese Workers' and Peasants' Red Army, was officially formed on 1 August 1927. It became known simply as the Red Army and fought several battles against the KMT's troops. It was further hardened during an epic military retreat from its old stronghold in Jiangxi in the south to Yan'an in Shaanxi in northern China in 1934–5. The Long March, as it came to be known, lasted for 370 days during which the Communist forces covered 9,000 kilometres. Only 8,000 made it to Yan'an, and of these, 7,000 were from the original 86,000 who had set out from the south in October 1934. Disease, hunger, and battles with government forces as well as armies led by local warlords had taken a heavy toll.

At the new, well-defended base area in Yan'an, the Red Army was rebuilt into a formidable fighting force. During the war against Japanese invaders, which lasted from 1937 to 1945, the Red Army was allied with Chiang Kai-shek's KMT forces. But fighting between the Communists and the Nationalists broke out again after the Japanese defeat in 1945, and the revolutionaries now came to be known as the PLA. By the time World War II was over and the civil war began, the Communist forces had over 900,000 regular troops and 2 million in militia units.[12]

The KMT was defeated and Chiang Kai-shek escaped to the island of Taiwan, where his Republic of China lived on along with the futile hope of reclaiming the mainland someday. That was not to be, and, on 1 October 1949 before hundreds of thousands of cheering people, the Communist leader Mao Zedong proclaimed the People's Republic of China, saying, 'Never again will the people of China be an enslaved people!'[13]

Mao has been hailed in official Chinese history as a military genius, but that is a myth which became part of the bizarre personality cult that was developed around him in the 1960s. Mao was a political rather than a military leader. The actual commander and founder of the Red Army and the PLA was Zhu De, a warlord in the southern provinces of Yunnan and Sichuan who had joined the Communists during the Nanchang uprising. Zhu had begun his revolutionary career as a Great Elder of a lodge of Gelaohui, one of China's most powerful secret societies. He was also an opium addict until he received treatment in Shanghai in the early 1920s. It was not Mao but Zhu who, despite his dubious personality, formulated the operational principles of mobile warfare summed up in the famous maxim:

> When the enemy advances, we retreat.
> When the enemy halts and encamps, we harass them.
> When the enemy seeks to avoid battle, we attack.
> When the enemy retreats, we pursue.[14]

Zhu remained the PLA commander-in-chief through 1954 and held several political positions until he was purged during the Cultural Revolution in the late 1960s. Mao may not have been a military commander, but his contribution to the Communist military doctrine was his famous slogan 'political power grows out of the barrel of a gun', which comes from a speech he gave at a meeting with the CCP's Central Committee in November 1938.[15] That phrase has since become the guiding principle for revolutionary movements all over the world. (And to support revolution even in other countries has been a Marxist dogma since Karl Marx himself coined the phrase, 'Workers of all countries, unite!')

The two armies, and their commanders, who clashed in the Himalayas in 1962 could not have been more different, and that is an important, and often overlooked, aspect of the war. It was a clash of civilizations, not only, or even primarily, a war for control of some remote mountaintops in the Himalayas or about where the border between India and China should be drawn.

Yaacov Y.I. Vertzberger, an Israeli scholar, argues that Nehru failed to understand the cultural and historical differences between India and China, and therefore grossly misjudged China's intentions. In Nehru's view, there was an objective, universally accepted, international legal system. If India only could back its case with maps and treaties, China would eventually recognize that India was legally in the right. China, on the other hand, has never paid any attention to international law, not at that time, as Vertzberger pointed out in his studies in his 1980s, and not much later, as we have seen in the South China Sea dispute. According to Vertzberger, Nehru did also not fully understand 'the basic differences between the process by which India had gained its independence and the one by which the Chinese were liberated from the Japanese and the domestic reactionary forces [the KMT]'.[16]

India had gained its freedom through civil disobedience campaigns, and thus with little bloodshed, which made it possible for the colonial power and the independence movement to part in what amounted to mutual friendship and respect. Mao Zedong's communists, on the other hand, had had an entirely different experience. According to Vertzberger, 'Thus, India could reject British colonialism as a general philosophy and yet adopt some of the trappings it had left behind, such as political culture, borders, and geostrategic thinking.'[17] Nehru had 'adopted British geo-strategic concepts, because for him there was a continuity between the past and present'.[18] There was no such concept of continuity on the Chinese side. Any agreement that had been signed with a foreign power before the 1949 Communist victory could be—and was—dismissed as 'an unequal treaty' that the new regime did not have to honour. Mao himself had made 'Abolish the Unequal Treaties!' one of the nine fundamental principles he outlined as early as 1925.[19]

While the Indian diplomats and academic researchers in the late 1950s and early 1960s were busy writing White Papers to prove that India's inter-pretation of the border issue was historically correct, China was preparing for war.[20] For the Chinese, the legal approach to the border problem was 'nothing but hypocrisy and fraud',[21] Vertzberger argues. China saw no rea-son to honour what it terms 'unequal, colonial treaties' and therefore never recognized the McMahon Line. China still lays claim to most of today's Arunachal Pradesh and continues to place the border along the foot of the mountains on all its official maps.

Those supporting China's claims, among them Neville Maxwell and Alastair Lamb, point out that this is also approximately where maps from British times, and some even after India's independence, show the border to be. Ironically, by referring to old maps and treaties, Maxwell and Lamb are making the same misjudgement as Nehru, but in reverse, with different interpretations. But not even the most ardent supporters of China's claims would argue that the line on those old maps was an international boundary between India and China with border gates manned by Indian or British Indian, immigration and customs officials on one side and the Chinese on the other. Even if one assumes that Tibet was part of China when India was a British colony, it would also be hard to argue that the area was under Lhasa's jurisdiction.

S. Mahmud Ali, former head of the Bengali language service of the British Broadcasting Corporation (BBC), states in his otherwise authoritative book about the Sino-Indian conflict that the NEFA, until 1951, had been 'administered by Tibetan lamas'.[22] That is a gross misrepresentation of the reality at the time. No Tibetan lamas ever ruled over the area now claimed by China. Tibetan tax collectors were stationed at Tawang and a few other areas in the far west and taxes were also collected from some village tracts in the immediate vicinity of the crest of the Himalayan ranges, which was as far as centrally-controlled Tibetan administration ever reached. Today, China refers to Arunachal Pradesh as 'South Tibet', a concept that never existed in the past.

The line at the bottom of the hills on British maps simply marked the limits of organized colonial administration. The non-Tibetan tribes in the areas between that line and the McMahon Line for the most part governed themselves, but had commercial and other contacts with the Brahmaputra plain. If they spoke any language other than their own, it would have been Assamese, or broken Assamese mixed with local expressions, which became known as 'Nefamese' when the NEFA was formed in the 1950s.

The only recorded presence of any Chinese, other than spies, in the area before the 1962 War was sometime between 1910 and 1912. In the late imperial era, the Chinese sent troops into Tibet. The invasion was led by General Zhao Erfeng, who earned the nickname 'Butcher Zhao' for his brutal suppression of the Tibetans. In 1910, his troops reached Lhasa, and according to historian John Rowland, '[a] pitiful force of Tibetan soldiers fought a rear-guard action while the God King [the Dalai Lama] and his entourage made good their escape to Sikkim on horseback'.[23] The

Dalai Lama sought refuge in India, where he was received by the British in Kolkata.

Butcher Zhao left Tibet in 1911 to suppress a rebellion in Sichuan and was later captured and executed by rebellious republican forces. But some Chinese officials remained in Tibet until 1912, and they crossed the Himalayas into the far eastern corner of what later became the NEFA. They erected some border pillars in the far eastern south of Walong, and then withdrew.

Those markers stood there until January 1914, when a British administrator called T. O'Callaghan removed them. He also crossed the watershed into Rima on the Tibetan side, conferred with Tibetan officials there, but saw no Chinese influence even in that area.[24]

A year before O'Callaghan removed the border markers, a British expedition led by Captains Frederick Marshman Bailey and Henry Treise Morshead had been sent to survey areas west and northwest of Walong. They found the Tibetan officials alarmed at the prospect of a British takeover of the area, and even of Tibet itself.

Bailey's account[25] of a meeting with a local Tibetan official says that,

> He asked if we were going to place officers in Mipi or in the Lohit Valley. I said that an officer was being stationed at Walong in Mishmi country. Were we then going to station officers in Tibet also? I assured him that we were not. I do not know if he believed me. He merely answered that in Tibet, their only experience of foreigners was of the Chinese and they were cruel people.

Memories of Butcher Zhao's rampaging were still fresh in people's minds.

Evidently, there were no Chinese administrators in the area at the time—they had left in 1912 when the occupation of Tibet ended and the Chinese troops had returned home—and, apart from being staunchly anti-Chinese, the Tibetans were of the opinion that the crest of the mountains was where their jurisdiction ended.

Maxwell, however, has a different version of the significance of the border markers and where the border should be, 'The Chinese...put up border markers in 1910, and the Tibetans maintained that the boundary lay there and not some twenty miles upstream where the McMahon Line put it.'[26] It is unclear on what Maxwell based his assertion of some kind of consensus between the Tibetans and the Chinese on the border issue. It is highly unlikely, and, in any case, those markers stood there for just over two years.

The Chinese invasion of Tibet in 1950 dramatically altered the geopolitics of the entire region. Tibet, which until then had had closer ties to India than China, was no longer a de facto independent country. One of the few in the Indian government who understood the profound significance of this change was the home minister, Vallabhbhai Patel, who, only a month before his death in December 1950, wrote to Nehru,

> We have to consider what the new situation now faces us as a result of the disappearance of Tibet, as we know it, and the expansion of China up to our gates. Throughout history, we have seldom been worried about our northeast frontier. The Himalayas has been regarded as an impenetrable barrier against threats from the north. We had a friendly Tibet which gave us no trouble. The Chinese were divided. They had their domestic problems and never bothered us about our frontiers.[27]

But the idealist Nehru, who failed to understand the mindset of Beijing's new communist rulers, continued to believe in friendship with China. India and China, in his view, were both countries which had risen from repression and should work together with all the newly liberated countries in Asia and Africa. And, in the 1950s, relations between India and China seemed to blossom under the Hindi slogan *Hindi Chini Bhai Bhai* or 'Indians and Chinese are brothers'.

India officially recognized Chinese sovereignty over Tibet for the first time through the 1954 Agreement between the Republic of India and the People's Republic of China on Trade and Intercourse between India and the Tibet Region of China'.[28] But India had, in effect, recognized Tibet as part of China in September 1952, when it formally agreed with the Chinese authorities, rather than with the Tibetans, to change the status of its mission in Lhasa to that of a Consulate General.[29] India had also been one of the first non-communist countries to recognize the People's Republic of China, and diplomatic relations at the ambassadorial level were established on 1 April 1950.

The Hindi Chini Bhai Bhai relationship was supposed to be cemented in a preamble to the 1954 agreement, which included the Five Principles of Peaceful Co-existence, known as the Panchsheel Treaty from *panch* meaning five, and *sheel* meaning virtues in Sanskrit. These were,

1. Mutual respect for each other's territorial integrity and sovereignty.
2. Mutual non-aggression.
3. Mutual non-interference in each other's internal affairs.
4. Equality and co-operation for mutual benefit.
5. Peaceful co-existence.

But China was still weak, and it was India, and especially its dignified statesman Nehru, that was the champion of the newly independent countries in Asia and Africa as old colonial empires, ruled by the British, the French, and other Western powers, crumbled. Nehru's Panchsheel also came to form the basis of the Non-Aligned Movement, which was born when leaders from 29 mostly newly independent Asian and African countries met in the Indonesian resort city of Bandung in April 1955.

Amidst its fruit orchards, Dutch-built canals, and colonial bungalows, it was Indonesia's President Sukarno who played host to an array of African and Asian leaders, including the mercurial Prince Norodom Sihanouk of Cambodia, Egypt's firebrand Prime Minister Gamal Abdul Nasser, Sir John Kotelawala of Ceylon (now Sri Lanka), Pakistan's Prime Minister Muhammad Ali Bogra, and Myanmar's Premier U Nu. As the black limousines carrying the dignitaries arrived at the meeting hall in Bandung, many expressed a greater fear of 'colonialism' than of communism.

China's Zhou Enlai was also there, invited at Nehru's insistence. But Zhou almost did not make it. The Kashmir Princess, the Air India plane that Nehru had sent to fly him from Hong Kong to Jakarta, crashed into the South China Sea on 11 April 1955. A bomb had been planted on the plane by KMT agents, and the target was obviously Zhou. But he had been delayed and was not on-board. Zhou left China three days after the crash and flew to Yangon in Myanmar to meet with Nehru and U Nu before continuing on to Bandung to attend the conference.

Between June 1954 and January 1957, Zhou paid four visits to India, and, in October 1954, Nehru flew to Beijing, where he met not only Zhou but also the supreme leader Mao. It was, as the *New York Times* stated, the first visit by the head of a non-communist government since the creation of the People's Republic of China. 'The six miles between city and airport were walled by unbroken banks of humanity, clapping, cheering and crying the inescapable Chinese slogan, "Long live peace", the newspaper reported.[30]

But the situation in Tibet was becoming serious as the Chinese occupation had turned brutal and bloody. According to Tibetan resistance fighter Gompo Andrugtsan, 'The Chinese collected large sums of money for taxes, locals were selectively arrested and publicly executed to arouse terror, monasteries were destroyed, and monks were imprisoned or executed without reason.'[31]

This led to an uprising among the Khampas, nomads of eastern Tibet, who had always been fiercely independent. They struck back, ambushing Chinese army convoys with whatever weapons they had. The resistance of the Khampas attracted the attention of the US Central Intelligence Agency (CIA), which airdropped supplies into Tibet; some Khampas managed to get out and were trained on the US-held pacific island of Saipan. The town of Kalimpong in northern West Bengal became a base for clandestine activities and intelligence gathering.

US–China scholar John W. Garver quotes in his account of the Sino-Indian conflict,

the closest study of India's decision-making process during this period, by Steven Hoffman [who concludes that] 'it is unclear how much India's government knew in 1958 or 1959 about the major CIA programme' ... [Indian security chief Bhola Nath] Mullik maintained in his memoir that Nehru told him that *armed* Tibetan resistance would be suicidal, counter-productive, and insisted that peaceful, non-violent resistance was the best way. [Tibetan historian] Tsering Shakya also concluded that Nehru and other Indian leaders were not aware until after the 1962 war of the extent of US activities in support of Tibetan armed resistance.[32]

On the other hand, authors Kenneth Conboy and James Morrison assert that Nehru and Mullik, at least, knew the general parameters of the programme and tacitly condoned it.[33]

The Chinese, unable to understand the genuine resentment and anger the Tibetans felt about the occupation, were convinced that India supported the resistance. Sino-Indian relations deteriorated even further when the Dalai Lama fled to India after the failed uprising in Lhasa in March 1959. At a CCP Politburo meeting on 17 March, Zhou stressed upon what he saw as a connection between the uprising and the Indian government, and he went on to speculate that both Britain and the United States had provided support for the rebels in collusion with India, and that, 'a commanding centre of the rebellion has been established in Kalimpong'.[34]

There was no more Hindi Chini Bhai Bhai and it was at this time that Deng Xiaoping argued that India had to be taught a lesson The incursions into Longju in August 1959 and Kongka La in October were most likely meant to probe India's defences. The American academic Donald S. Zagoria in his comprehensive study of the Sino-Soviet conflict has another explanation for the Chinese attacks in 1959; it once again shows that China's conflict with India was never mainly about border demarcation or whether or not old treaties should be honoured. He refers to what was said by a Polish delegation that visited Beijing in October 1959 for the 10th anniversary of the founding of the People's Republic of China,

> The Poles ... supposed that Chinese Communist resentment at being left out of high-level negotiations was one of the motivations behind Peking's (Beijing's) decision to stir up trouble with India over the boundary question. The October incident in Kashmir, where several Indian soldiers were ambushed and killed, was said to be intended as a reminder to India, the Soviet Union, and the West that there were important areas of the world where settlements could be reached only by direct negotiations with Peking.[35]

It was also becoming increasingly clear that Mao's—and China's— worldview was fundamentally different from Nehru's ideals of non-alignment and non-interference in the internal affairs of other countries. The Western concept of the Three-World Model, as formulated during the

Cold War, meant that the US and its allies belonged to the First World, the Soviet Union and its satellites to the Second, and neutral and non-aligned countries to the Third World. Mao's Three Worlds Theory was different. To him, the US and the Soviet Union belonged to the First World; Japan, Europe and Canada formed the Second World; and Asia, Africa, and Latin America were the Third.

Naturally, China aspired to become the leader of the Third World and dethrone India from the position it held throughout the 1950s as the main voice of the newly independent Asian and African nations. Wang Hongwei, a researcher from the Chinese Academy of Social Sciences, spelled it out in one of his studies, 'India after annexing more than 560 principalities, sent forces into Kashmir and embarked on expansionism … Since then the bourgeois elite of India stepped on the stage of contemporary Asian history and strived for power and hegemony, and acted as if they were leaders.'[36] And in order to change that, China had to show that it was militarily superior to India. That was achieved in 1962. India never recovered from the defeat—Nehru himself died a broken man in 1964, and China under Mao became the beacon for most of the Third World revolutionaries. As Mao had said, 'political power grows out of the barrel of a gun'.

The 1962 War also forced India to abandon its non-aligned status, first by seeking support from the US and later by allying itself with China's new enemy, the Soviet Union. Non-interference became history when Indian troops intervened in East Pakistan in 1971 and helped the resistance fighters there break away to form Bangladesh. Mahatma Gandhi's non-violent ideals had definitely given way to a militarized India, which expanded its armed forces and even exploded its own nuclear device in May 1974. China had won. India was no longer an example to follow for the Third World. China was.

Even a cursory look at the history of China's wars since 1949 shows that border disputes were never a main guiding principle in Beijing's foreign policy. Apart from the invasion of Tibet and bombardments of the nationalist-held islands of Quemoy and Matsu in the Taiwan Strait in the 1950s (which were meant to consolidate the new communist government over what it considered its rightful territory) China's wars have always been ideologically motivated, meant to show its superior strength vis-à-vis adversaries and to demonstrate socialist solidarity with its 'comrades-in-arms'. Respect for international boundaries has never been an issue.

In Korea in the early 1950s, hundreds of thousands of Chinese 'volunteers' streamed down the peninsula to support the communist regime in the North and its war against the US-allied South. The Korean War ended in an armistice in 1953, and a still-divided nation, a Chinese ally, the Democratic People's Republic of Korea in the North, and the pro-West Republic of Korea in the South. Chinese losses in that war were immense, as it resorted to 'human-waves tactics', i.e., sending wave after wave of inexperienced recruits to face the bullets and the artillery of the south. An estimated 152,000 Chinese died and 383,000 were wounded in that war, but China had for the first time showed that it was a military force to be reckoned with and that it would not hesitate to suffer heavy casualties if a political point could be made.

After the Mekong River Operation across the border into Myanmar in 1960–61, China embarked on a strategically even more adventurous campaign in the same region. In January 1968, thousands of Chinese crossed the border again into Myanmar—this time as 'volunteers' to fight alongside the insurgent Communist Party of Burma (CPB), which resorted to armed struggle against the Myanmar government shortly after independence in 1948. Since the early 1950s, more than 140 Myanmar Communists had been living in exile in China, but it was not until an unpredictable general, Ne Win, seized power in the capital Yangon in March 1962 that they began to receive substantial Chinese support for their cause. It is generally assumed by most Westerns scholars that the anti-Chinese riots in Yangon in June 1967 became the catalyst for China's decision to aid the CPB. But, like the border dispute with India, that was only a pretext for China to move into action.

CPB cadres had already begun surveying the border areas for possible infiltration routes in 1963. At the same time, they were introduced to a group of ethnic Kachin rebels who had also retreated into China in the early 1950s. As most of the Myanmar communists were urban intellectuals, that group of warlike Kachin tribesmen were to become the nucleus of the CPB army. But, until the early 1970s, Chinese 'volunteers' made up the bulk of the CPB's fighting force. Most of them were youthful Red Guards from China, who had received their political schooling during the Cultural Revolution. But among them were also more experienced PLA officers and political commissars.

Chinese support for the CPB continued until Deng Xiaoping, a political hardliner but an economic reformer, changed Beijing's foreign policy in the 1980s from support of revolutionary movements to bilateral trade with China's neighbours and other commercial activities. But the Chinese never completely abandoned the CPB. It was still a useful tool, which the Chinese could use to exert its influence inside Myanmar.

In March 1969, a border war broke out between China and the Soviet Union, ostensibly over the ownership of some sandbanks in the River Ussuri. But, as was the case with India in 1962, political motives were more important than the exact alignment of the border. Beijing wanted to show the Third World that revolutionary China was strong enough to stand up even against the 'Soviet revisionist renegade clique', as the Chinese called the Soviet leaders after Beijing had broken ties with Moscow in 1960. China, not the Soviet Union, was the true leader of all the oppressed peoples of the world.

Chinese support for North Vietnam and the communist guerrillas in the South was substantial until that war ended in May 1975. But centuries of mutual distrust between the Chinese and the Vietnamese let to strained relations, with Hanoi allying itself with the Soviet Union. When Vietnam invaded Cambodia, China's main ally in the region, in December 1978–Janaury 1979, it was time for Beijing to teach another neighbour 'a lesson'. In February 1979, Chinese troops—and they came from the same regiments as those that had taken part in the 1961 campaign against the KMT in Myanmar—crossed the border into northern Vietnam. But this time, the PLA was not as successful as it had been against India in 1962. The Vietnamese fought back, inflicting heavy casualties on the Chinese. No one really won that war—and it turned out to be the last of its kind that the PLA fought. Since then, efforts have been made to turn the PLA into a more modern and professional force, not the 'people's army' of the past.

But back in 1962, the PLA was still an ideologically motivated entity guided by the political commissars from the CCP, and it is clear that India, and Nehru in particular, did not realize that. Nehru's faith in Zhou was also misguided. George Patterson, a British Tibet expert who was fluent in several local dialects, writes in his *Peking Versus Delhi*,[37] which was published in 1963,

> There is another side to Chou [Zhou] which is not so well-known as the charming, brilliant, even 'moderate', exterior which he uses to win friends and influence people. In 1931, Kao Chen-chang [Gu Shunzhang], a member of the Communist Central Committee and Chief of the Communist secret police, broke with the Communists and informed to the police in Hankow [Hankou], a group of men led by Chou himself murdered the whole family, including servants and babies, by strangulation.

Gu himself was not among those killed, and the decision to punish the family was made as he had managed to escape from the clutches of the Party. When Gu had outlived his usefulness to the KMT authorities, he was executed by the police in 1935. Zhou, meanwhile, carried out many similar purges and killings of real or imagined traitors to the Communist cause. Zhou was as much a hardliner as the dreaded security chief Kang Sheng, who became notorious for his brutality during the Cultural Revolution in the 1960s.

Moreover, Chinese articles and documents show that Nehru's apparent fondness for Zhou was not reciprocated. The Chinese Communists always considered Nehru a bourgeois nationalist leader, and not even as a mild socialist. The earliest attacks on the Indian prime minister came even before the People's Republic of China was proclaimed on 1 October 1949. Nehru was a 'running dog of imperialism', according to an article on 19 August 1949 in *Shijie Zhishi* ('world knowledge'), a magazine published by the CCP's Culture Committee. In its 16 September 1949 issue, the magazine proclaimed, 'Nehru riding behind the imperialists whose stooge he is, actually consider[s] himself the leader of the Asian people... as a rebel against the movement for national independence, as a blackguard... as a loyal slave of imperialism, Nehru has always been made the substitute of Chiang Kai-shek by the imperialists.'[38]

Even if Nehru was unaware of what Zhou and his comrades were writing in their Chinese-language publications, and saying about him behind his back during the days of Hindi Chini Bhai Bhai, the CIA certainly knew what the Chinese were up to. A top secret CIA report from 2 March 1963,[39] which has only recently been declassified, states,

> The Chinese diplomatic effort was a five-year masterpiece of guile, executed—and probably planned in large part—by Chou En-lai [Zhou Enlai]. Chou played on Nehru's Asian, anti-imperialist mental attitude, his proclivity to temporize, and his sincere desire for an amicable Sino-Indian relationship. Chou's strategy was to avoid making explicit, in conversations and communications with Nehru, any Chinese border claims, while avoiding any retraction of those claims which would require changing Chinese maps. Chou took the line with Nehru in Peiping [Beijing] in October 1954 that Communist China 'had as yet had no time to review' the Kuomintang maps, leaving the implication but not the explicit promise that they would be revised. In New Delhi in November–December 1956, Chou sought to create the impression with Nehru that Peiping would accept the McMahon Line, but again his language was equivocal, and what was conceded with his left hand, he retrieved with his right.

The same CIA report says that the former prime minister of Myanmar, Ba Swe, had written a letter to Nehru in 1958, warning him to be 'cautious' in dealing with Zhou on the Sino-Indian border issue. At the same time, Myanmar was engaged in talks with the Chinese about their common border, which was eventually demarcated in 1960 after an agreement, which was not unfavourable to Myanmar, had been reached.

According to the report, 'Nehru is said to have replied by declaring Chou to be "an honourable man", who could be trusted'.[40] Nehru, and India, had to pay a heavy price for that trust when the PLA came storming across the Himalayas in October 1962.

Some analysts and historians have argued that China would have been willing to settle the border dispute with India through some 'give-and-take' on both sides. The Chinese would give up their claim to the NEFA in exchange for India's recognition of China's de facto control of Aksai Chin. After all, that was how China had settled its border disputes with Myanmar,

Nepal, and Pakistan. But this argument fails to make a distinction between Beijing's relations with smaller neighbours such as Myanmar and Nepal, and the importance of a strategic alliance with Pakistan, and the fact that China's disputes with India go way beyond drawing a line on the map and demarcating it on the ground. And, as noted, in the 1950s, China emerged as India's main rival for leadership of the newly independent nations in Asia and Africa.

Today, an entirely new situation has emerged. Bilateral trade between China and India—not across the closed border but by sea—is booming; in 2015–16, it stood at US$ 70.73 billion, but it should be added, India's trade deficit is US$ 52.68 billion. China imports minerals, ores, and cotton from India, while India buys electronic equipment, computer hardware, and chemicals from China.[41]

However, the rivalry between India and China is far from over, and the distrust between the two countries remains deep and profound. To China, Arunachal Pradesh is still 'South Tibet' and travellers from that part of India get their Chinese visas stapled into their passports. According to the Chinese, they are not foreigners, as they are coming from a part of China that is under Indian occupation. This is a gesture that serves no purpose other than to humiliate India and the Indians.

More alarmingly, China has not ceased its support to rebels in India's troubled northeast. Nagas, Assamese, and Manipuris have been able to buy weapons on what is euphemistically called 'the black market' in China. Paresh Baruah, the leader of the main outfit, the United Liberation Front of Asom [Assam] (ULFA), stays in Chinese towns and travels freely across the country. The Chinese may argue that they are only reciprocating India's act of providing sanctuary for the Dalai Lama, allowing the enemy of one country to stay in the other. But while the Dalai Lama is not the leader of a band of armed insurgents, Baruah certainly is.[42]

Bumla and other passes in the Himalayas may be quiet today, but there is growing concern over a cascade of dams the Chinese are planning to build on the Brahmaputra in Tibet, where it is called Yarlung Tsangpo in Tibetan and Yarlung Zangbo on Chinese maps. One dam, at Zangmu in southeastern Tibet, became operational in October 2015, and there are another 27 proposed dams on the Brahmaputra and its tributaries before the river enters India. Naturally, that plan has caused controversy as the Chinese have not consulted India and Bangladesh, the downstream countries that would be affected by these dams.[43] China's attitude towards its neighbours has been the same on the Mekong, where a number of dams have been built inside China without any consultation with Myanmar, Laos, Thailand, Cambodia, and Vietnam, through which that river also flows.

Despite the tension along and across the border, the centre of frictions between India and China today is not in the Himalayas but in the Indian Ocean. The Chinese are making inroads into what India has always considered its 'own lake', and that could lead to conflict. China wants to keep a close watch on the sea lanes used by its suppliers of oil in the Middle East, but that means challenging India's supremacy in the Indian Ocean. Recent joint naval exercises between India and the United States, and Japan's interest in those, show that there is a new Cold War, this time with China rather than the Soviet Union as the main adversary.

In the middle of this imbroglio lies Myanmar, which has always strived to be a neutral buffer state between regional rivals, but more often than not ended up as an area of conflict between players, indigenous as well as foreign, vying for power and influence. During the decade 1968–78, the Chinese poured more aid into the CPB in Myanmar than they had into any other communist movement outside Indochina. A 20,000-square-kilometre base area was established along the Chinese border in Myanmar's northeast. The Chinese built two small hydroelectric power plants inside the CPB's territory, and a clandestine radio station, 'the People's Voice of Burma', began transmitting from the Yunnan side of the border in 1971. It was later moved to the CPB's headquarters at Panghsang inside Myanmar, where the entire leadership resided in houses built by the Chinese.

On the Thai border, ethnic Karen, Shan, and Mon rebels were allowed to set up bases, and buy supplies and weapons from the Thai side. The Thais wanted a border buffer between themselves and their historical enemy, Myanmar, which had invaded their country in the past and had sacked the old capital of Ayutthaya in 1767. While such concerns may seem anachronistic in today's world, they were real enough for the Thais.

In the west, near the border with East Pakistan (later Bangladesh), Muslim guerrillas from the Rohingya community in Myanmar's Rakhine State have been active since Myanmar became independent from Britain in 1948. India never supported any rebel movement in Myanmar, but gave asylum to U Nu, who was ousted by General Ne Win in 1962. During a pro-democracy uprising in August–September 1988, the activists received moral support from Indian authorities.

The situation in Myanmar's border areas changed dramatically when, in March–April 1989, the once powerful CPB collapsed after a mutiny among the rank-and-file of the party's army, most of whom were Wa tribesmen. The Wa were headhunters who lived in the mountains straddling Myanmar's northeastern border with China and had been recruited into the communist army without having any clear idea of the ideology for which they were fighting and dying. Almost the entire old leadership fled to China, where they were given asylum. The CPB subsequently broke up into four ethnic armies, of which the United Wa State Army (UWSA) is by far the strongest.

The 1989 CPB mutiny actually suited China's interests, and there are strong suggestions that China's clandestine services actively encouraged the Wa and others to rise up against their leaders. In view of Deng's new polices, which emphasized trade and economic expansion, the CPB's old leadership, which remained staunchly Maoist, had become a liability.

In the years following the CPB mutiny, trade between China and Myanmar blossomed. China flooded Myanmar's markets with cheap consumer goods and imported mainly raw materials such as timber and minerals. The annual exchange of goods soon reached the US$ 1 billion mark. The surge in bilateral trade between Myanmar and China was facilitated by Western sanctions and boycotts, which at that time were in force because of the Myanmar government's gross violations of human rights. China did not have to face any competition and became Myanmar's most important foreign trade partner.

But China was not going to give up the foothold inside Myanmar that it had had since the late 1960s. In May 1989, the UWSA entered into a cease-fire agreement with the Myanmar government, which, on the one hand, suited China's new commercial interests, and on the other, also helped strengthen the UWSA. After all, the Chinese had had a long-standing relationship with most of the leaders of the UWSA, dating back to their CPB days. Thus, the UWSA has been able to purchase vast quantities of weapons from China, including heavy artillery, surface-to-air missiles, and armoured fighting vehicles.

Today, the UWSA is better armed than the CPB ever was. It can field at least 20,000 well-equipped troops as well as thousands of village militiamen and other supportive forces. Moreover, the top leaders of the UWSA are usually accompanied by Chinese intelligence officers who provide advice and guidance.

In recent years, Myanmar has mended its ties with the West, partly because the Chinese influence, even dominance, was becoming overwhelming, and sanctions have been lifted. China's sending of even more weaponry to the UWSA is a way of putting pressure on Myanmar's government at a time when its relations with Washington are improving. As China sees it, it cannot afford to 'lose' Myanmar to the US and the West. A strong UWSA provides China with a strategic advantage, and it is also a bargaining chip in negotiations with the Myanmar government.

When Aung Min, the then president office minister, visited Monywa, a town northwest of Mandalay, in November 2012, to meet local people protesting a controversial Chinese-backed copper mining project in the area, he openly admitted, 'We are afraid of China ... we don't dare to have a row with [them]. If they feel annoyed with the shutdown of their projects and resume their support to the Communists, the economy in border areas would backslide. So you'd better think seriously.'[44] By 'the Communists' he clearly meant the UWSA and its allies, among them the Myanmar National Democratic Alliance Army (MNDAA) in the Kokang area, another former CPB force in Myanmar's northeast, which indeed resorted to armed struggle in February 2015.

China, predictably, has denied any involvement in that conflict, but the fact remains that most of the MNDAA's weaponry and vast quantities of ammunition have been supplied by the UWSA. According to a well-placed source, China was indirectly 'teaching the Myanmar government a lesson in Kokang: move too much to the West, and this can happen.'[45] At the same time, China is playing another, 'softer' card by being actively involved in the so-called 'peace talks' between the Myanmar government and the country's multitude of ethnic rebel armies.

Whether China wants to export revolution or expand and protect commercial interests, it apparently feels that it needs to have a solid foothold inside Myanmar. There is no better and more loyal ally in this regard than the UWSA and its former CPB affiliates. Myanmar is China's 'corridor' to the Indian Ocean as an outlet for trade from Yunnan and other landlocked southwestern provinces, quite apart from Beijing's strategic interests in the region. Although there are no, and have never been, any Chinese bases there, as some Indian writers have suggested, China has helped Myanmar upgrade its own naval facilities—and that is worrying enough for India.

In April 2015, India eventually ran out of patience with Myanmar's turning a blind eye to the presence of Indian rebels on their soil. Indian commandoes crossed the border into Myanmar and destroyed a number of camps where Assamese, Manipuri, and Naga rebels were ensconced. The rebels were armed with weapons obtained from secret arms factories inside a former CPB area in Myanmar's northern Kachin State. Although located inside Myanmar, the machinery and the technicians came from China. The Chinese may have no interest in independence for Assam, Nagaland, or Manipur, but they evidently want to keep the Indians off balance—at least as long as the Dalai Lama is alive and the Tibetan exiles are being provided with sanctuaries in India.

Besides the broader issue of the vast differences in the respective cultures and worldviews to which the sign at Bumla refers somewhat presumptuously to as 'Two Old Neighbouring Civilisations', the question of Tibet remains at the heart of the conflict between India and China. And if the proponents of the Chinese version of the border dispute and the 1962 War had paid more attention to the Chinese source material, even they would have discovered that border demarcation was never the main issue. On 6 May 1959, only weeks after the Lhasa uprising against the Chinese occupation of Tibet, the official Chinese news agency Xinhua published an article titled 'The Revolution in Tibet and Nehru's Philosophy', accusing the Indian prime minister of having adopted 'the strategic aspirations of British imperialism'.[46]

According to US security expert and former CIA analyst Bruce Riedel, 'On the day the article attacking Nehru was published, Zhou Enlai said in a public forum that Nehru "had inherited England's old policy of saying Tibet is an independent country" and that this mentality was "the centre of the Sino-Indian conflict"'.[47] Vertzberger was obviously right in his conclusion that Nehru and the Chinese leaders had incompatible worldviews, and, in a more modern context, it can be argued that China and India are still worlds apart when it comes to culture and strategic thinking.

China may have been grossly mistaken in believing that Nehru, of all Indian leaders, wanted to seize Tibet. But, the Chinese fear of 'losing' what they have always considered an integral part of their country has been a factor that has determined relations between China and India for more than a century, and still does. And events first came to a head at Shimla in 1914—at a time when China was weak as millennia of imperial rule were being replaced by a new, chaotic republican order.

Notes

1. I visited Bumla Pass on 28 October 2015.
2. Interviews with Indian army personnel at Bumla, 28 October 2015. For a detailed account of the battle, see 'Operations on the Kameng Frontier Division (Tawang)', P.J.S. Sandhu, Bhavna Tripathi, Ranjit Singh Kalha, Bharat Kumar, G.G. Dwivedi, Vinay Shankar (eds.), *1962: A View from the Other Side of the Hill* (New Delhi: Vij Books India, 2015), pp. 82–3.
3. 'Operations in the Western Sector (Ladakh)', Sandhu et al., *1962*, p. 55.
4. Satyanarayan Sinha, *China Strikes* (London: Blandford Press, 1964), p. 77.
5. Cheng Feng and Larry Wortzel 'PLA Operational Principles and Limited War: The Sino-Indian War of 1962', Mark A. Ryan, David M. Finkelstein, and Michael A. McDevitt (eds.), *Chinese Warfighting: The PLA Experience Since 1949* (New Delhi: KW Publishers 2010), p. 188. This is an Indian reprint of the one published by M.E. Sharpe in 2003.
6. Sandhu et al., *1962*, p. 28.
7. For the life and philosophy of Dr Sun Yat-sen, see Bernard Martin, *Strange Vigour: A Biography of Sun Yat-sen* (London and Toronto: William Haeinemann, 1944).

8. Email communication with Pamela Kyle Crossley, an expert on the Manchu Dynasty, 14 April 2016.

9. For a complete list of the Indian Army's peace-keeping missions, see 'India and United Nations, Peacekeeping and Peacebuilding', available at https://www.pminewyork.org/pages.php?id=1985 (accessed on 8 April 82016).

10. For an account of the Lei Feng myth, see Evan Osnos, 'Fact-checking a Chinese Hero', *The New Yorker*, 29 March 2013, available at http://www.newyorker.com/news/evan-osnos/fact-checking-a-chinese-hero (accessed on 10 April 2016).

11. Fang Lizhi, *The Most Wanted Man in China: My Journey from Scientist to Enemy of the State* (New York: Henry Holt and Company, 2016), p. 228.

12. William Wei, '"Political Power Grows Out of the Barrel of a Gun": Mao and the Red Army', David A. Graff and Robin Higham, *A Military History of China* (Dehra Dun: Greenfields Publishers, 2012), pp. 244–5.

13. Quoted in, for instance, Roy Rowan, *Chasing the Dragon: A Veteran Journalist's Firsthand Account of the 1946–49 Chinese Revolution* (Guilford, Connecticut: Lyons Press, 2004) p. 217.

14. Wei, 'Political Power Grows Out of the Barrel of a Gun', p. 235.

15. Mao Zedong, *Quotations from Chairman Mao Tse-tung* (Peking [Beijing]: Foreign Languages Press, 1968), p. 61.

16. Yaacov Y.I. Vertzberger, *Misperceptions in Foreign Policymaking: The Sino-Indian Conflict, 1959–1962* (Boulder, Colorado: Westview Press, 1984), p. 217.

17. Vertzberger, *Misperceptions in Foreign Policymaking*, p. 217.

18. Vertzberger, *Misperceptions in Foreign Policymaking*, p. 217.

19. Wang Dong, *China's Unequal Treaties: Narrating National History* (Asia World, Lanham, Maryland: Rowman and Littlefield, 2005), p. 64.

20. From 1959 to 1962, the Indian government published more than a dozen White Papers with maps, documents, copies of treaties, and correspondence between the Indian and Chinese governments. Several of them are available at http://www.claudearpi.net/index.php?nav=documents&id=20&lang=1 (accessed on 16 June 2016).

21. Vertzberger, *Misperceptions in Foreign Policy Making*, p. 217.

22. S. Mahmud Ali, *Cold War in the High Himalayas: The USA, China and South Asia in the 1950s* (Richmond, Surrey: Curzon, 1999), p. xxviii.

23. John Rowland, *A History of Sino-Indian Relations: Hostile Co-Existence* (Princeton, NJ, Toronto, London: D. Van Nostrand Company, 1967), p. 42.

24. James Barnard Calvin, 1984, 'The India-China Border War (1962)', available at http://www.globalsecurity.org/military/library/report/1984/CJB.htm (accessed on 5 April 2016).

25. F.M. Bailey, *No Passport to Tibet* (London: The Travel Book Club, 1957), p. 71.

26. Neville Maxwell, *India's China War* (Harmondsworth, Middlesex: Penguin, 1972), p. 50.

27. Madhav Godbole, *The God Who Failed: An Assessment of Jawaharlal Nehru's Leadership* (New Delhi: Rupa, 2014), p. 312.

28. For the full text of the agreement, see http://www.mea.gov.in/bilateral-documents.htm?dtl/7807/Agreement+on+Trade+and+Intercourse+with+Tibet+Region (accessed on 5 April 2016).

29. CIA, 'The Sino-Indian Border Dispute Section 1: 1950-59', CIA document (2 March 1963, and declassified May 2007), available at https://e-asia.uoregon.edu/node/2570 (accessed on 29 March 2016).

30. See http://qz.com/404874/photos-when-indias-first-prime-minister-visited-china-in-1954/ (accessed on 5 April 2016).

31. Quoted in Yuliya Babayeva, 'The Khampa Uprising: Tibetan Resistance against the Chinese Occupation', Honours College Theses, Paper 31 (New York: Pforzheimer Honours College, 8 January 2006), p. 15, available at http://digitalcommons.pace.edu/honorscollege_theses/31/ (accessed on 7 April 2016).

32. John W. Garver, 'China's Decision for War with India in 1962', Alastair Iain Johnston and Robert S. Ross (eds.), *New Directions in the Study of China's Foreign Policy* (Stanford: Stanford University Press, 2006), p. 100.

33. Kenneth Conboy and James Morrison, *The CIA's Secret War in Tibet* (Lawrence: University Press of Kansas, 2002), pp. 95–6, 155–6.

34. 'The Politico-Diplomatic Prelude Part 2', Sandhu et al. *1962*, p. 23.

35. Donald S. Zagoria, *The Sino-Soviet Conflict 1959–1961* (Princeton, NJ: Princeton University Press, 1962), p. 280.

36. Wang Hongwei, *ximalayashan qingjie: zhongyin guanxi yanjiu* ('The Himalayan Sentiment: A Study of Sino-Indian Relations') (Beijing: China Tibetology Publications, 1998), p. 55. Quoted in B.R. Deepak, 'The Republic of India and the Republic of China 1947–1949', translated by B.R. Deepak, D.P. Tripathi and B.R. Deepak (eds.), *India and Taiwan: From Benign Neglect to Pragmatism* (Delhi: Vij Books, 2015), p. 52.

37. George N. Patterson, *Peking versus Delhi* (London: Faber and Faber, 1963), p. 51.

38. Quoted in Sandhu et al., *1962*, p. 5. *Shijie Zhishi* was a Shanghai-based fortnightly founded in 1934. The de facto editor was Hu Yuzhi, a secret CCP

member. The magazine moved to Hankou and then to Hong Kong in 1938, publishing there until it folded when the Japanese invaded the British colony in 1941. It resumed operations in Shanghai in December 1945, published by the CCP's underground Culture Committee, and was banned by the KMT government in March 1949. It resumed publication after the communist takeover of Shanghai in May 1949, before the People's Republic of China was proclaimed in Beijing on 1 October 1949.

39. CIA, 'The Sino-Indian Border Dispute Section 1', pp. 2–4.

40. CIA, 'The Sino-Indian Border Dispute Section 1', p. 4.

41. Press Trust of India, 'India's trade deficit with China jumps to $53 billion in 2015–2016', *The Economic Times*, 1 August 2016, available at http://economictimes.indiatimes.com/news/economy/foreign-trade/indias-trade-deficit-with-china-jumps-to-53-billion-in-2015-16/articleshow/53492853.cms (accessed on 6 June 2017).

42. Bertil Lintner, *Great Game East: India, China and the Struggle for Asia's Most Volatile Frontier* (New Haven: Yale University Press, 2015), p. 151.

43. Sana Hashmi, 'China Dams the Brahmaputra: Why India Should Worry', *Rediff News* (21 October 2015), available at http://www.rediff.com/news/column/china-dams-the-brahmaputra-why-india-should-worry/20151021.htm (accessed on 8 April 2016).

44. Bertil Lintner, 'Same Game, Different Tactics: The Myanmar Corridor', *Irrawaddy*, July 2015, pp. 14–19. Also available at http://www.irrawaddy.com/magazine/same-game-different-tactics-chinas-myanmar-corridor.html (accessed on 7 April 2016).

45. Lintner, 'Same Game, Different Tactics'. p. 19.

46. Bruce Riedel, *JFK's Forgotten Crisis: Tibet, the CIA, and the Sino-Indian War* (Delhi: HarperCollins India, 2016), p. 98.

47. Riedel, *JFK's Forgotten Crisis*, p. 98.

2

The Line

1912 was a year of upheaval and change throughout Asia. World War I had not yet broken out, but other forces were stirring throughout the continent. On the first day of the year, Asia's first republic was proclaimed, the Republic of China. After years of simmering discontent and local uprisings in various parts of China, a military revolt at Wuchang in Hubei province had broken out on 10 October 1911. 'Double Ten Day', as it became known among republican nationalists, served as the catalyst for a wider uprising against the ruling but increasingly inept Qing Dynasty.

The leader of the anti-Qing movement, Dr Sun Yat-sen, was not in the country at the time. He had been living in exile in for several years, organizing resistance among overseas Chinese in Hawaii, southeast Asia, and Japan. Accompanied by an American adventurer called Homer Lea, Dr Sun returned home on 21 December 1911 to oversee some of the most dramatic events in modern Chinese history. Eight days later, a gathering of delegates representing anti-Qing groups from all over the country elected Dr Sun the 'provisional president' of the republic, a role he assumed on New Year's Day. On 12 February 1912, the last emperor, six-year-old Pu Yi, was forced to abdicate.

But the end of more than two thousand years of imperial rule did not, as the revolutionaries and reformers had envisaged, usher in an era of modernity and prosperity in this vast and desperately poor country. Power struggles and intrigues led to chaos and instability. Dr Sun resigned after less than seven weeks in office and was succeeded by Yuan Shikai, a military officer and hardly a democratic reformer. In December 1915, Yuan even proclaimed himself emperor, a title he held for 83 days. Amidst several rebellions in his realm, Yuan had to relinquish his imperial title and died from a blood disease at the age of 56 in June 1916. Dr Sun was forced into exile in Japan, returning to China in 1917 when a republican form of government had been restored. By then the country had been plunged into even deeper chaos, with a weak central government and local warlords who were often little more than bandit-chieftains controlling their own fiefdoms in the provinces. Dr Sun tried in vain to reunify the fractured country. He died of liver cancer in March 1925 when he was only 58.

Lea, Dr Sun's American companion, who he wanted to make the chief of staff of the army of the Republic of China, had suffered a stroke in February 1912 and returned to the United States where he died in November. Dr Sun's revolutionary companions considered Lea an interloper, and strongly objected to the idea of having a foreigner as their army chief. Although China, as a country, was never colonized, European powers exerted their influence over the country from their colonial enclaves on the coast and that contributed to a deeply felt resentment of outsiders.

Hong Kong was British, the Portuguese were in Macau, and until the end of World War I the Germans had Qingdao. China was ruthlessly exploited by Western and Japanese commercial interests and the foreigners treated the Chinese as second-class citizens in their own country. It was hardly surprising that a Communist party was formed in 1921, and quickly gained support among urban intellectuals as well as from downtrodden peasants in the countryside.

Changes, albeit of a more peaceful nature, were also taking place in India in 1912. In June, the parliament in London promulgated the Government of India Act. Bengal, which had been divided in 1905 into a western part and the new province of Eastern Bengal and Assam, was reconstituted into three provinces—Bengal, corresponding to present-day West Bengal and Bangladesh, Bihar and Orissa, and Assam. Rather than being a centrally-ruled 'presidency' as before, reunited Bengal became a province under a governor. The creation of Assam as a separate province, which later got its own legislative assembly, meant that its borders had to be more clearly defined.

At that time, Assam included the present Indian states of Nagaland, Mizoram, Meghalaya, and Arunachal Pradesh. The two other northeastern Indian states of today, Tripura and Manipur, were princely states ruled by their own maharajas and never part of Assam. A centrally controlled Naga Hills District had been created as early as 1866 and gradually expanded to include more areas in the easternmost mountains. In 1912, the Naga Hills District was formally incorporated into the new province of Assam. The Lushai Hills, now Mizoram, were 'pacified'—colonial parlance for occupied—in the latter half of the nineteenth century and became part of British India in 1895. Today's Meghalaya consists of the Khasi, Jaintia, and Garo Hills, highlands south of the Brahmaputra Valley. Its present state capital Shillong served as headquarters for the entire province of Assam because the colonial administrators preferred to stay in the cool climate in the hills, rather than in the hot and humid tropical plains of the Brahmaputra. Shillong remained the capital of Assam from independence in 1947 until 1972, when Meghalaya became a separate state.

To the north of the plain around the Brahmaputra, there were other hill districts, not as firmly controlled as the Naga, Lushai, Khasi, Jaintia, and Garo, but nevertheless considered part of Assam and British India. Following several British military raids into the hills north of the Brahmaputra in the late nineteenth and early twentieth century, in 1912, Major General Hamilton Bower, the leader of one of those expeditions, recommended that those frontier areas should be divided into three tribal-dominated sections—western, central, and eastern. That led in 1914 to the formation of the North-East Frontier Tracts under the government of Assam.[1] Five years later, the central and eastern sections became the Sadiya Frontier Tract, and the western section was renamed the Balipara Frontier Tract.

While Assam and its outlying hill areas were being consolidated, administrative changes were taking place in other parts of British India as well. In 1911, King George V had visited India and he conveyed his impressions in a speech before the British Parliament on 12 February 1912. India was the jewel in the crown of the British Empire and, at the same time as the 1912 Government of India Act was passed, it was decided to move the capital from Calcutta (now Kolkata) in the east to a more central location at Delhi.

The foundation stone of a new city, called New Delhi, had actually been laid during King George V's visit, and the task of designing it was assigned to two prominent British architects, Edward Lutyens and Herbert Baker. However, because of the outbreak of World War I in 1914, the construction was delayed by several years. It was not until 15 February 1931 that the new grand capital of British India was officially inaugurated.

1912 was also a year of change in Japan. On 30 July, the Meiji Emperor died. He had ascended the throne in 1867 and his reign had seen the transformation of Japan from a feudal society to an industrialized world power. His funeral was described by the *Japan Advertiser* on 17 September as 'a fairy tale of lights' with old-fashioned 'frock-coated and silk-hatted gentlemen', and sacred oxen in front of the funeral car, and 'hundreds of men in peaked hats and gold laced uniforms' from the navy and army behind. 'The contrast between that which preceded the funeral car and that which followed it was striking indeed. Before it went old Japan; after it came new Japan,' the newspaper reported.[2]

The powerful Meiji Emperor was succeeded by his son Yoshihito, who assumed the imperial name Taisho. In sharp contrast to his father, the Taisho Emperor was weak and suffered from various neurological ailments, making it impossible for him to carry out his duties. Real power shifted to a group of older statesmen who ran the country without much interference from the emperor. Taisho's reign, from 1912 to his death in 1926, has therefore become known as the 'Taisho democracy'. There was room for political manoeuvre outside the imperial palace, but it did not amount to democracy in the western sense.

During World War I, Japan sided with the Allied powers, declared war on Germany, occupying the former German colonies in the Asia-Pacific, Qingdao on the Chinese coast, and the Carolines, the Marianas, and the Marshall Islands in the Pacific. Qingdao had to be returned to China in

1922, but, taking advantage of the weakened Republic, the Japanese expanded their influence over other parts of the Chinese mainland and adjoining areas. The Korean peninsula had already been annexed in 1910, now Japan took over German commercial holdings in Manchuria and Inner Mongolia.

When the Taisho Emperor died at the age of 47 in 1926, he was succeeded by his eldest son Hirohito, who became the Showa Emperor. Under Taisho's rather weak reign, the Japanese military had become the most powerful force in the country—and that would lead to more wars with China in the 1930s and 1940s. Japan was emerging as a military and political superpower in Asia.

The collapse of the Chinese empire, and the disintegration of the country that followed in its wake, provided non-Chinese vassals in the outlying areas with an opportunity to reassert the autonomy or de facto independence several of them had enjoyed even under the emperors. The Mongol tribes, which, under rulers such as Ghengis Khan and Kublai Khan, had conquered much of Asia in the thirteenth and fourteenth centuries, had gradually been subdued by the Chinese emperors. Under the Qing Dynasty, the land of the Mongols was divided into a more directly controlled 'inner' section and an 'outer' part on the steppes and highlands north of the Gobi desert, which was self-governing and corresponds to the modern state of Mongolia.

As early as 29 December 1911, only two-and-a-half months after the outbreak of the republican revolution in China, Mongolia declared its independence. The Mongols practised the same kind of Buddhism as in Tibet, with a clergyman titled 'Bogd Gegeen', or 'the Holy Enlightened One', as the highest religious authority in the country. He now assumed the title of 'Bogd Khan', 'Holy Ruler', of the new theocratic Mongolian state. Although governed by supposedly peaceful Buddhist clerics, the Mongols felt they had to build up an army to defend their newly won independence. Shortly after the declaration of independence, they launched a military campaign to 'liberate' Inner Mongolia also from the Chinese.

The Mongols turned to Russia to buy weapons for their fledgling armed forces, but Tsar Nicholas II was not interested in supporting a war against the newly proclaimed Republic of China. Unknown to the Mongols, the Russians had in the same year, 1912, concluded a secret agreement with the Japanese, delineating their respective spheres of influence in China's northern periphery. Southern Manchuria and Inner Mongolia came within Japan's sphere, while Japan recognized Russia's right to exert its influence over northern Manchuria and Outer Mongolia.[3]

Thus, no Russian weapons were ever sent to Mongolia, nor were the Russians prepared to annex any part of Mongolia despite the secret pact with Japan. But, on 3 November 1912 (21 October, according to the Russian calendar), Russia and Mongolia signed a treaty by which the Russians recognized Outer Mongolia's autonomy within the then newly constituted Republic of China. The Mongolian version of the treaty, however, said 'independence', which was interpreted by the Mongols as recognition of an independent 'Great Mongolian State'. In return, the Mongols granted the Russians commercial privileges in their country.

To add to the confusion regarding Mongolia's international status, a Sino-Russian treaty that was concluded shortly afterwards stated that Mongolia was 'under the suzerainty' of China, but with internal autonomy.[4] Under yet another treaty, signed by Russia, China, and Mongolia at Kyakhta in Buratiya in Russia on 25 May 1915, Mongolia was forced to recognize that suzerainty and agree not to conclude international treaties with foreign countries.[5]

Before the Treaty of Kyakhta was concluded, Mongolia had tried hard to gain formal recognition of its declaration of independence. A delegation was sent to St Petersburg, but it was prevented by the Russians from seeking further European contacts. An attempt to send a delegation to Tokyo was aborted when the Japanese consul in Harbin, Manchuria, refused to provide any assistance to the Mongols.

The only diplomatic success that the Mongols had was with their religious brethren in Tibet. On 11 January 1913 (29 December 1912, according to the Russian calendar), the Treaty of Friendship and Alliance was signed at Urga, now Ulaanbaatar, between Mongolia and Tibet. Mongolia was represented by its foreign minister, Da Lama Rabdan, and the commander-in-chief of the armed forces, Manlaibaatar Damdinsüren. Rabdan signed the agreement with Agvan Dorzhiev as a representative of Tibet's Dalai Lama. But the problem was that Dorzhiev hailed from Buryatia, a Mongol-speaking part of eastern Siberia, and was thus technically a Russian citizen. The validity of the treaty, therefore, has been questioned.[6]

Tibet also declared its independence during the turbulent first years of the Republic of China—although there is some confusion as to when, exactly, that declaration was made. In early 1910, the Qing had sent an expeditionary force to invade Tibet in a last attempt to assert authority over the territories they claimed to be within the boundaries of their empire. The Chinese marched into the Tibetan capital, Lhasa, on 12 February 1910 and deposed the thirteenth Dalai Lama. He fled to India and was invited to Kolkata by the then Viceroy, Lord Minto.

The Dalai Lama's flight to India helped restore his relations with Britain: Britain had, in December 1903, sent a force led by Francis Younghusband, a British India-born, Sandhurst-trained officer, into Tibet. Younghusband's brief but brutal occupation ended with a treaty signed in Lhasa in September 1904, which gave the British considerable privileges in Tibet.[7] The Dalai Lama had fled and then spent the years 1904–9 in exile in China and Mongolia to escape the British. Now, the Tibetans and the British were allies against the Chinese.

The Chinese occupation of Tibet was brief, and the troops had to withdraw after the fall of the Qing Dynasty in early 1912. It was during this occupation that Chinese troops for the first time in history crossed the watershed of the Himalayas and entered Walong, now in the northeastern-most corner of Arunachal Pradesh. After having erected a few border markers south of Walong, the Chinese left, never attempting to establish any administration in the area. The final withdrawal of the Chinese troops from the areas of Tibet they had occupied took place, somewhat ironically, through Kolkata. From there, they were sent by ship back to Chinese ports, as all overland routes from Tibet to China were blocked by Tibetan warriors.

With the Chinese gone from Tibet and the Dalai Lama back in Lhasa, it was time for the Tibetans to follow the example of the Mongols. On 13 February 1913, about a month after Avgan Dorzhiev had signed an agreement with Da Lama Ravdan and Manlaibaatar Damdinsüren at Urga, the thirteenth Dalai Lama issued a statement that amounted to a declaration of independence.

First, the Dalai Lama explained:

> A few years ago, the Chinese authorities in Szechuan [Sichuan] and Yunnan endeavoured to colonise our territory. They brought large numbers of troops into central Tibet on the pretext of policing the trade marts. I, therefore, left Lhasa with my ministers for the Indo-Tibetan border, hoping to clarify to the Manchu [Qing] Emperor by wire that the existing relationship between Tibet and China had been that of patron and priest and had not been based on the subordination of one to the other. There was no other choice for me but to cross the border, because Chinese troops were following with the intention of taking me alive or dead.[8]

Then came the clarification of Tibet's international status,

> Tibet is a country with rich natural resources; but it is not scientifically advanced like other lands. We are a small, religious, and independent nation. To keep up with the rest of the world, we must defend our country. In view of past invasions by foreigners, our people may have to face certain difficulties, which they must disregard. To safeguard and maintain the independence of our country, one and all should voluntarily work hard. Our subject citizens residing near the borders should be alert and keep the government informed by special messenger of any suspicious developments. Our subjects must not create major clashes between two nations because of minor incidents.[9]

But, as was the case with Mongolia's declaration of independence, Tibet's was also ignored by outside powers. Britain and other countries continued to recognize Chinese suzerainty over Tibet as well as Mongolia. But suzerainty does not amount to sovereignty. Originally a term used to define to the relationship between the Ottoman Empire and its surrounding areas, it simply means that a certain area recognizes the overlordship of a suzerain to whom it is supposed to be paying tribute. But, in reality, it often refrains from doing so. It means, in effect, internal autonomy with the suzerain power in charge of little more than foreign relations and, perhaps, defence. In the context of the chaos that reigned in China in the 1910s, it was a formal designation with no meaning. Both Mongolia and Tibet were if not de jure, at least de facto, independent nations.

In order to regulate the status of Tibet and to define its borders, British India's foreign office on 23 May 1913 sent an invitation to the Chinese government to a joint conference where representatives from the Tibetan government would also participate. The three parties eventually met at Shimla (then Simla), the summer capital of India in the foothills of the Himalayas, on 13 October 1913.

British India's chief negotiator, Henry McMahon, a Shimla-born colonial official, also served as the chairman of the conference. He was assisted by Archibald Rose, a former consul to China, and Charles Bell, the then British Political Representative to Sikkim on issues concerning Tibet. On the British side was also a remarkable man whose full name was Sonam Wangdel Laden La, or Laden La for short. He was an ethnic Bhutia from Sikkim and among the many languages he spoke were Tibetan and English. Laden La had accompanied Francis Younghusband during his military expedition to Lhasa in 1903–4, and was now a high-ranking police officer with security-related duties. Laden La had just returned from a trip to Britain when he was sent to Shimla to act as an interpreter for the Tibetan delegation during the final days of the conference. He arrived on 21 June 1914 and stayed until 21 July.[10]

Tibet sent Prime Minister Lama Lönchen Shatra to represent the Dalai Lama. The chief Tibetan negotiator was assisted by a delegation consisting of Trimon Norbu Wangyal and Khenchung Tenpa Dhargyal, two other high-ranking government officials. According to Tibetan sources, the conference was an opportunity the Tibetan government did not want to miss. They wanted recognition for their declaration of independence, and Lönchen Shatra and his men had collected documents in support of their case, which they presented before the British and Chinese representatives.[11]

China's main delegate was Chen Yifan, or Ivan Chen, a widely travelled diplomat who was fluent in English and had served for nine years in the Chinese Legation in London as counsellor. Designated as commissioner for Tibet, Chen was assisted by deputy commissioner Wang Haiping. But the power behind Chen and Wang was Lu Xingqi (Lu Hsing-chi), a more powerful officer who had played a crucial role in fostering divisions between the Dalai Lama and the second-most important lama in Tibet, the Panchen Lama, after the former had returned to Lhasa in 1912.[12]

In April 1913, the Chinese government had appointed Lu commissioner for Tibet. He was then ordered to leave for Tibet by sea via Kolkata. Lu was unable to proceed from there to Tibet and had to remain in the Indian city, which he knew quite well. At some time in the late nineteenth century, he had gone to Kolkata to study at a local Chinese school and later started a company called Tianyi Gongsi. Located in Tiretta Bazar in the city's Chinatown, it did business in fur imported from Tibet.[13]

Apart from being a successful businessman, Lu was all along an intelligence operative charged with Indian and Tibetan affairs.[14] Chen became the new, official face of the Chinese government for Tibetan affairs, although Chinese sources do not state when the post was shifted to him from Lu, if that happened at all officially.[15] Lu stayed in constant contact with Chen and the Chinese government throughout the proceedings in Shimla.

The conference ran into serious problems from the very beginning, as the Chinese wanted Tibet to be referred to as an integral part of China. Lönchen Shatra had hardly ever left his native land, but surprised the British and Chinese delegates with his grasp of political affairs as he presented his claims—and contradicted Chen's version or Tibet's status. Lönchen Shatra outlined the Chinese excesses during the 1910–12 occupation and, not surprisingly, continued to press for recognition of an independent Tibet:

> Tibet and China have never been under each other and will never associate with each other in the future. It is decided that Tibet is an independent State and that the Precious Protector, the Dalai Lama, is the ruler of Tibet, in all Temporal as well as spiritual affairs. Tibet repudiates the 1906 Anglo-Chinese Convention concluded at Peking on the 27th April 1906... as she did not send a representative for this Convention, nor did she affix her seal on it. It is therefore decided that this is not binding on the three governments.[16]

The 1906 Anglo-Chinese Convention stated that 'the Government of Great Britain engages not to annex Tibetan territory or to interfere in the administration of Tibet. The Government of China also undertakes not to permit any other foreign State to interfere with the territory or internal administration of Tibet.'[17] But Britain was entitled to lay down telegraph lines connecting Tibet with India. Tibet's communications with the outside world continued to be mainly via British India, not China.

The 1906 Anglo-Chinese Convention could be interpreted as British recognition of Chinese suzerainty over Tibet, but it was meant mainly to confirm Tibet's status as a neutral buffer zone between British India and the Russian empire. Therefore, the British could not agree to Lönchen Shatra's demand to repudiate the 1906 Anglo-Chinese Convention and recognize Tibet as a fully independent nation. Furthermore, a recognition of Tibet's independence would also be in violation of the 1907 Anglo-Russian Convention, which was concluded to settle disputes between Britain and Russia over spheres of influence in Persia, Afghanistan, and Tibet.[18] Under the terms of that Convention, both sides had pledged not to enter into any agreement with Tibet unless done through Chinese mediation. And China would not be willing to discuss the issue of Tibetan independence.

According to Charles Bell, there were also other reasons why the British were unwilling to concede to Lönchen Shatra's demands: the danger that an independent Tibet 'might be driven to seek assistance from Mongolia, and through Mongolia from Russia'.[19] As Pradip Phanjoubam, the editor of the *Imphal Free Press*, a newspaper in the northeastern Indian state of Manipur, has pointed out: 'British Tibet policy at the time was determined not by any fear of the Chinese, but of the Russians, in what was referred to as the Great Game.'[20]

The Chinese were actually not seen as important players in the Great Game, the struggle between Russia and Britain for hegemony over Central Asia, and they were invited to Shimla mainly because of the terms of the Anglo-Russian Convention signed in 1907, which, according to Phanjoubam, had been 'literally forced by the British on the Russians, weakened by a humiliating defeat at the hands of the Japanese'[21] in a war that ended in 1905. Russia had to promise to stay out of Tibet, but the rules of that Convention also applied to the British. Tibet, and also Afghanistan and Persia, were to remain neutral buffer zones between the Russian Empire and British India.[22]

Dutch scholar W.F. Van Eekelen opines that John Jordan, the British minister in Beijing, 'was primarily concerned with the danger of Tibet gravitating towards Russia, but British freedom of manoeuvre was also limited by the Anglo-Russian Convention of 1907'.[23] Jordan recommended that Britain should not become party to any final treaty reached at Shimla, as that would involve the conclusion of a new agreement with Russia. He recommended McMahon, 'to take an attitude of benevolent assistance and act as an honest broker'.[24]

The Russians had to be dealt with delicately. They were kept informed and the British went ahead with their plans to hold a conference at Shimla after the Russians had made it clear that they had no objection to it, and 'a more formal communication to Russia would only be required if the well-recognised frontier were rectified'.[25]

The main point of contention during the nine months of negotiations was where the border between China and Tibet should be, as many ethnic Tibetans lived in areas outside of Lhasa's political control. Technically, those areas were part of China, a country where central authorities at that time had difficulty controlling even less remote parts of the new republic. Perhaps influenced by the new arrangement for Mongolia, McMahon suggested that the Tibetan-inhabited areas should also be divided into 'inner' and 'outer' sections. Outer Tibet would be the part of Tibet traditionally under Lhasa's control and remain a self-governing entity. Inner Tibet, an integral part of China, would serve as a buffer between Tibet ruled by Lhasa and Russian-dominated Outer Mongolia.[26] Outer Tibet would correspond roughly to the central and western parts of Tibet, whereas Inner Tibet, bordering on China, would consist of Amdo and part of Kham.[27]

After nine months of strenuous and sometimes heated deliberations, a convention was signed by the British and the Tibetans on 3 July 1914. It stipulated that 'the Governments of Great Britain and China recognising that Tibet is under the suzerainty of China, and recognising also the autonomy of Outer Tibet engage to respect the territorial integrity of the country, and to abstain from interference in the administration of Outer Tibet (including the selection and installation of the Dalai Lama), which shall remain in the hands of the Tibetan Government at Lhasa'.[28] The text also states that 'the Government of China engages not to convert Tibet into a Chinese province. The Government of Great Britain engages not to annex Tibet or any portion of it'.[29]

The Tibetans did not get what they wanted, a full recognition of their independence, but China had to pledge to send only a 'high official' with 'suitable escort' that should 'in no circumstances exceed 300 men,' and 'it is also understood that the selection and appointment of all officers in Outer Tibet will rest with the Tibetan Government'.[30]

Chen had initialled the draft text of the Convention, but, in the end, refused to ratify it. According to historian John Rowland, his and his government's 'main reason for rejecting the Simla [Shimla] Convention stems from China's basic and traditional unwillingness to relinquish rights to territory which it considers to be eternally part of the "celestial" realm'.[31]

Although the question of the creation of an Inner and Outer Tibet and the demarcation of the boundary between the two areas were the main topics of debate at Shimla, the Indo-Tibetan border was also discussed. Among the articles in the Convention that Chen had initialled was the ninth article, which states that, 'For the purpose of the present Convention the borders of Tibet, and the boundary between Outer and Inner Tibet, shall be shown in red and blue respectively on the map attached hereto'.[32] The red line was the McMahon Line, which separated Tibet from British India, the blue one was the boundary between Inner and Outer Tibet. Thus, Rowland argues, 'it is unreasonable for China now to allege that the India-Tibet border was not taken up at Simla [Shimla]',[33] or that Chen did not approve of the red and blue lines on the map.

Nothing was negotiated behind the backs of Chen and his delegation, as the Chinese later claimed. But it could be argued that the Chinese were not party to discussions about the details of the demarcation of the Indo-Tibetan border, which was considered by the British and the Tibetans as a bilateral issue, and therefore not a Chinese concern.

According to Van Eekelen,

> Before the final drafts of the texts had been agreed the British and Tibetan
> delegates completed discussions on the north-eastern border of India, later
> to be known as the McMahon Line. The Chinese were not invited to take
> part and their specific acceptance was never sought. They were informed later
> when the line was embodied in the map annexed to the Convention drawing
> the borders of Tibet and the boundary between Outer and Inner Tibet.[34]

But if the Chinese and their supporters are to believed, the McMahon
Line was indeed the outcome of a conspiracy by McMahon. Chen and
his men were kept in the dark, as the British pressured the Tibetans
into accepting a new border with British India. Without consulting the
Chinese, the border was moved from the foot of the mountains, north of
the Brahmaputra, to the crest of the Himalayas. Then, for some unknown
reason—perhaps so as to not upset the Chinese—the agreement between
the British and the Tibetans was kept secret, or maybe even forgotten, for
decades, as Neville Maxwell and Alastair Lamb, among others, allege.

The 1914 Shimla Agreement and the separate Anglo-Tibetan
Declaration, which stipulated the McMahon Line, were not mentioned
in the 1929 edition of *Aitchison's Treaties*, a collection of 'treaties, engagements and sanads relating to India and neighbouring countries' that was
published in a series of volumes beginning in 1862. But, according to
Maxwell and Lamb, when the records from the Shimla Conference and the
Anglo-Tibetan border agreement were included in a 1938 reissue of the
1929 edition, it also had a 1929 publication date. The original 1929 edition was allegedly withdrawn from circulation.[35] In other words, it was an
outright deceit, according to Maxwell and Lamb.

In 1962, the Chinese communist government presented their version
of the Shimla conference and its aftermath in a book titled *The Sino-Indian
Boundary Question*.

> It was outside the Conference and behind the back of the representatives of the
> Chinese Central Government that the British representative drew the notori-
> ous 'McMahon Line' through a secret exchange of letters with the representa-
> tive of the Tibet local authorities, attempting thereby to annex 90,000 square

kilometres of China's territory to British India. The Chinese Government refused to recognise this illegal McMahon Line. So have all Chinese Governments since then. That is why even the British Government dared not publicly draw this Line on its maps before 1936 [sic]. The illegal McMahon Line was wholly imposed on the Chinese people by British imperialism.[36]

Maxwell asserts that Henry McMahon was transferred out of India after the Shimla conference with the implication that it was because of what he had 'done' in 1914.[37] In fact, McMahon, who spoke not only Hindustani and Persian but also Arabic, was awarded the post of High Commissioner for Egypt in 1915. This was hardly a punishment or even a demotion. From his base in Cairo, McMahon helped organize Arab leaders against the Ottoman Empire, which became a success when they rose up to fight for independence in 1916–17.

Maxwell also writes that, 'nothing more was done, or indeed heard, about the "McMahon Line" until 1935, when an official in Delhi, Olaf Caroe, happened upon the agreement with the Tibetans in old files and began to agitate within the government for making the Line the effective north-east boundary of India'.[38]

Caroe, also according to Maxwell, 'succeeded, with difficulty, in getting it [the McMahon Line] on to some official maps; and he arranged for the falsification of the published record of the Simla Conference of 1914 in *Aitchison's Treaties* so as to make it appear that there had been agreement there among all parties on the new "McMahon" alignment"'. It was only then, Maxwell asserts, that 'the British in India began slowly to move their administration forward, up towards the crest along which McMahon had drawn his line'.[39]

Lamb is more thorough and scholarly in his approach to the boundary issue than Maxwell, but he also blames Caroe for 'falsifying' documents and changing the border on his own accord. It was not easy for Caroe, Lamb states, 'to convince politicians that there really was a serious situation involving the security of territory which was technically British but about which the rulers of the British Empire had somehow managed to forget for more than two decades. If it was so important, how was it that it had slipped the official memory?'[40]

However, other scholars disagree with Lamb, and his interpretation of events is weak and debatable, to say the least. It is undeniable that a border agreement was indeed reached between the British and the Tibetans at Shimla, as documented by Leo E. Rose, a professor at Berkeley, and many others. And apart from criticizing Lamb for espousing overly pro-Chinese views, Rose also points at several more precise weaknesses in the British academic's writings on the McMahon Line. Rose takes Lamb to task on two major issues. Lamb asserts that the Tibetan government was not independent and could not enter into such an agreement without Chinese approval. He argues that Lamb

> ignores the fact that the Tibetan government had formally declared its independence from China in 1913, and had established effective authority throughout the state prior to the Simla Conference…The question whether the British and Tibetan governments were competent to conclude an agreement delineating the Indian-Tibet border…is dismissed [by Lamb] in short paragraph. Yet it is certainly legitimate to argue that the British and Tibetan governments were acting within the limits of their competence, and that the failure of the Chinese to ratify the convention is of no *legal* significance as far as the McMahon Line is concerned.[41]

And, besides, Chen had put his initials on the map accompanying the border agreement.

Lamb's argument, in a footnote in his book, that Tibet acknowledged Chinese 'suzerainty' in the Shimla Convention is, according to Rose,

> indeed curious given his general line of analysis, as apparently he would recognise the competence of the Tibetan government to make at least this kind of commitment for the Tibetan people. But he fails to note that this clause of the Convention would [according to the text] come into effect *only* after Chinese ratification. As the Chinese did not ratify the agreement, the whole argument is superfluous.[42]

Rose's other point is that Lamb's arguments are based on conventions signed by Britain and China and Britain and Russia, which would limit the capacity of the British to act in Tibet. According to Rose, 'While it may be argued that the British violated both those conventions [with Russia and China] in reaching an agreement with Tibet, it is indeed astonishing to conclude that a treaty signed under radically different circumstances is itself invalid under international law. The precedents against such an interpretation are overwhelming.'[43]

Reality is also much less convoluted and dramatic than the accounts of those who have accepted the Chinese version of events during and after the Shimla Conference. While Chen and his Chinese delegates were preoccupied with Tibet's status and the demarcation of the boundary between Tibet and China proper, it is evident from the records of the Shimla Convention that they had little or no idea where the Indo-Tibetan border was or should be. Chen deplored the absence of any 'accurate and detailed maps of the region on the various frontiers of Tibet'.[44] According to Pradip Phanjoubam, Chen 'was not sure where the Indian boundary was when McMahon asked him, and could only come up with an answer the following day and that too using French maps as evidence'.[45]

Furthermore, caution and then neglect on the part of the British rather than 'fear', as the Chinese claim, or secrecy and trickery, according to Maxwell and Lamb, should be seen the reasons why details about the Shimla Convention and the McMahon Line were not released immediately. World War I broke out shortly after the Convention was concluded and Britain obviously had other priorities and was preoccupied with more pressing issues than the demarcation of a border in a remote corner of India.

The fact that Britain did have an agreement with Russia on Tibet should also not be overlooked. It was an important consideration in the corridors of the Foreign Office in London.[46] However, it changed after the Bolshevik revolution in Russia in 1917 and the subsequent establishment of the Soviet Union. The 1907 Anglo-Russian Convention was now definitely dead and buried.

But it is at the same time incorrect to state, as Maxwell, Lamb, and the Chinese have done, that a border along the crest of the Himalayas was not shown on any British or other maps until the 1930s. Watersheds, mountains and rivers divided nations and states long before detailed maps with defined borders became a reality, and the crest of the Himalayas, rather than its southern foothills, has long been a natural dividing line between the Tibetan High Plateau and the Indian subcontinent.

When Charles Bell, the British officer in Sikkim who later took up the post as Britain's envoy to Lhasa, wrote his classic, *Tibet: Past and Present* in 1924, the accompanying fold-out map shows the Indo-Tibetan border at the heights of the Himalayas, or roughly along the McMahon Line.[47] The map of Tibet in *Atlas of the Chinese Empire*, published by the China Inland Mission in 1908, five years before the Shimla Conference, shows the border along the watershed of the Himalayas as well, and so does the map in the March 1912 issue of the *Geographical Journal*, published by the Royal Geographical Society in London. Even some maps printed in China place the border along the crest of the Himalayas. Among them are the official postal map which was used by the government of China in 1917 and a map of Tibet in the *New Atlas and Commercial Gazetteer of China*, published in Shanghai in the same year.[48]

Border demarcation in the west is even hazier than in the east, mainly because of the scarcity of people in the area and the absence of any significant trade across the mountains. Ladakh, though, was an independent kingdom inhabited by ethnic Tibetan tribes who practised the Tibetan form of Buddhism, maintained relations with Tibet as well as Bhutan. But in 1834, forces from the Sikh Empire of the Punjab plains annexed Ladakh, which finally lost its independence six years later. In 1846, Ladakh was incorporated into Jammu and Kashmir, a new princely state which under a treaty signed in Amritsar acknowledged British paramountcy within the Indian empire.[49] High mountain ranges and what was described as 'natural elements' became the frontier separating the Ladakh area from those to the north still under Tibetan or Chinese influence—but there were different views on exactly which 'elements' these should be.

According to the 1846 Treaty of Amritsar, the northern frontier with Tibet was to be defined by commissioners appointed by the British East India Company and Gulab Singh Dogra, the Maharaja of Jammu and Kashmir. William H. Johnson, a British surveyor, became the governor of Ladakh under the Maharaja, and, in 1865, he proposed a boundary through Aksai Chin that would touch the Kunlun range, the highest mountains in the area. This boundary was formally proposed to the government of British India in 1897 by the chief of British military intelligence in London, Major General Sir John Ardagh. Subsequently, it became known as the Ardagh-Johnson Line.[50]

The Chinese never recognized the Ardagh-Johnson Line, and, in 1892, one of their patrols erected some border markers at the Karakoram Pass, where there was an ancient caravan route between Xinjiang and Ladakh. Since then, the Chinese have continued to claim that the greater part of Ladakh's Aksai Chin region should be inside the territory claimed by them. The British did not pay much attention to the Chinese moves in this remote and inhospitable area, and, in order to create yet another buffer zone between the expanding Russian Empire and Tibet, a new boundary was drawn in 1893. It became known as the MacCartney-MacDonald Line and placed most of Aksai Chin on the Chinese side of the boundary. The new line was named after George MacCartney, the British consul in Xinjiang's main town Kashgar, and Sir Claude MacDonald, a British minister to the Qing rulers of China. MacDonald came to be better known as the man who negotiated and secured from China the 99-year lease of the New Territories to the colony of Hong Kong in 1898. It was when that lease expired in 1997 that the whole of Hong Kong reverted to Chinese rule.

According to Indian sources, by the end of World War I, the British Government had accepted the Ardagh-Johnson Line rather than MacCartney-MacDonald Line as the official boundary.[51] That is also the outer border of India on all its maps today, while China's claim follows roughly the MacCartney-MacDonald Line. Maps from the British colonial era are more ambiguous here than in the eastern sector, but those produced immediately before the partition of the British India into the independent nations of India and Pakistan in 1947 definitely show Aksai Chin, and today's Arunachal Pradesh in the east, as Indian territory.[52] But, contrastingly, the Ladakh boundary is shown on several older colonial maps as 'undefined'. Between 1921 and 1927, the government of British India made several representations to the authorities in Tibet, asking them to delimit the boundary between Ladakh and Tibet, but without any result.[53] Thus, that border was marked, at least until 1943, as no more than a dotted line on the map.

On the other hand, the outer boundaries of China are not accurate in any of the Chinese maps. The most imaginative one is the official map of the Republic of China, which is still in use in Taiwan. Although the old republic lives on only in Taiwan and some smaller nearby islands, the map that is still being used shows the boundaries of the Republic of China when it was proclaimed on 1 January 1912. The map's only amendment is from 1945, to include Taiwan, which had been under Japanese rule from 1895 until the end of World War II.

Tibet, of course, is part of the Republic of China on its official maps. So are Mongolia, the Republic of Tuva in Russia, Aksai Chin, Arunachal Pradesh, the northernmost part of Myanmar above Sumprabum in Kachin State, the islands in the South China Sea, and Diaoyudao Islands, which the Japanese also claim and call Senkaku, in the East China Sea.

The Republic of China never recognized Mongolia's independence, which was the reason why it could not, for many years, join the United Nations (UN). Mongolia became a UN member in 1961 only after the Soviet Union threatened to veto the admission of all of the newly decolonized states of Africa if the Republic of China used its veto, as it had done before. The Republic of China represented China in the UN, and served as one of the five permanent members of the Security Council, until the People's Republic of China occupied China's seat in 1971.

Mongolia had undergone some important changes since the declaration of independence in 1911. The old clerical state ceased to exist when the Russian Red Army occupied the country in 1921. The invasion had been prompted by the reign of terror that a former major-general in the Tsar's army had unleashed in the Russian Far East and adjoining areas. His name was Roman Fyodorovich von Ungern-Sternberg and he would today have been certified as a psychopath and locked up. Known as 'the Mad Baron', he had adopted Lamaistic Buddhism from Mongol horsemen in his cavalry unit. His Buddhist teachers had taught him about reincarnation, and he firmly believed that in killing feeble people he only did them good, as they would be stronger in their next life.

In the autumn of 1920, von Ungern-Sternberg led a motley force of 6,000 former members of the Tsar's cavalry, local Cossacks, and Mongol

horsemen into Mongolia. When they invaded Urga in January 1921, 'innu-
merable children of all ages, races and creeds were hacked to bits and bayo-
neted and shot and strangled and hung, and crucified and buried alive'.[54]

In Mongolia, von Ungern-Sternberg proclaimed himself 'Emperor
of all Russia' and vowed to plant ' an avenue of gallows' stretching from
Urga to Moscow, from which would swing 'Bolshevik and Jew alike'.[55] He
also declared that he would lead his men all the way to Tibet, where, he
believed, his 'empire' would forge a pact with the Dalai Lama.

The new Bolshevik government in Moscow clearly viewed the Mad
Baron as a threat, and not only because of the atrocities he committed. Von
Ungern-Sternberg's main benefactors were the Japanese, who saw him as a
useful tool to expand their influence in north-central Asia, especially after
their victory in the 1904–5 war against Tsarist Russia. The Japanese openly
backed von Ungern-Sternberg's plans for a 'Greater Mongolia', which they
had already earmarked as their own protectorate. It is uncertain whether
a conquest of Tibet was also part of the plan, but von Ungern-Sternberg's
Japanese-backed rampage in the region was cause for concern in New
Delhi and London, emphasizing the need to secure the northern borders
of British India.

In the end, it was the Russian Bolsheviks, not the British or any other
foreign power, that put an end to von Ungern-Sternberg's reign of terror. In
July 1921, 10,000 Red Army soldiers marched into Urga, and von Ungern-
Sternberg was captured and executed. Mongolia became a vassal of Moscow,
though, unlike some Bolshevik-run parts of Central Asia, it was not turned
into one of the republics of the Soviet Union when it was proclaimed on 30
December 1922. The Soviet Union had, at that time, friendly relations with
the Republic of China, and an annexation of Mongolia would have upset
those. The Soviet solution was what it considered a compromise. Mongolia
became a separate 'people's republic', the first communist-led country after
the Soviet Union itself. But all the maps of the Republic of China continued to include Mongolia within its borders.

Today's Tuvan Republic, now part of the Russian Federation, was
another area ruled by the Bolsheviks and claimed by China. Like Mongolia,
it also became a formally independent state. Then known as the People's

Republic of Tannu Tuva, it came into existence in August 1921, only to vanish from the map in 1944. Being smaller and not as strategically important as Mongolia, it was annexed by the Soviet Union. But, like Mongolia, it remains part of the Republic of China on its maps.

The official map of the Republic of China may be dismissed as being grossly out of touch with the realities on the ground, but the authorities in Taipei keep it because, if Mongolia were to be recognized as an independent country, what about Taiwan? There are strong forces on the island to shed the old name the Republic of China in favour of Republic of Taiwan. And if that happens, China has threatened to invade. Although Taiwan was ruled from the Chinese mainland for only four years since 1895—from the end of Japanese rule and reunification with China in 1945 until the communist victory in 1949 and the flight of the nationalist KMT government to the island—the People's Republic of China considers it part of its territory. The KMT also considers Taiwan part of China, but of the Republic of China. This view is not shared by the Taiwan-nationalist Democratic Progressive Party, the ruling party since May 2016, which wants to see an independent Taiwan separate from the mainland.

Maps printed by the People's Republic of China have fewer anachronistic anomalies than those produced by the Republic of China. But they nevertheless include areas which were never part of China or which have been occupied since the proclamation of the People's Republic on 1 October 1949. While the People's Republic of China does not claim Mongolia and the Tuvan Republic, Tibet and Aksai Chin were taken over by China's new communist government in the early 1950s. And the maps of the People's Republic of China also include Taiwan, today's Arunachal Pradesh, and the Spratlys in the South China Sea as well as the Diaoyudao Islands.

The communist government of China, on taking power, declared that it would 're-examine treaties concluded by its predecessors with foreign powers, and either recognize, abrogate, revise or renegotiate them'.[56] Between 1960 and 1963 new border agreements were concluded by China with Myanmar, Nepal, Mongolia, Pakistan, and Afghanistan, but not with India or the Soviet Union. Territorial disputes with the Soviet Union were not settled until agreements were reached in 1991, 2003, and, finally, in 2008.

In an accord signed on 1 October 1960, the People's Republic of China gave up old claims on the northern tip of Myanmar's Kachin State, which in any case had never been ruled by any Chinese authority. The 1960 border agreement went on to stipulate that in exchange for this 'concession', and for Myanmar's sovereignty over a 220-square-kilometre area on the Kachin-Shan state border called the Namwan Assigned Tract, which the British originally leased from China in 1897, China would get the three Kachin villages of Hpimaw, Gawlam, and Kamfang on the Sino-Myanmar border, and the Panhung-Panglao area in Myanmar's northeastern Wa Hills. The village tract in Kachin State encompasses 152 square kilometres and the Wa area that was ceded to China was 189 square kilometres in area.[57]

The deal was not unfair by international standards, but rumours soon spread across Kachin State, an ethnic minority area in Myanmar, to the effect that vast tracts of Kachin territory had been ceded to China, and, in 1961, a revolt broke out among the Kachins that continues to this day. Apart from the border agreement with China, the Myanmar government's decision in 1960 to make Buddhism the state religion also prompted widespread dissatisfaction among the predominantly Christian Kachin tribesmen, who began to fight for an independent, or at least a truly autonomous, state for themselves.

In a regional sense, the 1960 agreement between China and Myanmar was relevant to the conflict with India, as the border that was demarcated between those two countries follows the McMahon concept, i.e., the watershed principle. Myanmar's northern border is, in effect, a continuation of the McMahon Line, which China, evidently, does not see as an outcome of some old, colonial 'unequal treaty' or 'imperialist policies', the usual jargon that the Chinese government resorts to when the Sino-Indian border and other territorial disputes are mentioned.

The borders of Myanmar may have another bearing on India, and on the moves by the British in the 1930s to secure the McMahon Line. Myanmar, then known as Burma, had become a province of British India after the colonial conquest in the three Anglo-Burmese wars in the nineteenth century. But under the terms of the Government of India Act of 1935, Burma would become a separate colony. This happened in 1937, and according to Pradip Phanjoubam, this could have been 'one of the reasons why Olaf

Caroe was in a hurry to publish the McMahon Line in *Aitchison's Treaties*—which he ultimately did in 1938 under controversial circumstances—[because of] this imminent separation' of Myanmar from India.[58]

British rule in northernmost Myanmar, albeit comparatively light compared to other parts of the colony, did extend to the northern watersheds, so it would make sense to secure the actual McMahon Line as well. A declassified 1959 US Central Intelligence Agency (CIA) document states that 'despite the drawing of the McMahon Line in 1914, almost nothing was done thereafter to extend administrative control into the hills.'[59] While the hills north of the Brahmaputra were neglected by the British, it is not entirely true that nothing was done. The same CIA intelligence brief says that although the area was largely unadministered, 'before 1900, the British had made pacts with various hill tribes designed from keeping them from raiding the plains dwellers'.[60]

Those contacts were not insignificant. Expeditions were sent into the mountains north of the Brahmaputra, and tribesmen from there would not only raid the lowlands but also go there to buy certain daily necessities not available in the highlands. With the exception of the Tawang area in the northwestern corner of today's Arunachal Pradesh and Walong in the far east, which traded mainly with Tibet, any contacts between the tribals of the hills and the outside world were down to the plains in the south and not in a northerly direction over the highest mountain range in the world. And, as noted earlier, if those tribals spoke any foreign language, it would have been broken Assamese rather than Tibetan—and definitely not Chinese.

But there is some confusion and obvious contradictions not only in the writings of Maxwell and Lamb, but also in those of many other Western scholars with regard to an Inner and an Outer Line, which they claim existed beside and below the McMahon Line. Some of what is written is true, but much is fiction and not only misunderstandings but also distortions of the actual situation along India's northern frontiers. Maxwell claims that there was a 'de facto borderline' where the 'broad plains of the Brahmaputra River begins to rise into the foothills of the Himalayas...The Raj called this accepted limit to its rule "the Outer Line" and prohibited unauthorised ingress or egress across it'.[61]

This is utter nonsense. In 1873, as a by-product of the Bengal Eastern Frontier Regulation, a law was implemented that created what was termed an Inner Line between the plains of Assam and its surrounding hill areas. However, the administration made it clear that 'this line does not necessarily indicate the territorial frontier but only the limits of the administered area…it does not in any way decide sovereignty of the territory beyond'.[62]

As Phanjoubam points out, 1873 was the time the cultivation of tea was expanding rapidly throughout Assam 'and speculators in tea were hungering for more land'.[63] Those speculators were encroaching into the hills and the lack of control over the communication between them and the rent-paying population meant that 'the government was losing out on substantial amounts of revenue'.[64] On the other hand, the Inner Line was deemed necessary to prevent what the colonial authorities called 'the wild tribes' from raiding the lowlands. Territories outside the Inner Line were under the 1919 Government of India Act categorized as 'excluded areas', 'partially excluded areas', and 'backward tracts'. But they were considered parts of British India, not some alien land.

The Inner Line Regulation is still in force in parts of northeastern India, and it also prevents people from the lowlands settling permanently north of the line. Indian citizens who are not from the northeastern hill states need special permits to enter Nagaland, Mizoram, Arunachal Pradesh, and Sikkim. Non-Indian citizens have to register with the authorities when entering Nagaland and Mizoram, as well as Manipur, and apply for special permits for Arunachal Pradesh and Sikkim.

The Inner Line is clear, but there was never any official Outer Line. That is a figment of the imagination of several Western scholars. Lamb, in his *The China-India Border: The Origins of the Disputed Boundaries,* even has a map where a demarcated 'pre-1914 Outer Line' is marked.[65] Some old books and accounts do mention an outer line, but, as Phanjoubam points out, 'the British India government denied there was ever an official Outer Line, and that the implied Outer Line was always roughly where the McMahon Line was drawn in 1913–14'.[66] If there ever were an Outer Line, it would have been the crest of the Himalayas, as there would be no reason to have a third line between the Inner Line and the McMahon Line.

On Lamb's map, his Outer Line follows the foot of the hills, or some kilometres north of where the Inner Line is. It would hardly make sense to have two parallel lines that close to each other. Maxwell goes a step further and claims in his *India's China War* that, in 1910, 'the retiring Viceroy, Lord Minto was less tentative [than the Lieutenant-Governor of Bengal], proposing that the Outer Line should be extended to include all of the tribal territory… [and the new Viceroy] Hardinge took up Minto's proposal that the Outer Line should be pushed north'.[67]

Here, again, the implication is that there was an official Outer Line. The problem with Maxwell's account is that his footnote says 'Hardinge to Crewe', giving the impression that this was quoted from a direct communication Viceroy Charles Hardinge had with Lord Robert Crewe-Milnes, British Secretary of State for India in 1911, but the source, from where he got the quote, does not say that exactly.

According to the footnote in *India's China War*, the quote is reproduced from *History of the Frontier Areas Bordering Assam From 1883–1941* by Sir Robert Reid, the governor of Assam from 1937–41, and it says that

we do not propose to have a third or intermediate line between the existing Inner Line and the new external boundary, but it will probably be necessary during the course of the contemplated operations in tribal territory, to erect cairns at suitable points, such as trade routes leading into Tibet, to indicate the limits of our control, and to explain to the tribesmen the object of such marks.[68]

Hardinge refers in his dispatch to an 'outer line', but dismisses it as unnecessary, as a new, more precise boundary was being discussed. But in Lamb's and Maxwell's version of history, this imprecise 'outer line' becomes the official Outer Line. According to Phanjoubam, the territory between the Inner Line, which did exist, and the crest of the Himalayas 'was, for all practical purposes, treated as wild "no-man's" land till it was claimed officially and, in this case, by the McMahon Line'.[69]

Maxwell also gives the impression that the land beyond Assam was China and he refers to perceived threats in India by 'an active Chinese presence on the frontier of India', and that was the reason why the British wanted to expand north.[70] But apart from erecting a few border markers in a remote area in the vicinity of Walong during the brief occupation of Tibet during 1910–12, there were no Chinese officials or soldiers anywhere near India's northern frontier. Maxell also refers to Tawang as being 'unchallengeably Tibetan/Chinese', as if the Tibetans and the Chinese were happily administering the area together.[71] It is not inconceivable that some Chinese merchants did venture into or through Tawang in the early twentieth century, but no government officials from China were ever in that area. Equally misleading is Maxwell's reference to 'the sudden collapse of Chinese power in Tibet in 1911–12'.[72] He is, in fact, referring to the brief and failed Chinese occupation of Tibet during those years.

The colonial move into today's Arunachal Pradesh was prompted by other, more immediate concerns such as tribal raids into the lowlands of Assam, and planters wishing to extend their tea gardens into the hills north of the Brahmaputra. Several of the tribal chiefs north of the Inner Line were paid handsomely by the British Indian government to refrain from raiding the plains, resulting in a mutual dependence between them and the colonial power. The chieftains needed the British to keep outsiders away, and the British ensured themselves of a reasonable loyalty from the tribals by paying them annual subsidies.

Tibet, on the other side of the Himalayas, managed to maintain its de facto independence for decades after the 1913 proclamation by the thirteenth Dalai Lama, and even before that, as Tibet specialist Warren W. Smith points out, 'the nature of the [imperial] Qing relationship with Tibet was one between states, or between an empire and a semiautonomous state, not a relationship between a central government and an outlying province'.[73]

With the end of the limited influence the Chinese had enjoyed in Tibet, the Tibetans were now able to build a more truly independent nation. The border with British India was clear, as the Tibetan delegate at Shimla, Lönchen Shatra, had stated in a message to Henry McMahon,

As it was feared that there might be friction in future unless the boundary between India and Tibet is clearly defined, I submitted the map, which you sent me in February last, to Lhasa for orders. I have now received orders from Lhasa, and I accordingly agree to the boundary as marked in red in the two copies of the maps signed by you subject to conditions, mentioned in your letter dated 24th March, sent to me through Mr. Bell. I have signed and sealed the two copies of the maps. I have kept one copy here and return herewith the other.[74]

The 'boundary marked in red', of course, was the McMahon Line and 'Mr. Bell' was Charles Bell.

Thus, even the Tibetans would find it preposterous to claim that the McMahon Line was 'secret', and it is equally misleading to say that documents relating to it were 'discovered' by Caroe in the 1930s. Not much may have been done to establish any actual administration in the area between the plains of Assam and the McMahon Line, but in 1928, Captain Nevill, a political officer in the Balipara Frontier Tract, north of the Inner Line, informed the Indian government that in the event of a Chinese attempt to gain control over Tibet, Tawang would provide a 'secret and easy entrance into India'.[75]

Tawang was one of those areas where it was difficult to determine whether it was north or south of the McMahon Line. Henry McMahon's red line on the map puts the border roughly at Sela Pass, 78 kilometres south of Tawang. But according to the principle on which the McMahon Line was based—that it should be drawn along the highest peaks in the Himalayas and linked by watersheds—the border would be at Bumla Pass, northeast of Tawang. In his final memorandum at the Shimla Conference, McMahon discovered this, and briefly discussed the inclusion of Tawang in Indian territory, 'This secures to us a natural watershed frontier, access to the shortest trade route into Tibet, and control of the monastery of Tawang, which has blocked the trade by this route in the past by undue exaction and oppression'.[76]

The 'discovery' not of the McMahon Line as such, but of the ambiguity of some of its parts, should be credited not to Caroe, but to the British botanist and explorer Frank Kingdon-Ward, who made it to Monyul, or the Tawang area, in 1934–5. He noted that the Indian government had for a long time been paying an annual subsidy to the de facto rulers of Monyul (Tawang) under the impression that they were independent chiefs. Possibly they were at the beginning. But it has lately come to light that most of the subsidy went into the purses of the power at Tsona-Dzong (in Tibet) and hence to Lhasa...this practice dilutes the Indian claim to Monyul...a deal was effected in 1914; Monyul was to become part of the Balipara Frontier Tract.[77]

Kingdon-Ward held the Indian government responsible for this neglect. 'Had India been able to take up possession in 1914 no more could have been heard about the matter.'[78] Kingdon-Ward had a solution to the problem: 'effective occupation by 1939 or at the latest 1940'.[79] But World War II came in between, and it was not until the early 1950s that Tawang was eventually brought under the control of the central Indian government.

Kingdon-Ward's foray into Tawang caused some problems in relations between British India and Tibet. He was arrested by the local authorities, and the Tibetans protested to the British officer Derrick Williamson, then on a tour to Lhasa. After some negotiations with the Tibetans, Kingdon-Ward was sent back to the lowlands. It was after this incident that Olaf Caroe decided to make the Shimla agreements available to a wider public. Until then, they were known only to a limited number of frontier officials.[80]

Despite the Kingdon-Ward incident, relations between Tibet and the British in India remained cordial throughout the 1920s and the 1930s. Younghusband's foray into Tibet in 1903–4, the flight of the Dalai Lama, and the brutal humiliation of the Tibetans, were forgotten. In 1922, Laden La (the Bhutia Sikkimese officer, who had taken part in Younghusband's 'expedition' and later been an interpreter at the Shimla Conference) was sent by the British to Lhasa to establish a Tibetan police force. His efforts were extremely successful, and Colonel Frederick Bailey, a British intelligence officer, was able to report from a visit to Lhasa in 1924 that, 'Sardar Bahadur Laden La has organised a very credible police force for Lhasa city. The men are smart and dressed in thick khaki serge in winter, and blue with yellow piping in summer.'[81] Led by Laden La, the Tibetan Police Band entertained Bailey with the swirl of bagpipes and the beating of drums.

Those instruments, which would be considered exotic in a Tibetan context, had been brought in from India, along with most other foreign goods. The main trade route led south from Lhasa over Jelep La Pass on the Sikkim border, and on to Kalimpong and Laden La's hometown Darjeeling. From there, communications with Kolkata were excellent, and even included a railway that wound its way up the mountains from the plains of northern Bengal. Telegraph lines connected Tibet with India, Tibetan postage stamps and bank notes were printed, and coins were minted in the Tibetan currency. The currency included *srang*, which was divided into 10 *sho*, and, a lower denomination, the skar. There was also a *tangka*, divided into 15 *skar*. Monetary policies were the responsibility of the *kashag*, or Tibetan government. Electricity was introduced, though on a very small scale, and the first telephones and motorcars could be seen in Lhasa. Tibet also had its own national flag.

Chinese influence was basically non-existent in Tibet throughout the 1920s and 1930s. But China had not given up its claims to Tibet. In fact, one of the primary aims of Chiang Kai-shek was the 'reunification of China', and, according to him, both Mongolia and Tibet were part of the Republic of China. In 1928, Chiang established a Commission for Mongolian and Tibetan Affairs. But any attempts to seize Tibet by military means would have been disastrous given the fragmentation of China as a whole at that time. The Commission became what in modern terms could be called a government think-tank. After the Shimla Conference, nothing more was heard of Chen Yifan, perhaps because he had initialled the documents and thereby, in a sense, agreed to the British demands. But the wily Lu Xingqi is known to have continued to be working behind the scenes on Tibetan and Mongolian affairs well into the 1930s.[82]

But the thirteenth Dalai Lama's disenchantment with Tsarong Dzasa, the secretary of state and his pro-British military officers, did not go unnoticed in China. Intrigues began, and in late 1929, contacts with the Tibetans were established through the abbot of the Yunggün monastery in Beijing. Liu Man-ching, a young woman from the Commission for Mongolian and Tibetan Affairs, was sent to Lhasa, where she met the Dalai Lama. She conveyed Chiang's 'deep concern ... over the prevailing conditions in Tibet and his eager wish to see Tibet rejoin the family of the Republic as brothers'.[83]

The Dalai Lama's response was essentially the same as the position taken by the Tibetans at Shimla, but still somewhat conciliatory towards China. Tibet was an independent nation, but it was willing to accept some kind of nominal subordination to China as long as the Tibetans were able to run their own affairs. No agreement was reached, but for the first time since 1913, some official relations with China were restored.

If there were any friendly feelings between the Chinese and the Tibetans, these did not last long. Only two years later, in 1932, war broke out between China and Tibet when Tibetan forces tried to seize territory in Qinghai and Xikang, or the Kham region in Inner Tibet. The Tibetan army was defeated, and the Tibetans were warned not to cross the Jinsha River, the border between Inner and Outer Tibet, again.

Then, the following year, the thirteenth Dalai Lama died. Tibet scholar Melvyn Goldstein stated that 'the death of the strong-willed, autocratic and fiercely independent 13th Dalai Lama created new conditions that to the Chinese seemed promising for the restoration of what China considered its traditional superordination over Tibet'.[84] A mission, headed by General Huang Mu-sung of China's National Military Council, was sent to Lhasa to pay respects to the late Dalai Lama, but, more precisely, to try to reassert Chinese authority over Tibet. Among other stratagems, Huang emphasized the commonalities between China in contrast to the alien British.

No firm agreement was reached, but the Chinese were allowed to station an official and keep a wireless set in Lhasa, though only for the possibility of further dialogue. According to Goldstein, '[t]his decision again reflects the paradox of Tibet's China policy: a refusal to relinquish its de facto independence, but at the same time a refusal to make a complete break with China. China dangled the hope of a satisfactory settlement while refusing to yield on key issues.'[85]

China's attempts to lure the Tibetans into some kind of settlement continued as the search for a new Dalai Lama began shortly after the death of the thirteenth in 1933. There were indications that the exiled Panchen Lama, the second-most important lama in Tibet, was becoming a tool of the government of the Republic of China, now headquartered at Nanjing. The possibility of his return to Tibet was problematic for the British, but they made it clear that he was welcome back and, if necessary, they said they were even willing to mediate between him and the authorities in Lhasa. But, as the Chinese scholar Lin Hsiao-ting says, 'the British government would never agree to any Chinese troops entering Tibet...regarding it as a violation of the 1914 Simla Treaty, and their concerns were explicitly conveyed to the Chinese through diplomatic channels'.[86] Evidently, there was no 'fear' of referring to the Shimla agreements, as a couple of years before Caroe had supposedly 'discovered' those documents.

A new Dalai Lama, the fourteenth, was eventually found in 1937, a two-year-old boy whose birth name was Tenzin Gyatso. In 1939, when he was four years old, the new Dalai Lama was taken in a procession of lamas to Lhasa, where he was to spend his childhood in the Potala palace and the summer residence at Norbulingka. As the Dalai Lama was just a child, he was represented by a regent, Renting Rimpoche, the abbot of a monastery, who, together with the kashag, continued to rule the country. But lamas and officials in high positions in the clerical state were worried about the future, as they remembered the prophecy of the late thirteenth Dalai Lama. Before his passing, he is said to have uttered this ominous prediction for Tibet's future:

> Very soon in this land [with a harmonious blend of religion and politics] deceptive acts may occur from without and within. At that time, if we do not dare to protect our territory, our spiritual personalities including the Victorious Father and Son [Dalai Lama and Panchen Lama] may be exterminated without trace, the property and authority of our Lakangs [residences of reincarnated lamas] and monks may be taken away. Moreover, our political system, developed by the Three Great Dharma Kings [Tri Songtsen Gampo, Tri Songdetsen, and Tri Ralpachen] will vanish without anything remaining. The property of all people, high and low, will be seized and the people forced to become slaves. All living beings will have to endure endless days of suffering and will be stricken with fear. Such a time will come.[87]

The Chinese spectre was hanging over Tibet and the thirteenth Dalai Lama knew it. Latter-day Chinese accounts of the installation of the fourteenth Dalai Lama state that the KMT government, represented by General Wu Zhongxin, the acting director of the Commission for Mongolian and

Tibetan Affairs, presided over the ceremony and ratified the nomination at a ceremony in Lhasa on 22 February 1940. This, as many other Chinese claims concerning Tibet, its status and its borders, is utter nonsense. The British representative, Sir Basil Gould, who was also present at the same ceremony, asserts that Wu was just one guest among many and

> he did no more than present a ceremonial scarf, as was done by the others, including the British Representative. But the Chinese have the ear of the world, and can later refer to their Press records and present an account of historical events that is wholly untrue. Tibet has no newspapers, either in English or Tibetan, and has therefore no means of exposing these falsehoods.[88]

The fourteenth Dalai Lama was still an infant when World War II broke out and could not possibly have been aware of the changes it was going to bring to the region. Tibet's delicate status as a de facto independent buffer state between India and China was being challenged. For the first time in history, an alliance between China and British India was forged as they fought together against a common enemy—Japan. The Imperial Japanese Army had seized large tracts of territory in eastern China and, later, in December 1941, the British colony of Hong Kong was occupied as well.

Tens of thousands of Chinese troops retreated from China's inland through northern Myanmar into northeastern India. Many were cantoned at Ramgarh in Bihar, now in the state of Jharkhand. Britain and the United States were firmly behind Chiang Kai-shek's forces, and preparations were underway for them to be equipped and sent back to China to fight the Japanese. Sending supplies into China was another major task, as the Japanese had severed traditional routes through Myanmar and other neighbours.

Chiang Kai-shek and his allies saw the need to develop alternative supply routes, and those would have to be from India. After discussions between the Chiang's government and the British ambassador in the wartime Chinese capital of Chongqing, Chiang issued orders in February 1941 to build a new highway from Sichuan, where Chongqing is located, through the trading town of Rima in south eastern Tibet and on to Walong on the Indian side. From there, the road would continue to Assam, where high airfields were being constructed to support the war effort. The British ambassador, Horace James Seymour, supported Chiang's plan and recommended that 'in this matter we should not allow outmoded political conceptions to stand in the way of progress'.[89] Or Britain should not let its pledges to uphold Tibet's internal autonomy interfere with this strategically important highway project.

But the British Government of India opposed the plan because it would not substantially help the war effort and, besides, Tibet's position as a de facto independent buffer state with close ties to Britain and India would be affected. After the Japanese occupation of Hong Kong in December, Britain became willing to support the plan to build a supply road to China—but it would have to go through northern Myanmar, not Tibet. That eventually became the Stilwell or Ledo Road, named after the American General Joseph Stilwell, who led the campaign, or Ledo, the small town in north eastern Assam, the starting point for the new military supply route to China through Myanmar.

Although no road was built from Sichuan to Walong, the pressure was on from China's allies to assist the Allies by allowing supplies to be sent through Tibet as well. The British sent Norbhu Döndup, the assistant political officer in Sikkim, to Lhasa to try to persuade the Tibetan government to help Britain and China in the war against Japan.

The Tibetans were caught in a dilemma. On the one hand, they wanted to maintain their friendship with India and Britain, and, on the other, siding with China in the war would set a dangerous precedent. In the end, the National Assembly in Lhasa stated that Tibetan territory could not be used to transport supplies to China. The kashag also informed the British that Tibet wanted to remain neutral in the war.[90]

However, the war and the arrival of the Americans on the scene meant that Tibet's international status, and its hitherto isolation from the rest of the world, was being challenged. Stilwell was the chief military adviser to Chiang Kai-shek, who was determined to bring Tibet under Chinese rule. In 1942, the canny Chiang ordered one of his commanders, a Muslim called Ma Bufang, to prepare for an invasion of Tibet. Chiang also threatened to use his air force to bomb Tibet, if they, as he said, 'worked with the Japanese'.[91]

There is no evidence to support Chiang's suspicions of some collusion between the Tibetans and the Japanese. It was not until 1943 that the Japanese spy Hisao Kimura set out for Tibet disguised as a Mongolian monk, using the name 'Dawa Sangpo'. He did not reach Lhasa until September 1945, by which time the war was over.[92]

In July 1942, Tibet finally agreed to allow non-military goods to be transported through Tibet to China. But the issue was so sensitive that the kashag asked one of its representatives to sign the agreement without asking the National Assembly for approval. The route that was used also bypassed Lhasa. Supplies were to be sent through Tibetan trading companies on existing pack-animal trails via central Tibet. The Chinese, for their part, declared that they planned to station 'technicians' along the route through Tibet to 'facilitate transport'.[93]

The Tibetans refused. The Chinese government then tried another ruse. A representative of its Ministry of Communications would negotiate arrangements directly with Tibetan trading companies in Kalimpong in northern Bengal. The British agreed to this, but the Tibetans, once again, saw a hidden agenda behind the Chinese proposal and declared that no Tibetan trading companies would be allowed to enter into such agreements without the approval of the authorities in Lhasa.

Meanwhile, the Americans, through their Office of Strategic Services (OSS), proposed to send intelligence officers to Tibet to survey the terrain. The idea of constructing a motorable road from India and through Tibet to China had not been totally discarded. After some initial difficulties, two Americans, Ilia Tolstoy and Brooke Dolan, were granted entry to Tibet. The American position was to support the Republic of China and its territorial claims, but Tolstoy made promises to the Tibetans that probably went beyond official policy. He said that he would recommend to his government that Tibet should be represented at a peace conference, which was going to be held after the war. The kashag was excited, and saw it as the first opportunity since the Shimla Conference to push for international recognition of its independence.

The British, on the other hand, were watching China's manoeuvres with increasing concern. On 29 April 1943, the Foreign Office in London sent a proposal to the India Office that Britain should withdraw its previous recognition of Chinese suzerainty over Tibet. The Foreign Office stated in its letter that such a withdrawal would be in Britain's and India's interest, as it would then be easier to settle once and for all the question of the border between India and Tibet.[94]

In the end, Britain decided that altering its policy on the status of Tibet might provoke the Chinese to attack and even occupy Tibet. The Republic of China would probably have tried to invade Tibet anyway once World War II was over, but the civil war with the communists kept the KMT occupied on other, more crucial fronts. The communist victory and the proclamation of the People's Republic of China on 1 October 1949 changed all that—and that was when Mao Zedong made his famous pledge before the huge crowds who had gathered outside Tiananmen, the Gate of Heavenly Peace, about the never allowing the people of China to be slaves again.

China under the iron-fisted, communist rule of Mao Zedong was never a truly free nation but he did manage to unify the country in a way Chiang Kai-shek had never been able to. While China's new rulers recognized the independence of communist-ruled Mongolia, the clerical state of Tibet had to be brought under the control of the Chinese central government.

Though the United States may never formally have recognized Tibet as part of the Republic of China, as was claimed by successive Chinese governments, Washington treated it as such so as not to upset its relations with Chiang Kai-shek. But the American attitude was to change dramatically as the Communists were gaining ground in China. Already in January 1949, when it was becoming obvious that the days of Chiang's KMT government were over, the American ambassador to India suggested to the State Department in Washington that a review of its Tibet policy would be appropriate. In particular, the ambassador proposed that if Mao Zedong and his communists succeeded in taking control of China, the United States should be prepared to treat Tibet as independent, 'If the Communists gain control of China proper, Tibet will be one of the few remaining non-Communist bastions in Continental Asia. Outer Mongolia is already detached. Communist influence is strong in Burma and Communists are infiltrating Sinkiang [Xinjiang] and Inner Mongolia. Tibet will accordingly assume both ideological and strategic importance.'[95]

On 17 November 1950, the fourteenth Dalai Lama, then 15 years old, was formally enthroned as the ruler of Tibet—but his reign was not going to be a peaceful one. Prior to his enthronement, on 7 October, communist troops had crossed the River Jinsha and fought their first and perhaps most decisive battle with the tiny, ill-equipped Tibetan army. About 5,000 Tibetan soldiers are believed to have died in the fighting, which amounted to wholesale slaughter.

Ngapoi Ngawang Jigme, a governor who had been captured by the Chinese, was sent to Lhasa to negotiate with the Dalai Lama. After several months of deliberations, on 23 May 1951, Jigme signed the 17-point agreement for 'the Peaceful Liberation of Tibet' in Beijing. It was the first time, and long before Hong Kong reverted to Chinese rule in 1997, that China promised a model based on 'one country, two systems'. The agreement affirmed China's sovereignty over Tibet, but according to point four, '[t]he central authorities will not alter the existing political system in Tibet. The central authorities also will not alter the established status, functions and powers of the Dalai Lama. Officials of various ranks shall hold office as usual.'[96]

Rather ominously, however, in late 1951, the PLA set up a base in Lhasa. The Chinese occupation of Tibet proper had begun. And there were not going to be two systems under this arrangement. The official Chinese history also had to be altered. A Chinese propaganda book, published later in the 1950s, had no references to maintaining 'the existing political system in Tibet'. But it reproduced an editorial from the *Renmin Ribao* ('people's daily'), stating that,

> To protect the unification of the country and national unity, Premier of the State Council Chou En-lai [Zhou Enlai] has ordered the dissolution of the local government in Tibet, which organized the rebellion … actively assisted by the Tibetan people, both ecclesiastical and secular, the People's Liberation Army had swiftly stamped out the rebellion in the Lhasa area and is mopping up rebel bandits in some other places in Tibet.[97]

Almost immediately after the Chinese invasion, bands of Tibetans had taken up arms against the new rulers. Among the rebels were Khampa tribesmen, as well as the remnants of the Tibetan Army that had been crushed after the Chinese invasion. The Chinese retaliation was swift and harsh. Suspected resistance fighters were rounded up and shot, and monasteries were ransacked as the Chinese unleashed a reign of terror and repression all over Tibet.

Tibet was now under direct Chinese rule and, in the early 1950s, China became an immediate and, as it turned out, permanent neighbour of India, which it had never been before. The French researcher Bérénice Guyot-Réchard writes in her study *Shadow States: India, China and the Himalayas, 1910-1962* that, 'The PLA had appeared north of the McMahon Line in the last month of 1951. Dzayül, which had not seen Chinese soldiers since the 1910s, soon had a network of military camps, headquarters, and garrisons, including two near the Indian border. Around the same time, troops began to arrive north of Tawang.'[98]

But from the very beginning, the United States, then the main enemy of the newly proclaimed People's Republic of China, had to tread carefully because the old Republic of China lived on in the island of Taiwan, where Chiang Kai-shek sought refuge after his inevitable defeat. His government continued to represent China in the UN, including its Security Council, and remained a close American ally, now against the Chinese communists. And the KMT government in Taiwan, like the People's Republic, considered Tibet an inalienable part of China.

The intrigues that followed the Chinese invasion of Tibet, and the characters who were involved, put even the old Great Game to shame. As the Chinese were moving into Kham in the east and beginning to consolidate their grip on Tibet, the Americans began to take more interest in the Tibetan issue. In the spring of 1951, Larry Dalley, a young CIA officer at the US consulate general in Kolkata seeking information about China's designs for Tibet, contacted two young ladies in the city's diplomatic circuit. One of them was Pema Tseudeun, the older sister of the crown prince of Sikkim, Palden Thondup. She was a stunningly beautiful Himalayan lady who was married to a Tibetan nobleman and was more commonly known in her social circles as Coocoola. During World War II, while still a teenager, she had befriended Tolstoy and Dolan, the two OSS reconnaissance specialist officers then stationed in Lhasa. She and her husband owned considerable property in Lhasa, but the Chinese incursions had forced them to return to Sikkim, from where they then moved to Kolkata.[99]

Dalley's other contact was Coocoola's younger sister, the equally attractive Pema Choki, 'Kula' to her friends. She was also married to a Tibetan and her father-in law had been a high-ranking official at the Tibetan trade office in Kalimpong. Dalley asked the sisters if they thought the Tibetans would need any assistance from the United States, and a channel to the resistance on the other side of the Himalayas was opened.

According to American researchers Kenneth Conboy and James Morrison,

In June 1952, Kukula [Coocoola] approached the consulate with an oral message from the Dalai Lama. She had just returned from a visit to her in-laws in Lhasa, and although she had not personally met the Dalai Lama, she had been given information from Kula's father-in-law, Yurok Dazza, who had been in Lhasa at the same time, circulating among senior government circles. Kukula quoted the Dalai Lama as saying that when the time was propitious for liberation, he hoped the United States would give material aid and support.[100]

Discontent with the Chinese occupation was brewing throughout Tibet, and the young Dalai Lama was invited to Beijing in September 1954, ostensibly to lead a Tibetan delegation to an event to celebrate the inauguration of the first constitution of the People's Republic of China. Only 19 years old, he met all the important Chinese leaders of the time: Mao Zedong, Zhou Enlai, and Deng Xiaoping. Pictures of a smiling Dalai Lama with his seemingly friendly Chinese hosts were published in the official media, but Mao insulted the spiritual leader by telling him that religion was poison. Mao also told him that an entirely new body, the Preparatory Committee for the Autonomous Region of Tibet, was being created, effectively undermining the promises made under 17-point agreement of 1951. The Tibetans could forget about managing their own affairs.

When the Dalai Lama returned home to Lhasa, he found that the Chinese had built new roads into Tibet, including highways down to towns close to the Indian border. There were more PLA soldiers in the country than when he had left for Beijing. The Dalai Lama was distraught, realizing that whatever autonomy his beloved Tibet had enjoyed since the Chinese first entered Tibet would soon be gone. The Chinese were the new overlords. And the Communists would be much less tolerant of religious practices than their predecessors, Imperial China and the KMT, could ever have been had they extended their rule over Tibet.

There was an opening when, in late 1956, the Dalai Lama went on a pilgrimage to India. It was Buddha Jayanti, the birthday of the Buddha, and he received an official invitation from Jawaharlal Nehru to attend the celebrations at Bodh Gaya, where the Mahabodhi temple had been renovated for the event. The Dalai Lama and a 55-man strong Tibetan delegation entered India through Sikkim. But, to their astonishment, they found that Zhou Enlai was also in India on an official visit.

The Tibet issue was discussed and Nehru summoned the Dalai Lama to New Delhi. There would be no asylum for him in India, should he decide to escape from Chinese-dominated Tibet. India's new-won friendship with China was far more important and vital to the political stability of the entire region, the Indian prime minister had concluded. The Dalai Lama returned to Tibet, advised to do so by his two official soothsayers.[101]

It is not clear how much the Dalai Lama knew about the anti-Chinese resistance that was being formed or whether even Nehru was aware of what the CIA agents in Kolkata and their two royal Sikkimese lady friends were up to. In September 1952, the US consul general in Kolkata, Gary Soulen, had been on a trek in Sikkim with Princess Coocoola to survey the terrain. On his return to India, he contacted India's then spymaster, Bhola Nath Mullik, who was more steeped in the old colonial tradition than Nehru, a progressive politician. Contacts were made with two of the Dalai Lama's brothers then living in exile. The elder of the two, Thubten Norbu, already had CIA contacts through an obscure outfit called the Committee for a Free Asia. The younger, Gyalo Thondup, had settled in Darjeeling. Kalimpong, which was nearby, and on the main line of communication between India and Tibet, became a hub of covert activity, from where agents were sent across the border to collect intelligence on 'enemy troops movements' and local guerrillas resisting the Chinese occupation of Tibet were armed.[102]

By 1956, the Khampa rebellion was sweeping across eastern Tibet, and a group of warlike Khampas had congregated in Kalimpong. Getting them out of India posed a major problem, as Nehru and his government would have to be kept in the dark. But there was a way: across the narrow neck of Indian territory between Bhutan and East Pakistan. By the mid-1950s, Pakistan had become a close ally of the United States and would be more welcoming than neutral India to secret proposals from Washington. In 1954, Pakistan had joined an anti-communist defence organization called the Southeast Asia Treaty Organisation (SEATO), which included Australia, New Zealand, France, Thailand, and the Philippines, apart from the United States. In 1955, a parallel alliance had been formed in West Asia: the Central Treaty Organisation (CENTO), which brought together Britain, Iran, Iraq, Turkey—and Pakistan.

Then, in March 1959, an uprising broke out in Lhasa against Chinese occupation. The Dalai Lama had been invited by the Chinese to attend a theatrical performance at the PLA's military headquarters on the outskirts of Lhasa. He was advised not to bring his traditional armed escort, which made him and his men deeply suspicious. They suspected that the Chinese intended to abduct the Dalai Lama, and words to that effect spread throughout Lhasa. Thousands of people surrounded the Dalai Lama's palace to prevent him from leaving or being taken away by the Chinese.

On 12 March, people appeared on the streets of Lhasa, re-declaring Tibet's independence and fighting broke out between the PLA and Tibetan resistance forces. The PLA responded by deploying artillery pieces within range of Norbulingka, the Dalai Lama's summer palace. On 17 March, two shells were fired at the palace and that prompted the people around the Dalai Lama to prepare for his escape from Lhasa.

The uprising was brutally crushed by the PLA—but the Dalai Lama, escorted by resistance fighters, managed to slip out of the city under the cover of darkness at three o'clock in the morning. Their goal was to reach the Indian border. To what extent the CIA actually helped the Dalai Lama flee is still an open question, but they were certainly aware that he was heading for India in disguise within days of his escape from the Tibetan capital. Up in the mountains, the Dalai Lama's party caught up with the CIA's Tibetan resistance fighters inside Tibet, who were equipped with radios. They keyed a message to Okinawa, the US base on the Ryukyu Islands, which had not yet been handed back to Japan since their occupation during the final stages of World War II. The CIA also knew that the Dalai Lama, while on his way to the Indian border, had repudiated the 17-point agreement for 'the Peaceful Liberation of Tibet'.[103]

These messages from the CIA-trained Tibetan radio operators prompted the agency to ask India to grant the Dalai Lama asylum before he had reached the Indian border. The CIA's station chief in New Delhi went straight to Nehru with the request. After long deliberations about the possible negative impact of refusal on India's relations with the United States, the prime minister finally agreed, cutting layers of red tape to facilitate the process. Melinda Liu wrote in *Newsweek* in April 1999, 'A CIA-trained Tibetan even managed to film the odyssey with a 16-mm camera; it showed the spiritual leader, astride on a brown horse with richly embroidered saddlebags, and his retinue picking their way across Tibet's bleak hillsides, with the People's Liberation Army breathing down their necks.'[104]

On 30 March 1959, the Dalai Lama and his men crossed the last mountain pass on the border between Khenzemane and Zeimithang, northwest of Tawang. From there, weak from dysentery, the Dalai Lama rode into the salient Tawang, a green area in the rugged mountains, where he was met by Indian government officials and army personnel. He was safe. He and his entourage continued down to Tezpur in the Assam plains, where a media frenzy awaited him. The 24-year-old God King of Tibet had fled from communist China, and that was world news.

At Tezpur, the Dalai Lama boarded a train to Dehra Dun and continued by car to the hill station of Mussoorie on the western foothills of the Himalayas, where he met Nehru and other Indian dignitaries. A new place was chosen for the Tibetan leader, the much smaller hill station of McLeodganj in today's Himachal Pradesh, which has since 1960 also been the site for the Tibetan government in exile.

With the Dalai Lama and his entourage settled in India, the CIA could step up its support for the Tibetan resistance. The abandoned airstrip at Kurmitola north of Dhaka, which was built by the British during World War II, became the forward base for airdrops into Tibet and the place from which Tibetan resistance fighters were flown out to Okinawa, Clark Airbase in the Philippines, and the Pacific island of Saipan, the secret headquarters of the CIA's covert operations in the Asia-Pacific region. Nationalist Chinese, Korean, Lao, and Vietnamese commandos were already being trained there.

The secret Tibetan operation was codenamed ST CIRCUS and its aerial portion ST BARNUM. According to Conboy and Morison, because the planes would need to fly over Indian territory without permission, they had to factor in the radar at Kolkata. But the CIA had done their homework

> ... and knew that the Indian system had no compensation feature and could be defeated if the B-17 used the Himalayan massif as a radar screen. Flying north over Sikkim, the crew would go as far as the Brahmaputra [in Tibet] for the first drop, cut east across the Tibetan plateau to Kham for the second drop, then veer southwest through Indian territory back to East Pakistan.[105]

To conceal American participation in the scheme, in case one of the planes was detected or shot down, the pilots were all anti-communist Poles who had been given asylum in the United States.

Muslim guerrillas in Xinjiang also benefited from the CIA's largesse, as did the Nationalist Communist soldiers in secret camps in northern Myanmar. A covert war on China was being launched, but, as Conboy and Morrison point out, 'the agency had taken great pains to exclude ROC [the Republic of China] from its Tibetan operations'.[106] And it is doubtful whether the USA was actually in favour of Tibetan independence; the limited scope of the operation seems to indicate that the main purpose was to annoy the Chinese and keep their armed forces occupied.

Whatever the case may be, when the special training facility was established at Camp Hale not far from Leadville in Colorado, a group of tightly knit CIA officers were in charge of the Tibetan programme, and they developed a fondness for the Tibetans which was rather unique. They would later reminisce how the staunchly Buddhist Tibetans would carefully rescue flies that had fallen in their teacups even as they expressed a deadly desire to kill as many Chinese as possible. At Camp Hale, the Tibetans were trained in guerrilla warfare as well as covert operations such as spy photography, Morse code, and mine laying.

Details about the training were not revealed until the 1990s, when it was all over. According to Melinda Liu's 1999 cover story for *Newsweek*,

> The training took place in utmost secrecy. US officers made up stories about a top-secret nuclear research-project at Fort Hale, and guards deterred intruders with shoot-to-kill orders. In 1961, four dozen American civilians were temporarily detained at gunpoint when they inadvertently witnessed 15 Asians wearing camouflage fatigues being escorted onto a C-124 Globemaster with blacked-out windows. Defence secretary Robert McNamara personally intervened to persuade the *New York Times* to spike the story.[107]

The American agents who were sent to train the Tibetans were all very young for the formidable task that lay before them, which was to destabilize the most populous nation on earth. Some of them were smokejumpers from Montana, daring youth looking for adventure. After Tibet, many of them went on to take part in the CIA's secret war against the communist resistance in Laos. Among them was Thomas Fosmire, a former US army sergeant in his late 20s who had also served as an adviser to the border police in Thailand and, after Laos, remained in Vietnam until the communists marched into Saigon in April 1975. Another CIA operative, a Chinese linguist, and philosophy major at Stanford University, John 'Ken' Knaus later wrote a book about his experiences with the Tibetan guerrillas who underwent training in Colorado. He felt remorse in the end, for letting the Tibetans down. He felt guilt 'over our participation in these efforts, which cost others their lives, but which were the prime adventure of our own'.[108]

There was also the colourful Anthony Poshepny, better known by the short version of his name, Tony Poe. A former US marine who was wounded in Iwo Jima during the last battles against the Japanese during World War II, he joined the CIA as a paramilitary officer in 1951. He fought behind enemy lines in Korea and, in the late 1950s, tried and failed to foment an uprising in Sumatra against the Indonesian president Sukarno. Outgunned and trapped on the island, he and one of his companions fled on a fishing trawler that took them away to a waiting American submarine. At Camp Hale, Poe trained Tibetan guerrillas and even accompanied them to the airfield in East Pakistan from where they were flown and parachuted into Tibet.[109]

After Tibet, Poe went straight to Laos to train anti-communist guerrillas, a secret army of tribesmen raised by him and the other CIA operatives. In the mountains of northern Laos, he ran his own fiefdom, and soon became infamous for his brutality. He paid rewards for bringing in enemy ears, and higher remuneration if these were accompanied by a communist cap with a red star. He was also reported to have decapitated his enemies and put their heads on spikes to boost the morale of his own soldiers. Mentally unsound, Poe became the model for the renegade Green Beret Colonel Kurtz in the 1979 Hollywood movie *Apocalypse Now*, and as far as one could possibly get from the spiritual ideas of the Dalai Lama.

The Indians, meanwhile, were busy consolidating their territories after the partition of the former British possession into the secular but Hindu-majority Union of India and the Islamic state of Pakistan. The rulers of the princely states of the former British India could decide to which country they wanted to belong. The Hindu maharaja of Muslim-majority Jammu and Kashmir chose India, which marked the beginning of a conflict between Pakistan and India that continues to this day. The Muslim Nizam of Hyderabad, though, decided that he wanted to join Pakistan. This was unthinkable, as Hyderabad is located in southern India, far from any Pakistani territory. India's Home Minister Vallabhbhai Patel, who was in charge of integrating the princely states, sent the police to make sure no attempt to break away from India was made. The 'police action' lasted for five days. Hyderabad did not become part of Pakistan. Yet another Muslim ruler, the Nawab of Junagadh in Gujarat, chose to accede to Pakistan. Indian troops intervened, the Nawab fled to Pakistan and Junagadh joined the rest of India after a vast majority of the population voted to do so in a plebiscite in February 1948.

There was also the question of other, non-British possessions in India. The French had Chandannagar (then known as Chandernagore) on the banks of River Hooghly north of Kolkata, Mahe (Mayyazhi) on the Malabar coast in the south, and Puducherry (Pondicherry), Karaikal (Karikal), and Yanam on India's eastern coast. The French had no desire to remain in possession of those enclaves after India's independence and, especially after French Indochina became the independent states of Laos and Cambodia in 1953, and Vietnam in 1954. Chandannagar was merged with India in 1951, and the other four French possessions were transferred to Indian rule in 1954 and finally made part of India as a union territory in 1962.

The Portuguese, who ruled Goa, Daman, Diu, and Dadra and Nagar Haveli on the Indian west coast, proved to be more stubborn. The inland enclaves of Dadra and Nagar Haveli joined India in 1954 following requests from the local population. But the Portuguese refused to leave Goa, Daman and Diu. India decided to send in its army, and, in December 1961, launched Operation Vijay ('victory'). The 45,000 Indian troops who had been mobilized for the campaign had no difficulty defeating the Portuguese army of 4,000 and naval personnel in the territories. Those three former Portuguese colonies also became an Indian union territory, but on 30 May 1987, Goa was made India's 25th state, with Daman and Diu remaining a union territory.

The tribal rebellion in the Naga Hills showed no sign of subsiding. From cross-border sanctuaries in Myanmar and bases in the Chittagong Hill Tracts of East Pakistan, they carried on their quixotic armed struggle against the Indian Army and for an independent Nagaland. Even if the rebellion had no chance of success, it kept India's security forces busy in a remote and hostile terrain.

New Delhi's efforts to integrate all parts of the vast and ethnically and geographically diverse country, and to secure its borders, also included the area that is now known as Arunachal Pradesh. The British had at last, in 1943, decided to integrate the mountainous areas between the Inner Line and the Himalayas, and the North-East Frontier Tract was created. After independence, laws were introduced to regulate the administration of the Abor and Mishmi Hills Districts. Roads and civil administration began to reach villages and communities that previously had only limited contact with the outside world, which in this case would be the plains of Assam.

Tawang proved to be a problem. Nari Rustomji, an Indian administrative officer who spent years in the Himalayan region, wrote in his *Enchanted Frontiers: Sikkim, Bhutan and India's North-Eastern Borderlands* that

The region that caused us special anxiety was the region of Tawang in the extreme north-west corner of Kameng Frontier Division and across the 14,000 foot Se La Pass [Sela]. Although Tawang was undoubtedly south of the McMahon Line and therefore within the territory of India, the Tibetans had, for generations, felt a strong sentimental attachment to the area, partly as the birth-place of the sixth Dalai Lama. The office-bearers of the great Buddhist monastery at Tawang were sometimes selected from among the Tibetan lamas of the famous Drepung monastery near Lhasa and the culture of the region had affinities with Tibet as much as with India.[110]

Rustomji and his border officials decided it was time to make clear to which country Tawang belonged—something which had become especially important since the Chinese occupation of Tibet in 1950. In 1938, the British had sent a military expedition led by Captain Gordon Lightfoot to plant the flag at Tawang, though little had happened since then. But the Indians remembered Captain Nevill's warning from as early as 1928 that should the Chinese gain control over Tibet, which they now had, Tawang would provide a 'secret and easy entrance into India'.[111]

The local population in Tawang are known as Monpas and speak a language related to Tibetan, but they do not consider themselves ethnic Tibetans. In a confidential report, compiled by the secretariat of the Governor of Assam after Lightfoot's expedition, it was stated that the Monpas 'live in a state of virtual slavery... [and] that brutal punishments are inflicted on the British Monpas by irregular Tibetan courts... His Excellency is satisfied that inhabitants of the British area are from time to time murdered...under the orders of officials of the Tibetan Government.'[112] Apart from meting out harsh sentences against the local population, the Tibetan officials in the area did little more than collect money from the locals and send it to the Tsona (Cona) monastery in Tibet. Thus, it came hardly as a surprise to Lightfoot that the Monpas supported him against their Tibetan overlords when he entered the area.

The report from the Assam Secretariat suggested that the Tibetan Government should withdraw their officials from Tawang, and that the British should establish a more permanent presence in the district. That, however, did not happen because of the outbreak of World War II in 1939.

It was not until February 1951, three and a half years after India's independence, that a detachment of the paramilitary Assam Rifles marched over Sela Pass and into the salient Tawang. It was commanded by Major Ralengnao 'Bob' Khathing, a Tangkhul Naga from Manipur, and, according to Rustomji, 'Bob's entry into Tawang was, for them [the Monpas], a true liberation as they could no longer be bossed about and pressurized to sell their produce at anybody's dictation'.[113]

But, ironically, when the new Indian administration in Tawang did not collect any taxes at all, the local people were confused and, in the end, Khathing had to levy an annual house tax of five rupees on each Monpa household to convince them that they were indeed citizens of India, and not under Tibetan domination.[114]

Across the border in Tibet, although the first advance party from the PLA had entered Lhasa in November 1950, the Chinese did not take full control over the city until September 1951. So, the kashag was still in power in the Tibetan capital when Khathing took over Tawang. The Tibetans protested to the Indian diplomatic mission in Lhasa, but to no avail. Instead, New Delhi began to tighten its grip on all areas up to the McMahon Line. Apart from introducing government offices in previously unadministered areas, the Assam Rifles were reorganized to carry out patrols and surveillance work; intelligence units were deployed along the border; civil armed police forces were raised; and checkpoints set up along major roads and trails.

In January 1954, the North-East Frontier Tract became the North-East Frontier Area (NEFA), and Indian control had finally been secured all the way up to the McMahon Line, four decades after it had been drawn at the historic meetings at Shimla.

Notes

1. Pradip Phanjoubam, *The Northeast Question: Conflicts and Frontiers* (New Delhi, London and New York: Routledge, 2016), p. 34.
2. Excerpts from the article were reproduced in the *New York Times* on 13 October 1912, available at http://query.nytimes.com/mem/archive-free/pdf?res=9D05E3DB1F3CE633A25750C1A9669D946396D6CF (accessed on 14 April 2016).

3. For a comprehensive history of Mongolia, see C.R. Bawden, *The Modern History of Mongolia* (London: Weidenfeld and Nicolson, 1968).

4. For the text of the Russo-Chinese Agreement 1912, see www.claudearpi.net/maintenance/.../1913Russo-ChineseAgreeement.pdf (accessed on 16 April 2016). Reproduced from Pradyumna P. Karan, *The Changing Face of Tibet* (Kentucky: The University Press of Kentucky, 1976), pp. 87–8.

5. 'Treaty of Kyakhta 1915', available at https://www.revolvy.com/main/index.php?s=Treaty%20of%20Kyakhta%20(1915) (accessed on 12 June 2017).

6. For the text of the treaty, see https://www.mtholyoke.edu/acad/intrel/mongtib.htm (accessed on 16 April 2016) and Michael C. van Walt van Praag, *The Status of Tibet: History, Rights, and Prospects in International Law* (Boulder, Colorado: Westview Press, 1987), pp. 320–1. See also Matteo Miele, 'A Geopolitical reading of the 1913 Treaty Between Tibet and Mongolia', *Tibetan Review*, Jan–Feb 2015, available at http://www.tibetanreview.net/a-geopolitical-reading-of-the-1913-treaty-between-tibet-and-mongolia/ (accessed on 15 September 2016).

7. The British were allowed to trade in Yadong, Gyantse, and Gartok; the border between Tibet and Sikkim was delineated; Tibet was not to have relations with any foreign power other than Britain; and the Tibetans were forced to pay an indemnity of 7.5 million Indian Rupees to the British. For the text of the treaty, see http://www.tibetjustice.org/materials/treaties/treaties10.html (accessed on 15 April 2016).

8. For Tibetan and English versions of the declaration, see http://www.tibetjustice.org/materials/tibet/tibet1.html (accessed on 12 June 2017). See also, Tsepon W.D. Shakabpa, *Tibet: A Political History* (New Delhi: Paljor Publication, 2010 [a reprint of New Haven: Yale University Press, 1967]), p. 338.

9. Shakabpa, *Tibet*, pp. 339–40.

10. For a book about the life of Laden La, see Nicholas and Deki Rhodes, *A Man of the Frontier: S.W. Laden La (1876–1936: His Life and Times in Darjeeling and Tibet)* (Kolkata: Mira Bose, 2006). Laden La's role at the Shimla conference is mentioned on pp. 30–31.

11. Norbu Tsering, 'The Simla Convention of 1914—an appraisal', 9 November 2013, available at http://www.phayul.com/news/article.aspx?id=34200 (accessed on 15 April 2016).

12. For Lu Xingqi and his role, see Parshotam Mehra, *Essays in Frontier History: India, China, and the Disputed Border* (New Delhi: Oxford University Press,

2007), p. 58. See also Ravinder Makhaik, 'The 1913–14 Shimla Convention, McMahon Line and the Disputed India-China border', *The Hill Post*, 5 December 2011, available at http://hillpost.in/2011/12/1913-14-shimla-convention-mcmohan-line-and-the-disputed-india-china-border/36974/ (accessed on 16 April 2016).

13. Tan Chee-beng, *Routledge Handbook of the Chinese Diaspora* (Abingdon: Routledge, 2012), p. 222.

14. Mehra, *Essays in Frontier History*, p. 59.

15. Ya Hanzhang, *The Biographies of the Dalai Lamas* (Beijing: Foreign Languages Press, 1991), pp. 307–9. On page 307 it says that 'in April 1913 the Beijing government appointed Lu Xingqi commissioner for Tibet', and on page 309 Ivan Chen is referred to as 'Commissioner for Tibetan Affairs' when the Shimla Conference opened on 13 October 1913. Whatever the case, Lu was a chief intelligence officer charged with Indian and Tibetan affairs. Chen had to report to, and seek advice from, Lu before and during the Shimla Conference.

16. van Walt van Praag, *The Status of Tibet*, p. 54.

17. van Walt van Praag, *The Status of Tibet*, p. 305.

18. For the text of the 1907 Anglo-Russian Convention, see van Walt van Praag, *The Status of Tibet*, pp. 307–8, and http://avalon.law.yale.edu/20th_century/angrusen.asp (accessed on 10 May 2016).

19. Charles Bell, *Tibet: Past and Present*, (New Delhi: Asian Educational Services, 1992), pp. 148–9.

20. Pradip Phanjoubam, 'How McMahon Drew His Line, and Why China Wants It Changed', *The Wire*, 20 May 2015, available at https://thewire.in/2108/how-mcmahon-drew-his-line-and-why-china-wants-it-changed/ (accessed on 15 April 2016). For a comprehensive study of the border issue, see Pradip Phanjoubam, 'Neville Maxwell's "Facts" and Silences', *Economic and Political Weekly*, vol. 51, no. 46, 12 November 2016, available at http://www.epw.in/journal/2016/46/discussion/neville-maxwells-factsand-silences.html (accessed on 18 November 2016).

21. Pradip Phanjoubam, 'How McMahon Drew His Line and Why China Wants It Changed'.

22. 'Anglo-Russian Entente: United Kingdom-Russia [1907]', available at https://global.britannica.com/event/anglo-russian-entente (accessed on 14 April 2016). For the text of the clauses regarding Tibet in the Anglo-Russian Convention of 1907, see Melvyn C. Goldstein, *A History of Modern Tibet, 1913–1951: The Demise*

of the Lamaist State (New Delhi: Munshiram Manoharlal Publishers, 2007), pp. 829–31.

23. W.F. Van Eekelen, Indian Foreign Policy and the Border Dispute with China (The Hague: Martinus Nijhoff, 1964), p. 14.

24. Van Eekelen, Indian Foreign Policy and the Border Dispute with China, p. 14.

25. Van Eekelen, Indian Foreign Policy and the Border Dispute with China, p. 14.

26. John Rowland, A History of Sino-Indian Relations: Hostile Co-Existence (Princeton, NJ, Toronto, London: D. Van Nostrand Company, 1967), p. 47.

27. van Walt van Praag, The Status of Tibet, p. 55.

28. Melvyn C. Goldstein, A History of Modern Tibet, 1913–1951 (New Delhi: Munshiram Manoharlal Publishers [by arrangement with the University of California Press], 1989) p. 833.

29. Goldstein, A History of Modern Tibet, 1913–1951. pp. 833.

30. Rowland, A History of Sino-Indian Relations, pp. 33–6.

31. Rowland, A History of Sino-Indian Relations, p. 49.

32. Goldstein, A History of Modern Tibet, 1913–1951, p. 835.

33. Rowland, A History of Sino-Indian Relations, p. 49.

34. Van Eekelen, Indian Foreign Policy and the Border Dispute with China, pp. 16–17.

35. Neville Maxwell, India's China War (Harmondsworth, Middlesex: Penguin Books, 1972), p. 44, and Alastair Lamb, Tibet, China & India 1914–1950: A History of Imperial Diplomacy (Hertingfordbury, Hertfordshire: Roxford Books, 1989), p. 280.

36. The Sino-Indian Boundary Question (Enlarged Edition) (Beijing: Foreign Languages Publishing House, 1962), pp. 10–11.

37. Neville Maxwell, 'The Deadlocked Deadlock: Sino-Indian Boundary Dispute', Economic and Political Weekly, Vol. 16, No. 38, 19 September 1981, pp. 1548.

38. Maxwell, 'The Deadlocked Deadlock: Sino-Indian Boundary Dispute', p. 1548.

39. Maxwell, 'The Deadlocked Deadlock: Sino-Indian Boundary Dispute', p. 1548.

40. Lamb, Tibet, China & India 1914–1950, p. 429.

41. Lamb, Tibet, China & India 1914–1950, p. 133

42. Lamb, Tibet, China & India 1914–1950, p. 133.

43. Lamb, Tibet, China & India 1914–1950, p. 133.

44. Mehra, Essays in Frontier History: India, China, and the Disputed Border, p. 72.

45. Phanjoubam, 'How McMahon Drew His Line, and Why China Wants It Changed'.

46. W.F. Van Eekelen, 'Simla Convention and McMahon Line', *Journal of The Royal Central Asian Society*, Vol. 54, No. 2, 1967, p. 180: 'The Foreign Office … maintained its opposition to separate signing with Tibet on the ground that it would amount to tearing up the Anglo-Russian Convention of 1907.'

47. Bell, *Tibet: Past and Present.*

48. For reproductions of old and more recent maps of the Indo-Tibetan border, see Ministry of External Affairs, Government of India, *Atlas of the Northern Frontier of India* (New Delhi: Ministry of External Affairs, 1960).

49. John Bray, 'Introduction: Locating Ladakhi History', John Bray (ed.), *Ladakhi Histories: Local and Regional Perspectives* (New Delhi and Dharamsala: Library of Tibetan Works and Archives and Indraprashtra Press, 2011), p. 1.

50. Steven A. Hoffman, *India and the China Crisis* (Berkeley, Los Angeles, London: University of California Press, 1990), pp. 11–12.

51. K.L. Rao, *History of the Indian Army* (New Delhi: Manas Publications, 2016), p. 183.

52. See, for instance, Bina D'Costa, 'Partition: the price of freedom and the price paid by women', *South Asia Masala*, 6 August 2009, available at http://asiapacific.anu.edu.au/blogs/southasiamasala/2009/08/06/partition-the-price-of-freedom-and-the-price-paid-by-women/ (accessed on 20 May 2016).

53. George N. Patterson, *Peking Versus Delhi* (London: Faber and Faber, 1963), p. 192.

54. Jasper Becker, *The Lost Country: Mongolia Revealed* (London: Hodder & Stoughton, 1992), p. 75.

55. Becker, *The Lost Country*, p 134.

56. Francis Watson, *The Frontiers of China* (London: Chatto & Windus, 1966), p. 9.

57. For a map of the border and the areas which were ceded to China, see Josef Silverstein, *Burma: Military Rule and the Politics of Stagnation* (Ithaca and London: Cornell University Press, 1977), p. 174.

58. Pradip Phanjoubam, 'Why Removing the Historical Baggage of McMahon May Be More Important for China than the Line itself, *The Wire*, 26 May 2015, available at http://thewire.in/2015/05/26/for-china-removing-the-historical-baggage-of-the-mcmahon-line-may-be-more-important-than-the-line-itself-2509/ (accessed on 10 May 2016).

59. 'The Sino-Indian Border', *Current Intelligence Weekly Summary*, 17 December 1959, p. 17.

60. 'The Sino-Indian Border', p. 17.

61. Neville Maxwell, 'Olaf Caroe's Fabrication of the "McMahon Line"', *Economic and Political Weekly*, Vol. 51, Issue No. 32, 6 August 2016, p. 100.

62. Edward Gait, *A History of Assam* (Guwahati, Delhi: Spectrum Publications, 2011), p. 335.

63. Phanjoubam, *The Northeast Question*, p. 79.

64. Phanjoubam, *The Northeast Question*, p. 80.

65. Alastair Lamb, *The China-India Border: The Origins of the Disputed Boundaries* (London, New York, Toronto: Oxford University Press, 1964), p. 124. Maps showing 'the Outer Line' can also be found online on Wikipedia at https://en.wikipedia.org/wiki/McMahon_Line (accessed on 12 June 2017).

66. Phanjoubam, *The Northeast Question*, p. 110.

67. Maxwell, *India's China War*, pp. 30, 32.

68. Robert Reid, *History of the Frontier Areas Bordering Assam from 1883 to 1941* (Guwahati, Delhi: Spectrum Publications, 1997), pp. 227–8.

69. Phanjoubam, *The Northeast Question*, p. 112.

70. Maxwell, *India's China War*, p. 34.

71. Maxwell, *India's China War*, p. 30.

72. Maxwell, *India's China War*, p. 34.

73. Warren W. Smith, *China's Tibet? Autonomy or Assimilation* (Lanham, Boulder, New York, Toronto, Plymouth UK: Rowman & Littlefield Publishers, 2008), p. 8.

74. Goldstein, *A History of Modern Tibet, 1913–1951*, p. 841.

75. H.K. Barpujari, *Problem of the Hill Tribes North-East Frontier Vol. III: Inner Line to McMahon Line* (Guwahati: Spectrum Publications, 1981), p. 236.

76. Van Eekelen, *Indian Foreign Policy and the Border Dispute with China*, p. 182.

77. Barpujari, *Problem of the Hill Tribes North-East Frontier Vol. III*, p. 236.

78. Quoted in Barpujari, *Problem of the Hill Tribes North-East Frontier Vol. III*, p. 236.

79. Barpujari, *Problem of the Hill Tribes North-East Frontier Vol. III*, pp. 236–7.

80. Barpujari, *Problem of the Hill Tribes North-East Frontier Vol. III*, p. 238.

81. Rhodes and Rhodes, *A Man of the Frontier*, p. 39.

82. Mehra, *Essays in Frontier History*, p. 59.

83. Goldstein, *A History of Modern Tibet, 1913–1951*, pp. 214–215.

84. Goldstein, *A History of Modern Tibet, 1913–1951*, p. 223.

85. Goldstein, *A History of Modern Tibet, 1913–1951*, p. 245.

86. Lin Hsiao-ting, *Tibet and Nationalist China's Frontier: Intrigues and Ethnopolitics* (Vancouver, Toronto: University of British Columbia Press, 2006), p. 91.

87. Arjia Rinpoche, *Surviving the Dragon: A Tibetan Lama's Account of 40 Years under Chinese Rule* (Emmaus, Pennsylvania: Rodale Books, 2010), p. vii.

88. Charles Bell, *Portrait of a Dalai Lama* (London: Wisdom Publications, 1987, reprint, first published in 1946 by Wm. Collins, London), p. 454.

89. Goldstein, *A History of Modern Tibet, 1913–1951*, p. 379.

90. Goldstein, *A History of Modern Tibet, 1913–1951*, p. 382.

91. Yangdon Dhondup and Hildegard Diemberger, 'Tashi Tsering: The Last Mongol Queen of "Sogpo"' (Henan)', *Inner Asia*, vol. 4, issues 1–2, University of Cambridge, Mongolia and Inner Asia Studies, 2002, p. 204.

92. For a fascinating account of Hisao Kimura's exploits see Hisao Kimura, *Japanese Agent in Tibet,* as told to Scott Berry (London: Serindia Publications, 1990).

93. Goldstein, *A History of Modern Tibet, 1913–1951*, p. 387.

94. Goldstein, *A History of Modern Tibet, 1913–1951*, p. 399.

95. Quoted in Goldstein, *A History of Modern Tibet, 1913–1951*, p. 607.

96. The full text of the 17-point agreement is available at http://www.friends-of-tibet.org.nz/17-point-agreement.html (accessed on 12 June 2017). Ngapoi Ngawang Jigme, who passed away in Beijing in 2009 at the age of 99, became the first President of the newly established Tibet Autonomous Region in 1964. In an interview with *Asiaweek* magazine (20 October 2000), he predicted that 'nothing will change' when the present Dalai Lama dies, 'Without a Dalai Lama for 40 years, we've done quite well', available at http://www.tibet.ca/cms/en/library/wtn/archive/old?y=2000&m=10&p=16_2 (accessed on 13 June 2017). Many Tibetan exiles condemned Jigme as a traitor and collaborator. See Jasper Becker, 'Interview with Ngapoi Ngawang Jigme', *South China Morning Post*, 4 April 1998, available at http://www.tibet.ca/en/library/wtn/archive/old?y=1998&m=4&p=8_4 (accessed on 12 June 2017).

97. *Concerning the Question of Tibet* pp. 17–18.

98. Bérénice Guyot-Réchard, *Shadow States: India, China and the Himalayas, 1910–1962* (Cambridge: Cambridge University Press, 2017), p. 203.

99. For a detailed account of the two Sikkimese princesses and their CIA contacts, see Ken Conboy and James Morrison, *The CIA's Secret War in Tibet* (Lawrence: University Press of Kansas Press, 2002), pp. 21–23.

100. Conboy and Morrison, *The CIA's Secret War in Tibet*, p. 23.

101. Conboy and Morrison, *The CIA's Secret War in Tibet*, p. 35.

102. For Gyalo Thondup's own account of his activities in Kalimpong, see Gyalo Thondup and Anne F. Thurston, *The Noodle Maker of Kalimpong: The Untold Story of My Struggle for Tibet* (London, Sydney, Auckland, Johannesburg: Rider, 2015).

103. Conboy and Morrison, *The CIA's Secret War in Tibet*, pp. 91–2.

104. Melinda Liu. 'When Heaven Shed Blood', *Newsweek,*19 April 1999, available at http://www.newsweek.com/when-heaven-shed-blood-164864 (accessed on 13 June 2017).

105. Conboy and Morrison, *The CIA's Secret War in Tibet*, p. 61.

106. Conboy and Morrison, *The CIA's Secret War in Tibet,* p. 103.

107. Liu, 'When Heaven Shed Blood'.

108. John Kenneth Knaus, *Orphans of the Cold War: America and the Tibetan Struggle for Survival* (New York: Public Affairs, 1999), p. 325.

109. Richard Ehrlich, 'Death of a dirty fighter', *Asia Times Online*, 8 July 2003, available at http://www.atimes.com/atimes/Southeast_Asia/EG08Ae02. html (accessed on 13 June 2017).

110. Nari Rustomji, *Enchanted Frontiers: Sikkim, Bhutan and India's North-Eastern Borderlands* (Calcutta, Delhi, Bombay, Madras: Oxford University Press, 1973), p. 125.

111. Barpujari, *Problem of the Hill Tribes North-East Frontier Vol. III*, p. 236.

112. 'Letter from the Secretary of the Governor of Assam, No. 3851-G.S., dated the 7th September 1938: Report on the Tawang Expedition, 1938', The British Library's archives, London.

113. Rustomji, *Enchanted Frontiers*, p. 127.

114. Shiv Kunal Verma, *1962: The War That Wasn't: The Definitive Account of the Clash Between India and China* (New Delhi: Aleph Book Company, 2016), p. 11.

3

The Invasion

I t was entirely unexpected that the Chinese would attack. The Indians had observed a massive build-up across the border and there had been several encounters between the Indian Army and the Chinese PLA in the days before the main attack, including bombardment of Dhola and Khenzemane on 19 October 1962. But the ferocity and the sheer co-ordination of the Chinese attacks on 20 October 1962 and the days that followed stunned the Indian security establishment as well as international observers. At day-break on that day, artillery guns and mortars began intense bombardments across the Thagla Ridge.

According to Brigadier John Dalvi,

> At exactly 5 on the morning of 20th October 1962, the Chinese Opposite Bridge III fired two Verey lights. This signal was followed by a cannonade of over 150 guns and heavy mortars, exposed on the forward slopes of Thagla...this was a moment of truth. Thagla Ridge was no longer, at that moment, a piece of ground. It was the crucible to test, weigh and purify India's foreign defence policies.[1]

Dalvi called it 'The Day of Reckoning—20th October 1962'.[2] The all-out assault on Indian positions north of Tawang was on.

On the western front in Aksai Chin, the fighting was spread out over a swathe of land from north to south, covering a distance of approximately

600 kilometres. But the thrust of the Chinese towards the south was confined to a relatively narrow area, which measured approximately 20 kilometres from west to east.[3] Most of the attacks by the PLA seemed to be confined to dislodging Indian troops from the outposts that had been established as a result of the government's Forward Policy rather than for capturing territory. According to Indian military analysts, 'In the Western sector, [the] Chinese had a limited aim. They were already in occupation of most of the Aksai Chin plateau through which they had constructed the Western Highway connecting Tibet and Xinjiang. In this war, their aim was to remove the Indian posts which they perceived were across their 1960 Claim Line.'[4] They had no intention to move forward deep into Indian territory, as they did in NEFA.

The Aksai Chin plateau was and still is virtually unpopulated; this had made it possible for the Chinese to build their highway there in the mid-1950s without the Indians finding out about it until a year after it had been completed. The name Aksai Chin means 'the desert of white stones', and the altitude varies between 4,300 and 6,900 metres above sea level. In the past, some Ladakhi villagers used the area for summer grazing and made it part of the Cashmere wool trade, but otherwise there has been no commercial activity worth mentioning in the area. Whatever ancient trade routes that existed were secondary, and the only valley, if it may be called such, is along the River Chip Chap that flows from Xinjiang to Jammu and Kashmir. During the 1962 War, the Chinese captured several Indian positions in the valley and have since controlled most of the area.

During the weeks of fighting in this western sector of the theatre of the 1962 War, it became obvious that the Chinese knew exactly where the Indians were, how many there were at each position, and what kind of weaponry they had. As was the case in the NEFA in the east, pre-war intelligence gathering had been carried out in the Aksai Chin area by small teams of surveyors who could move freely and, presumably, undetected on the barren plateau.

A contentious issue on the eastern front was the location of the Indian outpost at Dhola in the River Namka Chu gorge, where the borders of India, Bhutan, and Tibet intersect northwest of Tawang. The post was created on 24 February 1962 and, according to the Henderson Brooks–Bhagat Report, the site 'was established north of the McMahon Line as shown on maps prior to October/November 1962 edition. It is believed that the old edition was given to the Chinese by our External Affairs Ministry to indicate the McMahon Line. It is also learnt that we tried to clarify the error in our maps, but the Chinese did not accept our contention.'[5] The Chinese, in any case, would not have paid much attention to Indian maps. Their objective was entirely different: to teach India a lesson.

This remark in the Henderson Brooks–Bhagat Report is anyway a far cry from the claim by Neville Maxwell and others that the establishment of the Dhola outpost triggered the 1962 War and that India was the aggressor. Chinese troops had crossed the Namka Chu on 8 September, surrounded an Indian outpost in the gorge, and destroyed two bridges on the river. The nearby Dhola Post was reinforced and firing from both sides continued in the area throughout September. Three Indian soldiers were wounded when the Chinese threw hand grenades at their position, but otherwise, there were no casualties.[6]

When the final attack came on 20 October, the Indians found that the Chinese had cut all their telephone lines the night before. In preparation for the assault, the Chinese had also taken up positions on higher ground behind Indian defences and were thus able to attack downhill on the morning of the attack. After the Chinese artillery barrage from the Thagla Ridge overlooking the Namka Chu, the PLA destroyed all Indian artillery positions and surrounding fortifications. The Indian border posts as well as Dhola and Khenzemane were overrun by ground forces within hours, and their defenders either lay dead or were captured alive. The strength of the Chinese attacking force was estimated at 2,000, while the Indians at those outposts numbered only 600.[7]

Simultaneous attacks were launched on other positions, and the 2nd Rajput Regiment, which was also in the area, suffered horrendously. Of the 513 members of all ranks, 282 were killed that day, 81 were wounded and captured alive, and 90 were captured unwounded. Only 60 men, mostly rear elements got away. A Gurkha regiment, also in the area, lost 80 men, with a further 44 wounded, and 102 taken prisoner by the

Chinese. The 7th Brigade lost a total of 493 men that fateful morning of 20 October.[8] The total strength of the PLA units that were deployed for the operation on the Dhola and Thagla front was at least 10,000, supported by heavy artillery and more sophisticated weaponry than the Indians had in their arsenal.[9]

After the Indian defences were crushed, the 7th Brigade commander, Brigadier John Dalvi, who remained a prisoner of war in China for almost seven months, described with a large degree of bitterness and in great detail how the chain of command had broken down, and how undersupplied his troops were. He quotes a fellow Indian Army officer as saying that their 'mission was the defence of a political instead of a tactical position. The troops slaughtered along the Namka Chu River were spread out in a thin line, difficult to supply and impossible to defend.'[10]

Apart from observing the camps that had been built by the Chinese for him and the other Indian prisoners of war, Dalvi also concludes that the 'Chinese preparations began in earnest from May 1962', so well before the incidents at the Dhola post.[11] The emphasis here should be on 'in earnest'; all available evidence points to the fact that intelligence gathering and construction projects began in the mid-1950s, when China wanted to challenge India's role as the leading voice of the newly independent countries in Asia and Africa. The Dalai Lama's flight to India in 1959 prompted the Chinese to switch from contemplating the possibility of a war with India to putting their ruminations into concrete action.

Dalvi also quotes, and ridicules, the Chinese version of events,

> The Chinese told the world that: 'At 7 o'clock (Peking time) in the morning of 20th October the aggressive Indian forces, under cover of fierce artillery fire, launched massive attacks against the Chinese Frontier Guards all along the Kachileng River and in the Khenzemane area.' The poor Chinese were driven to self-defence by the fire of two out-ranged para-guns with 400 rounds of ammunition![12]

Maxwell is not as extreme as the Chinese in his version of events, but his pro-Chinese account of what happened in 1962 would nevertheless have been equally dismissible if it had not been accepted as the truth and often referred to in writings about the war and the border dispute, even by former US Secretary of State Henry Kissinger himself.

The war on the eastern front in the NEFA was going to be very different from that in Ladakh. While the Chinese may not have encountered many civilians on the Ladakh front, interacting with the local population became an important issue for them in the NEFA, where they occupied several towns and villages. Once the road down from Bumla had been constructed by the Chinese, and Tawang was secured as a supply base, it became clear that not only had scouts been sent in advance by the PLA to collect crucial intelligence, but its soldiers and officers had also been trained in psychological warfare.

Most local people in Tawang, whether Monpas or Tibetans, had fled when the Chinese began attacking the border. They had heard from relatives and traders about the atrocities the PLA had committed inside Tibet and were, naturally, afraid. But there were always two sides to the PLA. As an ideologically motivated communist force, it tolerated no dissent or opposition to the rule that it imposed on local people anywhere. But, as a 'people's army', it was supposed to behave gently towards 'the oppressed masses'. According to the Maoist doctrine of the Eight Points of Behaviour, communist soldiers were ordered 'not to steal so much as a single needle or thread from the people'.[13]

British missionary and writer George N. Patterson observed that in some areas the Chinese soldiers who took part in the occupation of Tibet were also 'scrupulous in their behaviour, keeping to themselves and not oppressing the Tibetan population in any way. Heavy penalties were imposed on any Chinese soldier who was known to have made use of even a Tibetan prostitute. One Chinese soldier, accused by a Tibetan woman of raping her, was shot by his superior officer.'[14] In certain areas in Tibet, clinics and schools, where lessons were held in Tibetan as well as in Chinese, were built.

But there was a hidden agenda behind that kind of benevolent behaviour towards some of the Tibetans. According to Patterson,

> With all the beneficent and necessary reforms being introduced one ominous factor emerged, that the innovations were not being made on a national

scale but were limited strictly to the cities, towns and villages on the main route through Tibet to India. In effect, they were merely supplementary to the thrust to the Indian border; there was no attempt to develop the country outside the main arteries.[15]

That development began a year or two after the Chinese invasion of Tibet in 1950, indicating that China was prepared for action along the border even before Deng Xiaoping and Mao Zedong, in March 1959, pledged to 'settle accounts' with the Indians.[16]

Significantly, according to Patterson, 'in East Tibet their approach was more often on the accepted Communist pattern'.[17] That would inevitably mean harassment of local people and the execution of 'reactionaries' opposed to the new order. East Tibet was the home of the Khampas, where the first armed resistance against Chinese occupation broke out in the mid-1950s. When, in 1958, the Chinese authorities began forcing Tibetans in the central provinces to become collectivized in 'people's communes', the relations between the occupiers and the occupied deteriorated even further.[18]

The Chinese military historian Li Xiaobing, interviewing Li Weiheng, a PLA radio operator, describes the hostile reception the Chinese soldiers encountered when they entered Tibet, especially after the 1959 uprising, 'Sergeant Li Weiheng recalled that he and his comrades felt as if they were entering a foreign country when they went to Tibet. Religious and linguistic barriers, separatist propaganda, and a backward economy had created a seemingly irreparable rift between the troops and local Tibetans.' The sergeant told Li Xiaobing that one of the regulations for the PLA troops in Tibet was to refrain from talking to the Tibetan people without permission, 'Any communication between the village and the radar company had to be conducted by... the company commander through the village chiefs, one of whom spoke Chinese'.[19]

During his first six months of service in Tibet, sergeant Li Weiheng visited the village only twice. On the first visit, he and his comrades went there to see a local medicine man who had refused to come to the Chinese camp and insisted he would meet the PLA soldiers if they came to the village. Li 'could feel the hostility around them. Children vanished into their homes...no women could be seen. Several Tibetan men sat in front of the house with knives in their hands, staring at Li without saying a word. Li felt lucky that all firearms had been collected from the Tibetans after their rebellion in 1959. Nobody could legally have a gun.'[20]

Sergeant Li Weiheng's second visit to the village was different. It was during the 1962 War and when a temporary camp for the Indian prisoners of war (POW) had been built at the bottom of the hill below the village. 'Indian prisoners of war arrived in large numbers, more than the camp guard unit could handle...[Li] was surprised to see many Tibetan villagers visiting the Indian prisoners, bringing water, food and milk...Li even saw the old medicine man visiting sick and wounded Indian soldiers.'[21] Li and his platoon complained to the camp commander, who had been instructed not to let any Tibetans have contact with the Indian soldiers, 'but he had difficulty feeding the large number of prisoners. As a compromise, he had decided to allow Tibetan women and children to visit the Indian prisoners.'[22]

Despite being surrounded by an evidently hostile population, the PLA seems to have had no problem recruiting and educating enough Tibetan spies and interpreters for the campaign against India. It is often forgotten, particularly in the West, that some Tibetans, who were opposed to their country's medieval feudal system, did side with the Chinese, at least at the beginning of the occupation. A group of young intellectuals led by Bapa Phuntso Wangye had even set up a small Tibetan Communist Party in 1939. But, like several other progressive Tibetans, he became disillusioned with developments in the 1950s, and, consequently, the Chinese became suspicious of him. Bapa Phuntso Wangye was detained in 1958 and imprisoned in 1960.[23] Other Tibetans, however, worked for the Chinese and were fluent in their language. The thousands of porters, who the PLA mobilized during the months before the attack on 20 October, belonged to other segments of society. They were peasants who had been conscripted at gunpoint from villages all over southern Tibet.

In Tawang, the PLA quite naturally decided on adopting a 'benevolent' approach so as not to antagonize those who had remained in the town when almost the entire population had fled and the Indian soldiers had evacuated the area. There, the Chinese soldiers interacted with the local people and did their utmost to be friendly, according to Singye, a local Tibetan who was among the few who stayed behind.[24] Tawang was not in Tibet proper, but it was here that the sixth Dalai Lama, a Monpa, was born in 1683. He became the Dalai Lama in 1697 and reigned until he disappeared in 1706, presumably killed by an ally of the Chinese Kangxi emperor. Tawang, therefore, was a special place for followers of Tibetan Buddhism and the Chinese had to behave exemplarily.

According to Singye, Tawang's famous monastery was not destroyed or looted by the Chinese, as some rumours would have it. The PLA protected the monastery and gave one of the senior monks a rifle so that he could defend the monastery against looters, who were roaming the town after the Indian soldiers and most of the locals had departed. They even brought in a lama from the Rethang monastery in Tibet to lead and take part in religious ceremonies at Tawang. Private houses, which were empty because their owners had fled, were locked by the Chinese to prevent looting. Food that had been dropped from Indian aeroplanes and had fallen into Chinese hands was distributed to the locals. 'A gift from us to you,' the Chinese officers said.[25]

The Chinese also had other, cruder ways of showing that they, and not the Indian soldiers and administrators from the plains, were the ones the local population should trust and identify themselves with. Residents in the border areas recall that Chinese officers showed them photographs of a bearded Sikh in a turban, saying, 'Is this man or I your brother?'[26] A Chinese, of course, looks more like a local person in Tawang than a Punjabi ever would.

But those who stayed behind were still relatively few. Tens of thousands of local people had fled south towards the plains or across the border to Bhutan in the east. After the Chinese had broken through the Indian defences at the Sela Pass south of Tawang on 18 November 1962 , there was panic everywhere. A day later, when a PLA unit, in a flanking manoeuvre, reached the town of Bomdila, many Indians expected the Chinese to advance south and occupy Assam.

One of those who fled was Dorjee Khandu Thongdok from Rupa, a small town near Bomdila. He and his family trekked over the mountains for days with little more to eat than Tibetan *tsampa*, a porridge-like dish made from barley flour and mixed with butter tea. Once in the plains, they were taken by truck to makeshift refugee camps in the Brahmaputra Valley. Three such camps were built, at Barampur, Diphu, and Dansiri, where the refugees were housed in huts and barracks.[27]

Most local people in Bomdila and Rupa are Sherdukpens, who are related to the Monpas but still somewhat different. Consequently, they speak a dialect related to Tibetan as well. And, significantly, the PLA halted there because they would be lost further south, where they would not be able to communicate with any remaining locals through their Tibetan interpreters, and, more importantly, where the PLA's spies had not been able to gather intelligence during the years leading up to the 1962 War. The PLA troops could now benefit from those human intelligence operations, as it was clear that their knowledge of the terrain was remarkable in all the areas into which they intruded, in the west as well as in the east, in October and November 1962. Colonel Gurdial Singh, who was taken prisoner at Rupa, recalls that the Chinese kept asking him where the foothills were.[28] Bhalukpong, at the very foothills of the NEFA, was abandoned but never occupied.

The Indian Army was gone from all its former positions in the battle zones, and no less than two-thirds of the population of the garrison town of Tezpur on the banks of the Brahmaputra had fled by 20 November. Trains and trucks were full of people with baggage heading west, away from what they thought was an impending Chinese invasion. Prisons and hospitals were opened and patients and inmates were left to fend for themselves. This became a problem, as Tezpur had a major mental hospital, and suddenly severely mentally ill people were seen roaming about and staggering along the town's streets. Banks were closed after they had burnt their currency notes.[29]

But the panic was misguided. Because the PLA had no intention of occupying Assam, the same pattern as in western NEFA could be seen in the east. The attack on Kibihtoo right on the border on 22 October was probably meant to push all the Indian troops back to Walong, the main Indian base in the area located some 20 kilometres to the south. The final attack on Walong, which fell on 16 November, was also made possible because the Chinese possessed vital intelligence of the area and its terrain. Walong was attacked from all sides, even from the rear. Significantly, the local people there are the Meyor, who speak a dialect related to Tibetan and practise Tibetan Buddhism.

After the Chinese had captured Walong, India's defences in the eastern-most corner of the NEFA were obliterated. According to one Indian writer, 'The fall of Walong would mean the fall of Haiyuliang, and there after Tezu as well. From Tezu, it was the Brahmaputra Valley. After Tezu would be Tinsukia.'[30] But nothing like that happened. The Chinese did not advance beyond the River Yapuk, immediately south of Walong. That was as far as the Chinese had surveyed the area. South of the Yapuk is Mishmi country, where the people speak an entirely different dialect.

The Chinese incursion into Subansiri and Siang in the central NEFA commenced on 21 October, with a main offensive being launched on 16 November. The Indian defences, as understaffed and poorly equipped as elsewhere in the NEFA, put up a stiff resistance but, in the end, proved to be no match for the more heavily armed Chinese troops. This area forms part of Pemako, which today straddles the border with a major section located on the Indian side. Tibetan tax collectors were active here well into the 1950s, so intelligence was not a problem for the PLA.[31] But the Chinese did not capture any territory beyond it. The tribes in the areas south of Pemako would be Nyishis and Apatanis, whose languages are distantly related to Tibetan, but not close enough to be mutually intelligible.

The similarities between the Tibetan language and some of the local dialects had enabled Chinese agents to collect intelligence about the areas that had been selected for temporary occupation and, judging from the precision and swiftness of the operation, it is clear that this was done well before the PLA swung into action in October 1962. While the vast majority of the local population fled to the southern plains once the PLA had entered those areas, it was also important from a purely operational point of view that its officers could rely on their Tibetan-speaking interpreters to communicate with the few who had stayed behind.

After the unilateral ceasefire that the Chinese announced on 21 November, the withdrawal began and people could return home. Singye remembers how the Chinese soldiers packed up and marched single file along the road they had built from Bumla to Tawang. Chinese army trucks carried their equipment. Forty-nine days of occupation were over. The Chinese returned to their camps and bases north of the McMahon Line.

Dorjee Khandu Thongdok and his family were now able to return to Rupa. On the way from the Assam plains to their home in the hills, they saw burnt-out tanks and vehicles, and ammunition belts, mortars, rifles, and helmets left behind by soldiers who had died or retreated during the war. Once they reached their village, there was an eerie silence. Empty houses awaited them, and it was weeks before life returned to normal.[32] Thongdok notes wryly that, before the war, a portrait of the two countries' respective prime ministers, Jawaharlal Nehru and Zhou Enlai, had hung on the wall in the local school.[33]

But the end of the Chinese invasion of some carefully selected parts of the NEFA did not mean that anything had really changed on the ground. The McMahon Line became what the Chinese like to call the Line of Actual Control, while the Indians continue to refer to it as 'the traditional boundary'. But India was shattered and its pride lay in tatters. No one wanted to mention the Forward Policy and Nehru himself never recovered from the humiliation and what he and many others perceived as a betrayal by the Chinese.

Nehru felt that he was grossly misunderstood. Others would argue that Nehru had placed too much trust in sweet talk by Zhou Enlai who had hoodwinked him into believing that China was a friend of India, while the Chinese, as early as 1949, had denounced him as 'a running dog of imperialism' and a Chiang Kai-shek-like 'loyal slave' of the enemies of the revolution.[34]

To be fair to Nehru, he appears to have been unaware of what the Chinese were saying about him behind his back in the 1940s and 1950s. His Forward Policy was never meant to provoke the Chinese but to reassert what the Indians considered to be the traditional boundary and to check the continuing Chinese advance by connecting all the gaps and plugging the holes along the frontier by establishing new outposts and sending out patrols even to the remotest parts of Ladakh and the NEFA. Action was to be taken only if there were any new Chinese army camps south of where the Indians had decided that the McMahon Line should be.

Lieutenant Colonel Gurdip Singh Kler, an Indian Army officer who fought at the Sela Pass during the 1962 War, wrote after the events, 'Many of us compared the Forward Policy with police action whereby we could push the Chinese out of our territory. The action, we thought, would not lead to war.'[35] The officer also remarked that although some new army units were proposed to be raised—and some were—'insufficient funds were allotted to the Armed Forces for weapons, equipment and ammunition'. He found it 'strange' that in this state of affairs 'we had to confront with one of the world's strongest countries'.[36]

As the Chinese had been strengthening their positions in the mountains along the frontier in the late 1950s and early 1960s, the Indians decided to launch a military operation codenamed 'LEGHORN' on 8 October 1962 to secure its territorial claims. A bridgehead was established at Tsengjong, north of River Namka Chu, which was attacked by the PLA on 10 October. The Indians withdrew, but they were terribly undersupplied. Air-drops of supplies were landing in the wrong places; only a few days of rations were available for the troops; and many of the soldiers had only 50 rounds of ammunition each. Mortars and mortar ammunition were still in transit somewhere when the Chinese attacked across the Thagla Ridge 10 days later.[37] It is not certain exactly how many troops the PLA had in the area at this stage, but they vastly outnumbered those at the scattered Indian outposts along the McMahon Line.

In retrospect, much has been written about intelligence failures on the Indian side, that the government was not aware of the massive build-up the Chinese had been engaged in along the border since 1959. But Nehru's chief of intelligence, Bhola Nath Mullik, had actually repeatedly warned the government of Chinese manoeuvres along and across the border, 'In September 1960, we sent another report of widespread Chinese activities all along the frontier in Tibet and many instances of fresh intrusions. We also mentioned that new Chinese activities had been noticed in the area bordering South-East Ladakh, which had remained quiet until then.'[38]

But nor did Mullik entirely escape blame. The Henderson Brooks–Bhagat Report quotes 'the Director of the Intelligence Bureau', obviously Mullik, as saying that 'the Chinese would not react to our establishing new posts and that they were not likely to use force against any of our posts even if they were in a position to do so'.[39] That was obviously a gross miscalculation.

In the east, the Chinese had already advanced up to and even through the 'gaps' that the Indians wanted to connect—and that was long before Nehru announced his Forward Policy. The problem was that Nehru refused to believe that the Chinese were actually preparing for war against India. His firm belief in the friendship between India and China had even led him to dismiss reports of unrest in Tibet in the late 1950s. On 17 March 1959, Patterson, who was close to the Tibetans, was warned by Nehru himself in a speech in the Lok Sabha, the Lower House of the Indian Parliament, that he 'had accepted bazaar rumour for a fact'.[40] Patterson was guilty of sending 'misleading and exaggerated reports'[41] about the situation in Tibet, and was threatened with expulsion from India.

As Nehru was accusing Patterson of spreading falsehoods, revolt had already broken out in Lhasa. The heartbroken prime minister then had to admit in another speech in the Lok Sabha on 19 March that the revolt was real—and that Chinese bullets had struck the Indian Consulate-General in Lhasa. The Chinese, who apparently thought that the Indians were somehow involved in the uprising, ordered the diplomats to remain inside the Consulate until further notice. Patterson noted, 'Whatever India may have thought of China's friendship and good faith it became obvious that China placed very little value on India's goodwill'.[42] Even so, Nehru added in his speech that, 'India has no intention of interfering in the internal affairs of China, with whom, we have friendly relations'.[43]

Following the Dalai Lama's escape to India after the March 1959 uprising, Nehru was forced to re-evaluate that friendship. The Chinese authorities now began to openly accuse India of being behind the revolt.

The official, state-controlled Chinese media published reports saying that 'Indian expansionists and British imperialists have not given up their ambition to invade Tibet and enslave its people'. The 'commanding centre' for this grand conspiracy was the northern West Bengal town of Kalimpong, where the British imperialists and Indian expansionists were supposed to have connived with a 'traitorous clique' in Tibet to conduct 'a series of traitorous and subversive activities'.[44]

It is hardly any secret that the Tibetans, in collaboration with the Americans, were collecting intelligence from Kalimpong, and that some Tibetan resistance fighters had been trained and were supported by the American CIA, but, judging from Nehru's statements at the time, it is extremely doubtful that he was aware of these shenanigans. More alarmingly, although Nehru decided to grant the Dalai Lama asylum in India, he still believed that China was, in fact, a friendly neighbour and whatever problems there were between the two countries could be settled amicably. It was only at the eleventh hour that he took reports of massive build-ups of Chinese troops across the border seriously and then decided on a half-hearted, and many would argue, ill-conceived Forward Policy to counter China's advances. Whatever that policy was aimed to achieve, the tools and wherewithal were simply not available.

The Henderson Brooks–Bhagat Report, which Maxwell bewilderingly uses to 'prove' that India was the aggressor in 1962, stated that, 'it is obvious that politically the "Forward Policy" was desirable and presumably the eviction of the Chinese from Ladakh must always be the eventual aim. For this, there can be no argument, but what is pertinent is whether we were militarily in a position at that time to implement this policy.'[45] The still-classified report goes on to mention that

> the Chinese build-up in Tibet by the end of 1960 had substantially increased and was brought out in the Military Intelligence Review 1959–60. This required a fresh reappraisal of our forces and tasks ... [and] at the outbreak of hostilities if a coordinated plan had been made to meet the Chinese offensive our troops would perhaps have been more balanced and there would not have been any question of plugging holes at the last moment.[46]

It is also astonishing to note how many Western writers, not only Maxwell and Alastair Lamb, have decided to accept China's crude propaganda and fanciful interpretations of the border conflict and related issues such as the reason for the war in 1962. This could be because Lamb and the others who accept the Chinese view do indeed present the issues in 'much clearer and persuasive terms than the Beijing Government', to quote the Berkeley professor Leo E. Rose.[47] In other words, they present the general Chinese view minus crazed outbursts about 'Indian expansionists', 'British imperialists', and 'traitorous and subversive Tibetan cliques'.

The claim that Indian troop movements around the Dhola Post and some skirmishes between the Indians and the Chinese in mid-October determined the timing of the attack is part of this twisted interpretation of the causes of the 1962 War. A much more plausible explanation is that an event that was taking place far from the Indian subcontinent made the Chinese decide that 20 October would be the most appropriate day to launch an attack and that, of course, was the Cuban missile crisis, which lasted from 22 to 28 October.

From the Chinese point of view, it was a masterstroke to decide to wage war on India at the same time that the American President John F. Kennedy was preoccupied by such an immediate threat to national security. A direct American intervention supporting India in the war would be out of the question, but if it did happen, it would force India to compromise its commitment to non-alignment. On 26 October, as war was raging in the Himalayas, Nehru made an unprecedented appeal for international sympathy and support.[48]

Three days later, when the Cuban missile crisis was essentially over, the United States did decide to send military aid after Ambassador John K. Galbraith had had a private meeting with Nehru. The Soviets had agreed to withdraw their ballistic missiles from Cuba after a secret agreement had been reached according to which the United States would dismantle its missile bases in eastern Turkey, a North Atlantic Treaty Organisation (NATO) ally of the US.

The message was conveyed through Galbraith that Kennedy had agreed to send arms to India 'without strings and the terms would be settled later'.[49] Nehru is also reported to have requested American warplanes, and, on 19 November, India sought full defensive intervention by the United States.[50] That did not happen, but a US aircraft carrier had already set course for the Bay of Bengal, and a squadron of transport planes had arrived in India.[51] It is believed that Kennedy sanctioned supplies of a million machine-gun rounds, 40,000 land mines, and 100,000 mortar rounds to India, while *Time* magazine at the time reported that shipments had been even more substantial and were complete with US crews and maintenance teams.[52] But it was too little, and too late. The Chinese had already achieved their objectives by the time Western military assistance arrived.

China did not miss the opportunity to denounce Nehru as 'a lackey of US imperialism' and 'a pawn in the international anti-China campaign'.[53] The tone and content of the 15,000-word vitriolic article in the official party paper the *People's Daily* on 27 October was, according to British analyst Roderick MacFarquhar, 'consonant with that of Beijing's anti-Soviet polemics of 1960 and prefigured in its anti-Soviet polemics of 1963–64, thus marking it as a weapon in the ideological struggle with Moscow rather than in the military struggle with India'.[54]

Apart from condemning Nehru for seeking military aid from the United States, China also wanted to hit out at the Soviet Union, which had been closer to India than any other Western power before the conflict began—and the Soviet Union was China's main rival for control over what it termed 'The Third World'. The rivalry had begun in the 1950s and first came out in the open when Soviet leader Nikita Khrushchev and Peng Zhen, a leading member of the Politburo of the CCP, had an argument at the congress of Romania's ruling communist party in 1960. Khrushchev branded Mao 'a nationalist, an adventurist, and a deviationist', while the Chinese denounced Khrushchev as 'patriarchal, arbitrary and tyrannical', and, eventually, as a 'revisionist renegade' who had betrayed true Marxism-Leninism.[55] Khrushchev responded by withdrawing 1,400 Soviet experts and technicians from China and cancelling more than 200 projects in the world's most populous communist country.

In the beginning of the conflict between India and China, the Soviet Union had been cautious. Although Khrushchev's sympathies were with

India, he could not afford to get too tough with China. On the other hand, India's defence minister, Vengalil Krishnan Krishna Menon, who was known for his pro-Soviet leanings, was forced to resign on 31 October, after being held responsible for India's lack of preparedness for the 1962 War. In the midst of the crisis, Nehru himself temporarily took over the defence portfolio. The Soviets, who had provided India with defence equipment long before the war, found themselves in a severe dilemma. According to Mohan Ram, an Indian journalist and a specialist on Sino-Indian relations, the Soviets had begged the Chinese to stop their military operations and offered mediation, for which India was ready. 'They tried hard to prevent India from looking to the United States and Britain. Thus, years of striving for India's neutrality went to waste and capitalists were supplying arms to India thanks to the Chinese aggression.'[56]

Another disclosure, according to Ram, was the Soviet concern over the ouster of Menon from the Indian government. Ram quotes a rejoinder from the Soviets saying that 'Chinese aggression also had the consequences that we lost one of our most faithful friends among the Indian leaders, and that because he relied on our help'.[57]

Khrushchev had remained neutral during the skirmishes along the Sino-Indian border in 1959, which had angered the Chinese. As tension between India and China was brewing in 1962, the Chinese called upon the leaders of the Soviet Union to 'denounce the Indian bourgeoisie as a lackey of imperialism'—which they refused to do.[58] Instead, on 12 December, when the war was over, Khrushchev came out in support of India, saying 'we absolutely disallow the thought India wanted to start war with China'.[59] Thus, China managed to force India to seek help from the United States, and also put the Soviet Union in the same anti-Chinese camp. It was a masterstroke that placed China as the leader of the Third World.

According to MacFarquhar, 'Nehru's appeal for Western aid in his hour of need dented, if it did not destroy, India's image as a non-aligned nation, thus diminishing its status both in the Communist bloc and the Third World ... Beijing had also demonstrated to a deaf Moscow the unwisdom of choosing India over China as an ally.' But, most importantly, MacFarquhar states that rising tension with India even in early and mid-1962, which eventually led to outbreak of hostilities in October, 'had signalled to its erstwhile communist partner that the banner of militant Marxism-Leninism had once more been unfurled over Beijing'.[60] The year of 1962 saw China, with Mao back at the helm, successfully challenging both India and the Soviet Union and, in the end, becoming the leader of the Third World's progressive and revolutionary forces.

There has been much speculation among scholars and analysts as to why the Chinese decided to declare a unilateral ceasefire on 21 November and then withdraw to its former positions behind the McMahon Line. Some have suggested that the American decision to intervene was a factor, others that the Soviet Union had threatened to take action unless the Chinese halted their advance into Indian territory. Indian military analysts have pointed to that the fact that winter was approaching in the high Himalayas, making it impossible to maintain long and vulnerable supply lines from forward bases in Tibet.

But none of these explanations are consistent with the broader picture of China's overall policies and strategic ambitions at the time of the war. It was a limited action aimed at punishing India, dethroning it from its leadership position in the non-aligned movement, and at forcing the Soviets to take sides in the wider conflict that had been raging within the international communist movement since 1960. There is nothing to indicate that the Chinese ever intended to hold the territory it had captured in October and November 1962. China wanted to demonstrate its military might and superiority and, by withdrawing, it had showed its 'goodwill' towards its neighbours and the rest of the world, demonstrating that it was not an aggressive power bent on capturing land from other countries. It was against the backdrop of these events that China emerged as the winner and the road now lay open for China to become the leader of the Third World.

The Cuban missile crisis may help explain why the Chinese decided to attack India on that precise date, 20 October, putting into action a plan that had been on the drawing board since 1959. But there were also other, domestic, factors which made them hasten the decision to launch their blitzkrieg against India. After the dismal failure of the Great Leap Forward in the late 1950s, Mao was plotting to regain his former position as the undisputed leader of the Chinese communists.

His rivals in the Party would have to be sidelined, neutralized—or won over. Among those critical of Mao's policies were President Liu Shaoqi, Premier Zhou Enlai, and, most importantly, the powerful Defence Minister Peng Dehuai, a hero of the Chinese Revolution as well as the Korean War in the early 1950s who, wise from his experiences during the latter conflict, wanted to reform the PLA and make it more professional, along the lines of the armed forces of the Soviet Union. This ran contrary to Mao's doctrine of an ideologically motivated 'people's army' that would be indoctrinated by studying the writings of the Great Chairman. Mao's vision of a good soldier was to be embodied in Lei Feng, the fictitious character created later; the loyal fighter who wanted to be 'a stainless-steel screw for the Party'.[61]

The ideological aspect of the 1962 War and that it was part and parcel of power struggles within the CCP at the time have been highlighted by MacFarquhar in his study of China in the 1950s and 1960s, 'The question that remains unanswerable is: if Mao had still been in retirement, would Liu Shaoqi and Zhou Enlai have chosen to teach Mr Nehru a lesson in quite so brutal a fashion? Probably not, in the light of their support for *san he yi shao*.'[62]

'San he yi shao' was a notion advanced by Wang Jiaxiang, an erstwhile comrade-in-arms of Mao and a former Chinese ambassador to the Soviet Union. It can be translated as 'three peaceful acts and one reduction' and referred to his proposed conciliation with the imperialists (the United States), the revisionists (the Soviet Union), and the reactionaries (India), while reducing aid to the world's revolutionary forces.[63]

According to Sergey Radchenko, a specialist on Sino-Soviet relations, Mao was fiercely opposed to this idea.

Mao talked about national security and national pride. He wanted the world to know that China could not be intimidated, and that Beijing's stern warnings to India were not a bluff. He knew that the People's Liberation Army was in a position to inflict a shattering blow to the Indian Army and so assert China's claim to regional hegemony. National security concerns and illusions of grandeur were very good reasons for a war with India.[64]

India had been identified by everyone in the top leadership of the CCP as the main regional enemy as early as 1959, and could therefore serve as a unifying factor as well as a pretext for purging the Party of 'revisionists' and other 'undesirable elements'. At the time India was facing a highly disciplined and brilliantly efficient war machine in the Himalayas, it was not known that China was barely recovering from one of the worst famines in its history, a manmade disaster created by Mao's own disastrous policies.

Following the Communist takeover of China in 1949, big and small landlords had their land confiscated and distributed among poorer peasants. Collectivization of land had to wait because there would have been widespread opposition to it. It was not until the mid-1950s that the policy changed, and peasants were forced into agricultural co-operatives. By 1958, private ownership of land had been abolished altogether, eventually leading to the birth of China's hallmark people's communes, where thousands of farmers were expected to work together to achieve often unrealistic production quotas. Even before that happened on a massive scale, the CCP decided to replace old religious beliefs with communist ideology, which meant that old temples were abandoned and fell into disrepair, traditional festivals were banned, and old icons in people's homes had to be replaced with pictures of Mao, Zhu De, and other communist leaders.

There was widespread opposition to these measures and criticism of the new economic policies even from within the Party even during those early days of communist rule. In very basic terms, the state was unable to take care of the harvests and make sure that people had enough to eat. Mao's response was to launch a campaign to let a 'Hundred Flowers Bloom'.[65] Criticism was not only allowed, it was encouraged. In retrospect it seems that Mao wanted to let the flowers bloom in order to cut them down. Now, when the critics had made themselves known, they were arrested under a follow-up drive called 'The Anti-Rightist Campaign', which was launched in June 1957. At least half a million people suffered as a result. The lucky ones just lost their jobs or homes, those who were unlucky ended up in prison or were executed.

But Mao had grander plans for transforming life in China's rural communities and purging the critics opposed to his radical initiatives. He wanted China to become a modern, industrialized nation. The origins of these policies can be traced to the mid-1950s, when Mao began to advocate rapid industrial growth similar to what the Soviet Union had achieved under Stalin in the 1930s. This was in contrast to the modest, step-by-step industrialization and comprehensive balance as advocated by Chen Yun, a leading economist who tried—in vain—to moderate the Chairman's wild plans for later became termed as 'the Great Leap Forward' and turned out to be one of the worst man-made disasters in modern history.[66]

Mao refused to listen. In November 1957, he visited the Soviet Union and encouraged by Sputnik's recent launch into space, he declaimed, 'The east wind is now prevailing over the west wind'.[67] Mao was also impressed with the Soviet Union's massive steel production and Khrushchev's pledge to overtake the United States and Britain in economic production in 15 years. Mao wished to see this emulated in China, and, in a *People's Daily* editorial on 13 November, the slogan 'Great Leap Forward' was actually now used for the first time. Mao wanted to be even bolder than the Soviet Union and during the second Session of the 8th CCP Congress in May 1958 it was stated that China was to be 'going all out, aiming high, and achieving more, faster, better, and more economic results in economic construction'.[68] The goal was to overtake Britain in seven years and reach American levels in 15.

Millions of people all over the country were mobilized to turn China into the world's most modern and industrialized nation. Steelmaking was given top priority, but in the absence of raw steel, everything from tools and metal sheets to nails and doorknobs were melted down to meet the targets. At the same time wasteful irrigation projects were launched to increase agricultural production and the state-controlled media published fanciful reports of massive progress everywhere in the country.

The Henan Province became the vanguard of the Great Leap Forward policies for the supposedly marvellous progress it had achieved. In Shangqiu Prefecture alone, a million people were employed in home workshops under the slogan, 'Every household a factory, every home ringing with a ding-dong sound'.[69] The province's 38,473 collectives had been converted into 1,355 bigger people's communes with an average of 7,200 households each. Grain production, pig farming, and irrigation projects were booming, according to the state media. In October 1958, the provincial authorities announced that Henan also had 5.77 million people working at more than 220,000 smelting furnaces.[70]

Similar, though not quite as impressive strides forward were reported from other provinces as well. China was on the threshold of becoming the industrialized nation envisaged by Mao and summarized by the slogan 'Three Red Banners', i.e., 'go all out, aim high, and build socialism with greater, faster, better, and more economical results'.[71] But it was all pure fantasy. The people's communes were built on land previously owned by individual farmers who saw little or no reason to toil for the state and the Party in exchange for rations and handouts from the authorities. Millions of farmers who had been mobilized to make steel no longer worked in the fields. Not surprisingly, the production of grain in Henan actually declined during the Great Leap Forward.[72] Old food distribution networks also broke down under the weight of Mao's mass mobilization of people to industrialize the country, which was still a backward peasant society. The vast majority of the population lived off the land, even in the co-operatives that had been established after the communist victory in 1949.

In early 1959, the central authorities in Beijing received reports from the model province of Henan that many people there were 'stricken with edema or had died of starvation'.[73] One such letter, dated 20 January 1959, and sent by the masses north and south of the Liudiquan train station, is especially moving and graphic:

> On the day of the Spring Festival [the lunar New Year] people covered the grasslands of Xiayi and Yucheng searching for wild plants to eat, but there was nothing left. People have died of starvation in all of the villages on the border between the two counties. Some dropped dead while waiting in line to buy food; others perished while seeking wild herbs in the fields.[74]

The pattern was the same, or worse, all over China. People were dying from starvation everywhere, and there were frequent reports of cannibalism. In Xinyang prefecture in Henan alone, there were at least 20 cases of people eating human flesh. An 18-year-old girl drowned her five-year-old cousin and ate him. The boy's 14-year-old elder sister was also driven by hunger and ate her brother's flesh.[75] In Anhui Province there were 63 cases of cannibalism between 1959 and 1960. A couple strangled their eight-year-old son, and then cooked and ate him. In the same province, a man dug up a corpse, ate some of it, and sold a kilo as pork.[76] Those were not isolated incidents. Similar incidents were recorded in most of China's provinces, although it is only in recent years that the full scale of the disaster has come to light. There were also sporadic rebellions in some parts of the country, but those were quickly quelled and hundreds, perhaps thousands, of rebels and their ringleaders were executed by the police and the PLA.[77]

The drive to turn China into an industrialized country also failed miserably. The steel that the furnaces turned out was useless, and the irrigation canals, dykes, and dams that had been built in rural areas to modernize China's agriculture were of poor standard. Frank Dikötter, a professor at the University of Hong Kong who has written extensively about the Great Leap Forward, states that, 'more detailed reports by investigation teams confirmed that materials, tools and machinery were neglected or even deliberately damaged. In the Shijiazhuang Iron and Steel Company, for instance, half of the engines broke down frequently.'[78] Dikötter concludes that 'a culture of waste developed. In Luoyang, three factories alone had accumulated more than 2,500 tonnes of scrap metal that went nowhere. In Shenyang, sloppy streamlets of molten copper and nickel solution ran between heaps of scrap metal.'[79]

It was on 25 March 1959, in the midst of all this chaos, that the expanded Politburo of the CCP met in Shanghai. The issue that topped the agenda of the meeting was, naturally, the Great Leap Forward. But the Tibetan revolt had just been crushed, and the Dalai Lama had fled to India. So, that topic was also raised. Already before the conference, Zhou Enlai had accused both Britain and the United States of having provided support for the uprising. India, as a frontline state, must have been involved as well, according to Zhou.

At the Shanghai meeting, Deng Xiaoping reiterated what Zhou had stated, but argued that the time was not yet ripe for Beijing to condemn India openly.[80] While it was not yet clear exactly when China was going to 'settle accounts' with the Indians, this was an issue where everyone was in complete agreement. Deng, along with Liu Shaoqi, belonged to those who were advocating more realistic economic policies than those implemented by Mao. But Deng was as much a hardliner as Mao when it came to dealing with Tibet and what the Communist leaders considered to be national security issues. The question was only when India should be 'taught a lesson'.

Despite the consensus on issues relating to Tibet and India, Mao was still in trouble. The failures of the Great Leap Forward had shaken his leadership position and the Shanghai meeting endorsed his retirement from his post as the Chairman of the People's Republic, or the de facto head of state. That post was given to the much more moderate Liu Shaoqi. But Mao stayed on as Chairman of the Party and, to the best of his ability, continued to manipulate events from behind the scenes.

A major problem for everyone in the top leadership was that they could not trust their underlings in the provinces. To conceal the disastrous outcome of the Great Leap Forward, and perhaps in an attempt to avoid being punished for failures, production figures in all fields were falsified in reports sent to the centre in Beijing. But the figures were so gross and exaggerated that even Mao disbelieved them. In April 1959, after the Shanghai meeting, he sent a circular letter to the Party cadres denouncing 'mere bragging' and demanding production targets to be based on reality.[81]

The well-educated Zhou Enlai, who had no difficulty in understanding what was happening, had actually been one of the first to initiate a campaign against Mao's concept of 'rash advance' as early as 1956. But Zhou, perhaps feeling that his position in the top leadership was no longer secure as Mao steamrolled his policies through the CCP's Central Committee, soon turned around. In March 1958, he even undertook 'self-criticism' for opposing Mao's notions of rapid industrialization. 'I take the main responsibility for submitting the report opposing rash advance, in effect dashing cold water on the upsurge among the masses...at the time I lacked perception, and it was only later that I gradually came to understand that this was a directional error on the issue of socialist construction.'[82]

Here was the supposedly sophisticated statesman who had made such an impression on the public during his visits to India in the 1950s humiliating himself in front of the Party's inquisitors. Zhou was no doubt still critical of Mao's plans for a rapid industrialization of China, but, at the same time, he was an opportunist who had to survive in the increasingly bitter power struggles that emerged during and in the wake of the Great Leap Forward. This became obvious when the CCP convened a meeting of its Politburo and a plenum of the Central Committee at Lushan, a mountain resort in Jiangxi Province in July 1959.

Yang Jisheng, a Chinese writer and researcher, says, 'Obliged to defend the Three Red Banners and their consequences, Zhou felt deeply conflicted. This was manifested in his schizophrenic performance at the Lushan Conference as he exerted great effort to resolve practical issues while pandering to Mao at every opportunity.'[83] In retrospect, it seems implausible that Indian policymakers would have got anything sensible out of Zhou when he, at the very same time, was communicating with Nehru about the border and other outstanding issues China had with India.

Zhou's opportunism made it possible for him to survive the purges that Mao unleashed at the Lushan Conference. The most prominent leader to be ousted was Peng Dehuai, who, on 13 and 14 July, had written a private letter criticizing the Great Leap Forward. Although extremely cautiously worded, and saying that the 'accomplishments of 1958 Great Leap Forward are absolutely undeniable',[84] Mao took it as an attack on himself and his policies. But Mao also made the mistake of circulating Peng's letter, which meant that other critical voices were raised. Zheng Wentian, a party veteran and Politburo member, was outspoken in his criticism—or, rather, as outspoken as anyone could be in the CCP.

Mao's response was fierce and swift. Peng, Zheng, and others who were associated with them were branded 'rightists' and 'counter-revolutionaries' and were purged during and immediately after the Lushan Conference. Zheng was accused of having 'illicit relations with a foreign country', which, presumably meant the Soviet Union, and buckets of sewage water were poured over his head as he was ordered to confess his 'wrongdoings'.[85] In September, Peng was replaced as defence minister by Lin Biao, a Mao crony who himself would be purged later. Mao appeared to have emerged victorious in the power struggle, but even so, his position was not yet secure.

There was widespread dissatisfaction with him and his rule. The Great Leap Forward had led to famine on a scale not seen before in Chinese history. The exact number of deaths is difficult to determine. Dikötter believes that 45 million people died 'unnecessarily' between 1958 and 1962.[86] Yang quotes Jiang Zhenghua, a Chinese researcher, who puts the figure considerably lower at 17 million.[87] Whatever the exact number of deaths from starvation during the Great Leap Forward, it was a disaster of unprecedented magnitude. By comparison, approximately three million people died during the Bengal famine in 1943, the worst disaster that has affected India within the twentieth century.

Even with his main rivals out of the way, and Zhou licking his wounds and now following the Party line, Mao was disturbed by the opposition that he had had to face before and during the Lushan Conference. How many 'rightists' and 'revisionists' were there still in the Party? Who could he trust? The meeting was hardly over before Mao launched yet another vigorous 'anti-rightist' campaign to silence his remaining critics. Even the old marshal Zhu De, the real founder of the PLA, had tried to protect Peng at Lushan by criticizing him only mildly. That was enough for Mao, who had expected Zhu to denounce Peng. Zhu was dismissed from his post as vice-chairman of the Central Military Commission, but was allowed to retain some other, less important posts in the state and Party hierarchy.

It is plausible that it was at this time that Mao also decided to use the Tibet issue and the border dispute with India to enhance his still shaky position within the Party and the state. The Lushan Conference ended on 16 August, and on 25 August, a PLA unit launched a surprise attack on an Indian position at Longju on the NEFA border. Then came the firefight at Kongka La in Ladakh on 21 October. Lin Biao, the man Mao had put in charge of the military, was obviously doing his job. It is doubtful whether any of those attacks would have happened if the more professional, veteran officer Peng had still been in command of the PLA. On the other hand, China's battlefield achievements in 1959 as well as in Myanmar in 1961, and, especially, the victory in the 1962 War were made possible because the PLA had benefitted from initiatives taken by Peng to professionalize the officer corps and make the command structure of the armed forces more efficient. These were to be reversed under Lin Biao. It was under him that the Lei Feng concept was promoted and for political and ideological reasons turned into a nation-wide cult, which survives to this day.[88]

Mao's gradual climb back to a position of absolute power had begun. By 1961, the Great Leap Forward was buried along with all the people who had died during the three years it had lasted. Apart from the millions who had died from starvation, there were others who had been beaten to death by Party zealots or had been executed on accusations of sabotage and other imagined crimes. It was over, and the political legacy of the Great Leap Forward was that Mao decided to replace the old principles of collective leadership of the Party with his own rule, which was not to be disputed or even challenged. He would, from now on, not tolerate any criticism of his rule or of his person.

But his struggle for a political comeback was not yet over. So, how safe was he from plots and intrigues within the Party? Dr Li Zhisui, Mao's personal physician and confidante, wrote much later in his biography of the Chairman that his support within the Party was waning even after the Great Leap Forward. Mao was 'depressed over the agricultural crisis and angry with the party elite, upon whom he was less able now to work his will. Mao was in temporary eclipse, spending most of his time in bed.'[89]

But then came 1962. According to Dr Li, 'Nineteen sixty-two was a political turning point for Mao. In January, when he convened another expanded Central Committee work conference to discuss the continuing disaster, his support within the party was at its lowest.'[90] At the meeting, President Liu Shaoqi openly blamed the famine on 'man-made disasters'.[91] Liu wanted to bring back the leaders who had been purged for opposing the Great Leap Forward, which made Mao furious.

The sycophantic Lin Biao praised Mao, and the Chairman himself began counterattacking his enemies more vigorously by arguing that 'classes continue to exist even under socialism'.[92] The 'class struggle' had to be carried on and the notorious hardliner and spymaster Kang Sheng was put in charge of carrying out more purges of 'revisionist', i.e., anti-Mao elements within the CCP. Kang was almost inseparable from Jiang Qing, the former actress who in 1938 became Mao's fourth wife. Together with Lin Biao, they became instrumental in bringing Mao back to power and propagating his unique brand of Communism as well as the personality cult that was advanced in the mid-1960s.

The border dispute with India proved to be a useful distraction from the power struggle and an issue that would either silence Mao's rivals and critics or bring them back them into the fold. And that helps explain why the final preparations for a war with India began in early 1962. Lin Biao was put in charge of the operation and that alliance between Mao and his loyal de facto chief of the PLA made the attack on India possible.[93] With China's ultimate victory in the war, Mao's ultra-leftist line had won in China; whatever critical voices that were left in the Party after all the purges fell silent.

By now there was also no doubt that Mao's vision and ambitions went beyond China's borders. He wanted to become the leader not only of China but also of all the revolutionary movements in the world. And that became a reality after the victory over India in 1962. Two years later, Nehru died, humiliated by the Chinese, a broken man. Brigadier Dalvi noted this in his account of the 1962 War and its aftermath, 'Without a Nehru India ceased to be the moral leader of the non-aligned world. Whereas prior to 1962 she wielded immense power and influence despite her poverty and lack of military power, after the Chinese attack she was "cut to size" in the words of one unfriendly critic of Nehru.'[94]

China was encouraged by the victory over India, and, once again, united behind Mao. A more belligerent China also emerged from the ashes of the battlefields in the Himalayas. Bombastic revolutionary phraseology was nothing new in broadcasts by Radio Beijing and articles in the *People's Daily*, but the rhetoric in the Chinese media now became even more militant than ever before. And the message was directed at revolutionaries in the parts of the world Mao wanted to have on his side in the struggle against 'the imperialists', 'the revisionists', and 'the reactionaries'.[95]

Mohan Ram argues in his excellent study of events before and after the 1962 War that, by mid-1967, China 'thought the revolutionary situation had turned "excellent" amidst sharpening international class struggle' and with revolutionary flames being lit all over 'The Third World'.[96] Ram refers to an article in the *People's Daily*, which contained a fierce attack on the Soviet Union's then premier, Alexei Kosygin, and his call for 'an end to war' as well as a condemnation of 'the greater United States-Soviet collusion against revolutionary struggles'. The *People's Daily* concluded that 'the world is full of the smell of gun powder… to hell with the theory of "dying out" of wars!'[97]

Notes

1. John P. Dalvi, *Himalayan Blunder: The Angry Truth About India's Most Crushing Military Disaster* (Dehra Dun: Natraj Publishers, 2010), p. 364.

2. Dalvi, *Himalayan Blunder*, p. 364.

3. P.J.S. Sandhu, Bhavna Tripathi, Ranjit Singh Kalha, Bharat Kumar, G.G. Dwivedi, Vinay Shankar (eds), 'Operations in the Western Sector (Ladakh)', *1962: A View from the Other Side of the Hill*, (Delhi: Vij Books, 2015), p. 67.

4. Sandhu et al., 'Operations in the Western Sector (Ladakh)' in *1962: A View from the Other Side of the Hill*, p. 67.

5. The Henderson Brooks–Bhagat Report, available at http://www.indiandefencereview.com/wp-content/uploads/2014/03/TopSecretdocuments2.pdf (accessed on 15 April 2016), p. 54.

6. Sanjay Sethi, 'Confrontation at Thag La: Indo China War 1962', *Scholar Warrior*, Autumn 2013, p. 118.

7. G.S. Bhargava, *The Battle of NEFA: The Undeclared War* (Bombay, New Delhi, Calcutta, Madras, London, New York: Allied Publishers, 1964), p. 96.

8. Sandeep Unnithan, '1962 Indo-China war veteran Brigadier Lakshman Singh shares his experience', *India Today*, 18 October 2012, available at http://indiatoday.intoday.in/story/i-led-40-men-to-safety-brigadier-lakshman-singh-82/1/225265.html (accessed on June 1, 2016) and 'Battle of Namka Chu, 10 Oct–16 Nov 1962', available at https://www.facebook.com/notes/service-selection-board/battle-of-namka-chu-10-oct-16-nov-1962/347589408614911/ (accessed on 1 June 2016).

9. Cheng Feng and Larry M. Wortzel, 'PLA Operational Principles and Limited War: The Sino-Indian War of 1962,' Mark A. Ryan, David M. Finkelstein, and Michael A. McDevitt (eds.), *Chinese Warfighting: The PLA Experience Since 1949* (Armonk, NY: Sharpe, 2003), pp. 182–6.

10. Dalvi, *Himalayan Blunder*, p. 377.

11. Feng and Wortzel, 'PLA Operational Principles and Limited War', p. 152.

12. Dalvi, *Himalayan Blunder*, pp. 376–7.

13. Louise Chipley Slavicek, *Great Military Leaders of the 20th Century: Mao Zedong* (Philadelphia: Chelsea House Publishers, 2004), p. 37.

14. George N. Patterson, *Tibet in Revolt*, (London: Faber and Faber, 1960), p. 88.

15. Patterson, *Tibet in Revolt*, p. 88.

16. Patterson, *Tibet in Revolt*, p. 86–7 and 99–100.

17. Patterson, *Tibet in Revolt*, p. 88.

18. John Powers, *History as Propaganda: Tibetan Exiles versus the People's Republic of China*, (Oxford, New York: Oxford University Press, 2004), p. 120.

19. Li Xiaobing, *A History of the Modern Chinese Army* (Lexington: The University Press of Kentucky, 2007), pp. 202-03. .

20. Li, *A History of the Modern Chinese Army*, pp. 203–4.

21. Li, *A History of the Modern Chinese Army*, p. 204.

22. Li, *A History of the Modern Chinese Army*, p. 204.

23. See Melvyn C. Goldstein, Dawei Sherap, and William R. Siedenschuh, *A Tibetan Revolutionary: The Political Life and Times of Bapa Phuntso Wangye* (Berkeley, Los Angeles, London: University of California Press, 2005).

24. Interview with Singye (name changed for privacy), Tawang, 28 October 2015.

25. Interview with Singye, Tawang, 28 October 2015.

26. Interviews, with local residents, Tawang, 27–29 October 2015.

27. Interview with Dorjee Khandu Thongdok, Rupa, 26 October 2015.

28. E-mail communication with Shiv Kumar Verma, the author of *1962: The War That Wasn't* (New Delhi: Aleph, 2016), 18 March 2016.

29. Interview with Tilottoma Misra, Guwahati, 23 October 2015. Also see Brij Mohan Kaul, *The Untold Story* (Bombay, Calcutta, New Delhi, Madras: Allied Publishers, 1967), p. 427.

30. Mrinal Talukdar, *Sino-Indian Conflict*, translated by Deepika Phukan (Guwahati: Kaziranga Books, 2014), p. 216.

31. Interview with Tsering (name changed for privacy), Darjeeling, 12 March 2016. Tsering is the son of a Pemako aristocrat from the Tibetan side of the border.

32. Dorjee Khandu Thongdok, *War on Buddha: A Book on Chinese Aggression 1962* (Rupa, Arunachal Pradesh, 2012), pp. 18–19.

33. Thongdok, *War on Buddha*, p. 3.

34. Sandhu et al., *1962*, 'The Politico-Diplomatic Prelude Part-1', p. 5.

35. Gurdip Singh Kler, *Unsung Battles of 1962*, (New Delhi, London, Hartford WI: Lancer Publishers, 1995), pp. 94–5.

36. Gurdip Singh, *Unsung Battles of 1962*, pp. 95.

37. Sethi, 'Confrontation at Thag La: Indo China War 1962, p. 120.

38. B.N. Mullik, *My Years with Nehru: The Chinese Betrayal* (Bombay, Calcutta, New Delhi, Madras, Bangalore, London, New York: Allied Publishers, 1971), p. 307.

39. The Henderson-Brooks Bhagat Report, p. 8.

40. Quoted in Patterson, *Tibet in Revolt*, p. 167.

41. Patterson, *Tibet in Revolt*, p. 166.

42. Patterson, *Tibet in Revolt*, p. 161.

43. Patterson, *Tibet in Revolt*, p. 176.

44. Quoted in Patterson, *Tibet in Revolt*, p. 182.

45. The Henderson Brooks–Bhagat Report, p. 10.

46. The Henderson Brooks–Bhagat Report, p. 32.

47. Leo E. Rose, 'Review: The McMahon Line: A Study in the Relations between India, China and Tibet, 1904 to 1914, by Alastair Lamb', *Pacific Affairs*, Vol. 41, Issue no, 1, Spring 1968, p. 132. See also Introduction and Acknowledgements.

48. Paul M. McGarr, *The Cold War in South Asia: Britain, the United States and the Indian Subcontinent, 1945–1965*, (Cambridge: Cambridge University Press, 2013), p. 157.

49. Mohan Ram, *Politics of Sino-Indian Confrontation* (Delhi, Bombay, Bangalore, Kanpur, London: Vikas Publishing House, 1973), p. 122.

50. Ram, *Politics of Sino-Indian Confrontation*, p. 123.

51. Roderick MacFarquhar, *The Origins of the Cultural Revolution, Volume 3: The Coming of the Cataclysm* (New York and Oxford: Oxford University Press and Columbia University Press, 1997), p. 311.

52. Ramachandra Guha, *India After Gandhi: The History of the World's Largest Democracy* (New Delhi: Picador India, 2012), p. 340. *Time* claimed that Washington sent 60 planes loaded with US$5 million worth of automatic weapons, mortars, and land mines, and that 12 C-130 Hercules transport planes flew Indian troops to the battle zones; see 'India. Never Again the Same', *Time*, 30 November 1962, available at http://content.time.com/time/magazine/article/0,9171,829540,00.html (accessed on 27 September 2016). This is most likely an exaggeration of the extent of US military assistance to India in 1962. However, according to Bruce Riedel, 'The United States and the

United Kingdom responded very quickly to Nehru's request for armaments. U.S. Air Force (USAF) Boeing 707 aircraft, flying from bases in Europe and Thailand, began airlifting weapons and ammunition to India; by November 2, eight flights a day were each bringing in twenty tons of supplies to Calcutta. USAF C-130s then transported the arms from Calcutta to airfields near the front lines ... the Royal Air Force (RAF) also soon began airlifting supplies to India, and London was consulting with Australia, New Zealand and Canada on providing aid from the British Commonwealth.' See Bruce Riedel, *JFK's Forgotten Crisis: Tibet, the CIA, and the Sino-Indian War* (New Delhi: Harper Collins, 2016), p. 121.

53. MacFarquhar, *The Origins of the Cultural Revolution, Volume 3*, p. 310.

54. MacFarquhar, *The Origins of the Cultural Revolution, Volume 3*, p. 310.

55. Quoted in Alan Axelrod. *The Real History of the Cold War: A New Look at the Past* (New York: Sterling Publishing Co., 2009), p. 213. For the ideological conflict between the Soviet Union and China, see also Ram, *Politics of Sino-Indian Confrontation*, pp. 101–6.

56. Ram, *Politics of Sino-Indian Confrontation*, pp. 130–31.

57. Ram, *Politics of Sino-Indian Confrontation*, p. 131.

58. Ram, *Politics of Sino-Indian Confrontation*, p. 127.

59. Ram, *Politics of Sino-Indian Confrontation*, p. 133.

60. MacFarquhar, *The Origins of the Cultural Revolution*, pp. 311–12.

61. For an account of the Lei Feng myth, see Evan Osnos, 'Fact-checking a Chinese Hero', *The New Yorker*, 29 March 2013, available at http://www.newyorker.com/news/evan-osnos/fact-checking-a-chinese-hero (accessed on 10 April 2016).

62. MacFarquhar, *The Origins of the Cultural Revolution, Volume 3, p. 312.*

63. Sergey Radchenko, *The Suns in Heavens: The Sino-Soviet Struggle for Supremacy, 1962 to 1967* (Washington and Stanford: The Woodrow Wilson Center and Stanford University Press, 2009), p. 28.

64. Radchenko, *The Suns in Heavens*, p. 28.

65. This was a campaign that was launched after Mao Zedong had said in a speech made to a session of the Supreme State on 2 May 1956 that the party should 'let a hundred flowers blossom, let a hundred schools contend'. Referred to as 'the hundred flowers speech', it is mentioned and analysed in detail in Roderick MacFarquhar, *The Origins of the Cultural Revolution 1: Contradictions Among the People 1956–1957.* (New York: Columbia University Press, 1974), pp. 51–6.

66. For an excellent account of the origins and development of the Great Leap Forward, see Frederick C. Teiwes and Warren Sun, *China's Road to Disaster: Mao, Central Politicians, and Provincial Leaders in the Unfolding of the Great Leap Forward 1955–1959* (Armonk, New York and London: M.E. Sharpe, 1999). Chen Yun's criticism of Mao's policies is outlined on pp. 63–65.

67. Teiwes and Sun, *China's Road to Disaster*, p. xviii.

68. As quoted in Teiwes and Sun, *China's Road to Disaster*, p. xx.

69. Yang Jisheng, *Tombstone: The Chinese Famine 1958–1962*, translated by Stacy Mosher and Guo Jian (New York: Farrar, Straus and Giroux, 2012), p. 77.

70. Yang, *Tombstone*, p. 77.

71. Yang, *Tombstone*, p. 87.

72. Yang, *Tombstone*, pp. 80–81.

73. Yang, *Tombstone*, p. 81.

74. Yang, *Tombstone*, p. 81.

75. Yang, *Tombstone*, pp. 41–2.

76. Yang, *Tombstone*, p. 278.

77. For rebellions during the Great Leap Forward, see Yang, *Tombstone*, pp. 465–82, and Frank Dikötter, *Mao's Great Famine: The History of China's Most Devastating Catastrophe* (London, Berlin, New York, Sydney: Bloomsbury, 2010), pp. 226–8.

78. Dikötter, *Mao's Great Famine*, p. 146.

79. Dikötter, *Mao's Great Famine*, p. 146.

80. Sandhu et al. 1962, 'The Politico-Diplomatic Prelude Part 2', p. 23.

81. Teiwes with Sun, *China's Road to Disaster*, p. xxiii.

82. Yang, *Tombstone*, p. 100.

83. Yang, *Tombstone*, pp. 370–1.

84. Yang, *Tombstone*, p. 358.

85. Yang, *Tombstone*, p. 383.

86. Dikötter, *Mao's Great Famine*, p. x.

87. Yang, *Tombstone*, pp. 419–20.

88. In 1963, Lin Biao presented to the public a diary supposedly written by Lei Feng. Although this was done after the 1962 War, the basic concept of the loyal and ideologically motivated PLA soldier dates back to the Chinese civil war in the 1930s and 1940s. 'Lei Feng' gave a name and a persona to that concept.

89. Li Zhisui, *The Private Life of Chairman Mao: The Inside Story of the Man who Made Modern China* (London: Chatto & Windus, 1994), p. 356.

90. Zhisui, *The Private Life of Chairman Mao*, p. 385.

91. Zhisui, *The Private Life of Chairman Mao*, p. 652.

92. Zhisui, *The Private Life of Chairman Mao*, p. 652. See also Claude Arpi, 'Why Mao attacked India in 1962', *Indian Defence Review*, Vol. 26, Issue No. 3, July–September 2011, available at http://www.indiandefencereview.com/spotlights/maos-return-to-power-passed-through-india/ (accessed on 15 June 2017): 'At the beginning of 1962, as tension was increasing on the Indian border, did Nehru realize that China was a starving nation? Very few knew that, by the end of 1961 Mao was practically out of power.'

93. Claude Arpi, *India and Her Neighbours: A French Observer's View*, (New Delhi: Har Anand Publications, 2007), p. 194.

94. Dalvi, *Himalayan Blunder*, pp. 481–2.

95. Those 'enemies', and others, are identified in Mao Zedong, *Quotations from Chairman Mao Tse-tung* (Beijing: Foreign Languages Press, 1968), pp. 8–23.

96. Ram, *Politics of Sino-Indian Confrontation*, p. 184.

97. The quote about 'the smell of gun powder' and 'to hell with the theory of dying out of wars' comes from a broadcast over Radio Beijing on 1 July 1967 and quoted in Mohan Ram, *Maoism in India* (New York: Barnes & Noble, 1971), p. 7.

4

When the War was Over

The war was hardly over before the blame game began and heads started to roll. No one was surprised when Vengalil Krishnan Krishna Menon was sacked even as fierce fighting raged in the heights of the Himalayas. His left-leaning views were not a problem—many Indian politicians at the time leaned more to the left than to the right—but he was also the defence minister and was therefore criticized more than anybody else in the establishment for having underestimated the Chinese threat. According to Lieutenant General Brij Mohan Kaul, Chief of General Staff of the Indian Army during the 1962 War, India's intelligence gathering system 'compared unfavourably with that of the Chinese. They had systematically introduced agents into India in general and NEFA in particular (whereas we had lagged in this respect). Their agents built up a network for reporting back to the Chinese.'[1]

Even so, for several years before the attack in October 1962, intelligence reports had been pouring into the headquarters of the army—and Menon's ministry—about the Chinese military build-up across the northeastern border. Menon had at least three years' notice of the impending Chinese aggression.[2] Or, as the Indian journalist and political commentator D.R. Mankekar wrote in his book *The Guilty Men of 1962*, 'From 1959 onwards, Chinese belligerence was mounting up, until it burst out in a crescendo in October 1962'.[3]

Also according to Mankekar,

> Between the two schools of thought prevailing in the country at the time, Menon headed the one which played up the threat from Pakistan and underplayed the Chinese menace to India. Apart from his ideological bias in favour of China and other Communist countries, Menon had for long adopted Pakistan as his pet enemy, having for so many years monopolised the foot-lights in the glamorous role as a valiant gladiator over the emotionally-combustible Kashmir question.[4]

On 10 January 1962, Menon had issued a statement at Tezpur in Assam—a frontline position during the war that broke out nine months later—saying that 'the India-China border dispute was not of such a magnitude as could precipitate a war.'[5] In a sense, he was right. China would not go to war over the actual border dispute, but he failed to grasp the broader geopolitical and ideological context in which China decided to 'settle accounts with the Indians'.[6]

Menon was one of the most controversial, some would argue, divisive, figures in Nehru's cabinet. He was one of Nehru's oldest friends and closest political confidantes whose interests and actions were not always appreciated by the army. In 1959, the legendary General Kodendera Subayya Thimayya even resigned his post as the Chief of Army Staff over disagreements with Menon. Nehru, however, refused to accept Thimayya's resignation and persuaded him to stay on, which he did until his retirement in 1961.

A British observer even went as far as saying that Menon 'is felt to be one of the Nehru family (in a way no other Minister is or has been) … indeed Nehru behaved towards Menon in a manner so paternal to suggest that he saw in Menon the son he had always so much wanted to have'.[7] Other Westerners portrayed Menon as 'India's Rasputin', 'the Hindu Vishinsky', and 'India's Communist-cuddling roving ambassador'.[8]

Menon's anti-Western stance became an issue when India, during the height of the fighting in the Himalayas, saw it had no alternative but to turn to the United States for support. On 23 October, three days before Nehru made the official request for American support, the US ambassador in New

Delhi, John K. Galbraith, informed India's Foreign Secretary M.J. Desai that Menon's retention of the post as defence minister represented one of the 'more serious problems' standing in the way of American military aid to India.[9] Hence, he had to go. After a brief interlude with Nehru in charge of the defence ministry, Yashwantrao Balwantrao Chavan, who had played a prominent role during India's freedom struggle, became the new minister.

Despite the close friendship between Nehru and Menon, it is also clear that there were serious disagreements between the two. Nehru was perhaps more sceptical of the Chinese than he was prepared to show. As early as 1958, he is reported to have said in a private conversation with the Indian ambassador-designate to Beijing, G. Parthasarathi,

> I don't trust the Chinese one bit. They are a deceitful, opinionated, arrogant and hegemonistic lot. Eternal vigilance should be our watchword. You should send all your telegrams only to me, not to the Foreign Office. Also, do not mention a word of this instruction of mine to Krishna [Menon]. He, you and I all share a common worldview and ideological approach. However, Krishna believes, erroneously, that no Communist country can have bad relations with any Non-Aligned country like ours.[10]

That was Menon's most serious misjudgement. But as Kaul wrote in his book about the 1962 War and its aftermath, 'When Menon fell from grace, his many past services to India were forgotten and only his errors remembered'.[11] Menon was in fact one of the most brilliant minds and dynamic personalities ever to have held a ministerial post in the Indian government. He was a vegetarian, did not drink alcohol or smoke tobacco, and, as a minister, he lived in a small room in a modest bungalow full of books.

As a young man in the 1920s and 1930s, Menon had studied at University College, London, and the London School of Economics, where his professor of political science, Harold Laski, later described him as 'the best student I have ever had'.[12] After independence, Menon became India's first High Commissioner to the United Kingdom and, later, the Indian ambassador to the UN. He was also one of the brains behind the 1955 Bandung Conference and the creation of the Non-Aligned Movement. In fact, the very term 'non-aligned' was coined by

Menon in a speech at the UN in New York in 1953 to describe countries which were allied with neither the West nor the Soviet Union. But it was hardly any secret that Menon was more sympathetic to Moscow than to Washington and London.

When he took over the Defence Ministry in 1957, he was 'like a fresh breath of air, which blew away the cobwebs and layers of dust accumulated on the portfolio over the years'.[13] He was arrogant and not especially liked by his co-workers, whether subordinate or senior to him in the hierarchy, but, according to Kaul, 'He was a well-read man and an encyclopaedia on practically every subject under the sun such as science, philosophy, medicine, engineering, history, politics, economics, agriculture and animals. He had an intricate knowledge of the intricacies of aircraft engines, armoured vehicles, submarines and wireless sets. No expert felt safe in his presence.'[14]

Most importantly, however, he laid the foundations for India's own defence industries to make the country less dependent on imports and he restructured much of India's military command system, which under his tutelage came to be based on merit rather than seniority within the ranks. Menon was also the mastermind behind the annexation of the former Portuguese colony of Goa in 1961. In 1957, he set the record for the longest speech before the UN Security Council in New York. For eight hours, he defended India's right to sovereignty over Kashmir against Pakistan's claims to the same. Five years after he was forced out of the government, he left the ruling Congress Party and stood for several elections as an independent candidate. When he died at the age of 78 in 1974, the then Prime Minister Indira Gandhi stated that 'a volcano is extinct'.[15]

The next head to roll was that of General Pran Nath Thapar, Chief of Army Staff. On 18 November 1962, he flew back from Tezpur to Delhi, and went straight to Nehru's residence. Thapar told the prime minister that he was willing to resign. He said it was not his fault that the Indian Army had been routed in the Himalayas, but, as a professional soldier, he assumed responsibility for the disaster. Nehru said that he would consider it and, the following day, accepted Thapar's offer. Thapar then submitted a formal request for early retirement, which was granted.

Thapar was born in the western part of Punjab, which now belongs to Pakistan, and went to school in Lahore. Like so many other army officers of his generation, he was educated at Britain's Royal Military College at Sandhurst. He saw action in Myanmar, the Middle East, and Italy during World War II and later became Director of Military Operations and Intelligence. Thapar had a distinguished military career, and became army chief in May 1961. After his resignation from the military, he served for five years as India's ambassador to Afghanistan.

Thapar's successor as the Chief of Army Staff, General Jayanto Nath Chaudhury, a Bengali, was also a Sandhurst graduate who had taken part in the 'Burma Campaign', the British counteroffensive in Myanmar to recover the colony from the Japanese. Chaudhury had served as army chief for only two days when the Chinese declared a unilateral ceasefire. It fell to him to pick up the pieces and rebuild the shattered defences along the border.

Then, the turn came for General Kaul to go. He had also had a distinguished military career and served as Chief of General Staff and General Officer Commanding in the northeast during the war. Sandhurst-trained and, like all the others, brought up in the British Army tradition, he had seen combat in Myanmar during World War II and in Kashmir in 1948. In the early 1950s, he had served with General Thimayya for the United Nations Neutral Repatriation Commission. He was closer to Nehru, though, and was seen as one of very few Indian Army officers who may have had political ambitions. But the war in the northeast was his downfall.

Kaul was at the frontline when the first skirmishes occurred along the border in mid-October, but fell ill from altitude sickness up in the mountains and had to be evacuated from the area and flown to Delhi for medical treatment. He was not able to return to the northeast until 29 October and his absence from the theatre of war was seen by his detractors as a sign of cowardice. He had developed 'cold feet', they said, and was 'malingering'.[16] This was a highly unfair accusation, but given the political climate in India after the humiliating defeat that the Chinese had inflicted upon the Indian Army, he had no other choice but to bite the bullet and ask for an early retirement, which was duly accepted by the government on 11 December.[17]

Kaul was then only 50 years old. He eventually left the service, a bitter man, on 14 May 1963 and went on a year-long, personal tour of Europe, Japan, and the US. Had it not been for the blame he shouldered for the 1962 debacle, he would most probably have been looking forward to a future not only in the military but perhaps also in politics. The legendary American broadcaster Welles Hangen even saw him as a likely candidate to succeed Nehru as prime minister.[18]

There were also some unsung and largely anonymous victims of the war: India's ethnic Chinese community. The authorities suspected that they were a 'fifth column' that had provided the Chinese military with information prior to the 1962 War and they were treated as traitors to the nation. It is beyond doubt that China's Communist government had sent intelligence agents to India years before the 1962 War, but they were hardly to be found among India's own ethnic Chinese communities. India's Chinese had come during the British colonial era and most of them lived in Kolkata, where they worked as tanners, shoemakers, and carpenters, and owned restaurants, beauty parlours, shops, and other small businesses. If they had any political sympathies, it would be with the Nationalist Chinese government in Taiwan rather than the Communists in Beijing. The Overseas Chinese Association in Kolkata openly expressed support for the Indian government throughout the conflict and even urged it not to accept Beijing's 'dirty offer' of a ceasefire in November.[19]

Nevertheless, the Foreigners (Restriction of Chinese Nationals) Order, which was issued on 25 October, prohibited any person of Chinese descent from leaving his or her village for longer than 24 hours without written permission from local officials. Five days later, another order was issued making it possible to detain 'any person not of Indian origin who was at birth a citizen or subject of any country at war with, or committing external aggression against, India'.[20]

Then came the promulgation of the Foreigners (Internment) Order of 3 November under which the authorities in Assam and certain districts of northern West Bengal arrested all residents of Chinese descent and transported them over 1,500 kilometres away to an internment camp at Deoli in Rajasthan. By February 1963, according to the government's account, there were 2,165 ethnic Chinese at Deoli and an additional 143 detained in local jails.[21] Almost all of them had come from the northeastern border regions.

One of those interned was Yin Marsh, who was born in Kolkata and raised in Darjeeling, where her family ran a popular Chinese restaurant. She, her father, grandmother, and eight-year-old brother were all sent to Deoli, a harrowing experience which she has related in her book *Doing Time with Nehru: The Story of an Indian-Chinese Family*. The title alludes to the ironic coincidence that Nehru, who had authorized the mass arrests, had once been detained in Deoli by the British during India's struggle for independence.[22]

In the end, none of the detainees in Deoli, or any other Indian person of Chinese descent, was brought to trial for espionage or other charges.[23] But in 1963, 2,395 ethnic Chinese, of whom 1,665 were internees and 730 their dependents, were repatriated to China. For those who remained, the situation became untenable, and between 1962 and 1967 another 7,500 left India for Hong Kong, Taiwan, Canada, and other places, even Pakistan.[24] It was not until 1998 that ethnic Chinese were allowed to become naturalized Indian citizens.

The treatment of the ethnic Chinese hurt India's international image as a strong democracy and today no more than 2,000 persons remain of the once-thriving community in Kolkata, and even fewer in towns like Kalimpong and Darjeeling, and some districts of Assam where their ancestors were brought as indentured labourers by the British tea planters in the nineteenth century. In 2010, survivors of the Deoli camp went public saying that they wanted a monument to be raised at the site as 'an acknowledgement of the persecution of the ethnic Chinese' in 1962 and as a reminder of 'our loss of freedom'.[25]

But the main political casualty of the 1962 War was perhaps Nehru himself and his ideology of non-alignment. His health began to deteriorate after the war and, in 1963, he spent months recuperating in the highlands of Kashmir, from where his forefathers came. On 7 January 1964, Nehru suffered a stroke while attending a Congress Party meeting in

Bhubaneshwar, the capital of Odisha, in the eastern part of India. He collapsed while on stage and was rushed back to New Delhi for medical treatment. The Congress Party and the government began making arrangements to relieve him of some of his duties. He was not that old, only 75. But it was clear that his stamina was now disappearing fast.

There were two issues that Nehru had wanted to settle during his lifetime: his painful conflict with his old comrade Sheikh Abdullah over the status of Jammu and Kashmir and the ongoing tribal insurgency in the Naga Hills in the northeast, 'India's Little Vietnam', as it became known. But it was the defeat in the war with China that hurt him the most. Some historians believe that what he saw as a complete betrayal of trust on the part of the Chinese contributed to his declining health and hastened his death.[26] As the Indian writer Ramachandra Guha has pointed out, 'The China war had weakened Nehru's position not just in India or the world but within the Congress Party itself'.[27]

On 27 May, Nehru suffered another heart attack and died at his home, Teen Murti House in New Delhi. His daughter Indira Gandhi was by his side as heart specialists fought, in vain, to save him. At 2 p.m. that afternoon, cabinet minister C. Subramaniam told the lower house of the parliament, the Lok Sabha, 'The prime minister is no more. The light is out.' Subramaniam was paraphrasing Nehru's own statement after the assassination of Mahatma Gandhi on 30 January 1948: 'The light has gone out of our lives and there is darkness everywhere.'[28]

Although India had received some assistance from the West during the war, American and British offers of military aid came with strings attached. As the Indian historian Gyanesh Kudaisya points out in his account of Nehru's last days,

> Nehru was upset...India was now forced to accept outside mediation and to open a dialogue with Pakistan over the highly contentious issue of Kashmir. Both the US and UK governments had used the Himalayan crisis to put pressure on India to make concessions to Pakistan and to settle the Kashmir issue. Nehru's carefully nurtured policy of non-alignment suffered a setback and India's stature on the global stage, which he had worked so hard to build, diminished.[29]

Gulzarilal Nanda, an economist and a politician from the Congress Party, took over as interim prime minister until Lal Bahadur Shastri could be sworn in on 9 June. A former freedom fighter of some renown, Shastri was far from an unknown figure in Indian politics, but he was mild-mannered, soft-spoken, and lacked Nehru's charisma and stature on the world stage.

Nevertheless, he led India during the 1965 war with Pakistan, which the Indian Army won, and thus managed to restore some of the pride that had been lost in 1962. On 10 January 1966, a peace deal was signed in Tashkent in Uzbekistan, then a part of the Soviet Union. The Soviet Premier Alexei Kosygin moderated the meeting between Shastri and Pakistan's President Muhammed Ayub Khan. A day later, Shastri died from a sudden heart attack, which has led to all kinds of conspiracy theories. Was he poisoned and, if so, by whom? But there was never any evidence to confirm those speculations and Shastri's body was flown back to India to be cremated there.

Gulzarilal Nanda had to step in again and served as the acting head of the government until 24 January, when India got another new prime minister who would raise the country's profile in the region and across the world: Nehru's then 48-year-old daughter Indira Gandhi. Relations with Washington would become strained because of her criticism of the American bombing of Vietnam. She also steered India into a close friendship with the Soviet Union, which, from India's point of view, would be a more trustworthy ally than Western nations.

During the 1962 War, Ayub Khan had protested vehemently against American and British military aid to India, arguing that it would 'enlarge and prolong the conflict', and that the weapons would be used against Pakistan over the Kashmir dispute.[30] And the West could not afford to antagonize Pakistan, a member of the pro-Western Southeast Asia Treaty Organisation (SEATO) as well as the Central Treaty Organisation (CENTO).[31]

Pakistan was in the curious position of being a member of two Western-organized defence pacts while remaining a close ally of China. And India's alliance with the Soviet Union would inevitably accelerate the country's progression along the serious collision course it was already on with China. It is clear that India's decision makers felt the country needed a strong and decisive prime minister who could lead them through the extremely tangled situation in which the region was embroiled during these turbulent years. Furthermore, the choice of Indira Gandhi would ensure continuity. She was Nehru's daughter and, although not a relative, she had the same surname as the Mahatma.

In China, meanwhile, Mao Zedong was rapidly consolidating his grip on power. The 1959 Lushan Conference that had led to the purge of some of Mao's most prominent rivals and enemies was followed by intrigues and manoeuvrings which lasted well into 1962. If Mao was depressed in the beginning of 1962, as his physician Li Zhisui wrote in his book about the Chairman, it was not until a conference at the seaside resort town of Beidaihe in August of that year that 'the banner of militant Marxism-Leninism', in the words of Roderick MacFarquhar, could once again be 'unfurled over Beijing'.[32] Mao blamed the disastrous consequences of his Great Leap Forward on Liu Shaoqi, Zhou Enlai, Deng Xiaoping, Chen Yun, and other so-called 'moderates' within the party. 'We (meaning himself) had been talking about making agriculture the foundation, but this had not actually been practised by his [Mao's] colleagues ... in the four years from 1959 to 1962.'[33]

MacFarquhar points out that the last time a dispute over economic policy had been transmuted into political struggle was at the 1959 Lushan Conference, 'as Mao reminded them, and then it had resulted in the purge of four senior officials'.[34] The same pattern was repeated at the 1962 Beidaihe meeting. The Canadian professor Lorenz M. Lüthi argues that Mao then 'staged a brilliant comeback in daily policy making. He used this momentum to stamp his mark on Chinese foreign relations.'[35] This meant virulent condemnation of his new enemies, the 'Soviet revisionists', and getting ready for a war against India, although contingency plans for military action would have been discussed only among Mao's inner circle of trusted followers and behind closed doors and not during the actual conference. In other words, part of the plan was to sideline and marginalize what was left of the opposition to Mao within the Party and the state apparatus.[36] A major build-up of war materiel and an increase in the number of Chinese troops along the border could be noticed only a few days after the Beidaihe conference was concluded on 27 August.[37]

In November, as war was raging in the Himalayas, an article in the *Zhōngguó Qīngnián Bào* (*China Youth Daily*, the official newspaper of the Communist Youth League of China), stated that, 'the past ten years of practice in socialist construction ... have proven the unqualified correctness of Mao Tse-tung [Zedong]'.[38] Even more striking was an article in the 8 January 1963 issue of the newspaper. Mao was 'at all times standing higher and seeing farther than anyone else ... the way Chairman Mao Zedong looks at problems must be like standing on top of a skyscraper looking down on the streets and roads below. Each path, turn and curve comes into his views. How can it be possible for him to lose direction?'[39]

At the same time, the anti-Soviet rhetoric reached a crescendo. According to a declassified CIA document,

> In late September and early October [1962] Chinese Communist spokesmen were asserting that the CPSU [the Communist Party of the Soviet Union] had "given up" leadership of the world revolution ... [and] that this leadership had passed by default from Moscow and Khrushchev to Peiping [Beijing] and Mao Tse-tung [Zedong], and that although seemingly isolated, Communist China was now supported by a majority of people in the socialist camp and would pursue thereafter "uncompromising" struggle with the USSR.[40]

The CIA document goes on to refer to an editorial in the *People's Daily* of 15 November, which stated that Beijing claimed 'supreme doctrinal authority within the international Communist movement'[41]. The editorial concluded with a call for 'all Marxist-Leninists to resolutely carry on the struggle against modern revisionism to the end'.[42] The victory over India in the 1962 War had shown that China possessed enough military muscle to inflict a crushing defeat on another major Asian power. It had also, as intended, deprived India of its role as a major voice for the newly independent countries in Asia and Africa.

It was time for Mao and his trusted lieutenants, among them his wife Jiang Qing, Defence Minister Lin Biao, and the spymaster Kang Sheng to begin to purge the Party—and to assert China's role as the leader of not only the international Communist movement but also the entire Third World. But first, China needed a nuclear bomb.

China's interest in nuclear weapons began during the Korean War, when they learned that the United States was contemplating the use of atomic bombs to halt the advance of Chinese so-called volunteers, who came streaming down the peninsula in human waves. China had already in the early 1950s developed its own production of small arms, rockets, and artillery with technology imported from the Soviet Union and with the help of Soviet technicians. Then, in January 1955, Mao called a meeting of the Central Committee of the CCP to discuss starting a nuclear weapons programme. The following year, PLA Marshal Nie Rongzhen worked with the Chinese Academy of Sciences to establish a Nuclear Research Institute at an undisclosed location and the programme began to acquire content and direction.[43] Between 1955 and 1958, the Soviet Union and China signed six accords related to the development of nuclear science, industry, and weapons.[44]

In 1957, Marshal Nie Rongzhen travelled to Moscow to sign one of those treaties by which the Soviet Union pledged to provide aid in nuclear research, missile development, and aviation technology. That pledge included a prototype atomic bomb and related missile technology.[45] But a split between the Soviet Union and China was already developing, although it would not become public until 1961. Nie, however, was convinced that China would be able to progress with its nuclear programme even without Soviet assistance.

In 1958–60, when millions of people were starving to death throughout China, another high-ranking PLA officer, Chen Shiqu, moved 40,000 special engineering troops to Lop Nur, a former salt lake in the deserts of Xinjiang, to commence the construction of a nuclear testing site. Then, on 16 July 1960, the Soviet government scrapped 600 contracts it had signed with China and informed the government in Beijing of its decision to withdraw all its 1,390 experts in China between 28 July and 1 September.[46] But that did not deter the leadership in Beijing from going ahead with their nuclear programme, now entirely staffed with Chinese technicians and paid for with allocations from the state's military budget. On 16 October 1964, China conducted its first nuclear test. A second test was carried out on 14 May 1965, followed by a third on 9 May 1966. China had now established itself as a nuclear power.

Regarding Mao's own attitude to nuclear weapons, it was long speculated whether he had really said in his famous 'US imperialism is a paper tiger' speech before a meeting with the world's Communist parties in Moscow in November 1957 that, 'I'm not afraid of nuclear war. There are 2.7 billion people in the world; it doesn't matter if some are killed. China has a population of 600 million; even if half of them are killed, there are still 300 million people left. I'm not afraid of anyone.'[47] But in March 2013, the Chinese government's documentary TV channel, CCTV-9, ran an 18-part series on declassified Sino-Russian foreign affairs files dating back to the time Mao was in power. One episode showed him saying exactly that.[48]

Until then, many people—especially Chinese—had refused to believe that the leader of China could have been that callous. But the Chairman himself had actually refused to deny it when Edgar Snow, the American author of the famous book *Red Star Over China*, asked him about it in an 1965 interview. 'Mao would not deny anything he had said, nor did he wish me to deny for him the so-called rumour' (about China's millions' power of survival in a nuclear war).[49]

In the same month as the third nuclear test was conducted, May 1966, Mao decided the time was ripe to launch his Great Proletarian Cultural Revolution to purge the Party and the State of all 'counterrevolutionaries, revisionists and capitalist roaders'.[50] Already in December 1965, General Luo Ruiqing, a PLA veteran and its joint chief of staff, had been dismissed from his post for his reluctance to follow Mao's idea of emphasizing ideological training within the army, a line ardently followed by Mao and Defence Minister Lin Biao. Luo was lumped together with the CCP chief of Beijing, Peng Zhen, Propaganda Department Director Lu Dingyi, and senior CCP Central Committee member Yang Shangkun as part of an 'anti-Party clique'.

The country was thrown into turmoil as purges, mass meetings, and even killings of real and imaginary opponents to Mao became daily occurrences. Youthful and militant Red Guards roamed the countryside, terrorizing the population and destroying temples and anything else that could remind the people of pre-revolutionary days. Among those in a higher position to be humiliated in public and purged was Liu Shaoqi, once the second-most powerful man in the country after Mao. Deng Xiaoping was also targeted, purged, and sent to work as a regular worker at a tractor factory in Jiangxi province. His son, Deng Pufang, was tortured and thrown out of a window of a four-storey building. He became a paraplegic, bound for life to a wheelchair.

One of the masterminds behind the purges was Kang Sheng, the psychopathic opium addict who had played an important role in the CCP's intelligence network since the 1930s. Sidney Rittenberg, an American who was close to Mao and the entire leadership, described him as 'dark, devious and sinister'.[51] Calling India's Menon a 'Rasputin' was a clear exaggeration, but Kang Sheng certainly did live up to that epithet. According to Rittenberg, Kang Sheng was 'always holding something back, besides bragging about his ability to spot foreign agents … [he] carried himself as if he was wearing an invisible monocle surveying others with a superior and suspicious gaze.'[52]

Even the supposed 'moderate' Zhou Enlai, who Nehru once had trusted, was part of the leadership that unleashed a reign of terror in China. He made sure that the state machinery was functioning reasonably well during the years of upheaval. But he kept on the defensive, guarding his political backside, being challenged by Mao's vicious wife Jiang Qing. To make sure he was on the winning side during the Cultural Revolution, Zhou signed off on the documents used to expel Liu Shaoqi from the CCP in October 1968.[53] Rather than being an astute statesman, Zhou was the ultimate manipulator and opportunist.

Despite the few years of uncertainty after the death of Nehru, Indian politics remained, by comparison, a lot calmer than China's, though the 1962 War led India to also expand, modernize, and rearm all branches of its armed forces. For the defence of the north, new mountain divisions were formed and, according to Eric S. Margolis, 'Accurate surveys were begun of the hitherto uncharted Himalayan and Ladakh border regions. Disputed Kashmir suddenly assumed heightened strategic importance as Delhi worried that China had designs on the mountain state, or that it might join Pakistan in a coordinated assault on northern India.'[54]

The 1962 Sino-Indian War and the 1965 war with Pakistan, prompted India to improve its intelligence-gathering capabilities. The solution came in September 1968, when Indira Gandhi's government set up a new external spy agency, the Research and Analysis Wing, R&AW, better known to its operatives as simply 'RAW'. Its first head was Rameshwar Nath Kao, who had served under Bhola Nath Mullik in the Intelligence Bureau. His official designation was Secretary (Research) in the prime minister's cabinet secretariat, of which RAW was a 'wing'. He became India's first true spymaster and the organization he headed grew over the years to become one of the world's largest and most active intelligence agencies.

India's regular military forces were also strengthened. After the 1962 War, India ordered 400 T-54 medium tanks from the Soviet Union, which would be of no use in the mountains, but could be deployed against Pakistan. India's request to buy F-104 interceptor aircraft from the USA fell through because Washington did not want to antagonize its ally, Pakistan. But a factory to produce the Soviet's MiG-21 was already being planned. Now, in 1963, the first squadron of MiG-21Fs entered service in the Indian Air Force.[55] While Pakistan was still seen as the immediate threat, 'India's leaders were becoming convinced that China represented a long-term territorial rival. In 1963, India began secret development of a nuclear weapons program.'[56]

India's own defence industries, which had been established at the initiative of Menon when he was India's defence minister in the 1950s, were upgraded with the help of technical expertise mainly from the Soviet Union. The old garrison town of Bangalore, now Bengaluru, in the south, far away from India's troubled borders, was chosen as the site for the development of an indigenous electronics industry in the 1950s. Large research laboratories such as the National Aeronautical Laboratory and the Electronic Research and Development Establishment were established in

Bangalore. Bharat Electronics Limited was established in the city in 1954 and became India's premier defence electronics company and it grew to be so in the 1960s. Hindustan Aeronautics Limited was formed on 1 October 1964, having grown out of Hindustan Aircraft, a company established in 1940. What has today become 'India's Silicon Valley' began as a centre for the development of advanced defence material.

While the mainstream Indian economy was growing at an almost painfully slow rate in the 1960s and 1970s, the new friendship with the Soviet Union enabled the country to maintain a fairly advanced defence establishment. In August 1971, India and the Soviet Union concluded a Treaty for Peace, Friendship, and Cooperation, signed by India's minister of External Affairs, Swaran Singh, and his Soviet counterpart Andrei Gromyko. The Communist Soviet Union succeeded where imperial Russia had failed: to expand its sphere of influence down to the Indian subcontinent.

But there was a problem. In line with other socialist and some developing countries, India received from the Soviet Union preferential payment terms and could exchange Indian-made goods for military equipment and components. At the same time, defence analysts argue that 'the over-supply of Soviet equipment reduced India's incentive to develop its own weapons or seek other sources, alienating Western suppliers. India was prevented from selling its Soviet-originating but Indian-made arms on the international market, thus depriving India of a valuable source of military revenue.'[57]

It was not hard for India to come to the conclusion that the Soviet Union was an unreliable ally, thus strengthening the country's determination to develop its own armaments, including weapons of mass destruction. India's nuclear industry was actually not new. Research into using nuclear power for peaceful purposes began at the Tata Institute of Fundamental Research as early as 1944 under the renowned scientists Homi Jehangir Bhabha and Raja Ramanna. But it was not until after the 1962 War that the research was turned to the development of India's military arsenal. With plutonium produced in a reactor supplied by Canada, India managed to produce a nuclear device, which was tested on 18 May 1974 at the Pokhran Test Range in Rajasthan. It was supposed to be a 'peaceful nuclear explosion', but there was now no doubt that India too, 10 years after China's first test, possessed a nuclear weapons capability.

Ramanna, who is considered the father of India's nuclear programme, had been instrumental in setting up the facility at Pokhran, and in February of that year he is reported to have said, 'We are ready to tickle the dragon's tail'.[58] There could be no doubt as to who the 'dragon' was. After the successful explosion, a scientist at the site rang Prime Minister Indira Gandhi conveying a brief message, 'Madam, the Buddha has finally smiled'.[59] The test was set to coincide with the birthday of the Lord Buddha, and, thus, the operation had been codenamed the Smiling Buddha.[60]

India no longer had any reason to fear another Chinese attack and China's strategy after 1962 was, anyway, not to confront India directly. It would instead be a proxy war. The first anti-government force in India to receive support from China was the Naga rebel movement on the eastern border with Myanmar. Mowu Gwizan, a staunch Christian like most other Nagas, may have been surprised when, in June 1962, his Pakistani hosts in Karachi introduced him to a representative of Communist China promising support. There was a limit to how much aid and assistance Pakistan could provide to the Naga rebels without provoking a backlash from India. China had no such fears or qualms and even if the Nagas were Christians, they could prove to be a useful force in the efforts to destabilize India.

Back in the Naga Hills, Mowu discussed the offer with the other leaders of the Naga rebel army, and decided to take it up. Two men were selected to lead the first Naga trek to China, Thinoselie Medom Keyho, a veteran of the Naga struggle who had joined the Naga National Council (NNC) and its rebel army in the 1950s, and the much younger Thuingaleng Muivah, a Naga from Manipur who, despite his belief in Christianity, was inspired by Marxist ideology. In January 1967, after a four-month trek through northern Myanmar, they were well received at the Chinese border and, after some clarifications about their identity had been made, they were taken to the Chinese city of Tengchong in Yunnan. Thinoselie and Muivah were then flown to Beijing where they were lodged in the Beijing Hotel, while the 130 men who had followed them to China were stationed in a newly built training camp near Tengchong. In November 1967, Thinoselie and all the soldiers trekked back to India with new automatic rifles, machine guns, and rocket launchers. Muivah stayed behind in Beijing.[61]

A second contingent of Naga rebels reached China in March 1968, led by Isak Chishi Swu from the political leadership of the NNC and Mowu from the army. Four more groups also made it to China, bringing the total number of Naga rebels who underwent training in Yunnan to more than 700. Fierce battles were fought in the Naga Hills between the Indian Army and the Naga rebels. It was obvious that the Chinese had been much more generous than the Pakistanis, who had given them only old rifles and a limited number of machine guns.

Chinese support for the NNC is remarkable because of the Nagas' almost fanatical belief in Christianity. They were converted by Western missionaries in the late nineteenth and early twentieth centuries, and, although they arrived in China during the height of the Cultural Revolution, they were allowed to pray and sing hymns in their training camps in Yunnan. China wanted them to fight and destabilize India, and that was more important than their religious beliefs.

After the Nagas came other northeastern rebels. Mizo tribesmen, from another predominantly Christian tribe who fought for a separate state, trekked through northern Myanmar to China in the 1970s. The first group of 38 men arrived in China in 1973 and received military training at Kotong military post opposite Panwa Pass on the Yunnan frontier with Myanmar's Kachin State. A second batch of 109 Mizo rebels reached China in August 1975 and was trained at Meng Hai in southern Yunnan. The leader of the Mizo rebels, Laldenga, his foreign secretary Lalmingthanga, and a few others also visited China, including Beijing. But, they went by air from East Pakistan and did not trek through the Myanmar jungle.[62] But it was clear that China and Pakistan were colluding in their support for India's tribal revolutionaries. Laldenga's first visit to China in June 1968 was organized through the Chinese Consulate in Dhaka, and the Chinese had already then promised him military support. In September 1970, Laldenga was back in China where he met Premier Zhou Enlai and the promise of support was repeated.[63]

In April 1976, a smaller group of Manipuri revolutionaries made it via Nepal to Tibet, where they were trained by commanders of China's security forces. Like the Nagas, the Mizo rebels were also provided with arms by the Chinese, while the Manipuris received ideological training and some military instruction at a PLA camp near Lhasa.[64] After their return to Manipur, the militants unleashed a reign of terror in the Imphal Valley, killing Indian security personnel as well as suspected 'traitors' to its cause. Banks were looted and weapons snatched from police stations and other outposts. Evidently inspired by the regular Chinese military, the name of the new rebel group was the People's Liberation Army. In 1979, it formed a political wing called the Revolutionary People's Front, led by Nameirakpam Bisheswar Singh, one of the militants who underwent training in Lhasa in 1976.

According to a classified Chinese document entitled 'China Should Become the Arsenal for World Revolution' and dated 7 July 1967, Mao declaimed, 'The present situation is excellent. Nagaland in India is fighting against the Congress Party with armed struggle.'[65] Mao went on to stress the importance of the Communist Party of Burma (CPB). 'The geographic conditions in Burma are better than those of Vietnam, with more room to manoeuvre ... it is all better if the Burmese government chooses to oppose us; I hope it will sever normal relations with us. In that case, we can more openly support the Burmese Communist Party.'[66]

In the same speech, Mao went on to say, 'China is not only the centre of world revolution, it must also be the centre of world revolution military-ily and technically. When we give weapons, they will be Chinese weapons engraved with Chinese characters (except those to certain specific areas). We will support them openly; and China must become the arsenal for world revolution.'[67] India, naturally, was not pleased. India protested and pictures of weapons bearing Chinese markings that had been seized from Naga rebels were shown at the United Nations in New York. But China did not care, it was the centre of world revolution and India had become the enemy.

In 1960, Zhou Enlai had said in a speech before China's legislature, the National People's Congress, that, 'we place ardent hopes in friendly relations between China and India ... we deeply believe that the traditional friendship between the people's of China and India will shine forth brilliantly to the end'.[68] However, in an internal party report from December 1971, he was more explicit and perhaps more honest and forthcoming when it came to defining his views on China's relations with India.

> While the Soviet revisionists back India, we support Pakistan. When we say support Pakistan, we mean support her in resisting the aggression of India. But there are mistakes in the domestic policy of Pakistan, the massacres in Eastern Pakistan and the lack of national policy. India is the head of the reactionaries among the imperialists, revisionists and reactionaries. For all this, we still want to restore normal diplomatic relations with her at an opportune moment, for the purpose of furthering the people's revolution in India.[69]

That 'people's revolution', the Chinese believed, was going to be led by a political movement which at that time was sweeping across parts of the Indian countryside: the Naxalites, or, as they were officially called, the Communist Party of India (Marxist-Leninist) (CPI(ML)). At least, that was the intention until the situation got out of hand and the 'Indian comrades' were unable to live up to the expectations of the Chinese leadership.

The Communist Party of India (CPI), one of the biggest and best organized communist parties in Asia, had split after the 1962 War. The CPI's official line was to condemn the Chinese attack, as most of its leaders were pro-Moscow at a time when the international communist movement was split between those who supported the Soviet Union and a minority that sided with China. In 1964, the Communist Party of India (Marxist) (CPI (M)]) was formed. Without being entirely in favour of China's ideological line, it saw the 1962 War as a conflict between a socialist and a capitalist state.

But there was a group of Indian Communists who were openly pro-China and inspired by Mao's revolutionary ideology. They were led by Charu Mazumdar and Kanu Sanyal, both active in the plains below Darjeeling in northern West Bengal, where a peasant uprising broke out in May 1967. Mazumdar and Sanyal had for some time been preparing the tea garden workers and poor peasants in the area for armed revolution. The spark came when a sharecropper in a village called Naxalbari was evicted by a landlord without any legal basis. When he protested, he was beaten by the landlord's thugs and, in response, thousands of villagers armed with bows, arrows, and spears took over land holdings and granaries, basically running their and the neighbouring villages as a 'liberated' commune.

Between 15,000 and 20,000 peasants and workers participated in the movement which, by the end of May, reached the level of an armed uprising. The police were sent in and clashed with the peasants, who fought back with firearms and ammunition they had snatched from the landowners. The Chinese were quick to express their full support for the revolt. On 5 July 1967, the official newspaper, *People's Daily* ran an editorial titled 'Spring Thunder Over India',

> A peal of spring thunder has crashed over the land of India. Revolutionary peasants in the Darjeeling area have risen in rebellion. Under the leadership of a revolutionary group of the Indian Communist Party, a red area of revolutionary armed struggle has been established in India ... no matter how well the imperialists, Indian reactionaries and the modern revisionists cooperate in their sabotage and suppression, the torch of armed struggle lighted by the revolutionaries of the Indian Communist Party will not be put out. 'A single spark can start a prairie fire.' The spark in Darjeeling will certainly set the vast expanses of India ablaze.[70]

That same month, paramilitary forces were deployed in the Naxalbari area. Activists were beaten or arrested, or both. Some, like Mazumdar, escaped and went underground. The revolt lasted only a few months, but it had a far-reaching impact on the political scene in many of India's rural areas, as Sumanta Banerjee wrote in his classic *In the Wake of Naxalbari*. 'It helped expose the political failure of the parliamentary Leftists in power and unrolled a process of rethinking among the Communist ranks.'[71]

While the CPI(M), which was part of the United Front government that ruled West Bengal at the time, condemned the uprising, radicals led by Sanyal, who stayed behind in the area, met to discuss their future course of action. In September, probably encouraged by the editorial in the *People's Daily*, they decided to contact the Chinese through their diplomatic mission in Dhaka, East Pakistan. Sanyal crossed the border to East Pakistan, but did not make it to Dhaka.[72]

Back in northern West Bengal, they met again and assembled a four-man team headed by Sanyal which was to reach China via Nepal. The Nepalese border was only a few kilometres away from Naxalbari and the team had no problem going to Kathmandu by public bus. The Chinese Embassy in Kathmandu, the capital of Nepal, were at first hesitant to promise them anything, but after the staff contacted their superiors in Beijing, the ambassador himself informed them that they were welcome to China. They were even allowed to stay at the embassy until arrangements could be made.

Sanyal and his team were transported to the Chinese border by an embassy official, but had to walk the final stretch of the journey over the hills to avoid the immigration checkpoints. On the other side, PLA soldiers helped them get to a military camp near Lhasa. On 30 September, they went by a civilian flight to Beijing. Lodged at the Beijing Hotel, where the Nagas had also been staying, they were taken to see a PLA officer. According to Sanyal, 'Some 16 or 17 PLA commanders participated in the marathon meeting that lasted for well over two hours. They learnt about the happenings in Naxalbari at length; they wanted to know how it all began, how many weapons we had and what we planned to do next.'[73]

Over the next few weeks, the four Indian Maoists were introduced to Mao himself and they were then sent for military training. They learnt how use automatic rifles, machine guns, and hand grenades, and to plant mines and make explosive devices. Chinese-Hindi interpreters were at hand and they were also taught 'Mao Zedong thought' and how to apply it to Indian conditions. They were also told not to approach the Chinese Embassy in Kathmandu again but to establish a route through other parts of Nepal and Bhutan for what was described as 'future cooperation', which would include arms supplies.[74] The Chinese assured them that they would cover all the costs of setting up secret camps along the suggested route.

In mid-December, after spending three months in China, Sanyal and his team were driven back to Kathmandu in a Chinese army vehicle. They then returned to India by bus and, once on the other side of the border, caught a train for New Jalpaiguri near Siliguri in northern West Bengal.

It seemed like a promising beginning for a people's revolution in India and, throughout 1968, smaller, Naxalbari-type struggles erupted in different parts of India, especially in Srikalulam in Andhra Pradesh, an old revolutionary stronghold. On 22 April 1969, the 100th anniversary of the birth of Vladimir Lenin, the CPI (ML) was formed. The party's formation was announced nine days later by Sanyal at a massive May Day rally in the Kolkata Maidan. Mazumdar became its first general secretary. India now had its own pro-Chinese Communist party, different from both the CPI and the CPI(M) and much more radical and militant. Radio Beijing beamed more revolutionary bulletins from India and extracts from articles written by Mazumdar.

During the height of its struggle in 1969–70, CPI(ML) attracted a motley crew of supporters ranging from Bengali intellectuals to rural activists, and outright goons drawn from Kolkata's lumpenproletariat. Hundreds of 'class enemies' were 'annihilated' by the Naxalites, which meant that they were shot or bludgeoned to death. The victims of 'the Red Terror' included landlords, money lenders, policemen, and corrupt local officials, or just anyone who was opposed to the CPI(ML). Mazumdar, who was in hiding in Kolkata, was the driving force behind the 'left adventurist' line, whereas Sanyal remained faithful to his followers in the rural areas of northern West Bengal and stayed there.

On 9 April 1970, Radio Beijing announced, 'at present, the flames of peasants' armed struggle have spread to West Bengal, Bihar, Uttar Pradesh, Punjab, Himachal, Orissa, Assam and Tripura, and particularly Andhra Pradesh'.[75] Later that year, the CPI (ML) sent Sourin Bose, a senior cadre, to Beijing where he held talks with Zhou Enlai and Kang Sheng. By that time, Chinese enthusiasm for the Indian revolutionaries was beginning to wane. Kang Sheng reportedly told Bose that the CCP could not understand the meaning of the 'Naxalite' concept of 'annihilation', which he likened to the methods used in China by 'left adventurists' after the defeat of the Communists there in 1927. Mazumdar had also coined a phrase which Zhou criticized: *Chiner Chairman Aamader Chairman* (China's Chairman is Our Chairman).[76]

The Naxalites, as the Indian Maoists came to be known after the village where the 1967 rebellion occurred, were too radical even for the rabid ideologue and diehard Mao-supporter, Kang. Zhou told Bose that, 'we don't deny that Chairman [Mao] is [an] international authority... [but] to regard a leader of one country as the leader of another party is against the sentiment of the nation; it is difficult for the working class to accept it.'[77]

Bose flew back to Kolkata via London, bringing with him the depressing news from Beijing. At a meeting in Kolkata on 8 December 1970, the leaders of the CPI(ML) agreed not to disclose to their followers that the Chinese were critical of their polices, and that the party would get no support, moral, material, or otherwise, from China.[78]

It is quite possible that the Naxalites could have developed their movement into a more powerful force if Sanyal had managed to control it, and then Chinese aid would also most probably have been forthcoming. But before long, factionalism tore their tiny groups apart and the Chinese decided to disregard them when it became clear that they were not going to become a viable force in Indian politics.

On 16 July 1972, Mazumdar was betrayed by one of his comrades and captured at his hideout in Kolkata. Twelve days later, he died in police custody. No Chinese aid ever reached the CPI (ML). Instead, the Chinese continued to support Naga and Mizo rebels in the northeast. They seemed to be more trustworthy than the unruly Indian Maoists.

While the Chinese were determined to find and support proxies who could fight the war for them in India, the Indians had changed their attitude towards the Tibetan refugees—and the Tibetan resistance—after the 1962 War. Although relations between India and the Soviet Union became close and cordial in the 1960s, this did not prevent India's security services from cooperating with the CIA, which had provided clandestine support for the Tibetan resistance since the 1950s. After the 1962 War, the Tibetan guerrillas who had been trained at Camp Hale in Colorado were transferred to India where, according to the Tibetan historian Tsering Shakya, 'the Indians had established a secret Tibetan Army base near Dehra Dun at Chakrata, more commonly known to the Tibetans as Unit Twenty-Two.'[79] More than 12,000 Tibetans were brought to Chakrata, where many of them underwent military training. The Dalai Lama's government in exile at McLeodganj in the hills above Dharamsala provided leadership for the struggle, which, however, in the end amounted to more of an intelligence gathering expedition than an outright armed struggle against the Chinese occupation of Tibet.

The actual forward base for the resistance was not at the relatively short-lived camp in India but in Mustang, in a remote corner of Tibet, adjacent to the frontier. Mustang, ruled by a local feudal lord and sometimes described as a 'semi-independent Tibetan kingdom' inside Nepal, was surrounded on three sides by Chinese-occupied Tibet. It was sufficiently difficult to access by land, making it easy for the CIA to keep their operations secret. Soldiers from the regular Royal Nepalese Army also guarded all the mountain trails and passes leading into the area. Weapons and other supplies were airdropped from C-130 transport planes that had flown from Okinawa and through the Indian air space, and had been refuelled at Takhli airbase in Thailand. Before the 1962 War, the American planes dropping supplies and getting guerrillas in and out of Tibet had used obscure airfields in East Pakistan and then flown only across the narrow corridor of Indian territory between Nepal and Bhutan.

From a military point of view, though, Mustang was a bad choice for a rebel base. There were almost no villages on the barren and desolate Tibetan side of the border where the rebels could get food and other supplies, or organize an uprising against the Chinese. Then, in January 1972, Nepal got a new king, Birendra Bir Bikram Shah, who wanted to improve relations with China. In December 1973, he visited Beijing where the Chinese expressed their displeasure over the Tibetan bases in his country. In order to maintain a more independent stance towards India, Nepal's powerful southern neighbour, Birendra was willing to listen. The Chinese reciprocated by giving generous aid to Nepal.

In May 1974, a trade agreement was signed in Kathmandu between the Nepalese and the Chinese governments and, in July, the Nepalese military moved against the Tibetan camps in Mustang. They were disarmed without much resistance and their morale vanished almost completely after listening to a taped message from the Dalai Lama. He urged them, probably on instructions from the Americans, to lay down their arms and leave.

American support for the Tibetan resistance had come to an end after two historic visits to China by American dignitaries, that of the Secretary of State Henry Kissinger in July 1971 and of President Richard Nixon in February 1972. Despite their ideological differences, Washington and Beijing shared a common interest in countering the Soviet Union. National security policies were apparently more important than ideology, and the Tibetan resistance had to be sacrificed. China had agreed to normalize relations with the USA provided that it, among other things, stop all assistance to the Tibetans.

In India, China continued its support for ethnic rebel movements in the northeast until the death of Mao in September 1976 and the rise of the less ideologically rigid Deng Xiaoping. Deng had been branded a 'capitalist roader' during the Cultural Revolution—and that turned out to be correct. He introduced a number of free-market reforms, and China's economy began to grow at a breathtaking pace.

In Mizoram, a peace accord between the rebels and the Government of India was agreed upon in June 1986, paving the way for the union territory to become a full-fledged state within the Indian Union. Nagaland had achieved the same status in 1963, but disturbances continued there as well as in Manipur. In the late 1970s, serious disagreements over the validity of the armed struggle erupted within the old NNC, which led to the formation of the National Socialist Council of Nagaland (NSCN) in January 1980. Its main theoretician was Muivah, who had returned from China with a curious ideological blend of evangelical Christianity and revolutionary Maoism. But, since Muivah came from Manipur and not Nagaland, the official chairman was Isak Chishi Swu, a Sema Naga from Chishilimi village in Nagaland.

Its quaintly jumbled 'Manifesto', issued on 31 January 1980 and which was written by Muivah, quoted Mao emphasizing that a revolutionary organization must have 'correct policies', and went on to praise 'the Christian God, the Eternal God of the Universe'. The manifesto stated that 'to us the sovereign existence of our country, the salvation of our people is Socialism with their spiritual salvation in Christ are eternal and unquestionable' and went on to reject the idea of a multiparty system, paraphrasing Maoist jargon, 'To achieve socialism, the dictatorship of the people through a revolutionary organisation is absolutely indispensable.' That organization was, of course, the NSCN which promised to liberate the Nagas from 'the exploiting class…of reactionary traitors, the bureaucrats, a handful of rich men and the Indian vermin'.[80] Such mumbo-jumbo probably did not impress the Chinese, who had stopped providing the Naga rebels with military training in China after 1976. But links between them and the Chinese were never completely severed.

The only territory, and later state, in India's northeastern region that has never had any armed insurrection is Arunachal Pradesh, the erstwhile NEFA. One reason could be the ethnic diversity of the rugged and extremely mountainous area, where dozens of different tribes have for centuries lived more or less isolated from each other. Another possible explanation is that Western missionaries never went there. The missionaries had not preached separatism, but the introduction of written languages, a literature, and a firm belief in something other than a host of spirits had created a sense of nationhood among, for instance, the Nagas and the Mizos. This in turn led to local nationalist movements, which eventually became armed, anti-government forces.

Two entirely different personalities are closely associated with the emergence of the NEFA, Verrier Elwin and Nari Rostomji. Elwin, a British missionary who had married a tribal woman from central India, converted to Hinduism in 1935 and became an Indian citizen after independence. Rustomji was an Indian Parsi and a product of the Indian Civil Service, a meticulous bureaucrat with strong feelings for India's northern frontiers. Elwin was a close confidante of Nehru, who wrote the foreword to his book *A Philosophy for NEFA*, which was published in 1957.[81] The emphasis should be on education and economic development, Elwin stated, and not to isolate the tribal population despite the fact that the areas where they live lie behind the Inner Line.

Both Elwin and Rustomji travelled all over the NEFA and, after the Chinese established themselves in Tibet, the presence of a bureaucracy and organs of power such as courts and police stations became imperative. Local government offices, schools, libraries, dispensaries, and hospitals were constructed at major population centres, along with the establishment of crafts training institutes and cottage industries. Roads were built into the territory from Assam, to which the NEFA belonged until 1972. By 1955–6, NEFA counted 113 primary schools, 13 middle schools, and 3 high schools.[82] Knowing full well that it was a sensitive frontier area, India's intelligence networks were also strengthened in 1954 by the recruitment of candidates from 14 of the NEFA's many tribes. The main qualification when they were sent for training was that they should have had some basic education.[83]

With the help of Elwin and Rustomji, the NEFA began to take shape as a functioning administrative entity, but it was the 1962 War that laid the foundations for what was eventually to become Arunachal Pradesh. A crucial role in fostering a sense of belonging to India was also played by the Ramakrishna Mission, a volunteer organization founded by the Indian sage Ramakrishna's chief disciple Swami Vivekananda as early as 1897. It subscribes to the ancient Hindu Vedanta philosophy and promotes social work, education, tribal welfare, and health. Although a private charity, its move into the NEFA in the 1960s was no doubt encouraged and even supported by Indian authorities, especially the security services. It opened community centres and schools all over the NEFA, where Hindi language was taught along with basic education and the mission's firm roots in Hinduism were no doubt preferable to the central government than the introduction of Christianity into the hill country north of the Brahmaputra. The Inner Line regulation also prevented not only foreigners but also other Indians from entering the area without special permits.

The spread of Hindi into the hills was not entirely welcomed by everybody in India's northeast. As a by-product of the Ramakrishna Mission's activities, Hindi became the new lingua franca among the tribals instead of Assamese (the language spoken by those from the hills who had had interactions with officials, merchants, and others from the Brahmaputra Valley), and, more commonly, Nefamese (a pidgin kind of Assamese spoken by many tribals when they communicated with each other and with the people of the plains). As early as 1957, tribal leaders from the Lohit Frontier Division in the NEFA had submitted a memorandum to the Governor of Assam, saying that, 'Hindi may be taught to the students in the same school... [where the medium of instruction is] Assamese. It is known to your honour that in this Division seven classes of tribals are living such as Abor, Khamti, Edu, Miju, Digaru, Miri, Singpho and Tibetans. Assamese is the main language to exchange thoughts amongst ourselves.'[84] Whatever sympathy there might have been for their point of view in New Delhi in the late 1950s, there was much less of an incentive to promote Assamese language at the expense of Hindi in the NEFA after 1962.

The NEFA, previously a hill region of Assam, was converted into the Union Territory of Arunachal Pradesh in 1972 and proclaimed a state in 1987, thus becoming somewhat estranged from the plains with which the local people had had trade and other contacts for centuries. But the integration of the NEFA was more important than such local sensitivities for India's security planners. The new administrative entity was given a name in Sanskrit, meaning 'The Land of Dawn', and a new capital was established at Itanagar at the foothills of the Himalayas, close to the ruins of a fifteenth century fort built by Hindu kings from the plains.

Arunachal and the six other Indian states in the traditionally volatile northeastern region are connected with the rest of the country through a strategically sensitive corridor between Nepal, Bhutan, and Bangladesh called the Siliguri Neck, or more popularly, the Chicken's Neck, which at its narrowest point is only about 27 kilometres wide. The need to secure that area and the northeast became even more of a priority after the 1962 War. On 24 October of that year, the American ambassador John K. Galbraith had met the prime minister of Bhutan, who had told him that Chinese troops were massed on the borders of his kingdom. According to the former CIA analyst Bruce Reidel's account of the 1962 crisis, 'The miniscule army of Bhutan could not hope to stop a Chinese attack. If the Chinese broadened their offensive to include Bhutan and its even smaller neighbour Sikkim, they could easily drive south to cut off India's entire northeastern section—made up of NEFA and Assam—and link up with East Pakistan.'[85]

At the time of the 1962 War, China had no such intentions, the possibility of a move from the Chinese down to the corridor side was always in the minds of the security planners in New Delhi—and that made them more convinced than ever before that the tiny and isolated Himalayan kingdoms of Bhutan and Sikkim were of utmost strategic importance for the defence of India.

Notes

1. Brij Mohan Kaul, *The Untold Story,* (Bombay, Calcutta, New Delhi, Madras: Allied Publishers, 1967), p. 438.

2. See D.R. Mankekar, *The Guilty Men of 1962* (Bombay: The Tulsi Shah Enterprises, 1968), p. 122.

3. Mankekar, *The Guilty Men of 1962,* p. 120.

4. Mankekar, *The Guilty Men of 1962,* p. 122.

5. Mankekar, *The Guilty Men of 1962,* p. 126.

6. Deng Xiaoping stated: 'When the time comes, we certainly will settle accounts with them [the Indians].' Quoted in 'The Politico-Diplomatic Prelude Part-2', P.J.S. Sandhu, Bhavna Tripathi, Ranjit Singh Kalha, Bharat Kumar, G.G. Dwivedi, Vinay Shankar (eds), *1962: A View from the Other Side of the Hill* (New Delhi: Vij Books India, 2015) p. 24.

7. Paul M. McGarr, '"India's Rasputin?" V.K. Krishna Menon and Anglo-American Misperceptions of Indian Foreign Policy Making, 1947–1964', *Diplomacy and Statecraft,* Vol. 22, Issue no. 2, 9 June 2011, p. 224, available at http://www.tandfonline.com/doi/abs/10.1080/09592296.2011.576536 (accessed on 15 May 2016).

8. McGarr, '"India's Rasputin?" V.K. Krishna Menon and Anglo-American Misperceptions of Indian Foreign Policy Making, 1947–1964', p. 241.

9. McGarr, '"India's Rasputin?" V.K. Krishna Menon and Anglo-American Misperceptions of Indian Foreign Policy Making, 1947–1964', p. 254.

10. B.G. Verghese, '50 Years after 1962: A Political Memoir', *South Asia Monitor,* 23 September 2012, available at http://southasiamonitor.org/detail.php?type=yearsafter&nid=3844 (accessed on 12 August 2016).

11. Kaul, *The Untold Story,* p. 429.

12. Quoted in R.K. Bhatnagar. 'Was Krishna Menon a Sick Man ...' *Asian Tribune,* 17 October 2009, https://archive.li/itP4 (accessed on 21 September 2016).

13. Mankekar, *The Guilty Men of 1962,* p. 117.

14. Kaul, *The Untold Story,* pp. 204–5.

15. Bhatnagar. 'Was Krishna Menon a Sick Man ...'.

16. Mankekar, *The Guilty Men of 1962,* p. 104.

17. Kaul, *The Untold Story,* p. 451.

18. Welles Hangen, *After Nehru, Who?* (London: Hart-Davis, 1963), p. 242–72.

19. Jerome Alan Cohen and Shao-chuan Leng, 'The Sino-Indian Dispute over the Internment and Detention of Chinese in India', Jerome Alan Cohen (ed.),

China's Practice of International Law: Some Case Studies (Harvard: Harvard University Press, 1972), p. 276.

20. Cohen and Leng, 'The Sino-Indian Dispute over the Internment and Detention of Chinese in India', p. 274.

21. Cohen and Leng, 'The Sino-Indian Dispute over the Internment and Detention of Chinese in India', p. 277.

22. Yin Marsh, *Doing Time with Nehru: The Story of an Indian-Chinese Family* (New Delhi: Zubaan Books, 2015).

23. Cohen and Leng, 'The Sino-Indian Dispute over the Internment and Detention of Chinese in India', p. 277.

24. Cohen and Leng, 'The Sino-Indian Dispute over the Internment and Detention of Chinese in India', pp. 279–80.

25. Rahul Karmakar, 'Chinese seek 1962 war memorial', *The Hindustan Times*, 25 October 2010, http://www.hindustantimes.com/india/chinese-seek-62-war-memorial/story-ETOIvo6MY8sDcmqPMHpidI.html (accessed on 15 September 2016).

26. See, for instance, Ainslie T. Embree (ed.) *Encyclopedia of Asian History: Prepared under the Auspices of the Asia Society*, Vol. 3 (New York: Charles Scribner's Sons and London: Collier Macmillan Publishers, 1988), p. 99: 'The Chinese invasion in 1962, which Nehru failed to anticipate, came as a great blow to him and probably hastened his death'.

27. Ramachandra Guha, *India After Gandhi: The History of the World's Largest Democracy* (New Delhi: Picador India, 2012), p. 345.

28. 'Light Goes Out in India and Nehru Dies', *BBC*, 27 May 1964, available at http://news.bbc.co.uk/onthisday/hi/dates/stories/may/27/newsid_3690000/3690019.stm (accessed on 5 September 2016).

29. Gyanesh Kudaisya, 'Nehru: Death of a Democrat', *History Today*, Vol. 64, Issue No. 5, May 2014, available at http://www.historytoday.com/gyanesh-kudaisya/nehru-death-democrat (accessed on 15 September 2016).

30. Kudaisya, 'Nehru: Death of a Democrat'.

31. SEATO was set up in 1954 (and dissolved in 1977), and comprised Great Britain, France, USA, Australia, New Zealand, Pakistan, the Philippines, and Thailand. CENTO, also called the Baghdad Pact, was formed in 1955 (and dissolved in 1979) with Britain, Iran, Iraq, Pakistan, and Turkey as its members.

32. Roderick MacFarquhar, *Origins of the Cultural Revolution 3: The Coming of the Cataclysm* (New York and Oxford: Oxford University Press and Columbia University Press, 1997), p. 312.

33. MacFarquhar, *Origins of the Cultural Revolution 3*, p. 276.

34. MacFarquhar, *Origins of the Cultural Revolution 3*, p. 276.

35. Lorenz M. Lüthi, *The Sino-Soviet Split: Cold War in the Communist World* (Princeton, NJ: Princeton University Press, 2008), p. 219.

36. Lüthi, *The Sino-Soviet Split*, p. 219 and MacFarquhar, *Origins of the Cultural Revolution 3*, p. 302–3.

37. MacFarquhar, *Origins of the Cultural Revolution 3*, p. 303.

38. Quoted in a CIA report released in May 2007, 'Communist China's Domestic Crisis: The Road to 1964', OCI No. 1949/64, 31 July 1964, p. 130.

39. Quoted in 'Communist China's Domestic Crisis: The Road to 1964', p. 130.

40. 'Communist China's Domestic Crisis: The Road to 1964', pp. 117–18.

41. Communist China's Domestic Crisis: The Road to 1964', p. 118.

42. 'Communist China's Domestic Crisis: The Road to 1964', p. 118.

43. Li Xiaobing, *A History of the Modern Chinese Army* (Lexington: The University Press of Kentucky, 2007), pp. 151–2.

44. Dennis J. Blasko, 'Always Faithful: The PLA from 1949 to 1989', David A. Graff and Robin Higham (eds), *A Military History of China* (Dehradun: Greenfield Publishers, 2012), p. 252.

45. Blasko, 'Always Faithful: The PLA from 1949 to 1989', p. 252. For the early years of China's nuclear programme, see also the Central Intelligence Agency, 'The Chinese Communist Atomic Energy Program', *National Intelligence Estimate Number 13-2-60*, 13 December 1960 (declassified in May 2004), pp. 5–6, available at https://www.cia.gov/library/readingroom/docs/DOC_0001095912.pdf and accessed on 19 June 2017).

46. *China's Foreign Relations: A Chronology of Events (1949–1988)* (Beijing: Foreign Languages Press, 1989), p. 460.

47. Quoted in Peter Beinart, 'How America Shed the Taboo Against Preventive War', *The Atlantic*, 21 April 2017, available at https://www.theatlantic.com/international/archive/2017/04/north-korea-preventive-war/523833/ (accessed on 19 June 2017).

48. Ariel Tian, 'Mao's "Nuclear Mass Extinction Speech" Aired on Chinese TV', *Epoch Times*, 5 March 2013, available at http://www.theepochtimes.com/n3/4758-maos-nuclear-mass-extinction-speech-aired-on-chinese-tv/?utm_expid=21082672-12.InTAp1P_QWuf9wSnIRJAqg.0&utm_referrer=https%3A%2F%2Fwww.google.co.th (accessed on 20 September 2016).

49. Edgar Snow, 'Interview with Mao', *The New Republic*, 26 February 1965, available at https://newrepublic.com/article/89494/interview-mao-tse-tung-communist-china (accessed on 20 September 2016).

50. See Allan Todd, *History for the ID Diploma: Communism in Crisis 1976–1989* (Cambridge, New York: Cambridge University Press, 2012), p. 148, and César Landín, 'Mao's Cult or Personality and the Cultural Revolution: To what extent did Mao Zedong's cult of personality during the Cultural Revolution help him to regain authority over China?', available at http://share.nanjing-school.com/dphistory/files/2013/06/Extended-Essay_February_Cesar-Landin-2403vg5.pdf (accessed on 19 June 2017).

51. Quoted in John Byron and Robert Pack, *The Claws of the Dragon: Keng Sheng, the Evil Genius Behind Mao and his Legacy of Terror in People's China* (New York: Simon & Schuster, 1992), p. 328.

52. Byron and Pack, *The Claws of the Dragon*, p. 328.

53. Gao Wenqian, *Zhou Enlai: The Last Perfect Revolutionary*, translated by Peter Rand and Lawrence R. Sullivan (New York: Public Affairs, 2007), p. 180.

54. Eric S. Margolis, *War at the Top of the World: The Struggle for Afghanistan, Kashmir, and Tibet* (New York: Routledge, 2001), p. 131.

55. Ravi Rikhye, *The Militarization of Mother India* (New Delhi: Prism India Paperbacks, 1990), p. 48.

56. Margolis, *War at the Top of the World: The Struggle for Afghanistan, Kashmir, and Tibet*, p. 131.

57. Emrys Chew, 'Globalization and Military-Industrial Transformation in South Asia: An Historical Perspective', Geoffrey Till, Emrys Chew, and Joshua Ho (eds), *Globalization and Defence in the Asia-Pacific: Arms Across Asia* (London and New York: Routledge, 2009), p. 58.

58. Quoted in Deepti (blogger), *When the Buddha Smiled on India*, 2 August 2010, available at http://d-extracts.blogspot.com/2010/08/when-buddha-smiled-on-india.html (accessed on 19 June 2017) See also *India's Nuclear Program, Smiling Buddha: 1974*, available at http://nuclearweaponarchive.org/India/IndiaSmiling.html (accessed on 19 June 2017).

59. Deepti, *When the Buddha Smiled on India*. See also E.A.S. Sarma, *Will the sparrow ever return?* Undated self-published book, p. 90, available at http://eassarma.in/sites/default/files/Will_the_sparrow_ever_return_17-3-12.pdf (accessed on 19 June 2017).

60. For details about India's first nuclear test, see 'India's Nuclear Weapons Program - Smiling Buddha: 1974', available at http://nuclearweaponarchive.org/India/IndiaSmiling.html (accessed on 15 September 2016) and 'India's Nuclear Weapons Program- The Beginning: 1944–1960', available at http://nuclearweaponarchive.org/India/IndiaOrigin.html (accessed on 15 September 2016).

61. Interview with Thuingaleng Muivah at Kesan Chanlam (northwestern Myanmar), 21 November 1985, and interviews with Thinoselie Medom Keyho at Kohima, 18 October 1985 and 24 December 2009.

62. Bertil Lintner, *Great Game East: The Struggle for Asia's Most Volatile Frontier* (New Delhi: HarperCollins India, 2012), pp. 340. The figures and the names of places were the Mizos were trained were collected by the author through numerous interviews with Mizo, Naga, and Kachin rebel leaders in the 1980s, 1990s, and 2000s.

63. Vivek Chadha, *Low Intensity Conflicts in India: An Analysis* (New Delhi and London: Sage Publications, 2005), p. 344.

64. Interview with Soibam Temba Singh (one of the Manipuri rebels who went to Tibet in the 1970s) at Pa Jau, northern Myanmar, 22 April 1985.

65. 'China Should Become the Arsenal for World Revolution', Tsai Wei-ping (ed.), *Classified Chinese Communist Documents: A Selection* (Taipei: Institute of International Relations, National Chengchi University, 1978), p. 454.

66. Tsai (ed.), 'China Should Become the Arsenal for World Revolution', p. 454.

67. Tsai (ed.), 'China Should Become the Arsenal for World Revolution', p. 455.

68. See http://www.claudearpi.net/some-documents-on-the-1962-sino-indian-conflict (accessed on 19 June 2017).

69. 'Chou En-lai's Report on the International Situation, December 1971', Tsai (ed.), *Classified Chinese Communist Documents: A Selection* (Taipei: Institute of International Relations, National Chengchi University, 1978), pp. 477–8.

70. For the full text of the *People's Daily* editorial, see https://www.marxists.org/subject/china/documents/peoples-daily/1967/07/05.htm (accessed on 15 September 2016).

71. Sumanta Banerjee, *In the Wake of Naxalbari* (Kolkata: Subarnarekha, 1980), p. 118.

72. Bappaditya Paul, *The First Naxal: An Authorised Biography of Kanu Sanyal* (New Delhi: Sage Publications India, 2014), pp. 114–15. Paul's book is based on interviews with Sanyal and has an excellent account of the Naxalbari uprising and its aftermath.

73. Paul, *The First Naxal*, p. 124.

74. Paul, *The First Naxal*, p. 131.

75. Deepak Gupta, 'The Naxalites and the Maoist Movement in India: Birth, Demise, and Reincarnation', *Democracy and Security*, Vol. 3, 2007, pp. 157–88.

76. Banerjee, *In the Wake of Naxalbari*, p. 264 and Suniti Kumar Ghosh, *Naxalbari Before and After: Reminiscences and Appraisal* (Kolkata: New Age Publishers, 2009), p. 271.

77. Ghosh, *Naxalbari Before and After*, p. 332.

78. Ghosh, *Naxalbari Before and After*, p. 272.

79. Tsering Shakya, *The Dragon in the Land of Snows: A History of the Tibetan Struggle for Survival since 1947* (London: Pimlico, 1999), p. 359.

80. *Manifesto of the National Socialist Council of Nagaland*, Printed by the NSCN, 31 January 1980. The manifesto is also reproduced in Nandita Haksar and Luingam Luithui, *Nagaland File: A Question of Human Rights* (New Delhi: Lancer International, 1984), pp. 111–38.

81. Verrier Elwin, *A Philosophy For NEFA* (Delhi: Isha Books, 2009).

82. Bérénice Guyot-Réchard, *Shadow States: India, China and the Himalayas, 1910–1962* (Cambridge: Cambridge University Press, 2017), p. 131.

83. H.K. Barpujari, *Problems of the Hill Tribes North-East Frontier, 1873–1962, Vol. III: Inner Line to McMahon Line* (Guwahati: Spectrum Publications, 1981), p. 287.

84. Parag Chaliha (ed.), 'Tribal leaders Memorandum to Governor of Assam: Re-introduction of Assamese Language in NEFA Demanded', *The Outlook on NEFA* (Delhi: Facsimile Publisher, 2015), p. 49.

85. Bruce Riedel, *JFK's Forgotten Crisis: Tibet, the CIA, and the Sino-Indian War* (New Delhi: HarperCollins India, 2016), p. 118.

5

An Enchanted—and Endangered—Frontier

Not many people in the Western world, or even in Asia outside the Indian subcontinent, had paid much attention to Sikkim before 1963. But the marriage in that year of the *maharajkumar*, or heir to the throne, of Sikkim, Palden Thondup Namgyal, to Hope Cooke, a 23-year-old college student from New York, changed all that. The wedding took place in the Sikkimese capital Gangtok on 20 March. Cooke was led by two Buddhist lamas and accompanied by a 'fanfare of trumpeting, 10 ft-long Himalayan horns, braying conch shells, and booming bass drums' into the Tsuklakhang Royal Chapel and Monastery, where her husband-to-be was waiting.[1] Monks did not attend the wedding ceremony itself, as marriage would lead to birth and rebirth, which are to be avoided in accordance with Buddhist cosmology. The hall was lit with butter lamps and Tibetan prayer flags fluttered from tall bamboo poles outside. Among the guests were robed Sikkimese dignitaries as well as the US ambassador, John Kenneth Galbraith, and some other foreign diplomats from New Delhi.

Hope reminisced about the wedding in her autobiography *Time Change*: 'The TV and magazine photographers running around the crowd are bowled over by all the colour and beauty'. And there were groups of Nepali men in bright red tunics and jodhpurs, playing widely curled horns, Sikkim guards in scarlet jackets and striped kilts...Nepali and Sikkimese women wearing different national dress, who move around together, conscious of their impact on the photographers. Sound as well as sight overwhelms one, and the movie crews with audio equipment rush from the Sikkim Police Bagpipe Band to the Indian Army Band, which has been lent for the occasion to the various villagers performing on drums and horns.[2]

On 2 December, less than eight months after the wedding, Thondup's father, Tashi Namgyal, the ruler of Sikkim, died. Thondup was the new maharaja and Hope his royal consort. But the actual coronation had to wait for an auspicious time and date to be set by the court astrologers: 9.22 a.m. on 4 April 1965. The coronation attracted even more attention from the outside world than the wedding had done. Andrew Duff wrote in his excellent book about Sikkim, quoting Martha Hamilton, an Englishwoman who was there, 'The newspapers found ever more ways to romanticise Sikkim. "Americans are well aware that Monaco is touched by Grace," an editorial in the *Washington Post* read, "now Sikkim is radiant with Hope." Messages from Queen Elizabeth II and from Dean Rusk, the US Secretary of State, were proudly displayed in official programmes.'[3]

Thondup, however, was cautious, well aware of Sikkim's dependence on India. He said in his speech to the assembled guests, who included Indira Gandhi, then the minister for Information and Broadcasting, 'We recall with profound affection the memory of Jawaharlal Nehru, a true and steadfast friend of Sikkim, and we have confidence that the Government of India will continue to hold out to us the hand of friendship'. He then went on to say that, 'ours is a small country, but we have pride in our institutions, our way of life and cultural heritage', thus emphasizing that Sikkim had its own, distinct national characteristics.[4]

Thondup and Hope had met at the bar at the Windamere Hotel in Darjeeling in 1959 when she was a teenage student. He, then a widower for almost three years, was there to see his two sons at a boarding school in the town. He was nearly twice her age, but they were drawn to each other. They kept in touch after she returned to New York to continue her studies at the Sarah Lawrence College. Two years later, they were engaged and then the wedding took place in 1963 with pictures of the colourful ceremony appearing in glossy magazines, primarily in the US but also in other countries. They were referred to as the 'King and Queen of Sikkim', and it all seemed like a fairy tale come true. The Western media loved it, haunted by the setting of the romance: a small kingdom in the Himalayas with breathtaking scenery, where the people practised a form of tantric Tibetan Buddhism, and the mountains were replete with giant butterflies, pandas, and four hundred species of wild orchid.[5] It was exoticism at its best—or worst.

But what was Sikkim, really? An independent kingdom, as most Western publications preferred to describe it—or merely the last of the princely states, which had not yet been fully integrated into the Indian Union? Neither description would have been correct in the 1960s. But Sikkim was indeed once an independent kingdom and much larger than it is today. The area was settled in the thirteenth century by Tibetan herdsmen and swidden-cultivating Lepchas, but it was not until the seventeenth century that it came to resemble a state with its own administration. The first ruler is believed to have been Phuntsog Namgyal, who, in 1642, was consecrated as the first *chogyal* (king) of Sikkim. His ancestors came from Kham in eastern Tibet. Along with his lamas, Phuntsog converted the Lepcha people to Buddhism. He appointed 12 ministers to his government, all of whom came from the Tibetan-related Bhutia community, and another 12 men from the Lepchas were made heads in the same number of newly created, local administrative units. He also founded the Namgyal Dynasty, which continued to rule the country into modern times.

Some modern Tibetologists have questioned this official history, arguing that Phuntsog and his successors ruled over a much more loosely constructed entity, and that it was British expansion into the Himalayas in the early nineteenth century (and thus a foreign threat to Sikkim's sovereignty) that led to efforts to re-imagine Sikkimese history in 'an attempt to define Sikkim as a nation'.[6]

Whichever version of Sikkimese history one chooses to believe, Sikkim was a separate kingdom when the British arrived on the scene and it did once include the Chumbi Valley in present-day Tibet. It stretched westward to the Arun River in Nepal and southward to northern West Bengal, although the extent of Sikkimese influence over those areas waxed and waned with advances and retreats resulting from the chogyals' wars against their Nepalese and Bhutanese neighbours. Lots of territory was lost to the Nepalese Gorkha rajahs, but some of it was restored to Sikkim under two treaties signed in 1816 and 1817, the first between the British East India Company and the Nepalese and the other between the British East India Company and the chogyal of Sikkim.

The arrival of the British brought fundamental changes to Sikkim. In 1828, a group of East India Company officials, having settled a conflict between Nepal and Sikkim, found a place in the southern Sikkimese highlands which they deemed suitable for the location of a sanatorium for British servicemen and invalid servants. Seven years later, in 1835, a strip of territory was acquired for that purpose from the ruler of Sikkim, and the construction of a hill station began, which was named Darjeeling after a local monastery called Dorjeling ('the place of the thunderbolt') in Tibetan. More land was obtained after conflicts between the chogyal and the British—and, more importantly, between the British and the neighbouring state of Bhutan. By the early 1860s, the entire area of what today constitutes Darjeeling District of West Bengal was in British hands, including the important trading town of Kalimpong.

Under yet another treaty, this time signed in Tumlong in March 1861 between Sidkeong Namgyal, the chogyal, and Sir Ashley Eden representing the British, what remained of Sikkim became a de facto British protectorate. Subsequent civil and ecclesiastical friction, an invasion by Tibetan forces, and claims of Chinese suzerainty over Sikkim prompted the British Crown to annex the entire kingdom more formally as a protectorate in 1889.[7] A road and even a railway were built to Darjeeling, connecting the area with Calcutta, the capital of Britain's Indian Empire. Tea was introduced to the highlands and even to the plains below.

John Claude White, a British engineer, photographer, and later, author, became the first political officer for Sikkim, and, the first political officer for Sikkim residing in Gangtok. He had a magnificent mansion built, from where he reorganized the administration and chaired the council that advised the chogyal. That building is what became India House after 1947 and today serves as the residence of the governor.

Under British rule, Sikkim had a status similar to that of the other princely states and the ruler came to be referred to as 'maharaja', not 'chogyal'. The official India Office List names Sikkim as a 15-gun salute state along with 17 other principalities, among them Jaisalmer, Alwar, Kishangarh, Rampur—and Bhutan, which was also included in the dependencies of Britain's Indian Empire. But Sikkim was a frontier state, which the British treated somewhat differently from the other princely states.

The immediate problem after 1889 was that Sikkim was under-populated for Britain's designs for the region. It only had about 30,000 inhabitants, and manpower was needed for the construction of roads and portering of goods.[8] But there was a simple solution to that: the importation of labour from Nepal. According to Nari Rustomji, the Indian civil servant with perhaps the strongest attachment to the northern frontier areas, 'While it would be an overstatement to hold that the British deliberately and actively engineered the Nepalese immigration into Sikkim, there is no doubt that, in the earlier years, and particularly under the stewardship of Claude White, the first political officer of Sikkim, they encouraged and happily connived at it.'[9]

While labour was needed and few Sikkimese would want to be drafted into road construction crews or build houses in Gangtok and other towns being developed, the influx of Nepalese into Sikkim would also, Rustomji noted, be

> the surest guarantee against a revival of Tibetan influence. The Nepalese were mostly Hindus and their language was Sanskrit-based. Their culture and way of life had closer affinity with India than with Tibet … it was assumed by the British that settlement of a large bulk of an essentially Hindu-oriented population in Sikkim would preclude the risk of its looking northwards to Tibet for direction and support.[10]

Claude White's successors as political officer were more restrained when it came to encouraging Nepalese immigration, but the process he had set in motion could not be stopped. More Nepalese arrived and, already by the early twentieth century, they outnumbered the native population of Tibetan and Lepcha stock. Laws were passed to prevent the immigrants from owning land, but the influx continued unabated anyway. Many Nepalese also became engaged in various businesses. Francis Younghusband's military expedition to Lhasa in 1904 had opened Tibet for trade. Younghusband's troops had crossed the border at Jelep La Pass, which now became the main gateway for trade and other exchanges between Tibet and British India. Sikkim flourished in a way its eastern neighbour Bhutan, which remained isolated, did not. (The British political officer in Sikkim was also responsible for Bhutan as well as Tibet, although it was much bigger and an independent country.)

Then came India's independence and, on 5 December 1950, 'the President of India and His Highness the Maharaja of Sikkim' signed an agreement according to which 'Sikkim shall continue to be a Protectorate of India and, subject to provisions of this Treaty, shall enjoy autonomy un regard to its internal affairs'.[11] The government of independent India became responsible for the defence of Sikkim as well as all its external relations, 'The Government of Sikkim shall have no dealings with any foreign power ... [and] the Government of Sikkim shall not import any arms, ammunition, military stores or other warlike material of any description for any purpose whatsoever without the previous consent of the Government of India.'[12]

The maharaja could remain. But, just in time for Thondup's coronation, India agreed to his proposal to have the title changed to the old designation of chogyal. His wife, Hope Cook, became gyalmo (queen consort) and would now be addressed formally as 'Her Highness Hope La, the Gyalmo of Sikkim'. That was the beginning of the trouble. The very presence of Hope gave Sikkim a higher international profile. She brought Sikkimese handicrafts to New York, where they were exhibited and sold. Invitation cards were sent out in the names of 'Their Majesties the King and Queen of Sikkim'.[13] During her frequent trips to the US, she gave interviews to American journalists about her fabled kingdom in the Himalayas. The University of Kentucky produced a detailed contour map of 'the Kingdom of Sikkim'.

The international attention Sikkim received after 1963, and new signals from the palace in Gangtok, had an impact on the internal political scene as well. The Sikkim Guards were revived, the civil service was reorganized as a more formal hierarchy, and traditional features of Buddhist justice were incorporated into a partly new judicial system. A national anthem was composed and sung at official ceremonies where the national flag was prominently hoisted atop government buildings.[14] Demands were raised for Sikkim to issue its own postage stamps and passports, to be able to trade abroad on its own terms, and receive direct aid from countries other than India. Political parties, among them the pro-palace National Party, even began to ask for a revision of the 1950 treaty with India. 'We must remain Sikkimese,' its leader Netuk Tsering stated. 'There can be no merger with India, Tibet, Bhutan or Nepal.'[15]

In India, suspicions of Hope and her intentions had grown, and apprehension turned to fury when she, as early as 1966, that is, only a year after the coronation, wrote a controversial article for a local academic journal called the *Bulletin of Tibetology*. She argued that the 1835 treaty 'gave Darjeeling to the British for use as a sanatorium but had not intended an outright grant'. The British, Hope wrote, 'simply assumed the grant was outright and had begun to administer the area ... as part of their Indian possession'. By implication, Darjeeling belonged to Sikkim, not West Bengal. All the land that belonged to the chogyal and others, she argued, 'could have "usage" only', not actual ownership.[16]

Hope was probably not prepared for the reaction to her article. According to her, it 'stirred up a hornet's nest. "Sarah Lawrence girl claims Darjeeling for Sikkim." "American Trojan Mare in Gangtok." "CIA agent in borrowed plumage." "American wife plans missile base." The Indian reaction was vituperative, and I was remorseful, scared.'[17] She also noted that, 'afterwards, whenever the Indian papers wrote about Sikkim's wish for treaty revision, my article was trotted out as a further damning black mark against the country. The newspaper attacks seemed to be calculated to appear whenever any Sikkimese official was going to Delhi for talks.'[18]

Whether she was ignorant or simply naïve is hard to say, but she did indeed stir up a hornet's nest with her article and other antics, making it impossible for India to even consider a revision of the 1950 treaty, and this, at a time when the Chinese threat was becoming more intense. She could not have chosen a more inappropriate time to publish her article about Darjeeling and to encourage steps which were perceived as attempts to gain more independence from India.

But it was not entirely her fault that the bureaucrats in India House and New Delhi were not, to say the least, pleased with those moves. The Indian journalist Sunanda K. Datta-Ray, although a friend of the chogyal, wrote in his book *Smash and Grab: The Annexation of Sikkim*, 'The *Chogyal* was probably responsible for aiming at styles that denoted sovereign status internationally but Hope was the outsider, so she was blamed.'[19] And Hope was the one who had attracted international attention to an until then little-known corner of the world.

In spite of fears of the Chinese opening yet another front in the Himalayas during the 1962 War, there was then actually no fighting at the Sikkimese border. But according to a now declassified CIA report, compiled on 6 November 1962, as war was raging in NEFA and Ladakh, 'The Indian Army is increasingly concerned about a Chinese build-up in the Chumbi Valley opposite Sikkim.'[20] India sent troops to reinforce the small contingent of Indian Army personnel already stationed in Sikkim, which it had the right to do under the 1950 treaty.

Rustomji, who served as *dewan*, or the equivalent of a prime minister, of Sikkim between 1954 and 1959 noted in his book *Enchanted Frontiers* that the Chumbi Valley, a thin strip of Tibetan land between Sikkim and Bhutan, was historically part of Sikkim. 'Its inhabitants had close affinities in language, dress and social custom, with the people comprised within Sikkim's present day boundaries.'[21] It had also, because of its milder climate, been the summer headquarters of the Sikkimese ruler. But after the 1959 invasion of Tibet, Rustomji wrote, the Chinese took care 'to occupy the Chumbi Valley in strength lest the Sikkimese should harbour dreams of revising old claims'. The Chinese also 'accelerated the processes of "de-Tibetanizing" by deputing leading people of the area and brighter lights of the younger generation of China for "cultural integration".'[22]

What had been 'an enchanted frontier' when Rustomji was in Sikkim in the 1950s became, shortly after he had left, a tense and endangered frontier. The first skirmish with the Chinese PLA occurred even before the 1962 War. On 20 September 1960, a PLA patrol intruded into Sikkimese territory near Jelep La and, when the Indian side wanted to discuss the border between Sikkim and Tibet as part of the overall talks about the frontier, the Chinese said that, the issue did 'not fall within the scope' of those discussions.[23]

Tension escalated after the 1962 War as the Chinese amassed even more troops into the Chumbi Valley. In January 1963, the Chinese accused India of having built pill-boxes, communication trenches, and sentry posts to 'the southeast, northeast and north of Nathu La', demanding that India should dismantle all structures set up on 'Chinese territory.' India refuted the claim.[24]

All that had happened was that a new road had been built from Gangtok to Nathu La, a pass north of Jelep La, in 1958, at a time when cross-border trade between Sikkim and Tibet was still being conducted. But the Agreement on Trade and Intercourse between Tibet Region of China and India, which was concluded in 1954, expired on 6 June 1962, and, at a time when tension was mounting along the frontier, there was no interest on either side to have the agreement extended. All kinds of cross-border traffic were halted and the border was sealed. Indian troops had since then been stationed at the pass to guard the frontier, and possibly also to keep an eye on Chinese troop movements in the Chumbi Valley on the other side.

Chinese provocations continued in 1964. In August, a Chinese patrol intruded into Nathu La and on three occasions in December, Chinese soldiers were seen on the Sikkimese side of the pass. After the first incursion in August, China issued a statement 'refuting the rumours the Soviet Union fabricated in collusion with India that China had made "intrusion" into Sikkim'.[25] That was to become the standard line from the Chinese whenever there was an incident along the border—and there were many in the 1960s.

The Chinese, probably to annoy New Delhi, had also sent a condolence message on the death of Tashi Namgyal in 1963, and a congratulatory note on the April 1965 coronation of Thondup directly to Gangtok instead of forwarding it through the Indian government, which was responsible for Sikkim's external relations. This was perceived as a recognition of Sikkim's independence, and showed that China disapproved of Sikkim's status as India's protectorate.[26]

Only a few months after the coronation, war broke out between India and Pakistan. It had begun with a confrontation in Rann of Kutch in Gujarat in the beginning of the year, which ended with a ceasefire brokered by Britain in June. Likely encouraged by what Pakistan saw as a favourable outcome, about 30,000 Pakistani soldiers dressed as locals crossed the Line of Control in Kashmir in the first week of August. Fighting erupted with the Indian security forces who, for the most part, drove them back. Pakistan's response was a massive attack on 1 September 1965 across the Line of Control in Kashmir and the bombing of Indian airfields in an offensive codenamed 'Grand Slam'. But the belief that the Indian Army would crumble under the onslaught was short-lived. On 6 September, the Indian Army crossed the international border in Punjab and came within striking distance of Lahore.

The war witnessed some of the largest tank battles since World War II. The Indian Army had recovered from the defeat by China in 1962 and now had more men and weaponry. Although the Pakistan Army did occupy some positions inside India, Operation Grand Slam was not going as planned and expected. China had to come to the rescue by threatening to open a new front in Sikkim. If China could occupy a corridor between Tibet and East Pakistan via Sikkim, Darjeeling, and Siliguri, the entire northeastern region of India would be cut off from the rest of the country.

China began by sending protest notes to the Indian Embassy in Beijing, followed by an ultimatum on 16 September. It alleged that Indian troops had crossed the Sikkim-Tibet border and built fortifications on the other side. This was not a new claim, but the timing was no coincidence and, if India would not comply with the request within three days, China would take action. The note did not say exactly what would happen after those three days, but it was a provocation India could not ignore. China made it clear that it would 'strengthen its defences and heighten its alertness along the border' and that a chain of consequences would follow due to the 'criminal and extended aggression by the Government of India.'[27]

The objective was clear, as China openly linked its actions on the Sikkimese border to the ongoing war between India and Pakistan. China's Foreign Minister Chen Yi, on a visit to Karachi on 4 September, had declared its support for the 'just struggle of the Kashmiri people' who were resisting 'India's tyrannical rule.'[28] China was on Pakistan's side because it had only acted in self-defence against Indian aggression, the minister suggested.

China was forced to extend its three-day ultimatum when the UN intervened and Secretary General U Thant held meetings with Pakistan's President Ayub Khan and the Indian Prime Minister Lal Bahadur Shastri. Ayub Khan could not afford to let the war continue, as his forces were being crushed. China then issued a new note on 19 September, declaring its 'willingness' to put off the time limit to before the midnight of 22 September. The note also stated that the Chinese government 'gives all out support to the people of Kashmir in their struggle for the right of self-determination ... and to Pakistan in her just struggle against Indian aggression.'[29]

On 20 September, a PLA unit moved into position at the Dongchui La pass and opened fire on the Indian soldiers there. The following day, another PLA unit began firing at Indian positions at Nathu La. But it was too late for China to launch a new war against India. The UN Security Council passed a resolution demanding that India and Pakistan cease hostilities and withdraw all their soldiers back to the positions they had held before 5 August. This was accepted by India as well as Pakistan, leaving China in limbo. A late response from Beijing came in the shape of a bizarre note claiming that India has withdrawn the intruding troops within the specified time limit set by the Chinese government, and had 'dismantled these military works of aggression'. But since then, the note alleged, 'Indian troops, attempting to stage a come-back, have continued repeatedly to cross the boundary for reconnaissance, and even launched armed attacks against the Chinese frontier guards. It is perfectly clear that India has been using Sikkim's territory to commit ceaseless intrusions and provocations against China and create tension on the China-Sikkim boundary.' The note went on to remind people of the 'fact' that it is 'well known' that India had launched 'a massive attack on China' in October 1962'.[30]

India's Prime Minister Shastri could perhaps have extracted more concessions from Pakistan when he signed the deal brokered by the Soviet Union in Tashkent on 10 January 1966. That is debatable, but the appointment of Indira Gandhi as India's new prime minister definitely marked the beginning of a new and more assertive India. She was not going to tolerate any more provocations from China.

China did not attack, but, in July 1966, its troops opposite Nathu La installed six powerful loudspeakers blaring out propaganda at the Indian troops stationed at the pass. In August, loudspeakers were also put opposite Jelep La. Huge portraits of Mao Zedong were erected at both border passes, facing the Indians. But it is doubtful those manoeuvres had any impact on the morale of the Indian soldiers. The nuisance value was greater, as the noise from the loudspeakers may have deprived the soldiers of some sleep.

Small-scale incursions by the Chinese continued as well. Then, open confrontation broke out when, on 11 September 1966, the Indian troops announced over loudspeakers that they had no intention of intruding even one millimetre into Tibet. After the announcement was made, the Indian troops began putting up barbed wire along the border on the southern side of Nathu La. The Chinese then opened fire with automatic rifles and light-machine guns, killing and wounding several Indian soldiers. The Indian side returned fire and the Chinese upped the ante by firing 76mm and 122mm cannons. The Indians responded with their artillery, killing and wounding at least 36 PLA soldiers.

The Chinese Ministry of Foreign Affairs stated in a note given to the Indian Embassy in Beijing on 12 September, 'Do not misjudge the situation and repeat your mistake of 1962…the Chinese People's Liberation Army will certainly deal a crushing blow at any enemy who dares to invade us'.[31] But the Indian soldiers had not crossed into Tibet, nor had they vacated any of their positions along the border. This was not 1962 and the Chinese probably came to realize that after the exchange of fire at Nathu La.

In the late 1960s and early 1970s, the situation in Sikkim was becoming untenable for India: China was encroaching from the north; to the south of the Himalayan watershed, a second threat was posed by the Sikkimese ruler's quest for more independence; and then there was Naxalite activity in the strategically important Siliguri Neck just below the hills of Darjeeling. There were also intrigues within the Sikkim elite that had a destabilizing effect on the situation in this sensitive frontier area. Hope was certainly not a CIA agent, as some Indian tabloids had suggested. But she did not fit into Sikkimese society—and began to feel it. According to Datta-Ray, 'Hope's dream of queening it in the Himalayas cut off the *Chogyal* from his throne's traditional supporters and isolated him from Sikkimese society'.[32]

Hope had to compete for relevance with two other influential women: Thondup's sister Coocoola and Elisa-Maria Langford-Rae, the Scottish wife of Lhendup Dorji, a local landowner-turned-politician who came from an old Lepcha family. Nari Rustomji observed that 'Princess Coocoola saw in Hope a rival to her hold over the Prince, and Hope, in her turn, as soon made it clear that it was she, as Queen, who was the First Lady'.[33] Hope's contacts with powerful American senators prompted Coocoola to demonstrate to her brother that, 'she too was no less stalwart a champion of her country's cause. Her statements to the world press served however only to worsen the Prince's already sullied relations with the Indian authorities'.[34]

While the Indian journalists were speculating about Hope's possible CIA contacts, they forgot that it was Coocoola who had befriended American agents in Kolkata during and after World War II. But she was in her late teens and early twenties at that time and the agents she knew had most certainly already retired from active duty. Probably her main accomplishment in the U.S.A. was to arrange for two Sikkimese women to represent Sikkim at the Associated Country Women of the World conference in New York in 1967, a non-event for most Americans.

But there were concerns in India about possible American designs for Sikkim that could not be dismissed as tabloid gossip. After China's first nuclear test in 1964, a most peculiar, joint Indian-American espionage mission was undertaken in the Himalayas. The plan was to install a terrestrial communications device, powered by a nuclear electrical generator, on the top of Nanda Devi, a 7,816-metre peak in northern India, from where any unusual seismological activity in Tibet or Xinjiang would be registered. The generator, known as System for Nuclear Auxiliary Power (SNAP) 19C consisted of five elements—a hot fuel block, radioactive fuel capsules placed in its core, thermoelectric generators mounted around it, insulation material, and the block's outer casing.[35]

It was not a bomb and could not explode unless equipped with a trigger. But the device was powered by radioactive material, which could be harmful to humans who came close to it, and it was not meant to be lost somewhere on a remote mountain top. But that was exactly what happened. Because of bad weather, most of the equipment had to be abandoned during the first attempt to scale Nanda Devi. Today, half a century later, the generator is still at large in the vicinity of the mountain.

Indian interest in co-operating with the Americans in espionage missions—and to support the Tibetan resistance—decreased considerably after that affair. The U.S.A. could afford to take a hard line on China, but India was becoming weary of the consequences of provoking its northern neighbour. China's involvement in the wars in Nagaland and its interest in the Naxalite uprising were warning signals that India could not ignore. While the Dalai Lama and his government-in-exile were allowed to remain in McLeodganj, Indian support for the armed Tibetan resistance declined in the late 1960s. Mustang, not Chakrata in northern India, became the main stronghold for the American-supported Tibetan guerrillas.

With India adopting a more pragmatic approach towards China—and, at the same time, forging a close relationship with the Soviet Union—it was not impossible that Sikkim, especially if it gained more independence, could become a new base for American operations in the Himalayas. Whether those concerns were warranted or not is hard to say, but they certainly played a role in determining India's attitudes towards attempts to gain more independence for Sikkim. Hope, of course, was the weak link there, a gullible American lady who took pride in calling herself 'Her Majesty' and 'Queen'—and who was decidedly anti-Indian.

But Hope was far from safe on her throne and constant palace intrigues in Gangtok further weakened her power and influence. A far more formidable foe than her sister-in-law Coocoola was Langford-Rae. Her husband held the patrician honorific *kazi*. So, she took the title of *Kazini* of Chakung, a town in west Sikkim from where her husband's ancestors came. The kazi belonged to a group of people who were frustrated with Sikkim's 'byzantine electoral system', and with the kazini by his side—and more often behind the scenes—began to advocate for a more democratic order.[36]

In 1953, Thondup's father Tashi had introduced a mild form of constitutional monarchy with a State Council and an Executive Council. But the system was based on a Party Formula, whereby the seats in the State Council would be divided equally among the Bhutia-Lepcha and Nepalese communities, which meant that the constitution made the approximately 75 per cent Nepalese majority of the population equal to the 25 per cent Bhutia-Lepchas. This complicated voting system was replaced with an even more intricate method in 1958 and, in 1967, the strength of the State Council was raised from the initial 18 to 24, with the six additional seats to be nominated by the chogyal.[37]

There was widespread opposition to this undemocratic system, a movement that India encouraged because it would undermine the power of the chogyal, his American wife, and the nationalistic noblemen who supported them. India's involvement increased after a controversial election in January 1973, in which the pro-palace National Party won nine of the 18 contested seats. The two opposition parties, one of which was the kazi's Congress Party, claimed that vote rigging had taken place and demanded that the officials who were responsible for it be arrested. The demands were not met, and anti-chogyal demonstrations, some of them violent, were launched in Gangtok. A temporary solution was found in May, when the chogyal, India's Foreign Secretary Kewal Singh, and representatives of the political parties agreed to introduce a more democratic system. Under the agreement, the chief executive, or the head of the administration, was to be an Indian.[38]

Palace power was falling apart rapidly—and so was Thondup's marriage to Hope. There was infidelity on both sides and, on 15 August, she left with her son and daughter for New York. India's Independence Day was being celebrated in Gangtok. The writing was on the wall, and, in the 1974 election, the first that was really democratic, kazi's Congress Party routed the National Party by capturing 29 of the 32 seats in the new Assembly. One of the first resolutions it passed when it met in May was to reduce the powers of the chogyal. In June, some members of his Sikkim Guard tried, though unsuccessfully, to prevent the elected assembly members from entering the building where they were going to meet. On 4 September, the Indian parliament, the Lok Sabha, voted in favour of making Sikkim an 'associate state'.

Beijing perceived this as an Indian takeover of Sikkim and China's foreign minister, Qiao Guanhua, lashed out against India in a speech before the UN General Assembly on 2 October 1974. He also seized the opportunity to condemn the Soviet Union: 'The Indian Government's annexation of Sikkim has aroused the opposition of the Sikkimese people as well as the Indian people and met with condemnation by India's neighbours and world public opinion. The Soviet propaganda organs alone sing praises of India. This shows that the Soviet revisionist social-imperialism is the boss behind the scenes of Indian expansionism.'[39]

With the kazi as Sikkim's first democratically elected chief minister and the kazini by his side, events unfolded briskly. On 10 April 1975, the Sikkim Assembly decided to abolish the institution of the chogyal. Thondup was confined to his palace where he remained under virtual house arrest. Four days later, a referendum was held and an overwhelming majority voted for a final merger agreement with India. On 23 April, the Lok Sabha voted to make Sikkim the 22nd state of the Indian Union, a decision that went into effect on 16 May.

Predictably, the Chinese condemned the moves. On 29 April, the Chinese government issued a statement saying that it 'solemnly states once again that it absolutely does not recognize India's annexation of Sikkim and firmly supports the people of Sikkim in their just struggle for national independence and in defence of state sovereignty against Indian expansionism.'[40]

But there were few signs of any such 'struggle' by 'the people of Sikkim'. The relatively smooth merger of Sikkim with the rest of India occurred during the rise of the country's new external intelligence agency, the Research and Analysis Wing (RAW). As opposition to the rule of the chogyal was mounting, it sent agents to Gangtok, Mangan, Namchi, and Gyalshing, the headquarters of the then four districts of Sikkim, where they collected information and, India began supporting the opposition from behind the scene.[41] According to researcher Asoka Raina, RAW operatives established a close relationship with people who were opposed to the monarchy and in favour of a more democratic and representative government.[42] And it was not difficult for RAW to reinforce the idea that the chogyal had to go. Even the ethnic composition of Sikkim was heavily against the old monarchy. According to the 1971 census, the Nepalese formed an overwhelming majority of 134,000, with the Lepchas numbering only 25,000, and the Bhutias along with the related Tsongs made up about 23,000.[43]

Although achieved without military intervention, Sikkim could be seen the second major success achieved by India's security services. The first was scored during the much more violent creation of Bangladesh in 1971. India supported the freedom struggle launched by the Mukti Bahini fighters who wanted East Pakistan to break away and form an independent country, and RAW saw here a golden opportunity to secure the country's eastern frontiers, including the strategically important Siliguri Neck and the Sikkim corridor to the Tibetan frontier.

After the Indian intervention in the war, *The Sunday Times* of London reported in its 12 December 1971 issue, 'It took only 12 days for the Indian Army to smash through on its way to Dacca [Dhaka], an achievement reminiscent of the German *Blitzkrieg* across France in 1940. The strategy was the same—speed, ferocity, and flexibility.'[44] On 16 December, the Pakistan Army surrendered and, under international pressure, on 8 January 1972 Pakistan was forced to release the leader of the freedom struggle, Sheikh Mujibur Rahman, who had been arrested in March 1971 and flown to West Pakistan, where he was kept in solitary confinement. Now, he returned in a plane provided by the British Royal Air Force to Dhaka, where a million people were waiting to greet him. East Pakistan had finally become the independent nation of Bangladesh.

The Bangladesh operation also helped New Delhi's security services locate and apprehend insurgent leaders from India's northeast who were based in Dhaka. Among them were Thinoselie Medom Keyho, who, together with Thuingaleng Muivah, had led the first Naga mission to China in 1967 and Neidelie, another member of the top leadership of the Naga

National Council (NNC). The Mizo rebel chief Laldenga, who was also based in Dhaka at the time, managed to escape along with several of his men across the border to Myanmar. He later made it to Karachi in Pakistan with the help of the Pakistani consulate in Sittwe in Myanmar's Rakhine State.

The loss of their bases in erstwhile East Pakistan prompted the Mizo rebels to take the Chinese up on the offer of support Laldenga had received when he visited Beijing in 1968 and 1970. The first batch of rebels that reached China in early 1973 had left the Mizo Hills in mid-1972, and, like the Nagas before them, trekked through Myanmar's Kachin State to Yunnan. It was only later, when Bangladesh turned from friend to foe, that the Mizos and other northeastern rebels were able to re-establish training camps and other hideouts in the forests of the Chittagong Hill Tracts in Bangladesh. But by then, RAW had agents and informants in all of India's neighbouring countries, certainly including Bangladesh, regardless of whether an anti-India or an India-friendly party was in power.

When RAW was formed in 1968, its first officers came from the external wing of the Intelligence Bureau and the Special Branch of the police. The first chief, Rameshwar Nath Kao, had belonged to the colonial Imperial Police, which was renamed the Indian Police Service after independence in 1947. As the agency grew, recruits were taken from the police, the military, and the civil service while many were also graduates from India's universities. Basically, RAW grew out of the old establishment and its more modern offshoots.

By sharp contrast, China's intelligence services were formed during Mao's revolutionary struggle and the stormy decades before the Communist victory in 1949. The CCP was formed when, in the last week of July 1921, Mao and 11 of his comrades met in a nondescript, grey brick building on Rue Wantz (now Xingye Road) in the French Concession in Shanghai. In those days, the city consisted of three sections, each with its own administration and law enforcement. The French Concession was the most lightly policed, and therefore the safest place in the city for a band of dissidents to meet. The International Settlement, where the British and the Americans dominated, was too tightly controlled with Sikh policemen brought in from India patrolling the streets, while Shanghai's native, Chinese-run part of the city was in the hands of the KMT, which at that time was not the Communists' enemy—but was nevertheless a rival force that could not really be trusted.

Until 1927, the CCP and the KMT had actually constituted a United Front, but the relationship began to sour after the death of Sun Yat-sen in 1925. Chiang Kai-shek, his successor as the KMT supremo, was a staunch anti-Communist allied with the Green Gang of Du Yuesheng, nicknamed Big-Eared Du, Huang Jinrong, better known as Pock-Marked Huang, and other gangsters in Shanghai. Pock-Marked Huang also happened to be a senior officer in the French gendarmerie in Shanghai, which enabled him to carry out his criminal activities with near impunity. The CCP, on the other hand, gained a considerable following among the urban proletariat in Shanghai, China's most industrialized city, which, according to Marxist doctrine, should be their main power base.

The Communists were becoming powerful, threatening the KMT's tenuous hold on the city's administration. But Big-Eared Du came to the rescue of his old comrade Chiang Kai-shek. He mobilized hundreds of his and Pock-Marked Huang's hijackers, kidnappers, bodyguards, pimps, masseurs, manicurists, pick-pockets, gunmen, hawkers, waiters, and beggars, dressed them in blue and wrapped a band marked with the Chinese character for 'labour' around their arms. Guns were provided by Chiang's high command.

The attack began an hour before dawn on 12 April 1927, as the mobsters attacked a building where the Communist workers' militia were headquartered. The pickets surrounding the building were cut down in a hail of machine-gun fire. Other Communist offices and buildings were attacked as well, and, before the end of the day, seven hundred trade unionists were killed. It took eight truckloads and several hours to cart away the dead and the litter. With them went the last of the alliance between the KMT and the CCP.[45]

The bloody crackdown in Shanghai in 1927 crippled the CCP and forced it to shift its main area of operation from the city to the countryside where the vast majority of the Chinese people lived. It was going to be a peasants' revolution, not a struggle led by the urban proletariat, which anyway was too small to rely on for someone who wanted to seize power in China.

The CCP was revived by the mutiny among some of the KMT's troops in Nanchang and the subsequent formation, on 1 August 1927, of the Chinese Workers' and Peasants Red Army, the forerunner to the PLA. Although based mainly in the countryside, it still had to rely on information collected in the cities. The crackdown, and the Communists' struggle to survive, thus led to the strengthening of the CCP's intelligence capabilities.

According to China scholar David Chambers, the role of intelligence was actually crucial in preserving the CCP from extinction through the difficult years of the 1920s and early 1930s. Reliable intelligence enabled the Communists to stage the successful breakout from Jiangxi that began the Long March in 1934 as well as to penetrate the KMT's political and military establishment, which made the eventual seizure of power possible.[46] A close eye was also kept on dissident voices within the Party, which led to a climate of fear within their own ranks.

Before the 1949 communist takeover, the CCP had two intelligence agencies, Shehui Bu (the Social Bureau) and the Qingbao Bu (the Intelligence Bureau). This complex intelligence and security apparatus was headed by the notorious Kang Sheng between 1939 and 1946. He was, however, relieved of his command and stripped of other key posts when Mao and the top party leadership realized how much damage he had done to the Party with a 'Rectification Movement' in the early 1940s. Kang's campaign became especially vicious in 1943, when he detained over a thousand alleged 'spies' and 'enemy agents'. Among them were well-known intellectuals who had helped build the Party. Between 40,000 and 80,000 Party members were expelled and many of those went insane, while others committed suicide, either by hanging or drowning themselves in rivers or wells.[47]

But even with his ouster as intelligence chief, Kang remained a trusted member of Mao's inner circle and remained a close confidante of the Chairman after the Communist takeover. In November 1949, China's new rulers established the Ministry of Public Security, a new entity that was supposed to take over the internal counterespionage and security duties of the Shehui Bu, which would then be abolished. But, in practice, the Shehui Bu remained operational inside China until 1953, possibly until as late as 1954.

The system turned out to be too unwieldy. So, in 1955, the Investigation Department of the Chinese Communist Party (ID/CCP) was established as the principal civilian intelligence agency with the Second Department, the General Staff Department of the PLA in charge of military intelligence duties. Reigning over all this was a body called the Central Intelligence Committee, about which very little is known.[48]

Those sweeping changes came after yet another purge within the CCP. Chen Bo, once called by Mao 'the Sherlock Holmes' of Yan'an' for his able intelligence work, was accused of being a British spy and a KMT agent. In 1950, he was dismissed from his post as head of the Security Department of Guangdong province, and imprisoned for more than 20 years. Yang Fan, who had collected intelligence that facilitated the relatively peaceful takeover of Shanghai in May 1949 and later ran the city's counterintelligence operations, was sacked in 1951 and accused of being a KMT agent. Yang was imprisoned in 1955 and not released until 1978. Pan Hannian, a former CCP deputy intelligence chief who had led operations against the KMT in the early 1930s and against the Japanese during World War II, was arrested in 1955 and charged with having been a spy for the KMT as well as for Japan. He died in prison in 1977. According to Chambers, '[Pan] was the headline victim of an intelligence purge in which 800–1,000 cadres received compulsory job transfers, demotions or lengthy prison sentences, some committing suicide to avoid interrogation.'[49]

Perhaps fearing repercussions from other senior Party cadres he had purged in 1943 but which had then returned to power, Kang withdrew from public life after the Communist victory in the Chinese civil war, which enabled him to stay clear of the power struggles of the early 1950s. But then he re-appeared in 1956, now in charge of 'foreign relations', which meant meeting representatives of foreign fraternal parties and going on overseas trips. His first foreign visit was to East Germany in March as head of the Chinese delegation to the Third Congress of the ruling Socialist Unity Party. At home in China, he arranged to travel frequently with Mao, which gave him renewed access to the Chairman. Then, Kang became, of course, one of the masterminds and most brutal inquisitors of the Cultural Revolution in the 1960s and 1970s. He even led a thorough purge of the ID/CCP, which in March 1967 was placed under military control before being absorbed by China's military intelligence apparatus two years later.

Chaos reigned as Kang went berserk, accusing people of past and present 'crimes' such as being members of a 'Japanese Special Service Clique' during the 1937–45 war with Japan, and, in more recent years, of the 'Soviet Revisionist Special Service Group' or the 'Shielding the Hidden US-Chiang Kai-shek Organisation Group'.[50] The then ID/CCP de facto chief Zou Dapeng committed suicide with his wife, herself a senior intelligence operative, rather than having to face the kind of interrogation he had endured in the hands of Kang's men during the so-called Rectification Movement in 1943. In Shanghai, over 1,000 cadres from the Public Security Bureau, which would be the equivalent of the special branch of the police in most countries, were placed in custody and 147 were murdered during investigations of what was termed 'their past conduct'.[51]

It is somewhat of a mystery that this seemingly fatuous security apparatus with its chequered past was able, before, during, and after the 1962 War, to collect such precise intelligence about the Indian border and indeed about the situation beyond it. Before the war, India's more conventional intelligence services, as Lieutenant General Brij Mohan Kaul puts it, 'compared unfavourably'[52] with their Chinese counterparts. But Mao did succeed, most likely because it was of paramount importance for him to become the undisputed leader of China and the Third World. Moreover, India was seen not only as a geopolitical rival but also an enemy because it granted asylum to the Dalai Lama in 1959 and allowed him to set up base in McLeodganj, from where he continued to advocate Tibetan independence. Here, good intelligence work was needed. Cool heads prevailed and a distance was apparently kept from paranoid accusations against real and imagined 'enemies' within the CCP, which were rampant at the time, tearing the Communist establishment apart.

Beside the more traditional security services, a crucial role in China's intelligence gathering operations as well as outright subversive activities on behalf of the authorities was played by the International Liaison Department of the CCP Central Committee (ILD/CCP). Divided geographically into ten different bureaus, the third was responsible for India, Sri Lanka, Pakistan, Nepal, Indonesia, and Malaysia. According to a declassified CIA report, its initial duties consisted of 'finding, investigating and eventually supporting pro-Chinese splinter groups and malcontents, encouraging them to form so-called "Marxist-Leninist" parties in opposition to pro-Soviet "revisionist" parties'.[53] In this task, the CIA stated, the Department provided 'funds to keep the promising groups active, and offering political and organisational training on Chinese soil where it was deemed profitable'.[54]

Before the Cultural Revolution, the ILD's activities were supervised by Deng Xiaoping, Peng Zhen, and Liu Shaoqi, which meant that its entire leadership was purged in the mid- and late 1960s, after which it was replaced by a group of PLA officers appointed and controlled by Kang Sheng and his wife Cao Yi'ou, an equally rabid ideologue. According to the CIA, it was not until late 1970 that a new kind of ILD began to take shape with the reappearance of several veteran members who had been missing during the Cultural Revolution. Shen Chien, a civilian who had been put in charge by Kang, was sidelined and, the CIA noted,

> Kang's own disappearance shortly afterwards left a leadership vacuum. This was filled by Keng Piao [Geng Biao], Peking's [Beijing's] ambassador to Albania, who returned in January 1971 and was named to head the ILD in March. During this period, the military presence which had dominated the ILD was reduced.[55]

The 'new' ILD emerged at a time when the Cultural Revolution was running out of steam, and more infighting erupted within the CCP. After the clashes with the Soviet Union on the River Ussuri in March 1969, Mao's then right-hand man, Lin Biao, was at the height of his power. He was the one who had initiated the publication of Mao's famous *Little Red Book* and played a dominant role during the Cultural Revolution. But then, unexpectedly to most observers in the outside world, he died in an air crash in Mongolia on 13 September 1971. What actually happened is still unclear, but in the official version of events, Lin Biao, his wife Ye Qun, their son

Lin Liguo, and six subordinates were supposedly on their way to the Soviet Union following a failed coup attempt against Mao in China.

The circumstances of the alleged plot as well as the crash remain hazy to this day. The official Chinese version says the plane ran out of fuel. According to conspiracy theorists, however, the plane was shot down by a missile fired by either Soviet or Chinese forces. But a report on the crash compiled by Mongolia's intelligence agencies with help from Soviet experts after the crash suggests it was due to pilot error. The plane's three engines were not damaged before the crash, which would have been the case if it had been fired upon. The plane slammed into the ground at a speed of between 500 and 600 kilometres per hour, and the resulting explosion was followed by a fire that burned for a 'long time', the report said, suggesting there was plenty of fuel on board.[56]

It was at this time that the Indian intervention in East Pakistan, which led to the formation of Bangladesh, occurred—and it is worth noting that Islamabad got only limited support from Beijing in that conflict that was tearing Pakistan apart. According to another classified report compiled by the CIA after the Bangladesh war,

In fact, China did much less for Pakistan in 1971 than they had done during the Indian-Pakistani war of 1965. This time the Chinese avoided diversionary actions on the Indian-Chinese border. In contrast to 1965, they kept their border patrolling down, avoided moving bombers into Tibet, and made only pro forma protests of alleged Indian violations well after the event. In this way, the Chinese reduced any Indian concern about Chinese intervention—concern which, the Chinese reasoned, might induce New Delhi to allow the Soviets an enlarged role in South Asia.[57]

Another plausible reason for the Chinese inaction could be problems at home. The leadership in Beijing was shattered by the sudden death of Lin Biao, and Mao himself is said to have been depressed and become a recluse after the possible betrayal by someone who until then had been considered his anointed successor. Mao turned to some of his old comrades, ultra-leftists whom he had denounced in the past. Wang Hongwen, a 38-year-old cadre from Shanghai, was brought to Beijing and made

CCP vice-chairman. But Mao was ailing, and his wife, Jiang Qing, was in charge when he was unable to provide the CCP with any kind of coherent guidance. She brought in propaganda specialists Zhang Chunqiao and Yao Wenyuan—and the quartet later became known under the pejorative label 'The Gang of Four'. They saw Deng Xiaoping with his—by CCP standards—moderate views as the main threat to their grip on power. He was asked to take part in a series of self-criticism sessions, admitted to a number of ideological mistakes, and Mao, siding with his wife and her three companions, asked the CCP's Central Committee to 'discuss Deng's mistakes thoroughly'.[58]

At that time, the top leadership was getting decimated as one revolutionary veteran after another died. The first to pass away was the notorious Kang Sheng. He died of bladder cancer on 16 December 1975, and the official media spared no praise at his funeral. Kang was 'a proletarian revolutionary, a Marxist theoretician, and a glorious fighter against revisionism'.[59]

Zhou Enlai and Mao had been too weak to attend, and of those two, Zhou died first. He suffered from bladder cancer as well, and it took his life on 8 January 1976. Mao was absent, but Deng Xiaoping, who was on his way back into power, delivered a speech at this state funeral on 15 January. The death of Kang was probably not mourned by many, but in April, huge crowds gathered in Tiananmen Square in Beijing to honour Zhou. They openly criticized the Gang of Four, and indirectly, therefore, even Mao himself. The police, and later, security forces, intervened in this rare show of unauthorized public discontent.

Then came Mao's turn. He died on 9 September of the same year. His last public appearance had been on 27 May, when he had received the visiting Pakistani Prime Minister Zulfikar Ali Bhutto. After the death of the old Chairman, his official portrait was hung on the wall of the main gate at Tiananmen with a banner reading 'Carry on the cause left by Chairman Mao and carry on the cause of proletarian revolution to the end'.[60]

Inevitably, an intense power struggle followed the death of the old Chairman—and it was time for Deng to make his final comeback. Mao had appointed a loyal follower, Hua Guofeng, as his successor, but he was weak and unable to keep the fragmented CCP together. The first to come under attack was the Gang of Four. Before the end of the year, they were purged, arrested, and later put on trial.

Deng who had been in and out of power since the Cultural Revolution, was finally the new strongman by 1980. Hua was replaced by Zhao Ziyang as premier in 1980 and as CCP chief by Hu Yaobang the following year. Both were Deng supporters. Hu exonerated over three million people who had suffered during the Cultural Revolution. Zhao was one of the driving forces behind the new, more open economic policies that were launched in the early 1980s. The Mao era with its rigid ideologies and fanatical policies seemed to be over.

The return of Deng also heralded a new era in China's foreign policy. The Three Worlds concept was still very much alive, but now with a different tone and emphasis. 'China, though a big country, has never sought a special position in the third world. It is not the leader of the third world, not now and never will it be, because such a thing runs counter to the principles of China's relations with foreign countries.'[61] And China now sought friendly relations with as many foreign countries as possible. This was a definite departure from Mao's Three World theory, according to which friendly relations could be upheld even with capitalist nations if the common enemy was the Soviet Union, but where 'the people of the world support each other in their just struggles [62] ... the peoples of all countries are rising. A new historical period of struggle against US imperialism and Soviet revisionism has begun.'[63]

Cynics would argue that China under Deng began to aspire to become a global political and economic superpower rather than a revolutionary model for 'the oppressed masses' of the world. Chinese support for revolutionary movements in Asia gave way to business deals and trade agreements. Deng did indeed live up to his image during the Cultural Revolution as a 'capitalist roader', and began to transform China's peasant-based society into an industrialized nation.

India had to remain cool in its relations with such an unpredictable and volatile neighbour, which could swing from revolutionary belligerence in the early years of the People's Republic to total madness during the Cultural Revolution—and then on to cut-throat capitalism. The 1962 War and its aftermath were only symptoms of China's shifting perception of its role in world politics and, according to Mao himself, had nothing to do with the border dispute.

Meanwhile in Sikkim, the intelligence war between India and China continued unabated. But the days of confrontation, which had prevailed throughout the 1960s, were over. India and China began to negotiate the possibility of cross-border trade and, in June 2006, a historic agreement was signed to allow such trade. On 6 July, after 44 years of closure, border trade at Nathu La was resumed. The agreement allowed residents living in the border areas of the two countries to trade about 28 items mentioned in Sino-Indian border trade agreements of 1991, 1992, and 2003.[64] That list has since been changed several times, though it is still limited to certain items, and trade is not allowed all year round. But it has resulted in an influx of Chinese consumer goods to markets not only in Sikkim but also in West Bengal and northeastern India. Even in Tawang, in Arunachal Pradesh, close to the Chinese border, Chinese items for sale have been imported via Sikkim.

Trade, and not only with China, as well as tourism, cottage industry, and local entrepreneurship coupled with generous grants from the centre in New Delhi, have brought prosperity to Sikkim. It is among the smallest of India's states and union territories, but its per capita Gross Domestic Product (GDP) is the third highest in the country after Goa and Delhi. The literacy rate, which stands at 82.2 per cent, is also one of the highest in the country, well above the national average of 68.9 per cent.[65] It is not uncommon to see cars in Gangtok with the old Sikkimese flag as a sticker in the back window, but there is no secessionist movement in the state. Even Thondup's and Hope's daughter, Hope Leezum, has returned to Sikkim from New York and is married to a Sikkimese man. They live in Gangtok, where they help operate the Tsuklakhang Trust, which manages the palace and the old royal monastery.

Notes

1. Andrew Duff, *Sikkim: Requiem for a Himalayan Kingdom* (Gurgaon: Random House India, 2015), p. 105.
2. Hope Cooke, *Time Change: An Autobiography* (New York: Simon and Schuster, 1980), p. 107.

3. Duff, *Sikkim*, 2015, p. 117. 'Monaco touched by Grace' refers to Grace Kelly, the American actress who married Rainier III, the prince of Monaco and thus became the princess of Monaco.

4. 'Speech from the Throne of Denjong Palden Thondupo Namgyal', available at http://sikhim.blogspot.com/2009/04/april-4-1965-coronation-of-last-king.html (accessed on 5 October 2016).

5. See, for instance, Sunanda K. Datta-Ray, *Smash and Grab: The Annexation of Sikkim* (Chennai: Tranquebar, 2013), p. 93.

6. Saul Mullard, *Opening the Hidden Land: State Formation and the Construction of Sikkimese History* (Leiden: Brill, 2011), p. 186.

7. 'Ainslie T. Embree (ed.), *Encyclopedia of Asian History: Prepared under the Auspices of the Asia Society*, Vol. 3 (New York: Charles Scribner's Sons, and London: Collier Macmillan Publishers, 1988), p. 466.

8. Nari Rustomji, *Sikkim: A Himalayan Tragedy* (New Delhi: Allied Publishers, 1987), p. 10.

9. Rustomji, *Sikkim*, p. 10.

10. Rustomji, *Sikkim*, pp. 10–11.

11. For the full text of the treaty, see G.S. Bajpai, *China's Shadow over Sikkim: The Politics of Intimidation* (New Delhi, London, and Hartford, Wi: Lancer Publishers), pp. 231–7.

12. Bajpai, *China's Shadow over Sikkim*, p. 232.

13. Datta-Ray, *Smash and Grab*, p. 92.

14. 'Annexation of Sikkim: Demise of a Himalayan Kingdom', *Spotlight on Regional Affairs*, Vol. IV, Issue No. 6, June–July 1985 (Islamabad: Institute of Regional Studies), p. 26.

15. Quoted in Datta-Ray, *Smash and Grab*, p. 201.

16. Cooke, *Time Change*, p. 198.

17. Cooke, *Time Change*, p. 198.

18. Cooke, *Time Change*, p. 198.

19. Datta-Ray, *Smash and Grab*, p. 92.

20. Central Intelligence Agency, *Central Intelligence Bulletin: Daily Brief*, 6 November 1962, declassified in 2002, p vii.

21. Nari Rustomji, *Enchanted Frontiers* (Calcutta, Delhi, Bombay, Madras: Oxford University Press, 1973), p. 146.

22. Rustomji, *Enchanted Frontiers*, p. 146.

23. Bajpai, *China's Shadow over Sikkim*, p. 129.

24. Quoted in Bajpai, *China's Shadow over Sikkim*, p. 130.

25. *China's Foreign Relations: A Chronology of Events (1949–1988)* (Beijing: Foreign Languages Press, 1989), p. 247.

26. 'Annexation of Sikkim: Demise of a Himalayan Kingdom', p. 27.

27. Bajpai, *China's Shadow over Sikkim*, p. 143.

28. Bajpai, *China's Shadow over Sikkim*, p. 142,

29. Bajpai, *China's Shadow over Sikkim*, p. 153.

30. 'Note given by the Ministry of Foreign Affairs to the Embassy of India in China', Ministry of External Affairs, Government of India, *Notes, Memoranda and Letters Exchanged Between the Government of India and China, January 1965–February 1966, White Paper XII* (Delhi: Manager of Publications, 1966), p. 187.

30. Bajpai, *China's Shadow over Sikkim*, p. 129.

31. Quoted in Bajpai, *China's Shadow over Sikkim*, p. 189.

32. Bajpai, *China's Shadow over Sikkim*, p. 92.

33. Rustomji, *Sikkim*, p. 71.

34. Rustomji, *Sikkim*, pp. 71–2.

35. For an account of the espionage mission, see Bertil Lintner, *Great Game East: India, China and the Struggle for Asia's Most Volatile Frontier* (New Delhi: HarperCollins India, 2016), pp. 31–2.

36. Duff, *Sikkim*, p. 85.

37. J.R. Subba, *History, Culture and Customs of Sikkim* (New Delhi: Gyan Publishing House, 2011), pp. 67–8.

38. For the details of the agreement, see Satyendra R. Shukla, *Sikkim: The Story of Integration* (New Delhi: S. Chand & Co, 1976), p.86. 1976.

39. *Ch'iao Kuan-hua's Speech at the 19th U.N. General Assembly Session*, Warren Kuo (ed.), *Foreign Policy Speeches by Chinese Communist Leaders, 1963–1975* (Taipei: Institute of International Relations Press, 1976), p. 103. Although Ch'iao Kuan-hua (Qiao Guanhua in Pinyin) had been denounced as a 'counterrevolutionary' during the Cultural Revolution in the 1960s, he was protected by Zhou Enlai and survived the turmoil. In the early 1970s, he played an important role in talks with the American Secretary of State Henry Kissinger to normalize the relations between the United States and China. Qiao was purged from his post as foreign minister after the death of Mao Zedong in 1976, but remained an adviser to the Chinese People's Association for Friendship with Foreign Countries.

40. *China's Foreign Relations*, p. 248.

41. Asoka Raina, *Inside RAW: The Story of India's Secret Service* (Delhi: Vikas Publishing House, 1981), p. 68 and Duff, *Sikkim*, p. 188.

42. Raina, *Inside RAW*, p. 69.

43. Yadav, *Mission R&AW*. New Delhi: Manas Publications, 2014, pp. 69–70.

44. Quoted in Raina, *Inside RAW,* pp. 48–9.

45. For a detailed account of events in Shanghai in the late 1920s, see Bertil Lintner, *Bloodbrothers: Crime, Business and Politics in Asia* (Cows Nest, NSW, Australia: Allen & Unwin, 2002), pp. 35–40.

46. David Ian Chambers, 'The Past and Present State of Chinese Intelligence Historiography', *Studies in Intelligence*, Vol. 56, Issue no. 3, September 2012, p. 2.

47. John Byron and Robert Pack, *The Claws of the Dragon: Kang Sheng, the Evil Genius Behind Mao and his Legacy of Terror in People's China* (New York: Simon & Schuster, 1992), p. 182.

48. Communication with David Ian Chambers, on 13 October 2016.

49. Chambers, 'The Past and Present State of Chinese Intelligence Historiography', p. 4.

50. Chambers, 'The Past and Present State of Chinese Intelligence Historiography', p. 5.

51. Chambers, 'The Past and Present State of Chinese Intelligence Historiography', pp. 4–5.

52. Kaul explains: 'Our intelligence system compared unfavourably with that of the Chinese. They had systematically introduced agents into India in general and NEFA in particular (whereas we had lagged in this respect). Their agents built up a net-work for reporting back information to the Chinese ... the Chinese often knew about our military build-up in a particular area in advance whereas similar knowledge about them was denied us due to faulty intelligence.' See Brij Mohan Kaul, *The Untold Story* (Bombay, Calcutta, New Delhi, Madras, London, New York: Allied Publishers, 1967), p. 438.

53. Central Intelligence Agency, *Intelligence Report: The International Liaison Department of the Chinese Communist Party* (Reference title: POLO XLIV), December 1971, declassified in May 2007, p. i.

54. Central Intelligence Agency, *Intelligence Report*, p. i.

55. Central Intelligence Agency, *Intelligence Report*, pp. ii–iii.

56. Minnie Chan, 'Mongolian report blames Lin Biao plane crash on "pilot error"', *South China Morning Post*, 12 September 2016, available at http://www.scmp.com/news/china/article/2017978/mongolian-report-blames-lin-biao-plane-crash-pilot-error (accessed on 17 October 2016).

57. Central Intelligence Agency, *Research Study: Chinese-Indian Relations 1972–1975*, September 1975, Declassified on 29 June 2004.

58. Yuwu Song, *Biographical Dictionary of the People's Republic of China* (Jefferson, NC: McFarland, 2013), p. 62. For a more detailed account of the power struggle within the CCP at this time, see Roderick MacFarquhar, *The Politics of China: Sixty Years of The People's Republic of China* (Cambridge and New York: Cambridge University Press, 2011), pp. 275–98.

59. Byron and Pack, *The Claws of the Dragon*, p. 409.

60. Christine Quigley, *Modern Mummies: The Preservation of the Human Body in the Twentieth Century* (Jefferson, NC: McFarland, 1998), p. 41. Mao's body was embalmed after his death and placed in a mausoleum in Tiananmen Square.

61. 'The Third World Needs No Leader', Su Wenming (ed.), *China After Mao: A Collection of 80 Topical Essays by the Editors of Beijing Review* (Beijing: Beijing Review, 1984), p. 89. The article 'The Third World Needs No Leader' first appeared in *Beijing Review*, December 1982.

62. *Chairman Mao's Theory of the Differentiation of the Three Worlds is a Major Contribution to Marxism-Leninism* (Beijing: Foreign Languages Press, 1977), p. 53.

63. *Chairman Mao's Theory of the Differentiation of the Three Worlds is a Major Contribution to Marxism-Leninism*, p. 73.

64. 'Nathu La to open for Indo-China trade after 44 years', *The Economic Times*, 20 June 2006, available at http://articles.economictimes.indiatimes.com/2006-06-20/news/27445981_1_border-trade-trade-route-indo-china-trade (accessed on 15 October 2016).

65. Effective literacy rate in India in 2011 was 82.14 per cent for males and 65.46 for females (average 68.90 per cent), in Sikkim 87.29 per cent for males and 76.43 for females (average 82.20 per cent). See http://censusindia.gov.in/2011-prov-results/data_files/india/Final_PPT_2011_chapter6.pdf (accessed on 13 August 2017).

6

Gross National Happiness?

Bhutan, the last surviving Buddhist kingdom in the Himalayas, more than any other country in the world epitomizes the myth of Shangri-la. A small country with less than a million people, squeezed between the two most populous countries on Earth which are also regional rivals, Bhutan has managed to retain its distinctive cultural identity. Its landscape is breathtakingly spectacular, with ancient Buddhist monasteries scattered on the mountain tops, and, it was as a commitment to build a nation based on Buddhist spiritual values rather than crass materialism that King Jigme Singye Wangchuk coined the term Gross National Happiness (GNH) in the early 1970s. The country's national anthem, adopted in 1953, was written to sum up the spirit of a society that 'sprung from an aboriginal people and was enriched by Tibetan, Mongol, and Indo-Burman migrants'[1]:

> In the Thunder Dragon Kingdom adorned with sandalwood
> The protector who guards the teachings of the dual systems
> He, the precious glorious ruler, causes dominions to spread
> While his unchanging position abides in constancy
> As the doctrine of the Lord Buddha flourishes
> May the sun and peace and happiness shine on the people![2]

Buddhism has long been the state religion of Bhutan and the 'dual systems' refers to the combination and, until the early twentieth century, division, of civil as well as spiritual rule that throughout history has characterized the country's rather unique governance structure. But behind this romanticized and picturesque facade lies a turbulent past and a precarious present. Following several conflicts between Britain's colonial power in India and the Bhutanese, an agreement was reached in 1910 whereby Bhutan submitted 'to be guided by the advice of the British Government in regard to its external relations', while the British pledged 'to exercise no interference in the internal administration of Bhutan'.[3] On 8 August 1949, the governments of Bhutan and independent India entered into a similar agreement, which, in effect, reconfirmed Bhutan's status as a nation dependent on India but with a high degree of autonomy.[4]

But unlike Sikkim, Bhutan gradually managed to strengthen its independent status. In 1971, after being an observer for three years, Bhutan was admitted to the UN. And, in 2007, a revised treaty was signed, stating that 'the Government of the Kingdom of Bhutan and the Government of the Republic of India shall cooperate closely with each other on issues relating to their national interests. Neither government shall allow the use of its territory for activities harmful to the national security and interests of the other.'[5]

This special relationship between the two countries has made it possible for India to account for 75 per cent of Bhutan's total imports, while 85 per cent of its exports go to India. Bhutan's biggest export consists of hydropower from plants on rivers flowing down the Himalayas, and India is the sole importer. The Bhutanese currency, the Ngultrum, is tied to the Indian Rupee, with which it is on par. Strategically, Bhutan's border with China follows the crest of the mountains, which here and all along the Himalayan range separates the Indian subcontinent from the Tibetan plateau. The 1949 and 2007 treaties make no specific reference to India's defence of Bhutan but, as early as 1958, Prime Minister Jawaharlal Nehru declared that 'acts of aggression against Bhutan would be taken as acts of aggression against India itself'.[6] The Indian Army maintains a training mission, the Indian Military Training Team (IMTRAT) in Ha district, which is adjacent to the strategically important Chumbi Valley in Tibet, and Bhutanese army officers are sent for training at the National Defence Academy in Pune and the Indian Military Academy in Dehra Dun.

At the same time, Bhutan is the only neighbouring country with which China does not yet have diplomatic relations. But so as not to offend the Chinese, Bhutan remains one of the few Buddhist countries in the world that the Dalai Lama has not visited, although the population there practises a form of Buddhism similar to that of Tibet. Following the 1959 Lhasa uprising, 6,000 Tibetan refugees poured into Bhutan. They were allowed to stay on condition that they did not engage in any political activity. In 1981, the Tibetans were told to accept Bhutanese citizenship, or leave the country. Most of them left for India.

China has responded to Bhutan's delicate balancing act by deploying its new, post-Mao Zedong strategy in foreign affairs: soft diplomacy. In recent years, Chinese circus artistes, acrobats, and footballers have travelled to Bhutan and a limited number of Bhutanese students have received scholarships to study at universities in China. Tourism has also expanded. A decade ago, only 19 Chinese tourists visited Bhutan. In 2015, the figure was 9,399, or 19 per cent of the total.[7]

Not surprisingly, India is watching these developments with concern. In July 2014, Bhutan became the first international stop for Narendra Modi, two months after he became India's prime minister. Later that year, India's President Pranab Mukherjee visited Bhutan, underscoring the value that New Delhi places on its relations with the small but strategically located Himalayan kingdom. High on the agenda was discussion on China's attempts to gain a permanent presence in Bhutan. Diplomatically, the only contact between China and Bhutan are a series of talks to settle the border between the two countries. Today, China lays claim to two areas of Bhutan, a strip of territory adjacent to the Chumbi Valley and a large area in the north, while a 1961 map produced by Beijing showed larger areas of Bhutan as well as of Nepal and Sikkim as part of China. At one stage, China considered nearly 4,500 square kilometres of land on the northern and western regions of Bhutan to be disputed. In the 1930s, Mao openly declared that 'the correct boundaries of China' would include Bhutan, Myanmar, Nepal, Taiwan, Korea, and the Ryukyu Islands. But those remarks were later deleted from official records so as not to antagonize China's neighbours.[8]

Bhutan, high up in the Himalayas, may be considered an isolated kingdom, but its interaction with the outside world began as early as the seventh century when the Tibetan king Srongtsen Gampo converted to Buddhism and ordered the construction of two temples, one in Bumthang and the other in the Paro Valley. In the eighth century, the Buddhist sage Padmasambhava, who was also known as Guru Rimpoche and sometimes referred to as the Second Buddha, came to Bhutan from India at the invitation of one of the local kings who at that time ruled various parts of the country. Guru Rimpoche then travelled on into Tibet and, on his return to Bhutan, built new monasteries also in the Paro Valley and in Bumthang, where he set up his headquarters.

Guru Rimpoche is regarded as the founder of the Nyingmapa sect of the tantric Tibetan form of Mahayana Buddhism that spread throughout Bhutan in the eighth century. Nyingmapa is also known as the 'old sect' or the Red Hat sect.[9] But neither today's Bhutan nor Tibet had any properly organized central governments at that time. Local kings ruled different areas and were often at war with one another, and rival sects fought for spiritual supremacy over the subjects. Mongol warriors had also entered the scene and settled in some of the region's most fertile valleys, and, in Tibet, helped the first Dalai Lama gain political power.

By the fourteenth century, the power of the Mongol overlords began to decline, but, after a period of anarchy, the Gelugpa, or the Yellow Hat sect, which the Mongols supported, became the most powerful force in Tibet. As a result, monks of rival sects fled to eastern Tibet and headed south to Bhutan. Some of these monks built the first fortified monasteries, called *dzong*s, that still dot the Bhutanese landscape. Eventually, the practices of a subsect of the Red Hats called Drukpa became the dominant form of religious practice. The Drukpa school emerged as the most powerful force, especially in western Bhutan, and, as Bhutanese historian Karma Phuntsho writes, 'in later times came out victorious to become the ruling power and state religion'.[10]

But still, no reasonably centralized state structure existed until the Drukpa monk Ngawang Namgyel arrived in Bhutan in the early seventeenth century. He had fled the dominance, in Tibet, of the Yellow Hat sect, which was led by the fifth and most powerful Dalai Lama. Ngawang Namgyel assumed the title '*shabdrung*' (at whose feet one submits) and repelled repeated attempts by the Gelugpa rulers of Tibet to conquer his new realm. The most vivid account of the shabdrung's strong personality was compiled by a Jesuit priest from Portugal who met him in 1627. The priest, Estevao Cacella, was accompanied by another Jesuit, Joao Cabral, and these two Portuguese men were the first known Westerners to visit Bhutan. Cacella described the shabdrung as 'both King and highest lama in this kingdom'.[11]

Since the seventeenth century, the country has also been called Druk Yul, the land of the thunder dragon, to emphasize the Drukpa lineage. Bhutan, or 'Bootan', as it was spelled in the past, is most probably a derivative from the Indian term 'Bhutia' or 'Bhotay' in Nepali, which refers to peoples of Tibetan stock. But the Indo-Aryan term *bhot* could, in turn, be derived from the Tibetan word *bod*, which is what Tibet is called in Tibetan and Bhutanese dialects. The Tibetans call themselves *Bod-pa*, or inhabitant of Tibet.[12]

To strengthen his hold over his Thunder Dragon kingdom, the shabdrung built more and larger dzongs, which became centres of religious as well as secular power—the dual system of governance that is mentioned in modern Bhutan's national anthem and which is followed, at least in theory, even today. The colossal dzongs of Thimphu, Paro, and Punakha trace their origin to the time of the first shabdrung. According to the British historian and Tibetologist Michael Aris,

[e]very *dzong* was divided between an ecclesiastical wing occupied by state monks of the Drukpa school and a civil wing where the business of government was transacted and where the grain tax and other levies raised from the public could be deposited in storerooms[13] ... the effectiveness of his rule was demonstrated before his death by tribute missions from all over the country and by embassies from neighbouring Indian states, Nepal and several Tibetan principalities.[14]

The head of the civil, but still theocratic, government was a *druk desi* who was either a monk or a layman.

The succession of the shabdrung was supposed to be by reincarnation in the manner of Tibet's Dalai Lama. But when the first shabdrung died in 1651, his importance for the country was so great that his death was concealed for several years under the pretext that he was in a meditation retreat. And when his death became known, the search for a child into whose body he had been reborn began, with rival factions supporting at least five alternative reincarnations. The conflict was eventually settled when, in the 1730s, Bhutan was invaded by a military force from Tibet. According to Aris, this was 'the only successful invasion of Bhutan by Tibet... [but] the campaign was in fact brought to an end more by an appeal for peace issued by the leading Tibetan lamas of the day than by outright conquest.'[15]

The country was divided into two states and both sides appealed to the authorities in Lhasa for mediation. But they also had to submit their case to the Chinese emperor, who claimed sovereignty over Tibet. Emissaries from the two rival camps were sent to the Imperial Court in Beijing in 1734. Peace was achieved and the country was unified, but, as Aris points out, 'the submission to Chinese mediation entailed a theoretical loss of sovereignty'. At the same time, however, 'it led to the establishment of formal diplomatic relations with Tibet that helped to guarantee the fact of Bhutanese independence'.[16]

And it was not China but Britain that came to play an important role in the subsequent history of Bhutan. It began in the 1770s with the Bhutanese seizing control of the principality of Cooch Behar (now Koch Bihar) in the plains below the Himalayas. To rid the state of the invaders, the ruler of Cooch Behar appealed for help from the British East India Company. About 600 Bhutanese soldiers were killed in the first encounter on 22 December 1772 alone as British forces ousted them from the Cooch Behar fort.[17] Britain now replaced Tibet as the major external threat to Bhutan.

Boundary disputes continued to affect relations between the British and the Bhutanese. The British gained control over Assam after a war with the Myanmar kingdom in 1824–6, and proceeded to occupy the remaining Bhutanese-controlled areas in the plains. Several military encounters between British and Bhutanese forces came in the wake of colonial expansion into the Brahmaputra Valley. Bhutanese troops raided Cooch Behar and Sikkim in 1862, by which time the British Crown had taken over control of India from the East India Company. The British counterattacked, and, despite some battlefield victories for the Bhutanese, the conflicts ended with the Treaty of Sinchula, which was signed on 11 November 1865. Bhutan had to give up all claims to the Assam Duars, or foothills, in return for a subsidy of Rs 50,000. Article I of the Treaty also stated that '[t]here shall henceforth be perpetual peace and friendship between the British Government and the Government of Bhootan'.[18]

The loss of the plains dealt a severe blow to the Bhutanese economy and lead to civil strife within what remained of the country. While reincarnations of the shabdrung continued to be the spiritual head of Bhutan, the provinces were ruled by more worldly administrators who bore the title 'penlop' or 'pönlop'. The penlop of Tongsa was considered pro-British, while his counterpart in Paro was pro-Tibetan. Towards the end of the nineteenth century, Ugyen Wangchuk, the Tongsa penlop, emerged as the most powerful and managed to defeat his rivals after several civil wars and rebellions.

The British, naturally, welcomed this development, as peace on the Bhutanese border was not their only concern. According to a US government study, the British also wanted to offset potential Russian advances in Lhasa and open trade relations with Tibet. 'Ugyen Wangchuk saw the opportunity to assist the British and in 1903–4 volunteered to accompany a British mission to Lhasa as a mediator.'[19] That mission, of course, was Francis Younghusband's military expedition to Tibet, and for his services in securing the 1904 Anglo-Tibetan Convention, Ugyen Wangchuk was knighted by the British. The penlop of Tongsa became a knight commander of the Indian Empire at a ceremony at Punakha dzong in 1905 attended, apart from local dignitaries, by John Claude White, the political officer of Sikkim.

Ugyen Wangchuk emerged as the most powerful man in Bhutan. The penlop of Paro was removed and replaced by a relative, a member of the likewise pro-British Dorji family. The time had come for Bhutan to be a modern state, and when the then reincarnation of the shabdrung died in 1903 and a new one had not appeared by 1906, Ugyen Wangchuk assumed total control of the country. Although a new, nominal shabdrung was found, or rather two, one for his mind and the other for his body,[20] an assembly of leading monks, government officials, and heads of the country's most important clans and families elected Ugyen Wangchuk to the position of the first *druk gyalpo*, or Thunder Dragon King, of Bhutan. The fifty-seventh and last *druk desi*, or *deb raja* as he was also called, was forced to retire, and a hereditary, absolute monarchy succeeded the old theocracy. The Dorji family became hereditary holders of the position of *gongzim*, or chief chamberlain.[21]

This new system suited the British perfectly. Ugyen Wangchuk had visited Kolkata in 1906, where he met the prince of Wales. The two men met again in Delhi in 1911, when the prince had become King George V and Ugyen Wangchuk the king of Bhutan. This was a year after the signing of the new Anglo-Bhutanese Treaty, which had placed Bhutan's foreign relations under the control of the British Government of India while granting Bhutan internal autonomy.[22]

The 1910 treaty was signed and sealed by King Ugyen Wangchuk, Charles Alfred Bell, who was White's successor as political officer of Sikkim, and local Bhutanese administrators. Bell became political officer for Bhutan and Tibet as well, but continued to reside in Gangtok. Bhutan was left to manage its own internal affairs in a way Sikkim never was.

On the other hand, Britain was concerned about China, as its invading forces in Tibet were drawing close to the frontiers of India. In the 12 November 2016 issue of the *Economic and Political Weekly*, Pradip Phanjoubam wrote a lengthy critique of Neville Maxwell's version of events at the time. Maxwell had written in a previous article in the *Economic and Political Weekly* that a 'premortal, last-gasp expansionary impulse of the Manchu empire' in 1909–10 had driven 'its power closer to India's north-east'.[23] Phanjoubam retorted that not only did China overrun Tibet during that last-gasp impulse, but, 'it also began probing the neighbouring principalities, Nepal, Bhutan, Sikkim, and the un-administered region that the British considered its territory but lying beyond the Inner Line'.[24] The British were not worried about Nepal, which had a robust army, or Sikkim which had become a British protectorate, and not 'the un-administered areas in the north-east for it was unlikely China would covet these wild non-state, non-revenue hills'.[25] A couple of border stones south of Walong were the only signs of Chinese incursions into the northeastern areas.

The British were nevertheless 'extremely anxious about the possible fate of Bhutan', according to Phanjoubam, and hence the 1910 treaty, which formalized Bhutan's relations with British India and ensured that Bhutan would not undertake any foreign policy initiatives on its own. More importantly, the British wanted to pre-empt any attempt by the Chinese to expand their Tibetan conquest into Bhutan. But the collapse of the Imperial Manchu Dynasty during the 1911–12 revolution meant that it never happened. Tibet's role as a buffer between India and Bhutan on one side and China on the other was secured when the Chinese withdrew from the Tibetan highlands, and Lhasa could once again manage its own affairs.

The close relationship with India meant that the reign of the first druk gyalpo saw not only increased trade with the plains below the mountains but also the introduction of Western-style schools and improved internal communications. This development continued under his successor, his son Jigme Wangchuk, who became king in 1926. More schools, dispensaries, and roads were built. Monasteries and local governmental bodies were brought under central, royal control. But there was still a shabdrung, and he challenged, unsuccessfully, Jigme Wangchuk's accession to the throne.

In the spring of 1931, in a vain attempt to restore his powers, the then shabdrung, Jigme Dorji, sent his brother, Ckökyi Gyeltsen, with two servants to meet Mahatma Gandhi in Borsad in Gujarat, India. He was instructed to tell the Mahatma that Bhutan used to be ruled by the shabdrungs, but not anymore. Ckökyi Gyeltsen asked Gandhi for help. But, as Michael Aris points out, 'it is difficult to think of a person more unsuited to joining a plot of this kind than Gandhi'.[26] The shabdrung then began to make plans to go to Tibet and from there if necessary to China. According to Aris, '[t]he Panchen Lama Ckökyi Nyima was at that time expected by some to return from a long exile with the support of a strong contingent of Chinese troops, and the *Shabdrung* hoped now to obtain help in wresting power from the king'.[27]

The druk gyalpo found out about the plot and had the shabdrung detained at Talo monastery in Punakha, where he resided. Then, on 12 November 1931, the shabdrung died. Whether he was killed or committed suicide is unclear, but he was the last shabdrung to be recognized officially.

Since then there have been several claimants to the title of shabdrung, but they have all resided in India without any influence in Bhutan.

The first druk gyalpo had, before his death in 1926, sought and received British assurance that his family, the Wangchuks, would retain their prominent position in Bhutan. Thus, a royal lineage was established and the second druk gyalpo, Jigme Wangchuk, reigned unopposed until his death in 1952. He oversaw the transition of Bhutan's relationship with the British colonial power to the new agreement with independent India and personally ratified the 8 August 1949 Treaty of Perpetual Peace and Friendship between the Government of India and the Government of Bhutan. Indians made the same pledges as the British before them—to oversee Bhutan's foreign policy but leave internal governance to the Bhutanese—but some historians now believe that if India had been involved in a conflict with China at that time, as it was a decade later, it might not have agreed so easily to Bhutan's request for continuation of self-determination in its internal affairs.[28]

The third druk gyalpo, Jigme Dorje Wangchuk, was enthroned in 1952 and reigned until his death in 1972, some of the most tumultuous years in Bhutan's modern history. After it invaded Tibet in 1951, China was now a neighbour, and, as a consequence, Bhutan's relations with India grew even stronger. Jigme Dorje Wangchuk encouraged Indian investment in small-scale industry and agriculture, as it became more urgent than previously to speed up the modernization of Bhutan in order to counter Chinese encroachment into Tibet's border regions.

Slavery and serfdom were abolished and the third druk gyalpo also implemented a land reform to ensure more equal distribution of wealth. A 130-member National Assembly was established in 1953 and, in 1958, the position of gongzim, held by the Dorji family, was upgraded to that of *lonchen* (prime minister). The first steps towards a constitutional monarchy had been taken. Communications were also improved to break Bhutan's isolation from the outside world. Funded by India, a road was built in 1962 connecting Phuntsholing on the Indian border with the capital Thimphu. Until then, communications with India had been carried out on the back of yaks and mules. That was how Jawaharlal Nehru, accompanied by his daughter Indira, travelled into Bhutan during their visit to the country in 1958.

Bhutan nevertheless managed to maintain reasonably amiable relations with China—until the Chinese suppression of the 1959 Tibetan uprising. At the same time, enclaves in Tibet over which Bhutan had long exercised quasi-sovereignty, were taken over by the Chinese.[29] Then came the influx of 6,000 Tibetan refugees and the subsequent deterioration of relations between India and China. Bhutan closed its border with Tibet.

During the 1962 war with India, China stated that its troops would not enter Bhutan so long as it 'maintained its neutrality'.[30] Although some Indian troops did retreat from the Tawang area through Bhutanese territory, the Chinese refrained from crossing the border with Bhutan. Were that to happen, the tiny Bhutanese army would not have been able to repel any Chinese attacks, making it imperative for India to help Bhutan strengthen its armed forces and upgrade the roads from the lowlands to the interior.

Despite the progress it had made, Bhutan was still an almost medieval society with little contact with the outside world, except for India. But education came with development and many young Bhutanese attended school in India, primarily in the hill stations of Darjeeling and Kalimpong, but also at the prestigious Doon School in Dehra Dun. One of them was Jigme Palden Dorji of the Dorji family. His younger sister, Ashi Kesang, was married to the third druk gyalpo, Jigme Dorje Wangchuk. So, he was also considered a member of the ruling Wangchuk family.

Jigme Palden Dorji was appointed gongzim in 1952 and, when the title of lonchen was introduced six years later, he became the first to hold that title. He served as prime minister during the 1962 conflict with China and, according to his close friend Nari Rustomji, his most anxious concern at that time was that the Chinese would abduct the latest reincarnation of the shabdrung, then a boy of six residing in a monastery in the Tawang area of NEFA and use him as a puppet to challenge the authority of the druk gyalpo of Bhutan. Jigme Palden Dorji, remaining loyal to the king, told Rustomji that 'the institution of Dharma Raja [shabdrung] as dead as the dodo … and if any young lad was luckless enough to be identified as a potential Dharma Raja, the Bhutanese were adept in fixing an "accident" to hurry him to his Nirvana'.[31]

Rustomji, who was then adviser to the NEFA governor, received urgent appeals from Jigme Palden Dorji to locate the young shabdrung. He was found and brought to Shillong before the Chinese occupied Tawang. The boy was then sent to the Tibetan settlement in McLeodganj to study, where he would be safe under the tutelage of the Dalai Lama. It was never clear whether Jigme Palden Dorji's fears about a Chinese abduction of the shabdrung were real or just something he suspected, and therefore wanted to take precautionary measures against.

In Bhutan, Jigme Palden Dorji was determined to modernize the country, something which the third druk gyalpo was not necessarily opposed to. But he managed to antagonize elements within the clergy by attempting to reduce the power of state-supported religious institutions. As the druk gyalpo grew older, frictions between him and his dynamic prime minister became evident. Jigme Palden Dorji also made enemies within the military over the use of some military vehicles and the forced retirement of about 50 army officers.

All those who opposed modernization, especially the traditionalists, saw an opportunity in the growing conflict between the druk gyalpo and the Dorjis. On 5 April 1964, while the druk gyalpo was undergoing medical treatment in Switzerland, Jigme Palden Dorji was assassinated at Phuntsholing by an army corporal. The country was plunged into its most serious political crisis since the establishment of hereditary monarchy in 1907.

The druk gyalpo was rushed home from Switzerland, and with Indian prompting, the plotters were arrested and tried for treason. Some of them were executed, including the chief of army operations, Namgyal Bahadur, who happened to be the druk gyalpo's uncle. Others who had taken part in the plot escaped to Nepal. But that was not the end of the turmoil or the perceived power struggle between pro-Wangchuk loyalists and 'modernist' Dorji supporters. And the main issue may not have been an end to or lessening of the power of the monarchy but 'full freedom from Indian interference'.[32] Whatever the case, Jigme Palden Dorji's successor as prime minister, his brother Lhendup Dorji, was exiled along with members of his family in 1965. The druk gyalpo himself became prime minister and replaced the Dorji allies with more conservative men. His half-brother, Dasho Wangchuk, was made army commander to ensure the loyalty of the military. But the crisis was not over and in July 1965 there was an assassination attempt against the druk gyalpo himself. The Dorji camp was not implicated in the plot, and the would-be assassins were even pardoned by the druk gyalpo.

Even if some Bhutanese may have been dissatisfied with the heavy dependence on India, there was no way Bhutan could go its own way given the country's strategic importance to the Indians, especially after the 1962 War. In fact, in the words of a now declassified CIA report, 'the period after Jigme's assassination offered enhanced opportunities for the expansion of Indian influence'.[33] The same report states that 'India [now] provides Bhutan with military and intelligence training which is specifically aimed at countering Chinese subversion[34]...the Chinese...have some means of exploiting Bhutanese religious differences, particularly through the use of friendly Tibetans'.[35]

Efforts were also stepped up to develop Bhutan's economy and to strengthen the role of the monarchy as the pillar of the nation state. During the reign of the third druk gyalpo, Dzongkha, a dialect related to Tibetan, became the official language and Thimphu was made the sole, year-round capital. Punakha had, until 1955, served as the capital and after that as winter capital, while Thimphu, higher up in the mountains, was the summer capital. With the administration centred in Thimphu, the efficiency of the government could be improved.

Bhutan's leaders were also more astute in handling their relations with India than the controversial royal couple in Gangtok. Like Sikkim, Bhutan sought more direct, international links, but did so more discreetly and without antagonizing India. Without much ado, already in 1962, Bhutan joined the Plan for Cooperative, Economic, and Social Development in Asia and the Pacific, better known as the Colombo Plan. In 1966, the government in Thimphu notified India of its desire to become a member of the UN and, when that was granted in 1971, it was a major foreign policy breakthrough for Bhutan.

The third druk gyalpo, Jigme Dorji Wangchuk, who is seen as the father of modern Bhutan, died on 21 July 1972 while receiving medical treatment in Nairobi, Kenya. He was only 43, but had had a series of health problems and suffered several heart attacks before his death. The first druk gyalpo had adopted a unique symbol of his royal authority: a crown surmounted by the head of a raven, which represented the raven-headed Mahakala, Bhutan's guardian deity.[36] The Raven Crown was now passed on to Jigme Dorji Wangchuk's only son, Jigme Singye Wangchuk, who, on 24 July, became the fourth druk gyalpo. He was only a few months shy of 17 when he became the head of what was then still an absolute monarchy. But the young druk gyalpo was very well educated and more accustomed to the modernities of the outside world than any of his predecessors. After attending St. Joseph's College in Darjeeling, he continued his studies at the Heatherdown Preparatory School in England where, Prince Andrew, Prince Edward, and Britain's future Prime Minister David Cameron studied after him, and, later, at the Ugyen Wangchuk Academy in Paro.

The reign of the fourth druk gyalpo, which lasted until he abdicated in favour of his son Jigme Khesar Namgyel Wangchuk in January 2006, saw rapid economic and social development based on the export of hydro-electric power to India, high-end tourism, and cottage industry. This has enabled Bhutan's government to provide its citizens with free education and health care. A new middle class has emerged and even though farmers remain poor, they are, by and large, self-sufficient and there is no outright misery in the countryside.

The fourth druk gyalpo also introduced a form of democracy and negotiated the 2007 agreement with India, which established Bhutan as a truly independent nation. But it was also a time when relations with Nepal deteriorated over the expulsion of ethnic Nepalese in the early 1990s, when Indian anger grew at the presence of insurgents from northeastern India who trained at camps in southern Bhutan, and when China began to show renewed interest in the Himalayan kingdom.

In the outside world, however, the fourth druk gyalpo became best known for promoting his entirely new development concept, the GNH instead of the Gross National Product (GNP). Along with the GNH came a vigorous campaign to strengthen national identity. Known as *driglam namzha*, it sought to promote the national language, Dzongkha, and citizens of both sexes were instructed to wear Bhutanese national dress rather than western-style clothing.

This was not an easy task, given the fact that Bhutan is actually ethnically very diverse for such a small, sparsely populated country. In broad terms, the population consists of four major ethnic groups, which in turn are made up of several subgroups. The Ngalops are people who migrated to Bhutan as early as the ninth century. The name means 'earliest risen' or 'first converted' and they are related to the Tibetans, embraced Buddhism at early stage in history, and speak Dzongkha as their mother tongue. The Ngalops live in western and northern Bhutan and are the dominant political and cultural group in modern Bhutan.[37]

The Sharchops ('easterners') live mostly, as the name implies, in eastern Bhutan and are of mixed Tibetan and South Asian descent. They are believed to have migrated into Bhutan from Assam or possibly northern Myanmar over the centuries. Because of their proximity to Assam, many of them speak Assamese or even Hindi, apart from their own Tshangla, which, like Dzongkha, is a Tibeto-Burman language. The Sharchops are closely related to the Monpa of the Tawang area across the border in India. Although the Sharchops comprise the biggest single ethnic group in the country, they have become assimilated into the Tibetan-Ngalop culture.

Then there are aboriginal tribal groups living in scattered villages throughout Bhutan. They are mostly Hindu and related to tribal groups in Assam. Some of these groups are considered the most indigenous of Bhutan's various ethnic groups, while others are descendants of slaves who were brought to the country from similar tribal areas in India.

The fourth group consists of people of Nepalese origin. They are called Lhotshampas, meaning 'southerners', and most of them migrated to Bhutan from Nepal and the Darjeeling area in the early twentieth century. They were brought in to cultivate the tiny, and, until then, largely uninhabited, strip of lowland running from east to west between the mountains and the Indian border. Nepalese migrants turned the once inhospitable and malaria-infested jungles of southern Bhutan into a thriving agricultural region of rice fields, vegetable gardens, orange orchards, and cardamom groves. The highlands were supplied with food, and the government could levy badly needed taxes on the industrious migrants. The Lhotshampas are mostly Hindu, and speak Nepali, an Indo-Aryan language, and are quite easily distinguishable from the rest of the population by their South Asian looks. The Lhotshampas, however, did not fit into the new nation that the fourth druk gyalpo was going to build. Many Bhutanese remembered the fate of neighbouring Sikkim, where Nepalese migrants came to outnumber the indigenous Bhutias and Lepchas, and which eventually lost whatever independence it had once had.

The issue was actually not new. As early as 1942, the then British political officer for Sikkim, Bhutan, and Tibet, Sir Basil Gould, had warned the Bhutanese about the potential danger of immigrants taking over the country. The Bhutanese replied that since the settlers were not registered as subjects they would be evicted 'if need arose'.[38] In 1952, a party was formed by Lhotshampas who had left Bhutan and settled in West Bengal and Assam. It was called the Bhutan State Congress (BSC) and advocated the creation of a 'Greater Nepal' encompassing Nepal, Sikkim, northern West Bengal, and Bhutan. Two years later, they made an effort to expand their activities into Bhutan with a satyagraha (an Indian-style nonviolent resistance) in the Bhutanese village of Sarbhang. But few Lhotshampas joined in because they did not want to jeopardize their already tenuous citizenship status. The potential threat that the BSC could pose was neutralized by granting concessions to the Lhotshampas such as representation in the National Assembly.

Bhutan also introduced a Citizenship Act in 1958 to tackle the problem. Amnesty was given to all those who could prove that they had lived in Bhutan for at least 10 years prior to the enactment of the new regulations. Further immigration was also banned, but that became a problem when the highway from Phuntsholing to Thimphu was built in the early 1960s. Bhutan wanted to use a local workforce, while India saw that as impracticable because the country lacked the capacity to supply workers willing to take part in such projects. Unskilled labourers from India, most of them ethnic Nepalese, were brought in and, when the work was over, many of them decided to settle in villages inhabited by their kinsmen in the south.

But the extent of illegal immigration in the south did not become evident until the authorities conducted a nationwide census in 1988. The thought was to enforce the new Citizenship Act, enacted in 1985 and meant to clarify the 1958 Act by stating that only immigrants whose families had settled in Bhutan before 1958 were entitled to citizenship. The operation turned out to be a disaster. First, it was conducted thoroughly only in the south. Secondly, it was discovered that there were many more illegal immigrants than expected all over the southern districts.

The problem was especially evident in the Samtse (previously Samchi) district in southwestern Bhutan, which can be reached by car only from India, as most Bhutanese roads lead from the border with India in south to the Bhutanese interior in the north, with only one major east–west highway through the country. Further, Samtse is adjacent to Kalimpong, one of the worst hit areas of the 1986–8 agitation, which sometimes took a violent turn, for the establishment of an autonomous Nepalese region in northern India to be called Gorkhaland. Not surprisingly, the census showed that the population of Samtse had doubled during the 1980s. According to a brochure published by the Bhutanese government: 'The recently completed cadastral survey of Samchi [Samtse] district [also] revealed that the total illegal landholdings there was 47,235 acres, which is more than the total landholdings in Tashigang, the country's largest district.'[39]

The exact number of ethnic Nepalese residing legally and illegally in the country in the late 1980s is not known, but it could have been as many as 30–40 per cent of the population, then stated at 1.37 million. The response was a campaign to drive out all 'illegal immigrants'. Along with Dzongkha and English, Nepali used to be one of the three official languages of Bhutan taught in the country's schools. But in 1989, Nepali was dropped from school curricula, and ceased to be an official language.

Some Lhotshampas responded in 1990 by forming the Bhutan People's Party (BPP), which resisted the driglam namzha policies and said it was fighting for the rights of the people of the south. The BPP accused the government of arresting, torturing, and murdering many Lhotshampas suspected of indulging in anti-royal activities. In turn, the Bhutanese authorities alleged that the BPP's armed units—and it had some—had burned schools, bombed bridges, and assassinated village headmen and police officers. Between September 1990 and September 1991, more than 2,000 pieces of firearms as well as hand grenades, land mines, and gelatine explosives were seized from rebels in the south.[40]

Regardless of which side was right, the violence led to an exodus of ethnic Nepalese from Bhutan. As many as 100,000 fled. However, India, the only country, apart from China, that shares a border with Bhutan, did not want them: relations with the government of the strategically important Bhutan were more important than concern over the plight of the Lhotshampas. The refugees continued flow into Nepal, where they were housed in a string of refugee camps in Jhapa and Morang near the Indian border in the south. There, some of the Lhotshampas became involved with politicians from Nepal's various communist parties, among them the Maoists. In the early 1970s, Jhapa had been the scene of a Maoist-led uprising similar to that in Naxalbari across the border in India. Inspired by their Nepalese comrades, some Lhotshampas even set up their own Maoist party.

Needless to say, such activities made it impossible for Bhutan to accept what Nepal and many western countries demanded: the right of the Lhotshampas to return to the homes they had left behind. Nor could the Indians ignore the warning signs from the camps in southern Nepal. The CIA had stated as early as 1965 that the separatist activities by the Lhotshampas could create a situation

> capable of exploitation by the Chinese, even though they have no direct access to the *duars* [foothills] which are geographically contiguous to India. One access could be through Sikkim, where China is rumoured to have agents. There are also about 1,000 Communist Party of India members—most of them Chinese-oriented—in the Darjeeling district of West Bengal who could also be used to infiltrate the *duars* and to encourage subversion.[41]

There was no way back for the Lhotshampa refugees, and, despite several rounds of talks between Bhutan and Nepal, they were destined to remain in their squalid camps in Jhapa and Morang for many years to come. In Bhutan, those Lhotshampas who remained became careful not to engage in any anti-government activities. They knew the response would be expulsion from the kingdom.

No sooner had the refugee crisis died down than Bhutan was hit by another problem involving its neighbours. In the early 1980s, a student-led popular movement against illegal immigrants, primarily from Bangladesh, swept across Assam. While the movement's more moderate elements ended up forming a political party to contest state elections, some went underground and resorted to armed struggle for an independent Assam. The United Liberation Front of Asom [Assam] (ULFA), whose ideology was a mixture of Assamese nationalism and left-wing theories, during its heyday in the mid- and late 1980s, had base camps in various parts of Assam as well as a smaller presence across the border in Myanmar, where it co-operated with Naga and Manipuri insurgents who had established strongholds there, beyond the reach of the Indian Army.

Successive Indian Army operations in Assam in the early 1990s, among them Operation Rhino and Operation Bajrang, forced ULFA's armed cadre out of the state. New bases were established in Bangladesh and in southern Bhutan. ULFA shared some of the camps with three other groups of militants from India's northeast: the National Democratic Front of Bodoland and the Bodo Liberation Tigers Force, which were active among the Bodo plain tribals of Assam, and the Kamtapur Liberation Organisation which wanted to carve out a state called Kamtapur comprising areas of northern West Bengal and western Assam or the sensitive 'Siliguri Neck' between Nepal, Bhutan, and Bangladesh.[42] With camps and sanctuaries in Bhutan and Bangladesh, the insurgents had positioned themselves on both sides of 'the neck', posing a powerful threat to India's national security.

Some observers believe that the Bhutanese government 'invited' the militants from India's northeast to help them 'drive out' the Lhotshampas.[43] But there is little evidence to support this allegation. The insurgents actually moved into Bhutan after most of the Lhotshampas had left. The camps were also established in remote, forested areas in the hills above the southern plains where the Lhotshampas lived. A more plausible explanation is that Bhutan lacked the means to drive them out. And some of the tribal people living in the areas where the camps were located were related to those across the border in Assam, which made for a friendly environment for the insurgents.

Naturally, Bhutan came under pressure from India to take action against the intruders. The Bhutanese government tried, on several occasions, to resolve the problem through negotiations with the leaders of the insurgents. When that failed, only the military option remained. The Royal Bhutan Army, which has been trained and to a great extent also equipped by India, moved into action in December 2003. The operation, codenamed 'All Clear', was the Bhutanese army's first engagement in a major military campaign—and it turned out to be successful. Bhutanese troops seized ULFA's headquarters at Phukatong in Samdrup Jongkhar district on 15 December. The following day, 10 camps were destroyed and scores of insurgents were killed. The Indian Army did not participate directly in the operation, but deployed 12 battalions along the border with Bhutan to prevent the rebels from fleeing south. Indian helicopters also helped evacuate wounded Bhutanese soldiers, and, by the end of December, no insurgents from India's northeast remained in Bhutan.[44]

When Operation All Clear, which in Bhutan is also referred to as 'Operation Flush Out', was over, the Bhutanese had seized large quantities of assault rifles, rocket launchers, and mortars, communication equipment, and thousands of rounds of ammunition. Most of the equipment was made in China, obtained on what is euphemistically called the 'Chinese black arms market', and smuggled from ports in Bangladesh to Bhutan. The camps in Bhutan were lost, but ULFA and some other insurgent groups still had a presence in Bangladesh, which at that time was ruled by the anti-Indian Bangladesh Nationalist Party (BNP).

A further blow to ULFA came only four months after the loss of its sanctuaries in Bhutan, this time in Bangladesh. ULFA had placed a major order of weapons from its contacts in China, but it was seized when the ship carrying the lethal cargo arrived at port in Chittagong on 2 April. The shipment originated in Hong Kong and, at that point, involved only Chinese weaponry. From Hong Kong, the ship sailed on to Singapore, where more weapons of Israeli and US manufacture were added. According to the well-respected defence journal *Jane's Intelligence Review*: 'The shipment was then transported north through the Strait of Malacca to be transhipped in the Bay of Bengal to two trawlers, the *Kazaddan* and *Amanat*, which ferried the weapons to a jetty on the Karnaphuli river, Chittagong.'[45] The shipment included automatic and semi-automatic rifles, Kalashnikov-type assault rifles, rocket-propelled grenade-launchers, hand grenades, and a large quantity of all kinds of ammunition. The total value of the shipment was estimated at between US$ 4.5 and 7 million.[46]

It has never been made clear why the shipment was intercepted, but *Jane's Intelligence Review* speculated that, 'following a tip-off—understood to have probably come from Indian intelligence sources—the off-loading of the weapons was interrupted in the early hours of April 2 by the Chittagong Port Police and Bangladesh Rifles. Nine truckloads of munitions were seized, although it is believed that one loaded truck had left the jetty before the arrival of the port police.'[47] There is no question as to who the guns were destined to: the ULFA and the Bodo as well as Naga insurgents in India's northeast.

The new, commercially oriented China may not be interested in export-ing revolution to the rest of the world, but the arms trade is a lucrative busi-ness, and, as long as there are buyers, well-connected Chinese 'private arms dealers' are willing to sell. While the weapons actually come from Chinese arms manufacturers such as the state-owned North Industries Corporation (NORINCO), deals can be made through front companies in China or, more conveniently, Hong Kong, with its freewheeling economy and well-established financial institutions. Brokers in Thailand's capital, Bangkok, have also been identified as conduits for weapons from several countries, among them China.

ULFA was in serious trouble, and more was to come. The next setback was in November 2009, when Bangladesh's new government led by the Awami League, which, unlike its predecessor the BNP had no interest in supporting the Indian rebels, had ULFA chairman Arabinda Rajkhowa and its deputy commander-in-chief Raju Baruah arrested along with eight other Assamese militants. They were later handed over to India. In September 2010, Rajkumar Meghen, better known as Sana Yaima, leader of Manipur's United National Liberation Front, was arrested in Dhaka and bundled off to India. At about the same time, the main arms procurer of the Naga rebels and a frequent visitor to China, Thailand-based Anthony Shimray, was arrested at Kathmandu airport in Nepal and ended up in Indian custody.[48]

The loss of Bhutan and Bangladesh as sanctuaries has left northwestern Myanmar as the only remaining haven for India's northeastern rebels. ULFA and its Naga and Manipuri allies maintain several camps in the mountains north and northwest of Singkaling Hkamti in Myanmar's Sagaing Region. The main camp is at Taka on a western tributary of the River Chindwin, and some weapons from China are still reaching those bases, usually smuggled from Yunnan down to Mandalay and Monywa in central Myanmar, and from there to the Indian border. It is uncertain, however, whether China's security services are directly involved in this traffic, or if the weapons have been obtained on the Chinese black market. In any case, this has always been a grey area. When he is not paying occasional visits to Taka, ULFA commander-in-chief Paresh Baruah is based in Yunnan.

Baruah's presence in Yunnan and involvement with the 2004 Chittagong shipment, which although done through 'private arms dealers', was of such a quantity that it would have been impossible to conduct without at least the tacit approval of influential people, show that China's security services have not severed links with insurgents of northeastern India, and the relationship clearly goes beyond commercial deals. As long as the Dalai Lama and his Tibetan government in exile are based in India, China is not likely to give up those connections, which could be used simply to annoy India or, more specifically, for maintaining leverage inside India for purposes such as influencing border talks and other bilateral issues.

Bhutan is only a small pawn in this game, but not an unimportant one for China. While Mao Zedong once held that Bhutan should be part of China, Beijing settled for a different approach after Bhutan had joined the UN in 1971. The CIA analysed China's renewed interest in a 1975 report on Chinese-Indian relations. 'Not only was it meant to explore the possibility of increasing Bhutanese restlessness under Indian tutelage, but also to demonstrate, albeit in a low-key way, China's interest in preserving the status of Bhutan as a buffer between China and India.'[49]

Bhutan, along with India, voted in favour of the People's Republic of China taking over the China seat from the Republic of China in the UN in 1971. With Thimphu and Beijing both now having representatives at the UN headquarters in New York, direct contact between the two countries could begin. And the first major event that brought China into the equation with Bhutan was the coronation of Jigme Singye Wangchuk. Although he had been king since 1972, the coronation had to wait for an auspicious date chosen by astrologers. On 2 June 1974, the Raven Crown was bestowed upon the fourth druk gyalpo at a ceremony attended, among other dignitaries, by Ma Muming, chargé d'affaires at the Chinese embassy in New Delhi. Ma's visit was described by China's official news agency Xinhua as 'a new page in the friendly contacts between the two countries'.[50] The Chinese congratulatory message emphasized the 'desire of the Bhutanese government in developing its economy and safeguarding national independence'.[51]

The CIA concluded that 'the Bhutanese, in no position to alienate their big Indian brother, played down their new Chinese connection very lightly. The Indians, while disgruntled at the Bhutanese invitation to the Chinese, apparently believed that their hold on the small mountain kingdom— which includes responsibility for defence—was secure enough to let the incident pass.'[52]

In 1983, Chinese Foreign Minister Wu Xueqian and his Bhutanese counterpart Lyonpo Dawa Tsering met at the UN headquarters in New York for the first time. In April the following year, the first round of border talks between China and Bhutan was held in Beijing. The Chinese delegation was led by Vice-Foreign-Minister Gong Dafet and the Bhutanese by their ambassador to India, Dasho Om Pradhan. The two sides signed a joint communiqué on 20 April, 'expressing satisfaction with the first round of talks'.[53]

Since then, altogether 24 such talks have been held, but progress has been slow. China still claims parts of Bhutan and, in the 1990s, was carrying out road construction projects and logging in the disputed areas. Bhutan protested, but in December 1998, Bhutan and China signed an Agreement on Maintenance of Peace and Tranquillity in Bhutan-China Border Areas, which stated that China reaffirms that 'it completely respects the independence, sovereignty and territorial integrity of Bhutan'.[54]

The Chinese position on the border with Bhutan could be seen as an inadvertent recognition of the McMahon Line, as Bhutan is located south of the watershed at the crest of the Himalayas. But since the Sino-Bhutanese border has not been properly demarcated, the Chinese can always claim that the issue has not yet been settled. More importantly, one inconclusive round of border talks after another serves China's interest of improving its relations with Bhutan, which inevitably would be at India's expense. After the twenty-fourth round of talks in August 2016, the Chinese foreign ministry issued a statement saying that, 'although Bhutan and China have not established diplomatic relations yet, it will not hold back the mutually beneficial cooperation between the two countries. The Bhutanese side is willing to continue to deepen exchanges in such fields as tourism, religion, culture and agriculture to further lift cooperation with China.'[55]

China must also have been pleased with the Bhutanese decision not to allow the Dalai Lama into their country, though they did not do this to appease the Chinese. It has to be remembered that although both Bhutan and Tibet practise a similar form of Buddhism, the people of the two countries belong to different, and in many senses rival, schools of the Mahayana version of the religion. Most Tibetans who accepted Bhutanese citizenship did not pose any challenge to the established religious and political order, but a plot to assassinate the fourth druk gyalpo and burn down the Tashichhodzong in Thimphu was revealed in June 1974. It allegedly involved a number of Tibetan refugees and a Tibetan in Darjeeling.[56] Although there is nothing to implicate the Dalai Lama in the conspiracy, the plotters belonged to the Gelugpa sect and were therefore more loyal to him than to the Bhutanese monarch. While some of the conspirators managed to escape to India, about two dozen people were arrested and later pardoned. Whatever reasons were behind the plot, it underscores the fact that that the Bhutanese and the Tibetans are not natural allies against China.

As China's soft diplomacy continues, New Delhi remains concerned, but during the reign of the fourth druk gyalpo, Bhutan has regained its internal stability and also widened its areas of diplomatic contact to include smaller and medium-sized countries so as not to upset its relations with India. Apart from India, only Bangladesh and Kuwait have full diplomatic representation in Thimphu, but close ties have been established with countries such as Switzerland, Denmark, and Sweden. There is also a Bhutanese embassy in Bangkok, a favourite destination for many Bhutanese who want to send their children to be educated, or shop.

The Dorjis and the Wangchuks appear to have reconciled their differences, and even the descendants of the shabdrung have been included in the new order. At a mass ceremony on 31 October 1988, the fourth druk gyalpo wedded four sisters aged between 23 and 28, nine years after he had married them in private. The young women were daughters of Yab Ugyen Dorji, a descendant of both the mind and speech incarnations of the first shabdrung, Ngawang Namgyal. Yab Ugyen Dorji is the nephew of Jigme Dorji, who died under mysterious circumstances in 1931.

The official version of the fourth druk gyalpo's marriage was that it had been prophesied to him that he would marry four sisters, descendants of the first shabdrung, and he went through with it to go along with the prophecy. A more plausible explanation is that it was meant to neutralize any followers the shabdrung might still have. By marrying all four sisters, any kind of palace intrigues where one faction could use one daughter against another were also thwarted.

In a surprisingly candid book about the life of her father, one of the four queens, Ashi Dorji Wangmo Wangchuk, describes in detail how Jigme Dorji, her granduncle was, in fact, murdered. Three men entered his bedchamber, where 'they pinned him down, grabbed his throat and kicked him in the scrotum. Shabdrung struggled till the silken scarf stuffed down his throat suffocated him.'[57] Such a revelation would have been unthinkable only a generation ago, but Bhutan today is a different country from the medieval kingdom it used to be. It has entered the modern world with high educational standards, good roads that criss-cross the country; and, in June 1999 television and the internet were introduced to reflect 'the level of progress Bhutan has achieved in recent years', as the fourth druk gyalpo said at the time.[58] The launch coincided with the silver jubilee of his coronation, emphasizing the strong position that the monarchy has retained throughout all the economic and social changes the country has undergone over the last few decades.

A new constitution was presented in 2005, paving the way for elections and a more democratic system. Bhutan was about to become a constitutional monarchy with the monarch remaining an influential figure and, as Article 2 of the constitution states, the 'symbol of unity of the Kingdom and of the people of Bhutan'.[59] At this time, the fourth druk gyalpo announced that he was going to abdicate in favour of his eldest son, Jigme Khesar Namgyel Wangchuk, whose mother was the second youngest of the four sisters. On 9 December 2006, he succeeded his father and, on November 2008, the coronation of the fifth druk gyalpo took place at a colourful ceremony at Thimphu's Tashichhodzong. The new monarch had received his education in the United States, Britain, and India. Born in 1980, he belongs to a new generation of Bhutanese to whom the medieval past is distant history.

Yet, some of the old issues remain. The Lhotshampas who have remained in the country seem to have adapted to the new order so as not to jeopardize their citizenship status, and few remain in the camps in Nepal, as foreign countries have accepted them for resettlement. The United States has taken most of them—and, hardly by coincidence, after the 11 September 2001 terrorist attacks in New York and Washington. The US has laws requiring it to take between 60,000 and 70,000 refugees per year, but for several years after '9/11' that quota was never filled. The US had to look for 'suitable refugee populations', as a US government official said in a private conversation, which meant, not Muslim.[60] The choice fell on the Karen refugees from Myanmar in camps in Thailand, who are mostly Christian and Hindu Lhotshampas of Nepalese origin from Bhutan. This was never an official policy, but the fact that more than 80,000 Bhutanese Nepalese have been resettled in the US lends credence to the assumption that the choice was based on a desire to keep Muslim immigration to the US at minimum levels.

But other illegal immigration remains a problem. The English-language newspaper *Kuensel* reported on 10 June 2016, 'The rising number of illegal immigrants is a huge concern and rising threat to the safety and security of the country according to the National Council's legislative committee's report on illegal immigration presented to the house today'.[61] The 'illegal immigrants' are mostly Indian women working as housemaids in border towns and construction workers from India, some employed by IMTRAT (Indian Military Training Team) and DANTAK, the entity under India's Border Roads Organisation, which builds roads in Bhutan.

Thus, Bhutan's relationship with India is not without problems. While Bhutan is worried about illegal immigration, India sees China's charm offensive as the main concern, especially as the new, 2007, treaty between India and Bhutan gives the latter more independence than before. But India is not likely to act unless Chinese influence goes beyond what it sees as acceptable levels—and that did happen when, in June 2017, Chinese troops with earthmoving equipment entered the Doklam Plateau, an area claimed by both Bhutan and China near the Sikkim-Tibet-Bhutan border junction. The Chinese were going to build roads across Doklam, which they call Donglang and claim as theirs, but, inevitably, the move into this sensitive border area was perceived by India as a clear provocation. On 18 June, Indian troops entered the disputed area to prevent the road construction and, two days later, the government of Bhutan issued a formal diplomatic démarche to Beijing via the Chinese embassy in New Delhi, protesting China's incursion.

On 29 June, Bhutan protested again to the Chinese government, which on the same day released a map depicting the plateau as part of China. As evidence to support their claim, the Chinese referred to a border treaty signed by the Chinese and the British in 1890, which they claimed had been recognized by Jawaharlal Nehru. But that treaty defined only the northern part of the Sikkim-Tibet border, not the Sikkim-Tibet-Bhutan tri-border junction.[62] Meanwhile, India moved troops into Sikkim to strengthen its defences in the general border area. The stand-off heightened tensions along the border to a level not seen since the 1962 War.

Manu Balachandaran and Harish C. Menon, two Indian writers, wrote in an article on the website *Quartz India* that the issue was more than just a localized border dispute. 'China is testing the India-Bhutan relationship', they argued. 'If and when India falters, China will be waiting with open arms to take Bhutan into its fold, especially since the tiny country is now pursuing an independent foreign policy after decades of outsourcing it to India.'[63]

Bhutan was caught in a dilemma. On the one hand, relations with India are crucial for the country's economy, foreign trade, and defence, but, on the other, Thimphu cannot afford to antagonize its powerful northern neighbour. On 1 August, Bhutan's ambassador to India, Vetsop Namgyel, surprised the diplomatic community in New Delhi by attending a function at the Chinese embassy in the Indian capital to mark the 90th anniversary of the founding of the People's Liberation Army. His appearance at the event was highly remarkable, as Bhutan and China do not have diplomatic relations. But, as a commentator in a regional publication wrote at the time, it should be seen 'a subtle signal of Bhutanese goodwill to China.'[64]

The crisis was eventually resolved at the end of August, but India and China announced their respective decisions to withdraw troops from the Doklam Plateau in vastly different ways. In a statement on 28 August, India's Ministry of External Affairs said the 'expeditious disengagement of border personnel at the face-off site at Doklam has been agreed to and is ongoing'.[65] On the other hand, Xinhua, China's official news agency, announced that India had withdrawn its personnel and equipment 'that had crossed the border back to the Indian side ... Chinese personnel verified this at the scene [and] China will continue to exercise its sovereign rights and preserve its territorial sovereignty in accordance with historical border agreements.'[66]

Bhutan's attempts to strike a balance between its traditional friendship with India and China's attempts to gain more influence in the kingdom will be a major challenge for years to come. It remains to be seen how this is going to affect its internal stability, but, so far, Bhutan has continued to do well when it comes to social and economic progress. 'Gross National Happiness' may be a conveniently trite description of Bhutan's development model. Nevertheless, Bhutan has developed into a relatively prosperous welfare state, and, apart from China, the Himalayan kingdom is India's only stable neighbour. Pakistani politics is chaotic and often violent; constant mood swings among the public and power struggles within the elite make the future of Bangladesh unpredictable; Sri Lanka remains a wild card despite the end of Tamil insurrection in 2009; Myanmar is torn apart by civil war and ethnic conflicts; and Nepal is going from one political crisis to another. With China becoming an authoritarian-ruled but freewheeling capitalist society, most people in the world probably thought that orthodox Maoism was dead. That was until it resurfaced with a ferocity that few had predicted in Nepal in the 1990s.

Notes

1. Andrea Matles Savada, *Nepal and Bhutan: Country Studies* (Washington: Federal Research Division, Library of Congress, 1993), p. 253.

2. Savada, *Nepal and Bhutan*, p. 253. The website 'National Anthem of Bhutan', available at http://www.himalaya2000.com/bhutan/national-symbols/national-anthem.html (accessed on 5 November 2016) gives a slightly different English translation with 'consistency' instead of 'constancy', but that may be a typographical error.

3. For a complete text of the 1910 treaty, see Lyonpo Om Pradhan, *Bhutan: The Roar of the Thunder Dragon* (Thimphu: K Media, 2012), pp. 244–5.

4. 'Treaty of Perpetual Peace and Friendship Between the Government of India and the Government of Bhutan'. For a complete text of the treaty see, Pradhan, *Bhutan*, pp. 246–9.

5. 'India-Bhutan Friendship Treaty (2007)', Pradhan, *Bhutan*, pp. 260–2.

6. Quoted in Savada, *Nepal and Bhutan*, p. 335.

7. Bertil Lintner, 'China Turns on Charm Offensive for the Himalayan Kingdom of Bhutan', *Yale Global Online*, 22 September 2016, available at http://yale-global.yale.edu/content/china-turns-charm-offensive-himalayan-kingdom-bhutan (accessed on 25 September 2016). The article is based on information gathered in Bhutan in June 2016.

8. Thierry Mathou, 2004, 'Bhutan-China Relations: Towards a New Step in Himalayan Politics', *The Spider and the Piglet: Proceedings of the First International Seminar on Bhutanese Studies* (Thimphu: Centre for Bhutan Studies, 2004), p. 392, available at http://www.bhutanstudies.org.bt/pub-licationFiles/ConferenceProceedings/SpiderAndPiglet/19-Spdr&Pglt.pdf (accessed on 15 July 2016).

9. Savada, *Neoal and Bhutan*, p. 255: 'Following the guru's [Guru Rimpoche] sojourn, Indian influence played a temporary role until increasing Tibetan migrations brought new cultural and religious contributions.'

10. Savada, *Nepal and Bhutan*, p. 255. For a more detailed account of the sects and religious rivalries at the time, see Karma Phuntsho, *The History of Bhutan* (New Delhi, Random House, 2013), pp. 136–52. Phuntsho's massive, 663-page book is the best and most authoritative study of the history of Bhutan.

11. Quoted in Phuntsho, *The History of Bhutan*, p. 224.

12. Pradhan., *Bhutan*, p.15.

13. Michael Aris, *The Raven Crown: The Origins of Buddhist Monarchy in Bhutan* (London: Serindia Publications, 1994), p. 32.

14. Aris, *The Raven Crown*, p. 28.

15. Aris, *The Raven Crown*, p. 40.

16. Aris, *The Raven Crown*, p. 40.

17. Phuntsho, *The History of Bhutan*, p. 350.

18. For the text of the treaty, see 'Treaty of Sinchula - 1865', and https://bangalore-gorkha.wordpress.com/documents/treaty-sinchula/ (accessed on 10 December 2016).

19. Savada, *Nepal and Bhutan*, p. 261.

20. To minimize the power of the shabdrung, the druk desi decided not to recognize only one but several reincarnations of the same man. Even three reincarnations (body, mind, and speech) were sometimes referred to. See Ashi Dorji Wangmo Wangchuk, *Of Rainbows and Clouds: The Life of Yab Ugyen Dorji as told to his Daughter* (London: Serindia Publications, 1999), p. 13.

21. Savada, *Nepal and Bhutan*, p. 262.

22. For the text of the 1910 Anglo-Bhutanese Treaty, also called the Punakha Treaty, see Pradhan, *Bhutan*, pp. 244–5.

23. Neville Maxwell, 'Olaf Caroe's Fabrication of the McMahon Line', *Economic and Political Weekly*, Vol. 51, Issue 32, 6 August 2016, p. 101.

24. Pradip Phanjoubam, 'Neville Maxwell's "Facts" and Silences', *Economic and Political Weekly*, Vol. 51, Issue No .46, 12 November 2016, available at http://www.epw.in/journal/2016/46/discussion/neville-maxwells-factsand-silences.html (accessed on 18 November 2016).

25. Phanjoubam. 'Neville Maxwell's "Facts" and Silences'.

26. Aris, *The Raven Crown*, pp. 121–2.

27. Aris, *The Raven Crown*, p. 122.

28. Savada, *Nepal and Bhutan*, p. 263.

29. Central Intelligence Agency, *Intelligence Study: Bhutan between India and China* (OCI No. 1105/65), 2 April 1965, declassified on 19 December 2003, p. 19.

30. Central Intelligence Agency, *Intelligence Study: Bhutan between India and China*, p. 20.

31. Quoted in Nari Rustomji, *Bhutan: The Dragon Kingdom in Crisis* (Delhi: Oxford University Press, 1978), p. 92.

32. Savada, *Nepal and Bhutan*, p. 264.

33. Central Intelligence Agency, *Intelligence Study: Bhutan between India and China*,. p. 15.

34. Central Intelligence Agency, *Intelligence Study: Bhutan between India and China*, p. 16.

35. Central Intelligence Agency, *Intelligence Study: Bhutan between India and China*, p. 20.

36. Aris, *The Raven Crown*, p. 56.

37. Savada *Nepal and Bhutan*, pp. 273–5.

38. Sunanda K. Datta-Ray, *Smash and Grab: Annexation of Sikkim* (New Delhi: Vikas Publishing House, 1985), p. 51.

39. Bertil Lintner, 'Bhutan, India and the Nepalese Diaspora', *The New Asia-Pacific Review*, Vol. 3, Issue No. 2, 1997, p. 18.

40. Lintner, 'Bhutan, India and the Nepalese Diaspora' and Bertil Lintner, 'Stateless in Shangri-la', *Far Eastern Economic Review*, 25 July 1996, p. 30.

41. Central Intelligence Agency, *Intelligence Study: Bhutan between India and China*, p. 21.

42. For an account of the insurgency in Assam, see Bertil Linter, *Great Game East: India, China and the Struggle for Asia's Most Volatile Frontier* (New Haven and London: Yale University Press, 2015), pp. 144–203.

43. See for instance Ramtanu Maitra, 'Pakistan's Bhutan gambit worries India', *Asia Times Online*, 25 November 2004, available at http://www.atimes.com/atimes/South_Asia/FK25Df03.html (accessed on 15 December 2016) and S. Chandrasekharen, 'The ULFA and Bodo militants were invited into Bhutan', 2006, available at http://freu.blogspot.com/2006/08/ulfa-and-bodo-militants-were-invited.html (accessed on 15 December 2016).

44. For a detailed account of Operation All Clear see '2003: Operation all Clear', 2013, available at http://bhutannews.blogspot.com/2013/09/2003-operation-all-clear.html (accessed on 15 December 2016).

45. Anthony Davis, 'New Details Emerge on Bangladesh Arms Haul', *Jane's Intelligence Review*, August 2004 (closed website, copy provided to the author by Davis).

46. Davis, 'New Details Emerge on Bangladesh Arms Haul'. For a complete list of the seized equipment, see Lintner, *Great Game East,* p. 268.

47. Davis, 'New Details Emerge on Bangladesh Arms Haul'.

48. Mithu Chaudhury, 'NIA Report Reveals NSCN(IM)-China Link', *North East News Portal,* 14 January 2013, http://northeastnewsportal.-blogspot.com/2013/01/nia-report-reveals-china-link.html (accessed on 18 December 2016).

49. Central Intelligence Agency, *Research Study: Chinese-Indian Relations: 1972–1975,* September 1975, declassified on 29 June 2004, p. 7.

50. Quoted in Mathou, 'Bhutan–China Relations: Towards a New Step in Himalayan Politics', p. 399.

51. Quoted in Mathou, 'Bhutan–China Relations', p. 399.

52. Central Intelligence Agency, *Research Study: Chinese-Indian Relations: 1972–1975,* . p. 7.

53. *China's Foreign Relations: A Chronology of Events (1949-1988)* (Beijing: Foreign Languages Press, 1989), pp. 149.

54. For the text of the agreement, see Mathou, 'Bhutan–China Relations: Towards a New Step in Himalayan Politics', pp. 410–11.

55. 'China and Bhutan Hold 24th Round of Talks on the Boundary Issue', *Ministry of Foreign Affairs of the People's Republic of China,* 15 August 2016, available at http://www.fmprc.gov.cn/mfa_eng/wjbxw/t1389633.shtml (accessed on 20 August 2016).

56. Rustomji, *Bhutan,* pp. 145–7.

57. Ashi Dorji Wangmo Wangchuk, *Of Rainbows and Clouds,* p. 31. See also Norma Levine, *Love and Death: My Years with the Lost Spiritual King of Bhutan* (Kathmandu: Vajra Publications, 2011). The book is written by a Canadian woman who had an intimate relationship with the exiled (but not recognized) shabdrung who died in 2003. Some claim that he was poisoned, while the official version is that he died from cancer. He is considered by many as the last shabdrung, although some regard a young boy, born in 2003, as the newest incarnation. In early 2007, reports alleged that the boy, Pema Namgyen, along with his parents, has been held under house arrest in Bhutan since 2005 after being invited to there from his home in India, see 'Shabdrung', available at http://www.chinabuddhismencyclopedia.com/en/index.php/Shabdrung (accessed on 15 December 2016).

58. 'Bhutan TV follows Cyber Launch', *British Broadcasting Corporation (BBC),* 2 June 1999, http://news.bbc.co.uk/2/hi/south_asia/358230.stm (accessed on 15 December 2016).

59. *The Constitution of the Kingdom of Bhutan* (Printed at The Kuensel Corporation, 2008), p. 4. The constitution is also available at http://www.nationalcouncil. bt/assets/uploads/files/Constitution%20%20of%20Bhutan%20English.pdf (accessed on 15 December 2016).

60. A US government official, speaking on condition of anonymity, told me this in December 2014.

61. 'Illegal Immigration Concerns NC', *Kuensel*, 10 June 2016, p. 1.

62. A.S. Nazir Ahamed, 'Did Nehru really accept the Sino-British Treaty as final word on the border issue?' *The Hindu*, 5 July 2017.

63. Manu Balachandaran and Harish C. Menon, 'Fifty years after round one, Bhutan and China are stuck in another border face-off,' *Quartz India*, 4 July 2017, at https://qz.com/1020177/50-years-after-round-one-bhutan-china-and-india-are-stuck-in-another-border-face-off/ (accessed on 13 August 2017).

64. M.K. Bhadrakumar, 'China raps India over Doklam standoff, but dogs are on leash,' *Asia Times*, 3 August 2017, at http://www.atimes.com/article/china-raps-india-doklam-standoff-dogs-leash/ (accessed on 13 August 2017).

65. James Griffiths, 'India, China agree to "expeditious disengagement" of the Doklam border dispute', CNN, 29 August 2017, available at http://edition. cnn.com/2017/08/28/asia/india-china-brics-doklam/index.html (accessed on 1 September 2017).

66. James Griffiths, 'India, China agree to "expeditious disengagement" of the Doklam border dispute'.

7

Maoism Redux

13 February 1996 began as a fairly normal Tuesday throughout Nepal. No one, especially among the ruling circles in the capital Kathmandu, had expected that anything out of the ordinary would happen in any part of the kingdom. But, on that day, crowds armed with little more than daggers, old hunting rifles, and home-made bombs carried out simultaneous attacks on police stations in Rolpa and Rukum districts in the impoverished western part of the country, and in Sindhuli in the east. The stations were overrun and the attackers made off with guns, ammunition, and other equipment they had seized.

In Kavre, a local moneylender was captured and the attackers burned bond papers with the names of people who had borrowed money from him at extortionate rates. A similar event occurred in Gorkha district, where a local office of the Agriculture Development Bank was captured and its borrowers were declared free from debt. And in the Kathmandu Valley, Molotov cocktails were hurled at a Pepsi-Cola factory, partially damaging the building. Throughout the country, posters appeared and leaflets were distributed, urging people to support the uprising. Nepal's Maoists had launched their 'people's war' against the monarchy and for the establishment of a communist 'people's republic'.

But the uprising should not have come as a surprise. The year before, ultra-radicals led by Pushpa Kamal Dahal, alias Comrade 'Prachanda' (the

fierce one) and Baburam Bhattarai had broken away from Nepal's mainstream communist parties and fronts, denouncing them as 'renegades' and
'revisionists' because of their participation in the parliamentary process.
With the extreme left divided, and, its influence seemingly waning after
the announcement of the results of an election in 1994, the authorities
launched a campaign to crush what they thought were scattered remnants
of the movement. In November 1995, Operation Romeo was carried out
against the radicals' main stronghold in Rolpa. In what was to become
his last interview before going underground, Bhattarai told the weekly
Nepalese newspaper *The Independent* in December,

> Under this armed police operation around 1,500 policemen including a
> special trained commando force sent from Kathmandu have been deployed
> to let loose a reign of terror against the poor peasants of that rugged moun-
> tain district [Rolpa] in western Nepal. So far about 1,000 people have been
> arrested, of whom about 300 are kept in police custody or sent to jails under
> fictitious charges while the rest have been released on bail after severe torture.[1]

Shortly after the interview, Bhattarai left Kathmandu to link up with his
friend Prachanda. The Communist Party of Nepal (Maoist) (CPN-M) was
born, although the exact date of its formation is still a bit of a mystery. It
could have been set up as early as late 1994, before the police operations
began in the west, and whatever the name of the organization, a well-orga-
nized, underground Maoist movement was already in place well before the
attacks of February 1996. Resorting to armed struggle was also, according
to Prachanda, a 'decisive attack on revisionism which had been inflicting
[the] Nepalese Communist movement. In other words, this great process
started burning the heap of revisionist filth. The reaffirmation of the truth
of the ideology of the international proletariat in the form of Marxism-
Leninism-Maoism has been proved practically from February 13th.'[2]

It is clear that the actions taken on that day had been meticulously
planned for maximum impact and symbolism. The local police were organs
of the oppressive state, banks and moneylenders exploited the poor, and,
in the words of Prachanda, the attack on the Pepsi-Cola factory symbol-
ized the 'commitment to free the people from the exploitation of [the]

comprador bourgeois class which directly represents the imperialists'.[3] The struggle, Prachanda stated, 'started spreading throughout the country from February 14th onwards ... [and] actions against the feudals, goons in different parts of the country, especially against those from the rural areas started taking place continuously. The sky of Nepal reverberated with slogans such as "Long Live Maoism!", "Long live people's war!", "Long live New Democracy."'[4]

It became an extremely vicious civil war, with thousands of men and women fighting and dying for a cause that most people in the rest of the world would consider a total anachronism. Maoist-inspired uprisings in the Third World were not uncommon in the 1960s and 1970s—but in the late 1990s and the beginning of the twenty-first century? Even the turgid prose used by the Nepalese Maoists seemed to belong to a different era. But ultra-leftism and Maoism did have firm roots in Nepalese politics. The country's first communist party, called simply the Communist Party of Nepal (CPN), was formed when four young Nepalese intellectuals met in Kolkata on 22 April 1949. One of them, Pushpa Lal Shrestha, or Comrade PL, as he was known, became the party's first general secretary and is considered the father of Nepalese communism.

Nepal experienced a brief period of relative democracy during the first years of the reign of King Tribhuvan, who had ascended the throne as an eight-year-old boy in 1911. The Nepalese kings were at that time in any case powerless figureheads, as the country had been run by hereditary prime ministers from the Rana family, old allies of the British, since 1846. In later years, the king, with support from independent India, began to challenge the Ranas. A popular movement to end the oligarchy also broke out in 1950, and, in early 1951, a compromise was reached during a meeting in New Delhi between King Tribhuvan, who had been living in exile in India for a year and supported the movement, the Ranas, and representatives of the main opposition party, the Nepali Congress. The king would form a new government under his leadership, consisting of the Nepali Congress and the Ranas on an equal basis. The king returned to Kathmandu on 18 February, and, on the 21st, he declared an end to the rule of the Rana autocracy. Nepal had begun its first experiment with democracy.

The CPN, which had played an important role in the overthrow of the Ranas, became a legal political party. But when the Nepali Congress party's militia, called Raksha Dal, rose in revolt in 1952, and the uprising was crushed, the CPN, which had been sympathetic to the uprising, was also banned. It was only when the ban was lifted four years later that the CPN could openly hold its congress in Kathmandu, and adopted a revolutionary party programme that advocated an end to monarchy and the establishment of a republic. The period of political openness was brief: On 15 December 1960, the new king, Mahendra, staged a coup. He suspended the elected parliament and dismissed the government. An entirely new system called 'panchayat' was introduced, based on a hierarchical system of village, district, and national councils, with the king at the top. The CPN was banned again, this time with all other political parties.

The 1960 royal coup, the ban, and especially the Sino-Soviet conflict in the 1960s, caused the first of many splits in Nepal's communist movement. Its general secretary, Keshar Jung Rayamajhi, who was attending a meeting of communist parties in Moscow at the time, actually supported the monarch. A CPN plenum held in Darbhanga in India removed Rayamajhi from his position in March 1961. The following year, he was expelled from the CPN, but, refusing to accept the party's decision, he formed his own communist party. At the same time, while the 'mainstream' CPN remained loyal to Moscow, Comrade PL and his more radical comrades sided with China in the Sino-Soviet conflict. Thus the Communist Party of Nepal (Pushpa Lal) was born, and Comrade PL was its leader until his death in 1978.

The Naxalite-inspired rebellion in Jhapa in the early 1970s gave birth to yet another party, the Communist Party of Nepal (Marxist-Leninist) (CPN-ML). Formed in 1978, it became active in the area around Biratnagar in the southeastern plains. In the same year, another similar faction of the pro-China movement in the southeast formed the Nepal Workers' and Peasants Organisation. Yet another communist faction emerged from the turbulent 1970s. It was modelled after India's 'independent' communist party, the Communist Party of India (Marxist), and led by Manmohan Adhikari, a former CPN general secretary and erstwhile follower of Comrade PL. It named itself the Communist Party of Nepal (Marxist).

The troubled kingdom was thrown into a new crisis in the spring of 1990, when a popular uprising, called 'Jan Andolan' or people's movement, forced King Birendra, Mahendra's eldest son and successor, to agree to abolish what amounted to an absolute monarchy. More than 500 demonstrators were killed in violent clashes with the police in Kathmandu before the king eventually gave in to popular demands for an end to the old system. A multiparty system was introduced and elections were held to form a parliament in May 1991. The communist parties returned from underground. At first, even the most radical of them participated in the democratic process. Their front organization, the Samyukta Jana Morcha (United People's Front, UPF) emerged as the third largest party in the 1991 election, winning nine seats in the 205-member lower house. Led by Baburam Bhattarai, then a young intellectual, the UPF's not-so-radical slogans like 'down with corruption' and 'distribute the wealth of the country among the poor', appealed to many young disgruntled Nepalese.

The already tangled situation was further aggravated when Nepal's first democratically elected government, formed by the Nepali Congress, dissolved the parliament in July 1994. The elections in November of the same year led to the formation of a minority government headed by the Communist Party of Nepal Unified Marxist-Leninists (CPN-UML), which was formed in 1991 by uniting CPN-ML and the CPN-Marxist. The CPN-UML leader, Manmohan Adhikari, became Nepal's new prime minister, making Nepal the first country where communists came to power through elections, save for the tiny republic of San Marino in Europe.

Yet even the new left-wing government failed to improve the lot of the poor and clean up corruption. It fell after only nine months in power and gave way to a series of fragile and implausible coalitions, where the politics of gain rather than common ideologies motivated new alliances between parties. Nepal's return to democracy turned chaotic and the expectations of those who had taken part in the 1990 movement turned into despair and frustration.

Despite its name, the CPN-UML was not radical enough for many. It resembled a European social democrat party rather than a militant organization prepared to introduce any radical political or economic changes.

Throughout Nepal, revolutionary sentiments were still simmering, as they had done since the 1990 *Jan Andolan*. A clear indication of the direction in which Nepal's radicals were moving came in September 1992 when Abimael Guzmán, or Chairman Gonzalo, the leader of Peru's Shining Path guerrillas, an extreme Maoist group that had been engaged in a vicious armed struggle since 1980, was arrested in the capital Lima. The London staff of the International Emergency Committee to Defend the Life of Guzmán was astounded by the volume of mail they received from Nepal in his support.[5]

Nepal's Maoists were already tied to their Peruvian comrades through an obscure organization called the Revolutionary Internationalist Movement (RIM), which comprised Maoist groups from the United States, India, Iran, Turkey, Latin America, and Western Europe. RIM's periodical, *A World to Win*, a smart, glossy magazine that came out twice or thrice a year, contained information about the armed and unarmed revolutionary struggle in various parts of the world, including Nepal.

According to Stephen I. Mikesell, a research scholar writing in Kathmandu's *Himal* magazine,

> Appealing geo-cultural analogies can be drawn between Peru and Nepal. Both countries straddle mountain ranges of their respective continents, in which isolated valleys and high ridges have given way to a wide variety of cultural traditions. While neither country has a history of a recent foreign military conquest and occupation, as was the case in China in the 1930s, both have large rural indigenous populations subordinated to small ruling élites with whom they are divided by racism or casteism and regionalism.[6]

During the heydays of the Shining Path and the emergence of the militant Maoist movement in Nepal, Peru and Nepal both experienced sharp and growing divisions between the city and the countryside. In Nepal, despite the introduction of democracy and a more open economy since 1990, wages remained virtually stagnant, and GDP growth averaged an abysmal 2.3 per cent annually. This meant that the rapid annual increase in population of 2.4 per cent ate up all the achievements that the new governments brought in. According to a report by Kathmandu-based think-tank Nepal South Asia Centre, 71 per cent of wealth, even in the capital, was in the hands of 12 per cent of the households and only 3.7 per cent of the national income reached the poorest 20 per cent of the population.[7]

Regional disparities were also severe. The annual per capita income in Kathmandu averaged around 21,000 Nepalese Rupees (US$312) in the 1990s, while it was as low as 5,000 Nepalese Rupees in the poorest districts in the northwest, an area which was served by neither roads nor development activities. The International Centre for Integrated Mountain Development, a foreign-funded research institute, in its 1997 report, listed the western districts as 'the worst' in terms of literacy, child labour, landless households, and per capita food production.[8] Shyam Shrestha of the left-wing monthly magazine *Mulyankan* described Nepal's northwest as a 'poverty-stricken area … inhabited by Magars, a very "backward" ethnic group which continues to be sustained through migrant labour to India. A region ruled historically by feudal princelings, the area even today retains a medieval relationship between rich and poor—a classic setting for Maoist activity.'[9]

Shrestha hinted at a very important dimension to Nepal's 'people's war' apart from general disappointment at the widespread corruption, social and political instability, bickering politicians, and abuse of power instead of expected economic progress and greater equality that had come in the wake of the 1990 uprising: Nepal's intricate caste system and diverse ethnic composition. The vast majority of Maoist fighters came from the lower castes and the so-called 'backward' ethnic groups such as the hill-dwelling Mongol Magars and the Tharus in the narrow valleys closer to the lowlands. The arrival of the Maoists and their 'proletarian ideology' gave lower castes and tribes authority and power over the higher castes such as the *bahuns* (the local term for Brahmins), and the *chhetris* (Kshatriyas), the Indo-Aryan upper strata of society, which traditionally had treated them as second class citizens or worse. In the case of many of the Maoist foot soldiers, this explains why a seemingly anachronistic movement made such headway. The country needed a social revolution, and, for many, the CPN-M appealed as the only alternative to the old, repressive order.

Even Prachanda wrote in an assessment of the first two years of the war that

> Along with the development of the People's War a new consciousness for fighting for their own rights is spreading amongst many oppressed nationalities of the country such as the Magars, Gurungs, Tamangs, Newars, Tharus, Rais, Limbus and Madhesis...Similarly...a wave of organisation and struggle has been created among *Dalit* castes [low caste people] at a greater speed and wider scale. The *Dalits* are today rebelling against inhuman tyranny perpetrated upon them by the feudal state of high caste Hindus.[10]

But many of the leaders of the CPN-M, including Prachanda and Bhattarai, were actually bahun intellectuals. This is again a striking parallel with the Shining Path, whose leader, Guzmán, was a well-educated former professor of philosophy, while his followers were mostly poor people belonging to indigenous tribes of non-European descent. In the same vein, the dreaded, and likewise Maoist, Khmer Rouge in Cambodia was led by French-educated intellectuals whose foot soldiers, poor peasants from the countryside, were motivated by hatred of the better-off people in the cities rather than by ideology.

Prachanda was born in a village in Kaski district in 1954, the son of a farmer, but still a bahun. The would-be revolutionary received a diploma in science in agriculture from the Institute of Agriculture and Animal Science in Rampur in southern Nepal. Ironically, he was once employed by the United States Agency for International Development (USAID), at the project site in Jajarkot, which later became a Maoist stronghold.[11]

Bhattarai was also born in 1954, in Gorkha district in the hills, and, like Prachanda's parents, his parents also were bahun farmers. In 1970, he ranked first in the whole of Nepal in the School Leaving Certificate Exam of that year. He received further education in India, where he earned a Bachelors degree with honours in architecture from a university in Chandigarh and later a Ph.D. degree from the prestigious Jawaharlal Nehru University in New Delhi. His dissertation was titled *The Nature of Underdevelopment and Regional Structure of Nepal: A Marxist Analysis*.[12] While in India, he became the founding chairman of the All India Nepalese Students' Association.[13]

The road to armed rebellion they were going to tread on began when the powerful UPF split on the eve of the 1994 election. The main group, led by Bhattarai, decided to boycott the election while a smaller faction under Niranjan Govinda Vaidya participated but did not win a single seat—hence the assumption on the part of the authorities that the left was weak and divided, which turned out to be a monumental mistake.

After the first attacks in February 1996, the armed insurrection quickly spread to the neighbouring districts of Salyan, Jajarkot, and Kalikot, and soon to other parts of Nepal. The new slogan was much more militant than the relatively moderate rhetoric of the UPF, or even the Jhapa movement of the 1970s: 'War, war, and war! From the beginning to the end!'[14]

But having Peru's Shining Path as a role model did not endear the Nepalese Maoists to the Chinese. In December 1980, early risers in Lima began to find dead dogs hung from traffic lights and lampposts in the Peruvian capital. They were adorned with signs that read, 'Deng Xiaoping, Son of a Bitch!'[15] On 25 October 1989, car bombs exploded outside the Soviet and Chinese embassies in Lima in attacks that were attributed to the Shining Path, which believed that communist leaders in Moscow and Beijing had betrayed Marxism-Leninism. On 28 December 1992, Shining Path guerrillas detonated two more car bombs, this time outside Lima's Japanese and Chinese embassies. China was an obvious target for the Peruvian Maoists, and Peru's president at the time, Alberto Fujimori, was of Japanese descent and as such seen as a puppet of Japan's multinational corporations.

Prachanda, summarizing the experiences of the CPN-M's 'people's war' in 1997, stated that the first year of the armed struggle had established a firm relationship 'between the revolutionaries of South Asia, including India ... [the] Maoist people's war is getting support from tens of millions of people in India, who are waging national liberation struggles in various states ... similarly the communist revolutionaries of Bangladesh and Sri Lanka are giving support to the Nepalese people's war.'[16]

Conspicuously absent among all those allegedly supporting the CPN-M's 'people's war' was China. The party sparingly accused the new Chinese leadership under Deng Xiaoping of being revisionist, but Prachanda stated in one of his writings,

For the masses there is no alternative to rebellion and revolution, given the objective background of exploitation, repression and poverty prevalent in the semi-feudal and semi-colonial countries of the Third World. In Nepal, our first effort was to correctly grasp the science of Marxism-Leninism-Maoism. For this, we strove to link ourselves with the arduous and challenging ideological struggle waged by the genuine communist revolutionaries of the world against the Chinese counter-revolution after the death of Comrade Mao Zedong. Taking the synthesis of the Great Proletarian Cultural Revolution, the highest expression of conscious class struggle, as our starting point, we delved into serious study.[17]

Li Onesto, an American supporter and writer for the Chicago-based *Revolutionary Worker* weekly, echoed the same views in her book about the war in Nepal. 'The Maoists in Nepal denounce the current Chinese regime for overthrowing and dismantling socialism after Mao's death. The Chinese government has made clear that it supports the efforts to crush the insurgency, but China would be extremely concerned if India invaded Nepal to prevent the Maoists from seizing power.'[18]

It was far-fetched to suggest that India would 'invade' Nepal. India had other means of influencing Nepalese politics, for instance, through its close relationship with the Nepali Congress and other aboveground politicians. The Chinese, on their part, accused the CPN-M of distorting Mao's ideology and 'besmirching the name of Mao by calling their indiscriminate killing of civilians a People's War ... on February 3, 2005 Chinese Foreign Ministry spokesman Kong Quan expressed his indignation at foreign media who call Nepal's anti-government rebels "Maoists."'[19]

China's relationship with Nepal has always been motivated by geopolitical considerations rather than ideology, by the desire to build a strategic corridor in the Himalayas in order to counter India's influence in the border regions. China and Nepal established diplomatic relations in 1955 and the first direct talks between representatives of the Chinese and Nepalese governments were held in Kathmandu in August and September 1956. Immediately after those talks, Tanka Prasad Acharya became the first Nepalese prime minister in the post-Rana era to visit China, where he held talks with his Chinese counterpart Zhou Enlai. China agreed to provide 60 million Indian Rupees (which was more readily accepted in Nepal than the non-convertible Chinese renminbi) to help implement Nepal's first five-year plan.[20] In the same year, Nepal recognized China's sovereignty over Tibet and, in January 1957, Zhou Enlai visited Nepal. Relations between the two countries were cordial, a fact that did not really bother New Delhi at the time, since Sino-Indian relations had not yet turned sour.

China's policy towards Nepal saw a shift when a border dispute in 1959 led to the movement of Chinese troops towards the Nepalese border. Chinese maps showed Nepalese territory as part of China, and the Chinese made claims to Mt Everest, which they call Chomolungma.[21] The Tibetan uprising in that year also saw an influx of refugees to Nepal. Over 20,000 Tibetans fled to Nepal, where most of them remained, even as a significant number continued to India, where they were more welcome and freer to carry out their political activities.

The border issue was resolved when Nepal's Prime Minister Bishweshwar Prasad Koirala visited Beijing in March 1960 and signed a Treaty of Peace and Friendship with the Chinese, which included a provision to locate and demarcate the common border. Then, in September–October 1961, after the royal coup and the introduction of the panchayat system, King Mahendra and his queen paid an official state visit to China, where they met President Liu Shaoqi and Premier Zhou Enlai. A Sino-Nepalese boundary treaty was signed on 5 October, under which 'the formal delimitation of the entire boundary between the two countries would be made on the basis of the traditional customary boundary line in accordance with the principles of equality, mutual benefit and mutual accommodation.'[22]

On the last day of the king's visit, 15 October, an agreement was signed to construct a highway from Tibet to Kathmandu. The two governments would be responsible for the construction of the sections of the highway within their respective territories, but China pledged to provide Nepal with a generous grant to build the highway on the Nepalese side of the border. For several years, road construction crews blasted their way through the mountains. It was decided to name the highway after Araniko, a thirteenth century Nepalese who, according to legend, introduced Nepalese-style architecture to Tibet and China.

The road was officially opened in 1967, and although old yak tracks and caravan trails had followed approximately the same route for centuries, this was the first time a proper highway crossed the Himalayas. The newly built Chinese highway system in Tibet now extended not only down to the Indian border but also over the crest of the mountains. A bridge called the Sino-Nepal Friendship Bridge spanned the Sun Kosi border river, linking Kodari in Nepal's Sindhupalchok district with Zangmu in Tibet.

Before the road was built, in 1962, Nepal had withdrawn its ambassador from Tibet and substituted a consul general to please the Chinese and, on 22 January 1963, the border between the two countries was finally demarcated. During the 1962 War, Nepal had declared itself neutral although it had warned that it would not submit to aggression from any state. The message was directed to China, but Nepal continued to support China's application for membership in the United Nations and maintained contacts with Beijing.[23] In the wake of the 1962 War, India and Nepal concluded an Arms Assistance Agreement in which the Indians pledged to 'supply arms, ammunition and equipment for the entire Nepalese army [and to] replace existing Nepalese stock by modern weapons as soon as available and also to provide maintenance of and replacement for the equipment to be supplied by them.'[24]

By this time, however, Nepal had begun to play the China card to lessen its traditional dependence on India, which many Nepalese were acutely uncomfortable with, while China evidently saw Nepal as a weak link in India's northern defence that could be exploited to extend its influence over the Himalayas. Thus, as the highway to Tibet opened a new route for trade, India, to show its displeasure with the developments, responded by imposing a blockade on Nepal in 1970. It did not last long, but as a result economic growth in Nepal was limited to 1.7 per cent in the fiscal year 1970–1 from the previous year's 9.8 per cent.[25] After the blockade, much to the annoyance of India, relations between Nepal and China grew even closer.

Nepal was not Sikkim, which had no possibility of becoming more independent of India in how it conducted its foreign policy. Nor was it Bhutan, which played its cards more skilfully, managing to build its own identity without antagonizing its powerful southern neighbour. Nepal was beginning to become a pawn in the regional power struggle between India and China.

Not even the presence of Tibetan guerrillas, supported by the CIA, in Mustang seemed to have an adverse effect on the newly established friendly relations between the communist rulers in Beijing and the royal court in Kathmandu. King Birendra visited China in December 1973, and it was the cosy relationship that Nepal established with China in the 1960s and early 1970s that led its army to force out the Tibetan resistance from their Mustang sanctuaries in 1974. In the same year, Nepal fiercely criticized the Indian parliament's decision to make Sikkim an associate state, calling India 'an expansionist nation'.[26] The Chinese awarded Nepal with more road construction projects and, in April 1976, a trade agreement was made between Nepal and 'China's Tibet Autonomous Region'.[27]

China continued to have close relations with whoever was in power in Kathmandu, even during the upheavals of 1990 and the chaos that ensued after the abolishment of absolute monarchy. The situation in Nepal went from bad to worse when, on 1 June 2001, Crown Prince Dipendra stormed into the Narayanhiti palace in Kathmandu and opened fire on a monthly reunion dinner of the royal family. Nine members of the family were killed in the shooting, including Dipendra's parents, King Birendra and Queen Aishwarya, his brother Nirajan, his sister Shruti, and five other relatives. Dipendra then turned the gun on himself, survived and was king for a few days before he, comatose and in hospital, succumbed to his injuries on 4 June. Mahendra's son and Birendra's younger brother Gyanendra was proclaimed king.

Various conspiracy theories flourished in Kathmandu after the royal massacre, including fanciful accounts of Indian and even CIA involvement, but there is nothing to indicate that Dipendra was driven by anything but personal grudges against his family.[28] He was also heavily drunk and high on hashish when he grabbed a gun and killed those relatives. Dipendra had wanted to marry Devyani Rana, from the Rana family, who was also related to the Gwalior royal family in India, but his mother, Queen Aishwarya, disapproved of their relationship. Devyani Rana fled to India after the massacre to escape media attention, and now works for the United Nations Development Programme.

Meanwhile, a string of bank robberies and the extensive enforcement of 'revolutionary tax' from people in the areas under its control as well as in all major towns and even overseas had made the CPN-M one of the wealthiest rebel movements in Asia. According to the Nepalese-language daily *Rajdhani* published from Kathmandu, not even the poorest of farmers were spared from paying taxes. 'The families are forced to pay based on the value of their homes—tiled and tin roofs are taxed more than thatched ones. The rebels have also ordered NGOs and community-based organizations not to start any projects without their written permission.'[29]

Considerable amounts also came from 'collections' from Nepalese abroad, particularly the several million Nepalese workers in India. The main organization among them, Akhil Bharatiya Nepali Ekta Samaj (the All-India Nepalese Unity Society), was banned in July 2002 for links to the CPN-M. Indian authorities arrested its secretary, Bamdev Chhetri, then thought to be the most important contact for Nepalese Maoists in India, on 7 September and extradited him to Nepal.

Poverty, along with social and political unrest at home, had forced tens of thousands of Nepalese to emigrate. Reports emerged of a small but very active Maoist cell among the approximately 20,000-strong Nepalese community in Hong Kong and of forced 'revolutionary tax' collection there. In a more novel way, the CPN-M issued and sold trekking permits to foreign tourists in Nepal, along with a statement explaining their struggle for a communist republic. In 2002, it was estimated that the CPN-M had netted altogether between five and ten billion Nepalese Rupees (US$ 64–128 million).[30]

But no foreign power ever supported the CPN-M with funds or weapons. Its arms came exclusively from raids on army depots and out-posts and, to some extent, from clandestine gun factories in India's Bihar state. And by the early 2000s, Maoist-related violence had spread to all of Nepal's 75 districts. In the western districts, including Rukum, Rolpa, Salyan, and Jajarkot, the Maoist heartland in the hills, the government controlled little more than the district headquarters and strings of check-points on the roads leading down to the lowlands in the south. Even in Kalikot, Dailekh, Surkhet, Dang, and Pyuthan, adjacent to the Maoists' main strongholds, the government's presence was negligible outside major towns.

A Maoist takeover of Nepal did not seem an entirely unrealistic scenario, but, much to the relief of especially the Chinese, the CPN-M's 'people's war' came to an abrupt end when a peace accord was signed on 21 November 2006.[31] The 10-year insurgency had seen 15,000 people killed, more than 100,000 internally displaced, and the country's infrastructure reduced to shambles. The accord came after three years of talks and strenuous efforts at mediation by internal peacemakers. The combatants of the CPN-M's 'people's army' were to be confined to seven cantonments supervised by the United Nations. Their guns would also be stored at those cantonments. The combatants would then be 'rehabilitated', while their leaders were to be given adequate protection.

In return, the agreement stated,

No state powers shall remain with the king. The properties owned by the late King Birendra, the late Queen Aishwarya and their family members shall be brought under the control of the Government of Nepal and used in the interest of the nation through a trust. All properties (such as palaces at various places, forests and National Parks, heritages of historical and archaeological significance etc.) acquired by King Gyanendra in his monarchical capacity shall be nationalised.[32]

The agreement also stipulated that policies should be formulated to implement a land reform and

In order to end discriminations based on class, ethnicity, language, gender, culture, religion and region and to address the problems of women, Dalit, indigenous people, ethnic minorities (Janajatis), Terai communities (Madhesis), oppressed, neglected and minority communities and the backward areas by deconstructing the current centralised and unitary structure, the state shall be restructured in an inclusive, democratic and forward looking manner.[33]

The agreement fell well short of establishing the communist 'people's republic' that the CPN-M had been fighting for, but the party could now operate openly and take part in general elections. There was peace at last in Nepal and elections were held on 10 April 2008. The CPN-M emerged as the largest party in the constituent assembly with 220 out of 575 contested seats. King Gyanendra was forced to abdicate on 28 May, marking the end of the Shah Dynasty, which had ruled the country since 1768. The Assembly decided that Nepal was going to become a federal republic and on 23 July, it elected the country's first president, Ram Baran Yadav, a politician and physician who belonged to the Nepali Congress. At the same time as the monarchy was abolished, the last ruler of Mustang, Jigme Dorje Palbar Bista, also lost his royal titles, which he had held for half a century. As a young man, he had supported the CIA-funded guerrilla campaign to oust the Chinese from Tibet.

Prachanda, the revolutionary firebrand, was sworn in as Nepal's prime minister on 4 August 2008. His cabinet consisted of ministers from his own party as well as the CPN-UML, and the Madhesi Janadhikar Forum, a party representing the natives of the southern plains. Baburam Bhattarai became deputy prime minister and minister of Finance, while another deputy prime minister post was given to Bamdev Gautam from the CPN-UML. Somewhat alarmingly for the Nepalese military, Ram Bahadur Thapa Magar, a Maoist, was made minister of Defence. The former revolutionary assured the international community, especially India and China, that his party and government wanted to have good relations with everybody. He also pledged his commitment to elections and multi-party democracy. It seemed a complete turnaround from his earlier days and, not without reason, many of his comrades began to wonder if he also had joined those he himself had once termed 'revisionist filth'.

China began to re-evaluate its views of the CPN-M after the Maoists formed a new government. On 23 August 2008, Prachanda arrived in Beijing at the invitation of the Chinese government to attend the closing ceremony of the Beijing Olympics the following day. The minister for Information and Communications, CPN-M member Krishna Bahadur Mahara, and other government officials accompanied him to Beijing, where they remained for almost a week.

The leader of the Nepalese Maoists must have been impressed with China's economic progress. When he met Chinese Premier Wen Jinbao, he stated that the friendship between China and Nepal [has] endured the test of time. Historical changes are taking place in Nepal's domestic situation. The Nepali government and people [are] striving for national stability and development, and [hope] to get support and cooperation from China. Nepal would, as always, support China's efforts to maintain national sovereignty and territorial integrity.[34]

During a visit to New York in September 2008, Prachanda outlined his vision for Nepal's future in terms that were fundamentally different from his revolutionary rhetoric of the late 1990s: 'We are making a big experiment—not only for Nepal, not only for South Asia, but for the people of the world. We communists are more flexible and dynamic. We try to develop our ideology according to new conditions. We understand the dynamic of change.'[35]

Dengism rather than Maoism became Prachanda's new ideology when he entered mainstream politics. He began to emphasize the importance of economic growth through capitalism instead of heaping praise on Chairman Mao's revolutionary vision and glorifying the Cultural Revolution of the 1960s. 'We are not fighting for socialism,' he said in an interview while he was in Kathmandu negotiating the 2006 peace accord with the government. 'We are just fighting against feudalism. We are fighting for a capitalist mode of production. We are trying to give more profit to the capitalists and industrialists.'[36]

China could not have been more pleased. Senior Chinese leader Jia Qinglin assured Prachanda that his 2008 visit would have a 'positive and far-reaching impact on relations between the two countries as well as relations between the two parties'. [37] Having condemned the Nepalese Maoists as 'fakes', China now wanted to develop party-to-party ties with the CPN-M. China's willingness to accept Nepal's Maoists, who once had had Peru's anti-Deng Shining Path as their role model, should not have come as a surprise. In the post-Mao era, China's foreign policy has been guided by geostrategic considerations rather than ideology, and a close relationship with Nepal is undoubtedly in China's interest. Therefore, it would also have been surprising if China had not had some contacts with the Nepalese Maoists even during the years of civil war. Pragmatism, not dogmatism, was Deng's guiding principle, and, in that regard, his successors have followed in his footsteps.

But given the fractured nature of Nepalese politics, it was hardly surprising that Prachanda's government did not last long. In May 2009, after less than a year in office, he resigned after his move to sack Rookmangud Katawai, chief of the Nepalese army, was opposed by President Yadav. Prachanda was succeeded by CPN-UML's Madhav Kumar Nepal, who had been deputy prime minister in Nepal's first, 1994–5 communist government.

By then, the CPN-M had merged with another Maoist faction, the Communist Party of Nepal (Unity Centre) and become the Unified CPN-Maoist (UCPN-M). Eager to maintain good relations with their Nepalese comrades, the communist party leaders in Beijing invited Prachanda and other Maoist leaders to visit China in October 2009. Prachanda himself said before he and his delegation took off for Beijing, 'This will be one of the highest level meetings that has ever taken place between the two communist parties of Nepal and China. This visit will not only enhance ties between the two parties but will also contribute to strengthen Nepal's and China's age-old relationship.'[38]

Nepal's ambassador to China from 1998 to 2002, Rajeshwar Acharya said in an interview after the visit,

> It is indeed already assuming palpable significance. After the monarchy, the Chinese appear to be looking for a dependable ally in Nepal, and the Maoists seem to be willing to take on this role. Chinese policy needs to be analysed also in the context of Beijing's transparent desire to expand its contacts and linkages across the South Asian region.[39]

A Maoist became Nepal's PM again in August 2011, when Baburam Bhattarai took over the post. If there was any doubt that the Nepalese Maoists had abandoned their revolutionary ideals, his new economic policies settled it. Playing on anti-Indian sentiment in Nepal, Bhattarai wrote in a booklet published in 1998 that Nepal was 'India-locked' and went on to state that 'the biggest direct manifestation of world imperialist oppression and exploitation in Nepal is Indian expansionist exploitation and oppression'.[40] The way forward, he stated, 'would be to confiscate the means of production that have been in the hands of the reactionary classes … and then hand them over to the progressive forces'.[41]

No such thing happened during his premiership. Now Bhattarai wanted to strengthen the economy and improve the living standards of the people and, like Prachanda, he emphasized the importance of having good relations with both neighbours, China and India. Prachanda's first foreign visit as prime minister was to India in September 2008, and Bhattarai said on his visit to New Delhi as Nepal's PM in December 2011,

> We sincerely appreciate the Government and people of India for the continued cooperation in our development endeavors as a major development partner of Nepal…. we, in Nepal, have been keenly observing India's sustained and spectacular economic development in the midst of global economic stagnation. You have demonstrated by example that the leadership and determination backed with conducive policy environment stimulates economic development and prosperity which others too can emulate.[42]

In the same speech, Bhattarai mentioned the importance of having good relations with China as well:

> On the other side of our border, the People's Republic of China has equally made great strides in economic development. We are conscious of increased economic and trade interactions taking place between our closest two neighbours, India and China. We believe the dividends of prosperity across our borders should benefit our own people and business as well. From this perspective, we see great economic value and opportunities in developing Nepal as a vibrant bridge between our two neighbours on the way to shared prosperity.[43]

The new direction of Nepal's Maoist leaders did not, however, please everyone. In November 2012, Prachanda was slapped in the face and had his glasses smashed by one of his former guerrilla soldiers at a reception in Kathmandu. The attacker, 25-year-old Padam Kunwar, was whisked away by the police and was later seen drenched in blood after Prachanda's men had beaten him severely. After the incident, Kunwar said he had slapped

Prachanda to show his hatred towards the leaders who had betrayed the ordinary guerrillas who had fought in the mountains for an entirely different cause than the new, liberal policies of the Maoist party. The leaders should be 'beware of public anger', he said.[44]

According to some reports, Prachanda had ended up outside the mountains and the jungle with a red-brick mansion complete with a swimming pool and a badminton court. 'Comrade Prachanda has a war chest of more than a billion rupees and has achieved his own proletarian dream. It is just too bad for the rest of his supporters,' Pashupati Shumsher Rana, a former minister and the head of the Rana family, said in an interview.[45]

One of the key sticking points in the 2006 peace agreement was the rehabilitation of the approximately 19,000 men and women who had made up the CPN-M's 'people's army'—a task that had been neglected, perhaps because most of them, unlike some of their leaders, were low-caste people from the hills. The initial idea was to integrate them into the regular army, but Nepal's military commanders and the Nepali Congress were against it. As most of them were left to fend for themselves, it is hardly surprising that they felt abandoned and betrayed by their leaders. Prachanda became prime minister for the second time in August 2016, heading the 21st government since the 1990 uprising and the end of absolute monarchy.

Nepal's chronic political instability has put the country's two powerful neighbours, India and China, on a direct collision course with each other. Neither India nor China wants an unstable Nepal, but their respective strategic interests could not be more different. India's relationship with Nepal is, of course, much older and more profound than China's and, as in Sikkim and Bhutan, it began with the British East India Company.

Before Prithvi Narayan Shah, the ruler of Gorkha, unified the country in 1768, Nepal was divided into many smaller monarchies. He subdued them, and also managed to avoid the East India Company, which had sent an expeditionary force of 2,400 men into the hills to aid the traditional rulers in the Kathmandu valley. Many of the British soldiers succumbed to malaria before they even reached the valley and had to withdraw. Taking advantage of a religious festival, Prithvi Narayan Shah marched unopposed into Kathmandu, crowned himself king of the entire country, and established the Shah Dynasty, which, at least on paper, was to rule Nepal until 2008.

As the kings of Nepal expanded their territories—they occupied Sikkim in 1788 and sent military expeditions into Tibet in the 1790s—they were forced to confront their more powerful neighbours. The Tibetans appealed for help from the Chinese emperor Qianlong, who sent his army into Tibet in 1792. The Nepalese then turned to the East India Company for assistance, but the British did not want to challenge China, a country with huge trading opportunities. The Chinese drove the Nepalese out of Tibet and came within striking distance of Kathmandu. The Nepalese were forced to sign a humiliating treaty that deprived them of all their trading privileges in Tibet.

Nepal came into conflict with the British again when Kathmandu began to conquer territories south of the mountains. After Nepalese forces attacked a police station in Butawal in the southern plains and killed 18 officers in April 1814, war broke out. It ended two years later with the Treaty of Sagauli[46]: Nepal lost Sikkim and several southern areas that it had conquered; the king in Kathmandu was also forced to accept a British resident in his capital, which made the Nepalese fear for their independence. The British, however, found some of the areas in the south too difficult to govern and therefore turned them over to Nepal, which ended up confined within approximately the same boundaries as it has today.

Even so, the country was far from stable. Frictions within the royal family in the 1840s led to a massacre at Kot, where the military commander Jung Bahadur Rana killed about 40 men from the palace court—and subsequently introduced the hereditary premiership of the Rana family. The kings became mere figureheads.

In the following decade, China was weakened by a number of internal conflicts, the most serious of which was the Taiping rebellion in 1851–64. Kathmandu's already strained relations with Lhasa led to armed conflict with the Tibetans, and indirectly with the Chinese. In 1856, an agreement was negotiated with the Chinese resident in Lhasa under which Nepalese merchants were granted duty-free trade privileges in Tibet, while the Tibetans were forced to pay an annual tribute of 10,000 Nepalese Rupees to Kathmandu. A Nepalese resident was also allowed to stay in Lhasa. Nepal gave up its territorial claims in the north and agreed that it, as well as Tibet, would remain a tributary state subject to the emperor in Beijing, an agreement that did not please the Tibetans but which they grudgingly had to accept. But as China disintegrated further, Nepal, as well as Tibet, were able to shake off this subordination. And it was Britain rather than China that came to exert the most outside influence in Nepal and, to a lesser extent, on Tibet.[47]

As relations with the British improved—Nepalese troops had supported the British during the 1857–8 uprising, which the colonial power preferred to call 'the Sepoy rebellion'—the British came to accept the rule of the Ranas and the Nepalese were rewarded for their loyalty by being returned some territories in the southern plains. Nepal had built up a formidable military force centred on the Gorkha army of the first kings of the Shah Dynasty. Military techniques and technology were copied from British models, including an armaments industry. The British also discovered the fighting prowess of the Nepalese army and, after the British crown took over India from the East India Company after the rebellion, Nepal became an important source of recruits for the British military.

Although British influence remained strong, Nepal was able to preserve its national independence in a way Sikkim, and even Bhutan, could not. The country was bigger and more populous, and the Ranas were able to use their total control over domestic affairs to isolate Nepal from events in British India and the rest of the world. Political parties did appear in the country in the 1930s, but there were some based in exile in India where they could operate more freely. In Bihar, the exiles published a journal called *Janata* (the People), which advocated the overthrow of the Ranas in favour of a multi-caste, democratic government. But the Ranas' police managed to infiltrate the movement. Five hundred people were arrested in Kathmandu, accused of collaborating with the exiles. Four of the leaders were executed while the rest received long prison sentences.

Many of the exiles in India worked closely with the Indian National Congress, and, at a meeting in Kolkata in January 1947, the Nepali National Congress, dedicated to toppling the Rana dictatorship, was formed. Of the Nepali Congress leaders, Bishweshwar Prasad Koirala was the most prominent, and he met Jawharlal Nehru as well as Mahatma Gandhi. India's independence in 1947 provided a boost for the Nepalese opposition, for

India had no interest in preserving the old order. The days of the Ranas were numbered and ended with the king's return to prominence and the introduction of democratic rule in the wake of the 1950–1 uprising.

On 31 July 1950, when the Ranas were still nominally in power, though their grip over the nation was considerably weakened, India and Nepal signed a Treaty of Peace and Friendship. The governments agreed

> mutually to acknowledge and respect the complete sovereignty, territorial integrity and independence of each other ... [and that] each Government undertakes, in token of the neighbourly friendship between India and Nepal, to give to the nationals of the other, in its territory, national treatment with regard to participation in industrial and economic development of such territory and to the grant of concessions and contracts relating to such development.[48]

The agreement also stipulated that India and Nepal should award equal rights to citizens of the other country to reside in theirs. It went on to state that 'the Government of Nepal shall be free to import, from or through the territory of India, arms, ammunition or warlike material and equipment necessary for the security of Nepal. The procedure for giving effect to this arrangement shall be worked out by the two Governments acting in consultation.'[49]

India's influence increased during the 1950s. In 1952, an Indian military mission was established in Nepal and a memorandum signed two years later provided for the joint co-ordination of foreign policy, and outposts manned by Indian security personnel were established near the border with Tibet. Another agreement, which was concluded in 1952, amplified the privileges agreed upon in the 1950 agreement and gave Indian citizens the right to immigrate to Nepal and become Nepalese citizens and gave the same right to Nepalese citizens as well. This agreement, though, caused resentment in Nepal where many did not want to see large-scale Indian immigration, while many Indians, too, were opposed to Nepalese coming to work in their country. Dissatisfaction with India's influence led to Nepal looking north for closer relations with China. New Delhi, however, continued to give a high level of economic assistance to Nepal at the same time as

India provided a safe haven for the Nepali Congress, now operating almost exclusively in exile.

However, relations between Nepal and India were never going to be the same after the construction of the highway to Tibet and the 1970 blockade. New treaties for trade and transit rights were signed in 1978, but relations became even more strained when, in 1988, the Nepalese government signed an agreement with China to purchase weapons, including antiaircraft guns. A second road to Tibet was also going to be built west of the Araniko Highway.

According to US researcher Andrea M. Savada,

> In retaliation for these developments, India put Nepal under a virtual trade siege. In March 1989, upon the expiration of the 1978 treaties on trade and transit rights, India insisted on negotiating a single unified treaty in addition to an agreement on unauthorised trade, which Nepal saw as a flagrant attempt to strangle its economy. On March 23, 1989, India declared that both treaties had expired and closed all but two border entry points.[50]

Also in 1989, Nepal decided to decouple its rupee from the Indian Rupee, which until then had circulated freely in Nepal. India retaliated by denying the Nepalese port facilities in Kolkata to Nepal, thus preventing the delivery of oil from Singapore and other countries.

Relations improved after the 1990 Jan Andolan, which saw the return to power of the Nepali Congress. A joint Indian-Nepalese communiqué was issued in June 1990 announcing the restoration of the status quo and the reopening of all border crossings. The Nepalese leadership also said that 'lower cost' was the reason they had bought weapons from China, and China was advised to withhold its last shipment to Nepal.[51]

Then came the Maoist insurgency, to which both India and China found it difficult to relate. For China, the problem was embarrassment over the Nepalese revolutionaries' use of the Chairman's ideology as their guiding principle. The Indians, troubled by their own Maoist insurgency which had taken roots in tribal areas in central India, did not want to see a linkup between the revolutionaries of the two countries. The CPN-M already had close ties with the Communist Party of India-Marxist-Leninist

(People's War Group), which merged with the Maoist Communist Centre of India to become the Communist Party of India (Maoist) in September 2004. Apart from acquiring weapons from factories in Bihar, the CPN-M also trained some of its troops in Maoist camps in India. An alliance called the Coordinating Committee of Maoist Parties and Organisations of South Asia had also been formed in July 2001, comprising Indian, Nepalese, Sri Lankan, and Bangladeshi Maoist parties with the Communist Party of Bhutan (Marxist-Leninist-Maoist) holding what was called 'observer status'.[52]

Post-2008 developments and the mellowing of the CPN-M have allayed those fears, but have also led to a more intense tug-of-war between India and China for power and influence in Nepal. India suffered a severe setback after Nepal was struck by a third blockade in 2015, for which India was blamed. After years of wrangling and political bickering, Nepal's constituent assembly approved a new constitution on 20 September 2015, turning the country into a federal state made up of seven unnamed states. This led to violent protests by Madhesis and Tharus, historically marginalized groups in the southern plains adjacent to India.

The International Crisis Group (ICG) summarized the problem in this manner:

> There is disagreement over boundaries of the new states, electoral representation ... and citizenship-related issues. Supporters of the new constitution ... say an excessive focus on identity-based grievances threatens Nepal's unity, integrity and even sovereignty. The objections of those who demonstrated against it have their roots in long-running social disagreements on what it means to be Nepali and whether a homogenous conception of Nepaliness has led to structural discrimination against groups that do not conform to the behaviour and values of hill-origin, Nepali-speaking, upper caste Hindu communities.[53]

The 135-day blockade by Madhesi civil and political groups, which won sympathy from large segments of society in India, came five months after a devastating earthquake hit Nepal, killing nearly 9,000 people and injuring 22,000. Hundreds of thousands of people became homeless, entire villages were wiped out, and ancient temples in central Kathmandu were damaged. Both China and India, along with many other countries, provided assistance to the victims, but coupled with the blockade, 2015 was the worst year in Nepal's modern history. As a result of the blockade, there was a shortage of daily commodities, including fuel, in an already ravaged country.

After many Nepalese had blamed the blockade on India, which had criticized the lack of inclusiveness in the new constitution, some politicians in Kathmandu now began to accuse India of fomenting the movement among the Madhesis. According to the ICG:

> India's domestic policies were also a factor. When the blockade began, there was a common belief that the ruling BJP [Bharatiya Janata Party] was trying to win votes in Bihar state elections by appearing to project the interests of the Biharis' kin across the border. This fuelled the perception that Madhesi and Indian demands—and Madhesis and Biharis in India—were interchangeable.[54]

India denied the allegations, but that was to no avail. When the blockade ended on 8 February 2016, anti-Indian sentiment was running high in Nepal.

The Chinese, meanwhile, were pursuing a more subtle, behind-the-scenes policy—and one of their main concerns was the presence in Nepal of 20,000 Tibetan refugees, some whom had fled in 1959. According to an article for *Jane's Intelligence Review* written by Stephan Blancke, a German political scientist specializing in intelligence and organized crime: 'Internally, Tibet remains a key operational theatre. In Nepal, where the Ministry of State Security has established various non-governmental organizations (NGOs) and language institutes, delegations of Chinese intelligence operatives regularly meet in order to co-ordinate operations against the Tibetan community.'[55] *Jane's Intelligence Review* went on to quote a 23 May 2013 press statement released by the Central Tibetan Administration's Department of Security which 'claimed that Li Yuquan, in his capacity as head of the Public Security Bureau of Nangchu Prefecture in the Tibet Autonomous Region, recruited a Tibetan for the purpose of spying on Tibetan NGOs, and later in order to carry out the attempted murder of two dissidents.'[56]

On an official level, China has provided assistance to Nepal for establishing the National Armed Police Force Academy and built a well-equipped China Information Centre in Tatopani in Sindhupalchok to keep track of anti-Chinese activities along the Araniko Highway. The Chinese have also provided Nepalese police with a sophisticated Digital Radio Trunking System to enhance their communication capabilities. Since 2002, China has sent military officers to participate in 'adventure training' in Nepal and, from 2008, the Nepalese army has sent officers and soldiers for training at educational institutions in China.[57] As early as 1999, a China Studies Centre was set up in Kathmandu, with assistance from the Chinese embassy, to promote Chinese language and culture, a place where Nepalese can learn Chinese free of charge. The Nepal-China Media Forum is another organization involved in fostering closer relations with the Nepalese.

The Chinese-supported NGOs mentioned by *Jane's Intelligence Review* appear to include an outfit founded by CPN-UML leader Madhav Kumar Nepal and called the International Association of Shakya Buddha Faithful. Another NGO called ATOM, led by Normal Mahara, the son of CPN-Maoist Centre leader Krishna Bahadur Mahara, is also thought to be receiving Chinese assistance, as are the Nepal-China Mutual Cooperation Society (NCMCS), the Nepal-China Friendship Society, and an NGO headed by the wife of CPN-ML Chairman Chandra Prakash Mainali. The NCMCS, in turn, has provided assistance to the Himani Trust, which takes part in various social welfare activities.[58] China has even encroached upon what has traditionally been India's turf by providing assistance to the G.P. Koirala Foundation's earthquake relief programme.

When it comes to Nepalese politics, the Chinese have been actively trying bring about unity among Nepal's many communist parties. While the CPN-M, now the CPN-UML, may be their main choice, a high-ranking official from the International Department of the Communist Party of China met CPN-UML leader Khadka Prasad Oli before he became prime minister in October 2015, promising him a substantial economic package to consolidate his position. In September, just before Oli took over the premiership, another CPN-UML leader, Ishwor Pokhrel, visited China to seek support for the government they were going to form. In May 2016, the Chinese ambassador to Nepal, Wu Chuntai, presided over a meeting in Kathmandu of Oli, Prachanda, and Narayan Kazi Shrestha from the CPN-Unity Centre. There was yet another cabinet crisis and Wu was reported to have told Prachanda that it would be inappropriate for the Oli government to fall immediately after he had paid a visit to China. A leftist government should be in office when Chinese President Xi Jinping was scheduled to visit Nepal in October.

Oli survived as prime minister until 4 August 2015. Xi's trip was not cancelled, as some Indian newspapers predicted at the time, but postponed because of the political crisis in Nepal. In October Xi attended a BRICS-BIMSTEC (Brazil, Russia, India, China, South Africa and the Bay of Bengal Initiative for Multi-Sectoral Technical and Economic Cooperation) meeting in Goa, India, where he shook hands with Oli's successor Prachanda and pledged that he would visit Nepal 'at an earliest convenient date'.[59]

Even the Madhesis, who were thought to be close to India, turned to the Chinese for help. On 18 March 2016, a delegation from the Samyukta Loktantrik Medhesi Morcha went to the Chinese embassy in Kathmandu to hand over a memorandum expressing their opposition to the new constitution and seeking Chinese support to help put pressure on the then Oli government to address their grievances. A Madhesi-dominated political party, the Federal Socialist Forum, Nepal, and a faction of the Madhesi Jana Adhikar Forum, have also received support from the Chinese embassy for their activities, underscoring the fact that the Chinese always hedge their bets and never put all their eggs in one basket.

Politics in Nepal remains as messy as ever and became messier still when Bhattarai split with Prachanda and launched a new political party called Naya Shakti (New Force) in July 2016. It had been known for some time that differences existed between the two Maoist leaders, with the more intellectual Bhattarai feeling uncomfortable with Prachanda's consolidation of power in his own hands. But the actual policies of Bhattarai's new party are not quite clear other than that it intends to have a directly elected presidential system to solve the problem of constant crises and political chaos. Bhattarai also opposes the new constitution and has expressed support for the Madhesis, a position welcomed by India.

Even if India remains Nepal's main foreign trade partner and continues to give substantial foreign aid to the country, there is no doubt that China has developed a very special relationship with successive Nepalese governments as well as civil society in all spheres, politically as well as economically. China is also moving closer to Nepal in other respects. In 2005, China finished building a railway from Xining, the capital of Qinghai province, to Lhasa. Xining was already in 1959 connected with China's main rail network. In August 2014, the line was extended to Shigatse in southern Tibet, not far from the Nepalese border. There have been speculations about the railway being extended even farther, down to Zhangmu on the border and perhaps even to Kathmandu, which would be highly controversial considering India's sensitivities. China has also been increasingly involved in infrastructure projects inside Nepal such as in Lumbini, the birthplace of the Buddha right on the Indian border, and the construction of a road from Pokhara to Baglung, west of Kathmandu.

Nepal has sometimes been described as 'a jam between two boulders' and the Nepalese are without doubt looking to further strengthen their economic and other ties with China to fulfil the country's long-standing policy of being less dependent on India. But, as the French news agency Agence France-Presse (AFP) reported in August 2016, it will have a long way to go to accomplish that. 'Bilateral trade with India between July 2014 and June 2015 amounted to nearly US$4.5 billion, dwarfing China's US$882 million.'[60] But China's share is growing, and the AFP quoted Sujeev Shakya, chairman of the Nepal Economic Forum think tank as saying that 'the perception here is that the Chinese tend to deliver while India keeps talking. Over the years, China has gained more credibility in Nepal because of the pace at which they have put up infrastructure projects.'[61] But the problem for Nepal is that most of the labourers working on those projects are Chinese, and thus the projects have not created any job opportunities for the Nepalese. [62]

Nepal is likely to continue being the 'sick man of the Himalayas', with one political crisis after another and an economy that is heavily dependent on foreign aid. It is also likely to remain the country where India's geopolitical interests, more so than in any other neighbour, collide with those of an increasingly assertive China: India's seeking to protect its traditional influence in Nepal and to guard the crest of the Himalayas, and China look-ing to establish a string of 'friendly nations' in its periphery, a policy not unlike that of the old Chinese emperors who surrounded their realms with faithful satrapies and tributary states. But it is still in the east that India's and China's divergent interests could boil over into open conflict. And the tension is about much more than the border dispute. It is also about bilat-eral issues such as managing the water from the Brahmaputra, the wider geopolitical contest in the Indian Ocean—and, when it comes to armed conflicts, the presence of Chinese-allied insurgents from northeastern India in cross-border sanctuaries in Myanmar.

Notes

1. Quoted in Bertil Lintner, 'Nepal struggles to cope with diehard Maoist violence', *Jane's Intelligence Review*, June 1999, pp. 43–4.
2. Prachanda, *The First Glorious Year of People's War* (Kathmandu: Utprerak Publications, 1998), p. 25. ., p. 25.
3. Prachanda, *The First Glorious Year of People's War*, p. 24.
4. Prachanda, *The First Glorious Year of People's War*, pp. 25–6.
5. Lintner, 'Nepal struggles to cope with diehard Maoist violence', p. 43.
6. Stephen I. Mikesell, 'The Paradoxical Support of Nepal's Left for Comrade Gonzalo', *Himal*, March–April 1993, p. 31.
7. Quoted in Lintner, 'Nepal struggles to cope with diehard Maoist violence', p. 43. Nepal South Asia Centre can be reached at http://nepalsouthasia.org/remaining_of_intro.html (accessed on 14 August 2017). See also Udaya R. Wagle, 'Economic Inequality in the "democratic" Nepal', *School of Public Affairs and Administration*, Western Michigan University, Kalamazoo, avail-able at http://homepages.wmich.edu/~uwagle/IneqNepal.pdf (accessed on 14 August 2017).
8. Quoted in Lintner, 'Nepal struggles to cope with diehard Maoist violence', p. 43.
9. Shyam Shrestha, 'Nepali Cart Before Horse', *Himal*, September 1997, avail-able at http://old.himalmag.com/component/content/article/2721-Nepali-Cart-Before-Horse.html (accessed on 18 December 2016).
10. Prachanda, *Two Momentous Years of Revolutionary Transformation* (Kathmandu: Utprerak Publications, n.d.), p. 22. This book is undated,

but was most probably published in 1998 (at the second anniversary of the 1996 uprising).

11. For a detailed biography of Prachanda, see, Anirban Roy, *Prachanda: The Unknown Revolutionary* (Kathmandu: Mandala Book Point, 2008).

12. The dissertation is available at http://nepalitimes.com/news.php?id=11198#. WZFnXXcjFuU (accessed on 14 August 2017) and for purchase here https://www.amazon.com/Nature-Underdevelopment-Regional-Structure-Nepal/dp/8187392398 (accessed on 14 August 2017).

13. For a brief biography of Baburam Bhattarai, see 'Dr. Baburam Bhattarai's Biography', available at http://baburam-bhattarai.blogspot.com/2010/01/dr-baburam-bhattarais-biography.html (accessed on 23 December 2016).

14. Lintner, 'Nepal struggles to cope with diehard Maoist violence', p. 44.

15. Carlos Iván Degregori, 'The Origins and Logic of Shining Path: Two Views' Palmer, David Scott (ed.), *Shining Path of Peru* (London: Hurst and Company, 1992), pp. 33–4.

16. Prachanda, *The First Glorious Year of People's War,* p. 67.

17. Quoted in B. Raman, 'India & China: as seen by Maoists - part II', New Delhi: Observer Research Foundation, 15 February 2005, available at http://www.orfonline.org/research/india-china-as-seen-by-maoists-part-ii/ (accessed on 20 December 2016).

18. Li Onesto, *Dispatches from the People's War in Nepal* (London: Pluto Press, and London and Chicago: Insight Press Inc., 2005), p. 228. .

19. Raman, 'India & China: as seen by Maoists - part II'.

20. *China's Foreign Relations: A Chronology of Events (1949–1988)* (Beijing: Foreign Languages Press, 1989), p. 215.

21. Sanjay Kumar, *Nepal as a Factor in India's Security during Post Cold War Era* (Delhi: Mohit Publications, 2013), p. 62.

22. *China's Foreign Relations,* p. 216.

23. Andrea Matles Savada, *Nepal and Bhutan: Country Studies* (Washington: Federal Research Division, Library of Congress, 1993), p. 186.

24. Rajeev Ranjan Chaturvedy and David M. Malone, 'A Yam, between Two Boulders: Nepal's Foreign Policy Caught between India and China', Sebastian von Einsiedel, David M. Malone, and Suman Pradhan (eds), *Nepal in Transition: From People's War to Fragile Peace* (Cambridge: Cambridge University Press, 2012), pp. 294–5.

25. 'Over reliance on India has hit economy hard', *Kathmandu Post,* 22 November 2015, available at http://kathmandupost.ekantipur.com/printedition/news/

2015-11-22/over-reliance-on-india-has-hit-economy-hard.html (accessed on 20 December 2016).

26. Kumar, *Nepal as a Factor in India's Security during Post Cold War Era*, p. 22.

27. *China's Foreign Relations*, p. 218.

28. For a succinct account of the massacre, see Jonathan Gregson, *Blood Against the Snows: The Tragic Story of Nepal's Royal Dynasty* (London: Fourth Estate, 2002). See pp. 194–5: 'For a country whose history is littered with real conspiracies, it is second nature to accept anything at face value with extreme reluctance. The result is an admixture of credulity and distrust which permits no truth to be set in stone. Rather, it encourages the multiplication of different versions of an event to the point where it seems there are as many "true" variants as there are gods and goddesses in the Hindu pantheon.'

29. Quoted in Roy, *Prachanda*, p. 178.

30. Bertil Lintner, 'Nepal's Maoists Prepare for the Final Offensive, *Jane's Intelligence Review*, October 2002, p. 37.

31. For the full text of the peace agreement, see 'Unofficial Translation of the Comprehensive Peace Agreement concluded between the Government of Nepal and the Communist Party of Nepal (Maoist)', available at http://www.usip.org/sites/default/files/file/resources/collections/peace_agreements/nepal_cpa_20061121_en.pdf (accessed on 18 December 2016).

32. 'Unofficial Translation of the Comprehensive Peace Agreement concluded between the Government of Nepal and the Communist Party of Nepal (Maoist)'.

33. 'Unofficial Translation of the Comprehensive Peace Agreement concluded between the Government of Nepal and the Communist Party of Nepal (Maoist)'.

34. 'Chinese Premier meets Nepali PM', *Xinhua*, 24 August 2008, available at https://marxistleninist.wordpress.com/2008/08/24/prachanda-visits-china/ (accessed on 14 August 2017).

35. 'Prachanda in New York: A Maoist Vision for Nepal', *Links: International Journal of Socialist Renewal*, 22 October 2008, available at http://links.org.au/node/652/7040 (accessed on 20 December 2016).

36. Thomas Bell, 'Nepal's "fierce one" spurns Chairman Mao and claims centre ground in peace talks', *The Telegraph*, 31 October 2006, available at http://www.telegraph.co.uk/news/worldnews/1532891/Nepals-fierce-one-spurns-Chairman-Mao-and-claims-centre-ground-in-peace-talks.html (accessed on 20 December 2016).

37. 'Chinese top political advisor pledges closer ties with Nepal', CCTV.com, 12 October 2009, available at http://english.cctv.com/20091012/104634.shtml (accessed on 14 August 2017).

38. Quoted in 'Prachanda makes historic visit to China', *Lalkar*, November/December 2009, available at http://www.lalkar.org/article/837/prachanda-makes-historic-visit-to-china (accessed on 20 December 2016).

39. Quoted in Dhruba Adhikary, 'Maoists go on pilgrimage in China', *Asia Times Online*, 16 October 2009, available at http://www.atimes.com/atimes/South_Asia/KJ16Df03.html (accessed on 20 December 2016).

40. Baburam Bhattarai, *Politico-Economic Rationale of People's War in Nepal* (Kathmandu: Utprerak Publications, 1998), p. 7.

41. Bhattarai, *Politico-Economic Rationale of People's War in Nepal*, p. 35.

42. 'Nepal and India: Bhattarai and Singh address each other', *Nepal Monitor*, 21 December 2011, available at http://www.nepalmonitor.com/2011/10/nepal-india_bhattara.html (accessed on 20 December 2016).

43. 'Nepal and India: Bhattarai and Singh address each other'.

44. 'Padam Kunwar suggests leaders to 'beware of public anger' as he admits "unlawful act"', available at https://www.youtube.com/watch?v=X-xITPt-kKSo, (accessed on 20 December 2016).

45. Quoted in Lin Meilian, 'Maoism, borrowed and abandoned' *Global Times*, 25 March 2013, available at http://www.globaltimes.cn/content/770482.shtml (accessed on 20 December 2016).

46. For details of the treaty, see Buddhi Narayan Shrestha, 'What is Sugauli Treaty?', mimeograph available at https://indiamadhesi.files.wordpress.com/2008/11/what-is-sugauli-treaty.pdf (accessed on 14 August 2017). Sagauli can also be spelled Sugauli, See also 'Sugauli Treaty (1815) -East India Company and Nepal' at http://www.veergorkha.com/2012/01/sugauli-treaty-1815-east-india-company.html (accessed on 14 August 2017).

47. For a brief account of this period in Nepalese history, see Savada, *Nepal and Bhutan*, pp. 26–31.

48. For the full text of the agreement, see 'Treaty of Peace and Friendship Between the Government of India and the Government of Nepal', available at http://www.nepaldemocracy.org/documents/treaties_agreements/indo-nepal_treaty_peace.htm (accessed on 29 December 2016).

49. 'Treaty of Peace and Friendship Between the Government of India and the Government of Nepal'.

50. Savada *Nepal and Bhutan*, p. 182.

51. Savada *Nepal and Bhutan,* p. 183.

52. See 'Joint Statement of the Maoist parties and Organisations of South Asia', available at http://www.bannedthought.net/International/RIM/ AWTW/2001-27/AWTW-27-CCOMPOSA-Formation.pdf (accessed on 20 December 2016) and 'Coordination Committee of Maoist Parties and Organisations of South Asia', available at https://en.wikipedia.org/wiki/ Coordination_Committee_of_Maoist_Parties_and_Organisations_of_ South_Asia (accessed on 20 December 2016).

53. International Crisis Group (ICG), *Nepal's Divisive New Constitution: An Existential Crisis,* Crisis Group Asia Report No.276, (Brussels: ICG, 4 April 2016), p. i, available at https://d2071andvip0wj.cloudfront.net/276-nepal-s-divisive-new-constitution-an-existential-crisis.pdf (accessed on 20 December 2016).

54. ICG, *Nepal's Divisive New Constitution,* p. 23.

55. Stephan Blancke, 'Chinese whispers—Chinese intelligence Capabilities', *Jane's Intelligence Review,* 3 July 2013, available at https://www.researchgate. net/publication/255701947_Chinese_whispers_-_Chinese_intelligence_ capabilities (accessed on 20 December 2016).

56. Quoted in Stephan Blancke, 'Chinese whispers—Chinese intelligence capabilities'.

57. M.K. Singh, *Nepal Foreign Policy* (New Delhi: Sumit Enterprises, 2011), p. 244.

58. This and the information in the paragraph below comes from interviews with local security officials who requested anonymity, Kathmandu, 21–3 May 2016.

59. 'Xi Jinping "ready to visit Nepal at earliest convenient date"', *The Himalayan,* 15 October 2016, available at http://thehimalayantimes.com/nepal/xi-jinping-ready-visit-nepal-earliest-convenient-date/ (accessed on 20 December 2016).

60. Ammu Kannampilly, 'In Nepal's Himalayas, hopes of closer ties with China', *Agence France-Presse,* 25 August 2016.

61. Ammu Kannampilly, *Agence France-Presse,* 25 August 2016.

62. Chok Tsering, 'Kodari Road: Implications for Nepal, China and India: Analysis', *Eurasia Review,* 1 December 2011, available at http://www.eurasiareview.com/01122011-kodari-road-implications-for-nepal-china-and-india-analysis/ (accessed on 20 December 2016).

8

Borderlands and Oceans

With a total length of nearly 3,000 kilometres, the Brahmaputra is one of the longest rivers of the world. It originates in the Angsi Glacier north of the Himalayas, and then flows for more than 1,620 kilometres through Tibet before it enters India and cascades down to the Assam plains. It then flows through Bangladesh, joins the Ganges and other rivers with which it forms a delta, and, finally, empties into the Bay of Bengal. The Brahmaputra, known as the Yarlung Tsangpo in Tibet and the Jamuna in Bangladesh, is the lifeline of tens of millions of people. There was, therefore, alarm in India when it became known in 2009 that China was building a 116-metre-tall and 389-metre-long dam to support a 540-megawatt power station at Zangmu in Tibet. The Chinese had until then denied that it had any plans to build a mega dam just north of India and Bhutan. In January 2013, the Chinese government approved the construction of three more dams on the river, at Dagu and Jiexu upstream and at Jiacha below Zangmu Dam. Altogether 28 dam projects in Tibet have been proposed.

Causing more alarm, Li Ling, a Chinese scientist, published a book called *Save China, Through Water From Tibet*[1] in November 2005 in which he mentioned that Chinese water experts had conducted a survey on the viability of transferring water from Tibet's rivers to central China to alleviate water shortage there.[2] Most of China's big rivers originate in the Tibetan highlands, and the idea to divert waters from the tributaries and actually reroute the Brahamputra to the Yangtze-Huang He, or the Yellow River, was not even new. The PLA had entertained such ideas at least since the 1980s.[3] Although 70 per cent of the waters of the Indian stretch of the Brahmaputra comes from direct rainwater collected south of the border and from tributaries from Arunachal Pradesh, Sikkim, and Bhutan, the fact that China controls almost a third of it has been enough to cause serious concern in India. The Chinese view on the matter was expressed by a retired general, Guo Kai, in an interview with the official government paper *Global Post*. 'So much water in the Yarlung Tsangpo runs out of China, it's a waste'.[4] He went on to make the claim that India and Bangladesh get so much rainfall that they suffer from flooding, so if China diverted the water from the Brahmaputra, all three nations would benefit.

It is understandable that the fast-expanding Chinese economy needs vast amounts of electricity, but less so that the damming, and possible diversion, of the Brahmaputra is being done without consultations with the countries downstream. The initial Indian response to China's plans was meek. India's former minister for Development of the Northeastern Region, Praban Singh Ghatowar, told the British Broadcasting Corporation (BBC) in March 2014 that 'our foreign ministry has checked with China and we have been told that the flow will not be affected, and we will make sure that the people's lives are not affected by the dams'.[5] In response, a Chinese foreign ministry spokesman told the BBC that, 'all projects go through scientific planning and feasibility studies and the impact on both upstream and downstream will be fully considered'.[6]

But, many people remain sceptical, and even highly critical of the plans, as there is no water-sharing deal between India and China, just an agreement to share monsoon data. Information provided by the Chinese has also been incomplete and often contradictory, and, as the BBC pointed out, 'It is hard to know where the truth lies. The dams are hidden from view, on remote valleys and in deep mountain gorges. It is there that the never-ending tension between politics, development and environment is now being played out.'[7] Part of the equation is also that China controls the sources not only of the Brahmaputra but of other major Asian rivers as well, among them the Mekong and the Salween, and Chinese dams on the Mekong, known there as Lancang, have become a major problem for downstream countries by withholding water supply. A plan to build a cascade of at least five large dams on the Salween, known as the Nujiang in China, which flows into Myanmar and later in part marks the border between Myanmar and Thailand, was postponed only after vocal protests in Thailand and Myanmar, and even from Chinese NGO Green Watershed in Kunming.[8]

Spokesmen for the Chinese authorities claim that 'there are cooperation mechanisms for China and the five Southeast Asian countries (Myanmar, Laos, Thailand, Cambodia, and Vietnam) that can help co-ordinate sustainable use of water resources in the Lancang-Mekong River and share information'.[9] The problem is that there are actually very few such 'co-operation mechanisms' between China and the downstream countries. China is not a member of the Mekong River Commission, an intergovernmental body for co-ordinating water resources comprising representatives of Thailand, Laos, Cambodia, and Vietnam. Myanmar, which does not significantly rely on or tap the Mekong, attends meetings as an observer, as does China, but the Chinese only provide water level data to the Commission during floods. None of the downstream countries was consulted before China built its dams on the Mekong. China has built seven such dams so far, and plans to build 21 more.[10]

In Myanmar, Chinese plans to build a mega dam at Myitsone, where the Mali Hka and the Nmai Hka join to become the Irrawaddy River, rivers that do not flow from China, provoked mass protests until the country's new quasi-civilian government under President Thein Sein announced on 30 September, 2011, that the joint Myanmar-Chinese mega-hydroelectric project was suspended. The US$3.6 billion Myitsone Dam would have been world's 15th tallest dam, submerging 766 square kilometres of forestland, an area bigger than Singapore.[11] The suspension of the construction of the dam marked the beginning of rapidly deteriorating relations between Myanmar and China. Until then, Myanmar had been one of China's most faithful allies in Southeast Asia.

Hu Weijia, writing in the *Global Times* in October 2016, argued that 'it is understandable that India is sensitive to China's water exploitation on the Brahmaputra as a downstream country, but China is unlikely to use the waters of the river as a potential weapon ... China-India relations should not be affected by an imaginary "water war".[12] The problem is that there already is a 'water war', although it has not led to armed conflict and may never do so. But the dispute is bound to exacerbate the already strained relations between India and China.

India is building dams, too, to meet its growing needs for electricity: first in Bhutan and Nepal and now in Arunachal Pradesh. Revenue from the sale of electricity from dams built by India in Bhutan provides the Himalayan kingdom with a substantial source of income that has been used for the country's development. In Nepal, India has become the largest hydropower developer as well, most recently with an agreement signed in November 2014 to build a 900-megawatt dam and power station in the eastern part of the country. In August, Indian Prime Minister Narendra Modi signed a deal with the Nepalese for the first 900-megawatt dam, in western Nepal. The deals are not without controversy and some politicians and NGOs are demanding they be terminated.[13]

Hydroelectric development in Arunachal is also controversial. The state has a tremendous potential for generating electricity, and all its rivers flow down into the lowlands of Assam below the mountains. Construction of a dam on the Siang River, a tributary of the Brahmaputra that flows through Arunachal's Upper Siang District, began in April 2009 and, when completed, it will be the largest hydroelectric dam in the Indian subcontinent. In 2010, a local student organization appealed to the Indian government to scrap the Siang project and other dams that it has plans to build in Arunachal. The government responded by saying that the projects will not be cancelled and that necessary precautions will be undertaken to ensure minimal environmental impact.[14]

It is inevitable that those huge projects on the rivers flowing south from the Himalayas will adversely affect the environment. But there is a fundamental difference between hydroelectric power development in India and China. India is a democracy where such issues can be discussed freely, and it is legitimate to protest the government's decisions and plans. This is not the case in China. The suspension of the Salween dams was a rare

258 Chapter's India War

exception, but was possible because some of Green Watershed's organizers have high-level contacts and, therefore, some protection for their activities.

But India's strength, its democracy, also makes it vulnerable to unwanted, internal pressures. Protests against the plans to build dams in Arunachal have been exploited by India's Maoists. The Communist Party of India-Maoist (CPI-Maoist), which is engaged in armed insurrection against the Indian state, may be an unlawful organization, but it operates openly through a number of civil society groups and other fronts. Anti-dam activists have stalled the construction of a dam on the Subansiri River since 2011. In April 2015, *The Times of India* quoted Minister of State for Home Affairs Haribhai Parthibhai Chaudhary as saying that the Upper Assam Leading Committee of the CPI-Maoist is 'presently operating in Assam and Arunachal Pradesh and has been involved in the looting of weapons and extortion activities in the local villages'.[15] The minister went on to say that the CPI-Maoist had been engaged in recruitment and training of cadres for its units in Assam. 'These cadres have been involved in extensive propaganda against mega dams in Assam. Against this backdrop, the Assam-Arunachal border has emerged as another theatre of Maoist activity,' the minister said.[16]

India's Maoist movement may be dwindling and is not as strong as it was in the first decade of the twenty-first century. But it is still active mainly in the tribal belt in central India—and it has been able to find new fertile ground for its revolutionary message among some tribal communities in Arunachal precisely because the state is developing fast, and hydroelectric power generation is part of economic development. As Akhil Ranjan Dutta, a professor of political science at Guwahati University, explains, the projects have been marred

> by pursuing aggressive corporate friendly development paradigm as is evident in the case of commissioning of large river dams in the region. Relative egalitarian societies have ... witnessed a transition towards hierarchical class divisions once the political elites have joined hands with the Indian ruling class ... along with it has evolved a new middle class—the contractors, clerks etc. who have gradually disassociated from the communities.[17]

The extent of Maoist penetration of Arunachal became known in August 2011, when arrested Maoist cadres told their interrogators that they used to hold regular 'revolutionary meetings' at their hideouts in Lohit and Lower Dibang Valley districts in Arunachal. Such meetings were attended by between 150 and 200 villagers and cadres, the captured Maoists said.[18] The CPI-Maoist has, over the past few years, also established links with ULFA and leftist rebels in Manipur. According to ULFA commander Paresh Baruah, 'if the Maoists can launch a successful war against the Indian state, it will be beneficial for ULFA. We have a strategic understanding with the Maoists on our common enemy.'[19] Most Manipuri rebels have been leftists since the days of their hero Hijam Irabot, who formed the first revolutionary movement in the state in the 1940s.

Even so, the possibility of a widespread CPI-Maoist insurgency in Arunachal is extremely remote. And, as was the case in Nepal during the Maoist insurrection there, the Chinese have shown little interest in the Indian Maoist movement and are unlikely to support it, with 'Maoism' being an anachronism even in China. It is an entirely different matter with India's ethnic, northeastern insurgents who have a long-standing relationship with China's intelligence services. After the death of Mao Zedong in 1976 and the introduction of Deng Xiaoping's market-oriented reforms, China was no longer exporting world revolution—only consumer goods and other products from its fast-growing industries. But China's secret services did not, as the April 2004 arms bust in Chittagong clearly showed, give up their contacts with India's ethnic rebels. And contacts had to be maintained through northwestern Myanmar, to where the Naga rebels in the 1970s, and ULFA in the 1980s, had retreated after successive Indian military operations in the northeast. Headquartered at their camp in Taka, northern Sagaing Region, they have been able to carry out cross-border attacks into India.

Myanmar's military, preoccupied with its own ethnic insurgencies elsewhere in the country, has paid little attention to the presence of rebels from India on its turf. Undisturbed by nearby Myanmar Army outposts, a meeting of Assamese, Naga and, Manipuri rebels took place at their camp at Taka near the Chindwin River in April 2014. They formed a new outfit with the peculiar name, the United National Liberation Front of Western Southeast Asia (UNLFWSA), to co-ordinate their activities— and to emphasize their ethnic affinity with the peoples of southeast Asian roots rather than with those in India. The chairman of the new alliance, Shangwang Shangyung Khaplang, a Naga from Myanmar, had been fighting for self-determination for his Myanmar Naga tribes for several decades. In the late 1960s, Khaplang met and escorted Indian Nagas on their way to China for training. When the Indian Nagas could no longer maintain camps on their side of the border, a joint-Naga base area was established on the Myanmar side.

Khaplang sided with Thuingaleng Muivah and Isak Chishi Swu, both China-trained rebels, when the Naga movement split in the late 1970s. When the NSCN was formed in 1980 with Isak as its chairman and Muivah as general secretary, Khaplang was appointed vice-chairman. But it was an alliance that was doomed to fail. The Myanmar Nagas, tired of being treated as serfs by their Indian cousins, drove them out of the area in 1988. The NSCN then split into NSCN (Isak-Muivah), or NSCN-IM, and NSCN (Khaplang), or NSCN-K.

After the loss of its sanctuaries in Myanmar, the NSCN-IM had little choice but to enter into peace negotiations with the Indian government, with which it agreed to a ceasefire in 1997. But, ignoring the accord, Anthony Shimray, the NSCN-IM's main arms procurer who was arrested in 2010, continued to acquire guns from China and other sources until the 2004 Chittagong arms haul put an end to any attempts to get any large shipment of weapons into Nagaland on the Indian side. Shimray first visited China in 1995 and made his initial contacts with the Chinese arms manufacturer North Industries Corporation (NORINCO) as well as a firm based in the coastal province of Guangzhou called the Xin Li Yuan International Investment Company, which was to act as a middleman for weapons purchases. Shimray also held regular meetings in Ruili in Yunnan with Chinese intelligence officers, including one who used the name 'Allan Chang'.[20] In Thailand, Shimray dealt with a local gunrunner called Wuthikorn 'Willy' Naurenartwanich, and through him attempted to procure a huge consignment of Chinese-made guns. In other words, Wuthikorn was another middleman for China's 'grey' arms market, acquiring weapons from a Chinese front company in Bangkok known only as TCL.[21]

But the deal fell through. And, two years after the arrest of Shimray, the Indian government managed to persuade Thai authorities to extradite Wuthikorn to India.[22] Since then, the NSCN-IM's activities have been confined to occasional murders of opponents in Manipur and 'tax collection' from businesses, government officials, ordinary citizens, and some local politicians in Nagaland. Under the ceasefire agreement with the Indian government, the group cannot engage in any violence in Nagaland. The NSCN-IM's troops are confined to a number of camps, where they carry out drills using mostly wooden guns.

The NSCN-K also entered into a ceasefire agreement with the Indian government in 2001 and with Myanmar in April 2012, making it the only insurgent group in the country to have ceasefire agreements with the governments of two sovereign states. Since the late 1980s and early 1990s, the Myanmar government has made peace with a number of ethnic rebel armies within its borders while engaged in war with others such as the powerful Kachin Independence Army (KIA) in the far north of the country.

The NSCN-K kept its ceasefire agreement with Myanmar, but abrogated its peace deal with India in March 2015, and ambushes on the Indian side began. The UNLFWSA guerrillas' fiercest strike occurred on 4 June, when 18 soldiers were killed and 15 wounded in an ambush on an Indian military convoy in Manipur's Chandel District. The guerrillas, who had come from across the Myanmar border, retreated to their sanctuaries on the other side after the ambush.

For years, Indian authorities had tried to press the Myanmar military to take action against the rebels from India, but to no avail. Suggestions that the armies of the two countries should carry out joint, or at least co-ordinated, operations against the rebels were also ignored. But the Chandel ambush prompted Indians to take matters into their own hands. So, on 9 June, Indian soldiers crossed into Myanmar and attacked camps belonging to the UNLFWSA.

It is clear that as long as the Indian rebels do not bother the Myanmar Army, they are left alone. According to a testimony by an Indian soldier, who took part in the June 2015 cross-border raids, which was published in the Indian press, the operation was kept secret even from the Myanmar Army officers in the area so they would not tip off the Indian rebels in advance. Several of those officers were collecting protection money from the Indian rebels, the soldier alleged. It is also clear that the Myanmar government was not informed about the Indian cross-border raid until after it had taken place.[23]

It is unclear, however, what prompted the NSCN-K's decision to scrap the ceasefire agreement with the Indian government. The brain behind the ULFWSA, however, was not Khaplang, who was in his mid-70s when he was made the official head of the alliance only because of his age and stature in the Naga Hills of Myanmar, but the younger and much more dynamic ULFA leader Paresh Baruah. A charismatic former footballer from Dibrugarh who has been with the Assamese underground movement since the early 1980s, Baruah is now known to be spending most of his time in Ruili in Yunnan as well as in other parts of China. He was, for instance, spotted at an International Trade Fair in Guangzhou in November 2009. Ruili, just north of Muse in Myanmar, is also the base for several Manipuri rebels. Khaplang died on 9 June 2017 and although one of his closest associates, Khole Konyak, has taken over as NSCN-K leader, a new chairman of the UNLFWSA has not yet been appointed.

Weapons not made in China are acquired from a gun factory at Pangwa, just across the border inside Myanmar's Kachin state. Pangwa is in an area controlled by Zakhung Ting Ying, a former commander of the CPB who made peace with the Burmese government in 1989 and then went on to head a local government-recognized militia force. Before the November 2015 election in Myanmar, Ting Ying was also a member of the Amyotha Hluttaw, the upper house of the national parliament. As a former CPB commander, he also has contacts in China. No one from the tribal communities in his area would know how to make sophisticated weaponry, which is why technicians from China have to handle the Chinese machinery at the factory.

Ting Ying's factory is known to be capable of producing automatic rifles, pistols, revolvers, and shotguns and, among his customers are the rebels from India's northeast. The guns are transported in vehicles along the road down to Myitkyina and on to Mogaung and the jade mining area at Hpakant. From there, in order to bypass areas controlled by KIA rebels, who would levy 'taxes' in cash or in kind on the shipments, the guns are transported along smaller roads to Singkaling Hkamti and beyond. Guns acquired in China are smuggled across the Myanmar border at Ruili and then trucked via Lashio, Mandalay, and Monywa up to the Indian border.[24]

ULFA is also known to have contacts within the United Wa State Army (UWSA), which China arms and uses to provide leverage when dealing with the increasingly pro-Western Myanmar government. The well-equipped, 20,000–30,000-strong UWSA keeps most of its new, Chinese arsenal to itself, but is known to have sold old stocks to other rebel groups, including those from India's northeast. And the UWSA would not be permitted to sell anything without the approval of the Chinese security officers who always accompany its leaders. While Chinese support for the UWSA is mainly aimed at maintaining a solid foothold inside Myanmar, it cannot be ruled out that the group could also be used as a middleman for arms supplies to organizations like ULFA, as it has already supplied its ally, the Myanmar National Democratic Alliance Army, and some other Myanmar groups with weapons.

So, to what extent is China involved with the Indian rebels? Mostly indirectly through arms dealers, but it is evident that Chinese security services, at the very least, are turning a blind eye to the traffic, which serves China's geopolitical interests in the region. Apart from sheltering Baruah, Chinese intelligence officers are also known to have visited the camp near Taka on more than one occasion.

The Chinese may not want to set India's northeast ablaze, but it is in Beijing's interest to cause frictions and disruptions in Myanmar's relations with India. Since the suspension of the Myitsone dam project in 2011, Myanmar has distanced itself from its old ally China and established closer contacts not only with the West but also with India. But a closer, more cordial relationship between Myanmar and India is not in China's interest. Instability along the border—rebel raids into India and retaliatory, Indian cross-border attacks—would serve that purpose. It is also to

China's advantage that Myanmar's authorities are paying only scant interest to events along the country's western border. It keeps Myanmar closer to China, which has not given up hope of improved relations.

For this and other more compelling reasons such as its own ethnic insurgencies, it is highly unlikely that Myanmar would ever agree to take part in any joint operations with the Indian Army against the rebels from India's northeast. On the formal level, the Myanmar government continues to have a ceasefire agreement with the NSCN-K—and while attacks in India and cross-border raids by the Indian Army into Myanmar were taking place, Khaplang himself was recuperating in a hospital in the old capital, Yangon, where he was visited by Aung Min, then a government minister who was also engaged in ongoing peace talks with Myanmar's many rebel groups.[25]

The borderlands between India and Myanmar are more likely to be the scene for further military action rather than the Himalayas. The only potentially serious conflict on the border between Arunachal and Tibet since the 1962 War began in July 1986, when an Indian patrol found about 40 Chinese soldiers erecting what appeared to be permanent buildings in the Sumdorong Chu Valley, an area which the Indians believed was on their side of the border or straddling it. Reinforcements were sent in to keep an eye on developments and, by August, the Chinese had constructed a helipad in the area.

In order to diffuse the situation, India suggested that if the Chinese vacated the area during the coming winter, Indian troops would not enter it the following summer. Beijing rejected the proposal.[26] The Indian army chief at the time, General Krishnaswamy Sundarji, decided it was time for India to show its teeth and sent an entire brigade into Zeimithang just south of the border. Operation Falcon had begun. A helipad was constructed on a hilltop overlooking the Sumdorong Chu Valley, heavy guns were placed in position, and long-range patrols were sent into surrounding areas. According to an Indian Army officer who was on active duty along the border at the time, 'Sundarji wanted to show the Chinese that this is not 1962. He wanted to flex his muscles and demonstrate to the Chinese that it's a different Indian Army they are facing today.'[27]

Indian Prime Minister Rajiv Gandhi was alarmed at the developments along the northeastern border and came to the area in October. But he was unable to visit Zeimithang because, the officers said, 'the weather was bad'. Helicopters could not land there. The prime minister had to be content with a briefing at the army camp in Tawang. He reportedly said, 'A nice presentation, but I'm not convinced'.[28] Sundarji did not back down and sent more troops and heavy artillery into the area.

By early 1987, the Chinese had moved 20,000 of their troops to the mountains overlooking the Sumdorong Chu Valley, and Indian and Chinese soldiers were also standing literally face-to-face at Bumla and other mountain passes. The situation was not defused until Narayan Dutt Tawari, then Indian minister of External Affairs, stopped over in Beijing in May of that year on his way to North Korea's capital, Pyongyang. As a result, the two sides met at Bumla on 5 August and decided to solve problems over border incidents through talks rather than armed confrontation.

It is extremely rare for an Indian army officer to challenge the elected government like Sundarji did in 1986–7, but that was such an occasion. When Sundarji died in 1999, *India Today* published an obituary saying that his

> place in history will probably rest on the lesser-known Operation Falcon …Western diplomats predicted war and Prime Minister Rajiv Gandhi's advisers charged that Sundarji's recklessness was responsible for this. But the general stood firm, at one point telling a senior Rajiv aide, "Please make alternate arrangements if you think you are not getting adequate professional advice." The civilians backed off, so did the Chinese.[29]

The Chinese were far more careful in their dealings with Indians after the confrontation in the Sumdorong Chu Valley. Rajiv Gandhi, invited by his Chinese counterpart Li Peng, paid an official visit to China between 19 and 23 December 1988. It was the first such visit by an Indian prime minister, since his grandfather Jawaharlal Nehru travelled to Beijing in October 1954. Rajiv Gandhi held meetings with China's top leaders, climbed the Great Wall, and, at official banquets, the exquisitely carved vegetable decorations were in the shape of a dragon, symbolizing China, a peacock, symbolizing India, and two doves, symbolizing peace.[30] Perhaps because of the recent incidents along the border, the Indian prime minister was received with utmost respect. China had certainly changed a lot since 1962, but so had India.

Rajiv Gandhi's landmark visit marked the beginning of a thaw in Sino-Indian relations. In December 1991, Chinese Premier Li Peng reciprocated Rajiv Gandhi's visit by going to New Delhi. High-level visits became routine in the 1990s and, when, in September 1993, Pamulaparti Venkata Narasimha Rao, then prime minister, visited China, agreements were signed on maintaining peace and tranquillity along the crest of the Himalayas. In November 1996, China's President Jiang Zemin visited India, and the two countries agreed to a set of confidence-building measures to be implemented along the common border.[31]

After decades of confrontation, Sino-Indian relations were improving. While significant progress was made, it also became clear, once again, that China and India were fundamentally different civilizations with incompatible political systems. During Rajiv Gandhi's visit, many had hoped for a breakthrough on the border question. But that was not to come. In 1960, China had proposed a straight east-west territorial exchange, including India, abandoning Aksai Chin in the west in return for China accepting the Himalayan crest line or the McMahon Line in the east. In other words, the Line of Actual Control would become a new, demarcated border.[32]

It would not have been difficult for the Chinese to agree to such a deal, as no one in China would dare oppose the government's policies on matters of vital strategic concern. India, on the other hand, is a democracy where leaders and politicians have to face the public in general elections. It would be political suicide for any Indian politician to suggest that India should give up Aksai Chin, an area which it considers part of its territory, in return for recognition of sovereignty over land it already controls, that is, the NEFA. Complicating matters even further, since 1985 China has extended its claim to include a demand for territorial concessions in the Tawang area. India perceives this as part of a broader encirclement strategy, which includes inroads into Bhutan, and would make India more vulnerable than it already is.[33]

In October 2014, Narendra Modi's new government announced a plan to build 2,000 kilometres of new roads in Arunachal to improve its infrastructure and help develop remote, neglected areas in the state. The government also pledged to allocate more resources to build schools, clinics, and bridges, and to improve telecommunications. The Indian minister of State for Home Affairs, Kiren Rijiju, who is a native of Arunachal, later told *Bloomberg* that 'the people along the border have migrated down where amenities are available. People native to the region should not have to move out.'[34] None of the roads, however, would link the state with China. 'I don't want to link it with China,' Rijiju told *Bloomberg*. 'We are not doing anything to disturb relations. It's not in terms of challenging or competing with China, but in terms of securing our own territory.'[35]

The Chinese authorities reacted immediately to India's plans. On 14 October, Chinese foreign ministry spokesman Hong Lie said, 'We still need to verify the specifics. The boundary issue between China and India is left by colonial past. We need to deal with this issue properly ... Before final settlement is reached we hope that India will not take any action that may further complicate the situation.'[36]

In February 2015, after Modi paid a visit to Arunachal's state capital, Itanagar, Chinese Vice-Foreign Minister Liu Zhenmin said that 'the Chinese government has never recognised the so-called "Arunachal Pradesh" unilaterally set up by the Indian side'.[37] The official Chinese news agency *Xinhua* reported in the same vein, 'The so-called "Arunachal Pradesh" was established largely on the three areas of China's Tibet—Monyul, Loyul and Lower Tsayul, currently under Indian illegal occupation. These three areas, located between the illegal "McMahon Line" and the traditional customary boundary between China and India, have always been Chinese territory.'[38]

Even if the rhetoric these days is not quite as gross and bombastic as it was in the 1950s and 1960s, the Chinese position remains the same and, in essence, it has not changed since the 1913–14 Shimla conference. But the Chinese are unlikely to do anything more nowadays than issuing such official statements every time India does something noteworthy in Arunachal Pradesh, and sending occasional patrols across the border to show that they still do not recognize the McMahon Line. And India's defences along the border are stronger than ever, making such incursions little more than irritants. The stalemate in the border negotiations is, therefore, likely to continue with no solution in sight.

A much stickier point in bilateral relations is the status of Tibetan exiles in India. During Rajiv Gandhi's 1988 visit, his Chinese hosts devoted most of the time to the Tibetan issue. A communiqué was signed at the end of the visit, which said that 'The Chinese side expressed concern by anti-Chinese activities by some Tibetan elements in India. The Indian side reiterated the long-standing and consistent policy of the government of India that Tibet is an autonomous region of China and that anti-Chinese activities by Tibetan elements are not permitted on Indian soil.'[39]

Then the wording of joint Sino-Indian declarations became even stronger. According to American China specialist John W. Garver,

> By the time of Li Peng's December 1991 visit to India, the Chinese expression of "concern" in the final communiqué had expanded from fourteen words in the 1988 communiqué to forty-nine words: "The Chinese side expressed concern about the continued activities in India by some Tibetans against their motherland and reiterated that Tibet was an alienable part of Chinese territory and that it was firmly opposed to any attempt and actions aimed at splitting China and bringing about 'independence' of Tibet".[40]

By linking Tibetan activities in India to 'splitting China,' Beijing was actually intensifying pressure on New Delhi rather than defusing the situation.

Despite declarations of friendship and collaboration, the differences between China and India were obvious even on this issue. Cracking down on demonstrations and other forms of popular protest is standard practice in China, but, as Garver points out, India could agree on such restrictions of free speech only to a limited degree: 'India's core political values are, after all, liberal, holding such things as free expression and travel to be intrinsic human rights'.[41]

India can, at most, restrict, but not ban, political activities by the Tibetan exiles who want the world to know what is happening in their homeland. Between September 1987 and March 1989—that is, before, during, and after Rajiv Gandhi's visit to Beijing—Tibet was rocked by a series of pro-independence protests, which proved that Tibetans, despite the region's economic development, had not become any more pro-Chinese than they had been in 1959. Demonstrators were killed and injured during the riots, and all foreigners, including journalists, were expelled from Tibet.

The bloodiest incident took place in March 1989. Officially, only about a dozen people were killed when Chinese security forces clamped down on the protesters. But a former Chinese journalist, who was in Tibet during the unrest as a representative of the Chinese Journalists' Association, told reporters after he had got out of China and settled in France that he had a copy of a report from the Chinese Public Security Bureau and the Tibet Military District Command, dated 11 March 1989, stating that '387 Lhasa citizens have been killed ... the majority by bullets ... 721 were injured, 2,100 have been arrested or detained ... 354 have disappeared ... 82 religious people have been killed, 37 injured, 650 arrested or detained'.[42]

Concern over Tibetans and the activities of the Dalai Lama and his followers in exile is another reason, apart from geopolitical interests in Myanmar's borderlands, why China retains contacts with India's northeastern rebels: it is a means of putting pressure on India, and it gives China some leverage on other bilateral issues, including the sharing of water resources. The Chinese may not admit this, but the very fact that they are permitting Paresh Baruah and his comrades access to China, and to its not-so-black arms bazaar, is enough to keep India on edge. Chinese authorities, much to the annoyance of Indians, also continue to give stapled visas to residents of Arunachal Pradesh when they want to visit China.

On the other hand, rapid economic development in both countries has created an entirely new dimension to Sino-Indian relations. Trade between the two countries is booming. China has become India's largest trading partner and they co-operate as members of the trading association BRICS (Brazil, Russia, India, China, South Africa). Bilateral trade between India and China stood at US$70.73 billion in 2015–16. Major imports from China include telecom instruments, computer hardware and peripherals, fertilizers, electronic components, consumer goods, chemicals, and raw materials for drugs, while exports to China consist of ores, iron and steel, tin, raw hides, leather, plastics, and cotton. But it is a trade where China is the main beneficiary. India's trade deficit with China rose to US$52.68 billion, from US$48.48 billion in the previous fiscal year.[43] China's increasingly assertive economic—and, therefore, political—role in the Asia-Pacific has inevitably caused concern among other countries in the region. The conflict in the South China Sea between China on the one side and Southeast Asian countries and the United States on the other has received much international attention, as has the ongoing a tug-of-war between the United States and China for influence over small island territories in the Pacific with huge, surrounding economic zones. But there is also what could be described as a new Cold War emerging in the Indian Ocean. And, it is there that China's strategic interests collide with India's and an informal alliance is emerging between India, Japan, the US, and Australia.

China's interest in opening a corridor down to the Indian Ocean was first articulated in September 1985 as the country was moving from rigid socialism to a market-oriented economy. In an article in the official mouthpiece *Beijing Review*, Pan Qi, a former vice-minister of communications, outlined the possibility of finding an outlet for trade for China's landlocked southwestern provinces of Yunnan, Sichuan, and Guizhou, with a combined population of 160 million people, through Myanmar down to the Indian Ocean.[44] The article mentioned the Myanmar railheads of Myitkyina and Lashio in the north and northeast, and the Irrawaddy River as possible conduits for Chinese exports.

The first border trade agreement between Yangon and Beijing was signed in early August 1988, only days before a nationwide uprising for democracy broke out in Myanmar. After the movement had been crushed, and Western sanctions put in place, China moved in with trade, loans, and credits to a regime that otherwise would have crumbled under internal and external pressure. Apart from becoming Myanmar's largest foreign trade partner, Beijing exported more than US$1.4 billion worth of military equipment to Myanmar and helped upgrade its naval facilities in the Indian Ocean. In return, the Myanmar junta gave Beijing access to signals intelligence from key oil shipment sea lanes collected by the Myanmar Navy, using equipment supplied by China. The strategic balance of power in the region was shifting in China's favour. Not only India but also the United States was watching these developments with increasing concern. The construction of oil and gas pipelines from the Myanmar coast to China added to the anxieties in the West and India.

Western sanctions may not have caused Myanmar's economic and strategic push into the hands of the Chinese, as many foreign observers have argued. But Western policies certainly made it easier for China to implement its designs for Myanmar. This, in turn, caused the West to rethink its Myanmar policy. US strategic concerns were outlined as early as June 1997 in a *Los Angeles Times* article by Marvin Ott, an American security expert and former CIA analyst. 'Washington can and should remain outspokenly critical of abuses in Myanmar. But there are security and other national interests to be served ... it is time to think seriously about alternatives,' Ott concluded.[45]

Geostrategic concerns, rather than issues such as human rights and democracy, caused a shift in Washington's Myanmar policy at the same time as many staunchly nationalistic Myanmar military officers were becoming increasingly dissatisfied with their country's heavy dependence on China. In order to understand Myanmar's policy shift, it is also instructive to look behind the façade of democracy that was introduced after the 2010 election. A classified military document written by Lieutenant Colonel Aung Kyaw Hla, who is identified as a researcher at Myanmar's prestigious Defence Services Academy, was completed and circulated internally as early as August 2004. Entitled 'A Study of Myanmar–US Relations', the main thesis of the 346-page dossier is that Myanmar's recent reliance on China as a diplomatic ally and economic patron had created a 'national emergency' that threatened the country's independence. According to the dossier, Myanmar would be able to normalize relations with the West only after implementing political reforms and electing a government instead of being ruled by a junta. In this way, the regime can deal with the outside world on more acceptable terms, Aung Kyaw Hla suggested.[46]

And it worked, although the turn took some doing. It was not until a general election had been held in Myanmar in November 2010 that relations with the United States improved. In early December 2011, US

Secretary of State Hillary Clinton paid a high-profile visit to Myanmar, the first such trip by a top-ranking US official in more than 50 years. This was followed by a visit by President Barack Obama in November 2012, and, in May 2013, Thein Sein became the first Myanmar president to visit the United States since 1966.

Diplomatic exchanges between Myanmar and the West—and especially Myanmar's scrapping of the Myitsone dam—prompted China to start searching for new ways to salvage the relationship. In 2012, academic-style journals in China ran several articles analysing what went wrong with Beijing's Myanmar policy and what should be done to rectify it. One proposed measure has been to launch a public relations campaign in Myanmar aimed at overhauling China's current negative image in the country and to extend promises of help with the government's peace process. Many countries support this process financially and a host of Western NGOs are involved as advisers to the government's peace committee—but only China can wield a carrot as well as a stick: aid, loans, and trade and guns to the UWSA.

China cannot give up its newly-won access to the Indian Ocean and Myanmar's strategic importance to Beijing cannot, therefore, be overestimated. More than 60 per cent of the world's oil shipments pass through the Indian Ocean, from the Middle East's oil fields to China, Japan, and other strong economies in the region, as does 70 per cent of all container traffic to and from the Asian industrial countries and the rest of the world. While traffic across the Atlantic has diminished and that across the Pacific is static, trade across the Indian Ocean is increasing. Parts of the ocean, especially in the west around the Horn of Africa and next to the Strait of Malacca in the east, are areas where pirates are active and terrorists have been shipping arms to various conflict zones in the region, which has prompted tighter regional co-operation. But there are more fundamental, geopolitical, threats to stability in the Indian Ocean. Not only the United States but also Japan and India distrust China. For India, it began with the border conflicts which culminated in the 1962 War and Japan has for decades been involved in a dispute with China on the ownership of a group of islands in the East China Sea, called Senkaku in Japanese and Diaoyutai in Chinese.

With two nationalists now as prime ministers of their respective countries, Shinzo Abe of Japan since December 2012 and Narendra Modi of India since May 2014, the battle lines and alliances have become clearer. Although regional naval co-operation actually began in 2007 with annual joint exercises, called Exercise Malabar, by India, Japan, Australia, Singapore, and the United States, they were initially held with relatively informal arrangements in the sea off Japan. But, in 2015, Exercise Malabar was upgraded, with more participants after an agreement between Modi and Obama, and a joint naval exercise was held by the United States, India, and Japan in the Bay of Bengal.

India's fleet is the strongest in the region, with aircraft carriers, submarines, and over 90 other kinds of ships. The Indian Navy is currently undergoing a modernization drive to upgrade its submarines and other vessels, especially those that can detect foreign submarines. Meanwhile, China has invested in a number of port projects in the region: Kyaukphyu in Myanmar, Chittagong in Bangladesh, Hambantota in Sri Lanka, and, most important of them all, Gwadar in Pakistan. The deep-sea port in Gwadar combined with the Karakoram Highway, which was opened in 1979 and connects northern Pakistan with Xinjiang, gives western China a direct outlet to the Indian Ocean. China is basically a huge inland empire with a relatively short coastline for a country of its size and its landlocked inland provinces depend on outlets through neighbouring countries for trade with the outside world. Kyaukphyu in Myanmar was designed to fulfil the same function for Yunnan and other southwestern Chinese provinces, from where it is a long way to China's own ports. Chinese plans to open a trade route from Tibet through Sikkim down to the port of Kolkata have not been met with enthusiasm in India, and may never materialize.

The future of the Kyaukphyu port facility, and pipelines for oil and gas that China has built from there to Yunnan to bypass the potential chokepoint at the Malacca Strait, through which most of its oil supplies now have to go, is also not clear since the Myanmar government has adopted a new foreign policy and the country no longer wants to be seen as a Chinese client state. So, while arms continue to flow to the UWSA, here, too, as in India's northeast, China does not want to see another war break out. It is

China's way of putting pressure on its neighbours in order to exert its influence over them in the post-Mao era.

It may seem as if China's interests are only about trade and economic development, but given the importance of the transportation of China's oil supplies from the Middle East, it is hardly surprising that Beijing is also pursuing a defence umbrella to secure such vital lines of communication. In 2005, the US consulting firm Booz Allen Hamilton coined the expression 'String of Pearls' to describe China's port projects in the Indian Ocean, which now also include Obock in Djibouti in the Horn of Africa. China calls the new initiatives 'The Maritime Silk Road' and the 'One Belt One Road' and reiterates its assertion that its only aim is to peacefully promote trade in the region.[47]

The port project in Obock will, according to China's own admission, become a base for anti-piracy operations which its fleet carries out in the area and, therefore, represents no threat to other powers. But Obock will nevertheless be China's first military base abroad, as Chinese planes will be stationed there. Even Gwadar will have an airfield and combined with the facility at Obock, this means increased freedom of movement for the Chinese Air Force outside the country. The US is already in the area, in Djibouti as well as on Diego Garcia, a British possession in the Indian Ocean where it established a large air and naval base in the 1970s. Diego Garcia has been used extensively during the United States' wars on Afghanistan and Iraq.

Meanwhile, Chinese submarines have already been observed in the Indian Ocean, mainly around the Andaman and Nicobar Islands, north of the entrance to the Strait of Malacca. The Indian Navy says it encounters Chinese submarines at least once a month, which is not so surprising given the volume of Chinese trade and oil supplies through the Indian Ocean. But it is a completely new development in a maritime region where, only two decades ago, China was not present at all. India and the United States now co-operate to detect and identify Chinese submarines.

France is another, almost unknown, Indian Ocean power with close relations to India and the United States. There are two inhabited French *départements d'outre-mer* (overseas departments) in the Indian Ocean,

Mayotte and Réunion, which thus also are part of the European Union. In addition, France controls the relatively large Kerguelen Island, the smaller St. Paul and Amsterdam Islands, the Crozet Archipelago, and a series of small islands around Madagascar. Only Mayotte and Réunion have permanent populations, but there are French scientists and military personnel on the other islands and Kerguelen has a satellite monitoring station. In total, France's Economic Exclusive Zone in the southern Indian Ocean consists of more than 2.5 million square kilometres.

Australia, another partner in the informal alliance, possesses Christmas Island, south of Java and, further out in the Indian Ocean, the Cocos (Keeling) Islands. These territories have a combined population of just over 3,000, but there is a big airstrip on the Cocos, as well as extensive installations for electronic surveillance.[48] The United States reportedly has plans to use the Cocos as a base for drones to monitor sea traffic in the region, an action which the Chinese certainly would perceive as directed against them. Proposals have also been made in Australia to allow the Indian Navy to use the facilities on the Cocos.

China's long-term plans for its presence in the Indian Ocean are still unclear, especially as to whether there will be more ports and if those will actually be used by the Chinese military. But the fact that China is now there, in all probability to stay, has prompted India to upgrade its Indian Ocean fleet and to co-operate with other countries in the region. Although the situation in the Indian Ocean is nowhere near as worrisome as in the South and East China Seas, there can be no doubt that it is about to become a new focal point in the cold war that few want to talk about but that everyone knows is already a reality.

Some Western scholars have dismissed the notion that there is a new 'Great Game' being played out in the region.[49] But, as Colonel Stuart Kenny at the Australian Defence College in Canberra points out, there is indeed a New Great Game 'founded on historic mistrust and current competition'.[50] It has to do with border disputes in the Himalayas, the competition for influence in Nepal, Bhutan, and Myanmar, cross-border insurgencies, the sharing of water resources, and strategic rivalries in the Indian Ocean. And this time, it is not between Imperial Russia and the British Empire, but, after a long, complicated, and often violent history, between an independent India and China, a communist-ruled country that has risen from famine, chaos, and anarchy to become the world's new economic superpower.

Notes

1. Li Ling, *Xizang zhi shui jiu Zhongguo: Da xixian 'zai zao Zhongguo' zhanlüe neimu xianglu* [Save China through water from Tibet: a detailed record of the inside story of the Great Western Route 'Rebuild China' strategy] (Beijing: Zhongguo Chang'an chubanshe, 2005).

2. Binoda Kumar Mishra, 'China Eyes Brahmaputra Waters', *Lookeast,* September 2010, p. 23. See also Marcus Nüsser (ed.), *Large Dams in Asia: Contested Environments between Technological Hydroscapes and Social Resistance,* available at https://storage.googleapis.com/vjaystnboufufn.appspot.com/large-dams-in-asia-contested-environments-between-technological-hydroscapes-and-social-resistance-advances-in-asian-human-environmental-research-PDF-a9a66.pdf (accessed on 26 December 2016).

3. Brahma Chellaney, *Water: Asia's New Battleground* (Washington: Georgetown University Press, 2013), p. 135. See also Michael Buckley, *Meltdown in Tibet: China's Reckless Destruction of Ecosystems From the Highlands of Tibet to the Deltas of Asia* (New York: Palgrave MacMillan, 2014), p. 193.

4. Quoted in Buckley, *Meltdown in Tibet,* pp. 194–5.

5. Quoted in Navin Singh Khadka, 'Megadams: Battle on the Brahmaputra', *BBC,* 20 March 2014, available at http://www.bbc.com/news/world-asia-india-26663820 (accessed on 26 December 2016).

6. *BBC,* 'Megadams: Battle on the Brahmaputra', 20 March 2014.

7. *BBC,* 'Megadams: Battle on the Brahmaputra', 20 March 2014.

8. Tom Fawthrop, 'Southeast Asia's Last Undammed River in Crisis', *thethirdpole.net,* 26 October 2016, available at https://www.thethirdpole.net/2016/10/26/southeast-asias-last-major-undammed-river-in-crisis/ (accessed on 20 December 2016).

9. Hu Weija, 'No Need for Concern in India over China's Blockage of Brahmaputra River Tributary', *Global Times,* 10 October 2016, available at http://www.globaltimes.cn/content/1010346.shtml (accessed on 10 December 2016).

10. World Rivers Review, 'Understanding the Impacts of China's Upper Mekong Dams', December 2014, available at https://www.internationalrivers.org/resources/8477 (accessed on 20 December 2016).

11. Bertil Lintner, Burma Delivers its First Rebuff to China, *YaleGlobal Online*, 3 October 2011, available at http://yaleglobal.yale.edu/content/burma-delivers-its-first-rebuff-china (accessed on 23 December 2016).

12. Hu, 'No Need for Concern in India over China's Blockage of Brahmaputra River Tributary'.

13. Ramesh Bhushal, 'India and Nepal Sign deal to Build another Mega-dam', *thethirdpole.net*, 27 November 2014, available at https://www.thethirdpole.net/2014/11/27/india-and-nepal-sign-deal-to-build-another-mega-dam/ (accessed on 21 December 2016).

14. *Sify News*, 'Assam Dam Project May Continue: Jairam Ramesh', 12 August 2010, available at http://www.sify.com/news/assam-dam-project-may-continue-jairam-ramesh-news-national-kimpEcidiaa.html (accessed on 23 December 2016).

15. Prabin Kalital, 'Subansiri dam is the new theatre of Maoist activity', *Times of India*, 30 April 2015, available at http://timesofindia.indiatimes.com/city/guwahati/Subansiri-dam-site-is-new-theatre-of-Maoist-activity/articleshow/47101239.cms (accessed on 26 December 2016).

16. Prabin Kalital, *Times of India*, 30 April 2015.

17. Akhil Ranjan Dutta, 'Equitable Justice Development and Rise of the Maoists in Northeast India', Wasbir Hussain (ed.), *Northeast India: The Maoist Spread* (Guwahati: Worldweaves India, 2014), p. 41.

18. Wasbir Hussain and Arunav Goswami, 'Maoists in Assam: Filling the Void Created by Rebels in Peace Talks And Truce', in Wasbir Hussain (ed.), *Northeast India: The Maoist Spread* (Guwahati: Worldweaves India, 2014), p. 108.

19. Quoted in Dutta, Equitable Justice Development and Rise of the Maoists in Northeast India', p. 44.

20. Interview with a Southeast Asian security officer who wished to remain anonymous, 15 October 2016.

21. For a detailed account of the arms deal, see Bertil Lintner, *Great Game East: India, China and the Struggle for Asia's Most Volatile Frontier.* (New Haven: Yale University Press, 2015), pp. 220–1.

22. Rahul Tripathi and Dipanjan Roy Chaudhury, 'Extradited Thai National Wuthikorn Naruenartwanich sent to NIA's custody till December 21', *The Economic Times*, 11 December 2015, available at http://articles.economictimes.indiatimes.com/2015-12-09/news/68899905_1_naruenartwanich-bangkok-extradition (accessed on 20 December 2016).

23. Bertil Lintner, 'Mysterious Motives: India's Raids on the Burma Border', *The Irrawaddy*, 30 June 2015, available at http://www.irrawaddy.com/news/

ethnic-issues/mysterious-motives-indias-raids-on-the-burma-border.html (accessed on 10 December 2016).

24. Lintner, 'Mysterious Motives: India's Raids on the Burma Border'.

25. For a picture of the meeting, see Lintner, 'Mysterious Motives: India's Raids on the Burma Border'.

26. Claude Arpi, 'The Sumdorong Chu incident: a Strong Indian Stand', *Indian Defence Review*, 4 May 2013, available at http://www.indiandefencereview. com/the-sumdorong-chu-incident-a-strong-indian-stand/ (accessed on 22 December 2016).

27. Interview with retired Colonel Ashish Das, Kolkata, 26 February 2013.

28. Interview with retired Colonel Ashish Das, Kolkata, 26 February 2013.

29. Manoj Joshi, 'Warrior as Scholar', *India Today*, 22 February 1999, available at available at http://indiatoday.intoday.in/story/general-krishnaswami-sundarji-passes-away/1/253281.html (accessed on 27 December 2016).

30. Dilip Bobb, 'Breaching the Wall', *India Today*, 15 January 1989, available at http://indiatoday.intoday.in/story/prime-minister-rajiv-gandhi-visit-to-china-marks-a-new-beginning-in-bilateral-relations/1/322962.html (accessed on 27 December 2016).

31. John W. Garver, *Protracted Contest: Sino-Indian Rivalry in the Twentieth Century* (Seattle and London: University of Washington Press, 2001), p. 7.

32. Katherine Richards, *China-India: An Analysis of the Himalayan Territorial Dispute* (Canberra: Australian Defence College, Centre for Defence and Strategic Studies, 2015), p. 11, available at http://www.defence.gov.au/ADC/Publications/IndoPac/Richards%20final%20IPSD%20paper.pdf (accessed on 20 December 2016).

33. Richards, *China-India*, p. 11.

34. Quoted in Natalie Obiko Pearson, 'India is Spending Billions to Populate a Remote Area Claimed by China', 26 October 2015, available at https://www. bloomberg.com/news/articles/2015-10-25/india-spending-billions-to-populate-remote-area-claimed-by-china (accessed on 20 December 2016).

35. Pearson, 'India is Spending Billions to Populate a Remote Area Claimed by China'.

36. Quoted in 'China reacts to India's road construction plan, says don't complicate border issue', *The Indian Express*, 16 October 2014, available at http:// indianexpress.com/article/india/india-others/china-reacts-to-indias-road-construction-plan-says-dont-complicate-border-situation/ (accessed on 23 December 2016).

37. *Xinhua* in *China Daily*, 'China "unhappy" on Modi's visit to disputed territory', 21 February 2015, available at http://usa.chinadaily.com.cn/china/2015-02/21/content_19630989.htm (accessed on 23 December 2016).

38. 'China "unhappy" on Modi's visit to disputed territory'.

39. Garver, *Protracted Contest*, p. 72.

40. Garver, *Protracted Contest*, pp. 72–3.

41. Garver, *Protracted Contest*, p. 73.

42. 'Chinese Said to Kill 450 Tibetans in 1989', *New York Times*, 14 August 1990, available at http://www.nytimes.com/1990/08/14/world/chinese-said-to-kill-450-tibetans-in-1989.html (accessed on 23 December 2016).

43. 'India's trade deficit with China jumps to $53 billion in 2015-16', *The Economic Times*, 1 August 2016, available at http://economictimes.indiatimes.com/news/economy/foreign-trade/indias-trade-deficit-with-china-jumps-to-53-billion-in-2015-16/articleshow/53492853.cms (accessed on 27 December 2016).

44. Pan Qi, 'Opening to the Southwest: An Expert Opinion', *Beijing Review*, 2 September 1985.

45. Marvin Ott, 'Don't Push Myanmar into China's Orbit', *Los Angeles Times*, 17 June 1997.

46. A copy of the document is in the author's possession.

47. Zhou Bo, 'The String of Pearls and the Maritime Silk Road', *China.org.cn*, 12 February 2014, available at http://www.china.org.cn/opinion/2014-02/12/content_31445571.htm (accessed on 23 December 2016).

48. Bertil Lintner, 'Australia's strategic little dots', *Asia Times Online*, 25 June 2010, available at http://www.atimes.com/atimes/China/LF25Ad01.html (accessed on 23 December 2016).

49. For an unusually naïve account of the rivalry, see, for instance, Sunniva Engh, 'India's Myanmar Policy and the "Sino-Indian Great Game"', *Asian Affairs*, 9 March 2016, available at http://www.tandfonline.com/doi/abs/10.1080/0306 8374.2015.1130307?journalCode=raaf20 (accessed on 25 December 2016).

50. Stuart Kenny, *China and India: A 'New Great Game' founded on historic mistrust and current competition* (Canberra: Australian Defence College, 2015), available at http://www.defence.gov.au/ADC/Publications/IndoPac/Kenny_IPS_Paper.pdf (accessed on 26 December 2016).

Chronology

1903–4
Lieutenant Colonel Francis Younghusband leads a British military expedition to Lhasa.

1906
27 April: An Anglo-Chinese Convention is signed in Beijing. Both China and the British agree not to interfere in the internal administration of Tibet.

1907
31 August: Russia and Britain sign a convention in St Petersburg relating to Persia, Afghanistan, and Tibet.
17 December: Bhutan becomes a unified kingdom under Ugyen Wangchuk.

1910–12
China invades Tibet.

1910
8 January: Bhutan and British India sign a treaty which gives Britain control over Bhutan's foreign affairs; Bhutanese retains control over its internal affairs.

1911
10 October: A republican uprising breaks out in China.
29 October. Mongolia declares its independence.

1912

1 January: China is declared a republic and the Manchu (Qing) Dynasty is deprived of all its powers on 12 February.

1913

13 February: Tibet declares its independence.

13 October: A conference to settle bilateral issues between British India, China, and Tibet convenes in Shimla.

1914

3 July: A Convention is signed in Shimla. China and Britain agree not to occupy Tibet. The McMahon Line is drawn between northeastern British India and Tibet. Britain and Tibet sign the agreement, while the Chinese delegate Chen Yifan, or Ivan Chen, only initials it. China does not recognize Tibet's independence, while Britain establishes close relations with Lhasa.

1928

China establishes a Commission for Tibetan and Mongolian Affairs in order to re-assert its influence on those two de facto independent nations.

1932

War breaks out between China and Tibet. China defeats the Tibetans who, however, manage to retain their de facto independence.

1941–2

Nationalist Chinese troops arrive in India for a joint British–US campaign to drive the Japanese who had occupied the British colony of Myanmar out of the country. The Chinese want to build a supply road through Tibet, which is not approved by the Tibetans. Instead, the Allies, led by the British and the Americans, built a road is built from Ledo in northeastern India to northern Myanmar.

1947

15 August: India becomes independent from British rule.

1949

8 August: The governments of India and Bhutan enter into an agreement reconfirming Bhutan's status as a nation dependent on India but with a high degree of autonomy.

1 October: Mao Zedong proclaims the People's Republic of China in Beijing, ending the Chinese Civil War between the Communists and the Nationalist Chinese Kuomintang (KMT). The KMT and its followers flee to Taiwan, where the Republic of China lives on. Some KMT troops withdraw to mountainous regions in northeastern Myanmar.

1950

7 October: Communist Chinese troops enter Tibet.

November: The first contingent of Chinese troops arrives at Lhasa.

5 December: The president of India and the maharaja of Sikkim sign an agreement according to which 'Sikkim shall continue to be a Protectorate of India.'

1950–3

In the Korean War, China sends 'volunteers' to support North Korea, while India participates in the UN-backed support for South Korea.

1951

February: A detachment of the Assam Rifles, led by Ralengnao 'Bob' Khathing, enters Tawang, to secure the border with Tibet after the Chinese had occupied it.

23 May: The 17-point 'Agreement for the Peaceful Liberation of Tibet' is signed between the Chinese and a representative of Tibet's Dalai Lama.

September: The Chinese army takes control of Lhasa.

1954

January: The North-East Frontier Tract becomes the North-East Frontier Area (NEFA).

29 April: China and India sign an agreement regarding Tibet. India recognizes Tibet as a region of China. Zhou Enlai visits New Delhi and

Jawaharlal Nehru visits Beijing. Relations between the two countries are close and cordial.

September: The Dalai Lama visits Beijing where he meets Mao Zedong, Zhou Enlai, and Deng Xiaoping.

1955

April: An array of newly independent nations meets in Bandung, Indonesia, to establish the Non-Aligned Movement.

1956

February: The Khampas of Tibet begin to resist the Chinese occupation. The US Central Intelligence Agency clandestinely supports them.

March: A rebellion breaks out among the Nagas in easternmost India.

November–December: The Dalai Lama goes on a pilgrimage to India.

1957

India discovers that China has built a highway through Aksai Chin. China also builds new roads inside Tibet, including roads towards the Indian border.

1958

Mao Zedong launches his 'Great Leap Forward' to modernize the Chinese economy. It turns out to be a disaster.

1959

10 March: An uprising breaks out in Lhasa against China's occupation of Tibet. The Dalai Lama flees to India. In the same month, a split begins to occur between the Soviet Union and China.

25 March: Deng Xiaoping states that China will 'settle accounts' with India. China begins to prepare for war with India by sending Tibetan-speaking spies into NEFA's Tibetan-speaking areas where they survey the terrain and collect other intelligence.

25 August: Chinese troops attack an Indian position at Longju in NEFA, killing two Indian soldiers.

21 October: Chinese troops attack an Indian position at Kongka La in Ladakh, killing 17 Indian soldiers.

1960

June: The split between China and the Soviet Union is final. The Soviets withdraw 1,400 experts and technicians from China and cancel 200 projects.

1 October: China and Myanmar sign a border agreement. The border follows the crest of the mountains, i.e., the McMahon Line.

The Chinese begin to move thousands of troops to areas close to the Indian border.

1961

February: Thousands of Chinese troops cross the border into northeastern Myanmar to attack KMT forces ensconced on the other side.

2 November: Indian Prime Minister Jawaharlal Nehru convenes a meeting in New Delhi and announces his Forward Policy to consolidate the border areas.

15 October: China and Nepal sign an agreement to construct a highway from Tibet to Kathmandu. The road is officially opened in 1967.

December: India takes over Goa and other Portuguese colonies on its west coast.

The Great Leap Forward ends and as many as 45 million people may have died from starvation and other hardships. Mao is blamed for the disaster.

1962

June: Naga rebel leaders meet a Chinese official in Karachi. He promises them help.

October: Chinese troop movements are observed near the McMahon Line. Mao appears to have reasserted power.

19 October: The Chinese begin to bombard Indian positions along the border.

20 October: China launches an all-out attack on Indian positions in NEFA and Ladakh. Tawang falls on the 24th. In the east, Kibihtoo is attacked.

26 October: Nehru appeals for international 'sympathy and support'.

16 November: The Chinese capture Walong.

19 November: Chinese troops reach Bomdila.

21 November: China declares a unilateral ceasefire and begins to withdraw its troops from the areas that it had occupied.

1963

1 December: The Naga Hills become Nagaland, an Indian state, but the insurgency continues.

1964

27 May: Nehru dies a broken man embittered by what he saw as a Chinese betrayal.

August: Chinese troops intrude into Nathu La in Sikkim, followed by more incursions in December.

October 16: China conducts its first nuclear test.

1965

April: Skirmishes between Pakistan and India lead to war between the two countries in August. Pakistan is defeated and moves closer to China.

1966

24 January: Indira Gandhi becomes India's prime minister and strengthens the country's relationship with the Soviet Union.

26 February: A rebellion breaks out among the Mizos on India's border with Myanmar.

16 May: Mao launches his 'Great Proletarian Cultural Revolution' to purge any remaining opponents to his rule.

20 September: Chinese troops open fire on Indian soldiers on the border with Sikkim.

24 October: The first batch of Naga rebels sets off from India on foot through northern Myanmar to China.

1967

27 January: The first batch of Naga rebels reaches China. They are followed by many more Nagas as well as rebels from Mizoram and Manipur.

May: A Maoist-inspired peasant uprising breaks out in Naxalbari in northern West Bengal.

1968

January: China begins to give massive military support to the Communist Party of Burma (CPB). Thousands of Chinese volunteers join Myanmar communists who until then had been living in exile in China. The CPB takes over vast areas of northeastern Myanmar.

1969

2 March: China troops ambush Soviet border guards on an island in the Ussuri border river. Chinese and Soviet troops fight a brief war for control of the island

1970

February: The China-supported CPB takes over more areas in northeastern Myanmar.

India imposes a brief blockade on Nepal in response to the Chinese construction of a road from Tibet to Kathmandu. India demands a new look at the trade transit treaty with Nepal.

1971

26 March: East Pakistan declares its independence from Pakistan and a bloody war breaks out. The new country is called Bangladesh.

22 April: A Naxalite-style rebellion breaks out in Jhapa and other districts in southeastern Nepal which leads to the formation of the Communist Party of Nepal (Marxist-Leninist).

21September: Bhutan becomes a member of the United Nations.

3 December: India intervenes in the civil war in Bangladesh.

16 December: Pakistan's armed forces surrender in Dhaka and Bangladesh becomes a truly independent nation.

1972

20 January: NEFA becomes the union territory of Arunachal Pradesh.

21 January: The old princely states of Manipur and Tripura, until then Indian union territories, become states. The erstwhile Khasi, Garo, and Jaintia Hills of Assam, which had been an autonomous state within Assam since 2 April 1970, become the state of Meghalaya.

1973
January: An election is held in Sikkim. The anti-palace opposition claims it is rigged, the opposition against the local ruler, the chogyal, gains momentum.

1974
18 May: India tests a nuclear device.
4 September: Sikkim becomes an Indian 'associate state'.

1975
16 May: Sikkim becomes India's 22nd state after the chogyal is deposed and a referendum is held.

1976
9 September: Mao Zedong dies. A power struggle ensues which ends with Deng Xiaoping's return to power.

1979
April: A movement, which became known as 'the Assam Agitation', begins in Assam against illegal immigrants. The more militant activists form the United Liberation Front of Asom (Assam).

1983
18 February: More than 2,000 people are killed in Nellie in Assam when mobs attack villages inhabited by Muslims. The violence was seen as a fallout of the decision to hold state elections in 1983 in the midst of the 'Assam Agitation', and after Indira Gandhi's decision to give four million migrants from Bangladesh the right to vote.

1986

30 June: The Government of India and the Mizo National Front sign an accord, paving the way for Mizoram to become a fully fledged state within the Indian Union.

October: The Indian Army launches 'Operation Falcon' to secure the border between Zeimithang in India and Khenzemane on the Tibet-China side.

1987

January: The Chinese respond with a build-up on their side of the border. Tension runs high but does not lead to war.

20 February: Arunachal Pradesh and Mizoram become Indian states.

27 December: An anti-Chinese demonstration is held in Lhasa. Protesters set fire to a police station and the police open fire on the crowd.

1988

11–13 May: India carries out a series of underground nuclear tests.

August: A nation-wide uprising breaks out against the dictatorship in Myanmar. India supports the pro-democracy forces. China stays close to the government in Yangon.

10 December: Further anti-Chinese riots in Lhasa. Several people are killed.

19–23 December: Indian Prime Minister Rajiv Gandhi visits China.

1989

March–April: The rank-and-file of the insurgent Communist Party of Burma mutinies against the party's old, Maoist leadership and drives them into exile in China. China supports the mutiny and provides the new United Wa State Army with state-of-the art weaponry at the same time as it maintains cordial relations with Myanmar's military government.

5–6 March: Chinese police attack pro-independence protesters in Tibet. At least 469 people, including 82 Buddhist monks, are killed and 721 are injured, according to an independent Chinese journalist.

1990

September: Clashes occur between ethnic Nepalese and the Royal Bhutan Army in southern Bhutan. The violence escalates, prompting approximately 100,000 ethnic Nepalese to flee. Most of them end up in refugee camps in south-eastern Nepal.

1991

December: Chinese Premier Li Peng visits India, bilateral relations begin to thaw.

1993

September: India's new Prime Minister P.V. Narasimha Rao visits China.

1996

13 February: A Maoist rebellion breaks out in Nepal.

1998

8 December: Bhutan and China sign the Agreement on Maintenance of Peace and Tranquillity in Bhutan-China Border Areas. This states that China reaffirms its commitment to respect Bhutan's independence, sovereignty, and territorial integrity.

2003

December: The Bhutanese army drives Assamese and Bodo rebels from India out of their sanctuaries in southeastern Bhutan.

2004

2 April: A huge consignment of mainly Chinese weapons is seized in Chittagong, Bangladesh. The weapons were destined for ethnic rebels in India's northeast.

2007

8 February: India and Bhutan sign a new bilateral agreement. The two countries pledge to work closely on 'issues relating to their national interests', but Bhutan gets more independence.

2008

March: Lhasa is rocked by anti-Chinese protests. The Chinese government says 22 people during the rioting; Tibetans in exile claim many more people were killed during the protests and subsequent crackdown.

2010

27 September: Anthony Shimray, the main arms procurer for the Naga rebels, is apprehended at Kathmandu airport and later ends up in jail in India. He was in charge of a gun-smuggling network spanning Bangladesh, Thailand, the Philippines, and China.

2011

30 September: Myanmar's new, quasi-civilian government led by Thein Sein decides to suspend a mega-hydroelectric, joint project with China at Myitsone in northern Myanmar. Relations between China and Myanmar begin to sour.

2015

March–April: Assamese, Naga, and Manipuri rebels meet to form the United National Liberation Front of Western Southeast Asia with its headquarters in northwestern Myanmar. Weapons are acquired from gun factories on the Myanmar-China border.
9 June: Indian commandos cross the border into Myanmar and attack camps belonging to rebels from northeastern India.

2016

11 August: Bhutan's Foreign Minister Damcho Dorji arrives in Beijing for the 24th round of border talks between his country and China. The Chinese foreign ministry issues a statement saying that 'although Bhutan and China have not established diplomatic relations yet, it will not hold back the mutually beneficial cooperation between the two countries. The Bhutanese side is willing to continue to deepen exchanges in such fields as tourism, religion, culture and agriculture to further lift cooperation with China.' But no agreement is reached on the demarcation of the border between the two countries.

2017

9 June: The Naga rebel leader S.S. Khaplang dies at his camp in northwestern Myanmar. An Indian Naga, Khole Konyak, succeeds him as chairman of the National Socialist Council of Nagaland (Khaplang). The rebel group remains based in Myanmar.

18 June: Indian troops enter the Doklam Plateau, which disputed between China and Bhutan, following an attempt by China to built a road through the area.

20 June: The Bhutan government issues a formal diplomatic démarche to Beijing protesting the Chinese incursion into an area the Bhutanese claim as theirs.

29 June: Bhutan issues another protest against the construction of the road.

1 August: The Chinese foreign ministry issues a 15-page document accusing India of using Bhutan as a 'pretext' to interfere in boundary talks between China and Bhutan. The confrontation leads to a stand-off between Indian and Chinese forces on the Doklam Plateau.

28 August: India and China agree to withdraw their respective forces from the Doklam Plateau.

Additional Reading

Adams, Barbara. 2006. *Nepal: Crisis Unlimited—Reflections from the Crucial Years.* New Delhi: Adroit Publishers.

Adhikari, Aditya. 2014. *The Bullet and the Ballot Box.* London and New York: Verso.

Adhikari, D.P. 1998. *The History of Nepalese Nationalism.* Kathmandu: Romila Adhikari Acharya.

Adhikari, Pushpa. 2012. *China: Threat in South Asia.* New Delhi, Frankfort, IL: Lancer Publishers.

Agrawal, Ajay B. 2003. *India and Tibet: The Role Nehru Played.* Mumbai: N.A. Books International.

Allen. B.C., E.A. Gait, C.G.H. Allen, and H.F. Howard. 2012 [1905]. *Gazetteer of Bengal and North-East India.* New Delhi: Mittal Publications.

Appadorai, A. 1955. *The Bandung Conference.* New Delhi: The Indian Council of World Affairs.

Aris, Michael. 1994. *The Raven Crown: The Origins of Buddhist Monarchy in Bhutan.* London: Serindia Publications.

Arpi, Claude. 2008. *Tibet: The Lost Frontier.* New Delhi, Olympia Fields IL: Lancer Publishers.

Arpi, Claude. 2009. *Dharamsala and Beijing: The Negotiations that Never Were.* New Delhi, Olympia Fields, IL: Lancer Publishers.

Arpi, Claude. 2013. *1962 and the McMahon Saga.* New Delhi, Frankfort, IL: Lancer Publishers.

Avedon, John F. 1985. *In Exile from the Land of Snows.* London: Wisdom Publications.

Bagchi, Romit. 2012. *Gorkhaland: Crisis of Statehood.* New Delhi: Sage Publications.

Bailey, F.M. 1945. *China-Tibet-Assam: A Journey, 1911.* London: Jonathan Cape.

Bains, J.S. 1962. *India's International Disputes.* New York: Asia Publishing House.

Bajpai, G.S. 1999. *China's Shadow over Sikkim: The Politics of Intimidation*. New Delhi, London, Hartford, Wi: Lancer Publishers, Spantech & Lancers.

Bakshi, K.N. 2012. *I was a Prisoner of War in China*. New Delhi: Lancer Publishers.

Barber, Noel. 1969. *From the Land of Lost Content: The Dalai Lama's Fight for Tibet*. London: Collins.

Bareh, H.M. 2001. *Encyclopaedia of North-East India: Sikkim*. New Delhi: Mittal Publications.

Barkataki, Meena Sharma. 2011. *British Administration in North-East India 1826–1874: A Study of Their Social Policy*. Guwahati, Delhi: Spectrum Publications.

Barpujari, N.K. 2008. *Seven Sisters: North East India Profile*. Delhi: Sumit Enterprises.

Barua, Lalit Kumar. 2010. *India's North-East Frontier: The Colonial Legacy*. Guwahati, Delhi: Spectrum Publications.

Basnet, Lal Bahadur. 1974. *Sikkim: A Short Political History*. New Delhi: S. Chand & Co.

Basu, Gautam Kumar. 1996. *Bhutan: The Political Economy of Development*. New Delhi: South Asian Publishers.

Becker, Jasper. 1996. *Hungry Ghosts: Mao's Secret Famine*. New York: Henry Holt and Company.

Bell, Charles. 1991 [1928]. *The People of Tibet*. New Delhi, Madras: Asian Educational Services.

Bhanot, Madan. 2015. *Escape from Namka Chu: A Love Story Based on India-China War 1962*. New Delhi: KW Publishers.

Bhattacharyya, Rajeev. 2014. *Rendezvous with Rebels: Journey to Meet India's Most Wanted Man*. Noida: HarperCollins Publishers India.

Bhushan, Ranjit. 2016. *Maoism in India and Nepal*. New Delhi, London, New York: Routledge.

Bhutani, Sudarshan. 2004. *A Clash of Political Cultures: Sino Indian Relations [1957–1962]*. New Delhi: Roli Books.

Bhuyan, S.K. (compiled, trans., and ed.). 1933. *Tungkhungia Buranji or A History of Assam 1681–1826 A.D.* London, Bombay, Calcutta, Madras: Oxford University Press.

Bista, Dor Bahadur. 2001. *Fatalism and Development: Nepal's Struggle for Modernization*. Hyderabad: Orient Longman.

Borah, Swapnali, Deke Tourangbam, and A.C. Meitei. 2010. *Encyclopaedic Studies of North-Eastern States of India: Arunachal Pradesh*. New Delhi: New Academic Publishers.

Bower, Ursula Graham. 1953. *The Hidden Land*. London: John Murray.

Bray, John (ed.). 2011. *Ladakhi Histories: Local and Regional Perspectives*. New Delhi and Dharamsala: Library of Tibetan World and Archives & Indraprastha Press.

Cederlöf, Gunnel. 2014. *Founding an Empire on India's North-Eastern Frontiers 1790–1840*. New Delhi: Oxford University Press.

Central Intelligence Agency. 1965. *Intelligence Study: Bhutan between India and China*. OCI No. 1105/65, April 2. Directorate of Intelligence, Office of Current Intelligence.

Chakravarti, P.C. 1961. *India–China Relations*. Calcutta: Firma K.L. Mukhopadhyay.

Chakravarti, P.C. 1971. *The Evolution of India's Northern Borders*. London: Asia Publishing House.

Chakravarti, Sudeep. 2008. *Red Sun: Travels in Naxalite Country*. New Delhi: Penguin Books.

Chakravarty, L.N. 1989. *Glimpses of the Early History of Arunachal*. Itanagar: Director of Research, Government of Arunachal Pradesh.

Chapman, F. Spencer. 1940. *Lhasa: The Holy City*. London: Readers Union and Chatto & Windus.

Chaudhury, Mithu. 2013. 'NIA Report Reveals NSCN (IM)-China Link', *North East News Portal*, 14 January.

Choudhary, Shubhranshu. 2012. *Let's Call Him Vasu: With the Maoists in Chhattisgarh*. New Delhi: Penguin Books.

Chowdhury, J.N. 1990. *The Tribal Culture and History of Arunachal Pradesh*. Delhi: Daya Publishing House.

Coelho, V.H. 1970. *Sikkim and Bhutan*. New Delhi: Vikas Publications.

Craig, Mary. 1992. *Tears of Blood: A Cry for Tibet*. New Delhi: Harper Collins Indus.

Crossette, Barbara. 1995. *So Close to Heaven: The Vanishing Buddhist Kingdoms of the Himalayas*. New York: Albert A. Knopf.

Dalai Lama. 1964. *My Land and My People: The Memoirs of His Holiness the Dalai Lama of Tibet*. London: Panther Books.

Dalai Lama. 1982. *His Holiness the Dalai Lama: Collected Statements, Interviews and Articles*. Dharamsala: The Information Office of His Holiness the Dalai Lama.

Dalai Lama. 1990. *Freedom in Exile: The Autobiography of the Dalai Lama*. New York: HarperCollins.

Damodaran, A.K., and U.S. Bajpai (eds). 1990. *Indian Foreign Policy: The Indira Gandhi Years*. New Delhi: Radiant Publishers, the Nehru Memorial Museum and Library.

Das, B.S. 1995. *Mission to Bhutan: A Nation in Transition*. New Delhi: Vikas Publishing House.

Das, Gautam. 2009. *China-Tibet-India: The 1962 War and the Strategic Military Failure*. New Delhi: Har-Anand Publications.

Das, Gautam. 2013. *Understanding the Sino-Indian War 1962*. New Delhi: Har-Anand Publications.

Das, Gurudas, C. Joshua Thomas, and Nani Bath (eds.). *Voices from the Border: Response to Chinese Claims over Arunachal Pradesh*. New Delhi: Pentagon Press.

Das, Smriti. 2005. *Assam–Bhutan Trade Relations 1865–1949: A Socio-Economic Study*. Delhi: Anshah Publishing House.

Dash, Arther Jules. 2011 [1947]. *Bengal District Gazetteer: Darjeeling*. Siliguri: N.L. Publishers.

Datta, Saikat. 2011. 'The Great Claw of China', *Outlook*, 7 February. Available at http://www.outlookindia.com/article.aspx?270223 (accessed on 29 March 2016).

Dave, Shri A.K. 2006. *The Real Story of China's War on India, 1962*. Occasional Paper No 1. New Delhi: Centre for Armed Forces Historical Research.

De Vore, Howard O. 1999. *China's Intelligence and Internal Security Forces*. Surrey: Jane's Information Group.

Deane, Hugh. 1987. 'The Cold War in Tibet', *Covert Action Information Bulletin*, No. 29 (Winter): pp. 48–50.

Dhar, Maloy Krishna. 2005. *Open Secrets: India's Intelligence Unveiled*. New Delhi: Manas Publications.

Dikötter, Frank. 2013. *The Tragedy of Liberation: A History of the Chinese Revolution 1945–1957*. New York, London, New Delhi, Sydney: Bloomsbury Press.

Dixit, Kanak Mani, and Shastri Ramachandaran (eds). 2002. *State of Nepal*. Kathmandu: Himal Books.

Dixit, Kanak Mani. 2011. *Peace Politics in Nepal: An Opinion from Within*. Kathmandu: Himal Books.

Dorji, C.T., 1995. *History of Bhutan*. Thimphu: Sangay Xam.

Dozey, E.C. 2012. *A Concise History of the Darjeeling District since 1835 with a Complete Itinerary of Tours in Sikkim and the District*. Kolkata: Bibliophil.

Dunham, Mikel. 2004. *Buddha's Warriors: The Story of the CIA-backed Tibetan Freedom Fighters, the Chinese Invasion, and the Ultimate Fall of Tibet*. New York: Jeremy P. Tarcher and Penguin.

Dutta, S., B. Tripathy (ed.). 2008. *Sources of the History of Arunachal Pradesh*. New Delhi: Gyan Publishing House.

Eftimiades, Nicholas. 1994. *Chinese Intelligence Operations*. Essex: Frank Cass.

Elleman, Bruce A., Stephen Kotkin, and Clive Schofield (eds). 2013. *Beijing's Power and China's Borders: Twenty Neighbours in Asia*. New Delhi: Pentagon Press.

Elwin, Verrier (ed.). 1962. *India's North-East Frontier in the Nineteenth Century*. London, Bombay: Oxford University Press.

Elwin, Verrier. 1964. *The Tribal World of Verrier Elwin: An Autobiography*. New York, Bombay: Oxford University Press.

Elwin, Verrier. 2009. *The Oxford India Elwin: Selected Writings*. New Delhi, New York: Oxford University Press.

Elwin, Verrier. 2014. *Democracy in NEFA*. Itanagar: Directorate of Research, Department of Cultural Affairs, Government of Arunachal Pradesh.

Epstein, Israel. 1983. *Tibet Transformed*. Beijing: New World Press.

Faligot, Roger, and Rémi Kauffer. 1990. *The Chinese Secret Service*. London: Headline Book Publishing.

Fang, Percy Jucheng, and Lucy Guinong J. Fang. 1986. *Zhou Enlai: A Profile*. Beijing: Foreign Languages Press.

Fisher, Margaret W., Leo E. Rose, and Robert A. Huttenback. 1963. *Himalayan Battleground: Sino-Indian Rivalry in Ladakh*. New York, London: Frederick A. Praeger.

Fleming, Peter. 1987. *Bayonets to Lhasa*. Hong Kong, Oxford, New York: Oxford University Press.

Ford, Robert. 1957. *Captured in Tibet: An Epic of Endurance*. London: Pan Books.

French, Patrick. 2011. *Younghusband: The Last Great Imperial Adventurer*. London: Penguin Books.

Fürer-Haimendorf, Christoph von. 1955. *Himalayan Barbary*. London: John Murray.

Fürer-Haimendorf, Christoph von. 1962. *The Apa Tanis and Their Neighbours*. London: Routledge & Kegan Paul.

Gaige, Fredrick H. 1975. *Regionalism and National Unity in Nepal*. Berkeley: University of California Press.

Gait, Edward Albert. 2011. *A History of Assam*. Guwahati, Delhi: Spectrum Publications.

Garver, John W., and Fei-Ling Wang. 2010. 'China's Anti-encirclement Struggle', *Asian Survey*, 6(3) 238–61.

Gautam, Kul Chandra. 2016. *Lost in Transition: Rebuilding Nepal from the Maoist Mayhem and Mega Earthquake*. Kathmandu: Nepal-Laya.

Gautam, Rajesh, and Asoke K. Thapa-Magar. 1994. *Tribal Ethnography of Nepal, Volume I*. Delhi: Book Faith India.

Gautam, Rajesh, and Asoke K. Thapa-Magar. 1994. *Tribal Ethnography of Nepal, Volume II*. Delhi: Book Faith India.

Gearing, Julian. 2000. 'Lama Wars: Can the Dalai Lama hold his divided people together—and keep China at bay?', *Asiaweek*, October 20.

Gearing, Julian. 2003. 'The tale of two Karmapas', *Asia Times Online*, December 24. Available at http://www.atimes.com/atimes/China/EL24Ad02.html (accessed on 29 March 2016).

Gelder, Stuart, and Roma Golder. 1964. *The Timely Rain: Travels in New Tibet*. New York and London: Monthly Review Press.

Ghosh, Suniti Kumar. 2009. *Naxalbari: Before and After*. Kolkata: New Age Publishers.

Goldstein, Melvin C., Dawei Sherap, and William R. Siebenschuh. 2004. *A Tibetan Revolutionary: The Political Life and Times of Bapa Phüntso Wangye*. Berkeley, Los Angeles, London: University of California Press.

Goldstein, Melvyn C. 2007. *A History of Modern Tibet Volume 2: The Calm before the Storm, 1951–1955*. Berkeley, Los Angeles, London: University of California Press.

Goldstein, Melvyn C. 2014. *A History of Modern Tibet Volume 3: The Storm Clouds Descend, 1955–1957*. Berkeley, Los Angeles, London: University of California Press.

Graff, David A., and Robin Higham (eds). 2012 *A Military History of China*. Dehra Dun: Greenfields Publishers.

Gupta, Karunakar. 1982. *Spotlight on Sino-Indian Frontiers*. Calcutta: New Book Centre.

Gupta, Ranjit Kumar. 2004. *The Crimson Agenda: Maoist Protest and Terror*. Delhi: Wordsmith.

Gupta, Shishir. 2014. *The Himalayan Face-Off: Chinese Assertion and the Indian Riposte*. Gurgaon: Hachette Book Publishing.

Guruswamy, Mohan, and Zorawar Daulet Singh. 2009. *India China Relations: The Border Issue and Beyond*. New Delhi: Viva Books and the Observer Research Foundation.

Halper, Lezlee Brown, and Stefan Halper. 2014. *Tibet: An Unfinished Story*. London: Hurst & Company.

Hamilton, Angus. 1912. *In Abor Jungles: Being an Account of the Abor Expedition, the Mishmi Mission and the Miri Mission*. London: G. Bell & Sons.

Harrer, Heinrich. 1956. *Seven Years in Tibet*. London: Pan Books.

Harrer, Heinrich. 1998. *Return to Tibet: Tibet After the Chinese Invasion*. New York: Penguin Putman.

Hazarika, Joysankar. 1996. *Geopolitics of North East India*. New Delhi: Gyan Publishing House.

Hoftun, Martin, William Raeper, and John Whelpton. 1999. *People, Politics & Ideology: Democracy and Social Change in Nepal*. Kathmandu: Mandala Book Point.

Hopkirk, Peter. 1982. *Trespassers on the Roof of the World: The Race for Lhasa*. Oxford: Oxford University Press.

Huberman, Leo, and Paul Sweezy. 1963. 'A Fool's Game: The China-India Border Dispute', *Monthly Review*, 14 (9) (January): 465–86.

Hussain, T. Karki. 1977. *Sino-Indian Conflict and International Politics in the Indian Sub-Continent, 1962–66*. Faridabad: Thomson Press (India) Ltd.

Hutt, Michael (ed.). 2004. *Himalayan People's War*. London: Hurst & Company.

Jeffrey, Robin, Ronojoy Sen, and Pratima Singh. 2012. *More than Maoism: Politics, Policies and Insurgencies in South Asia*. New Delhi: Manohar and the Institute of South Asian Studies.

Jha, Prashant. 2014. *Battles of the New Republic: A Contemporary History of Nepal*. New Delhi: Aleph Book Company.

Johri, Sita Ram. 1968. *The Chinese Invasion of NEFA*. Lucknow: Himalaya Publications.

Johri, Sita Ram. 1969. *The Chinese Invasion of Ladakh*. Lucknow: Himalaya Publications.

Jose, Vinod K. 2010. 'Spies in the Snow: How the CIA and Indian Intelligence Lost a Nuclear Device in the Himalayas', *The Caravan*, December.

Joshi, H.G. 2004. *Sikkim: Past and Present*. New Delhi: Mittal Publications.

Joshi, P.C. 2012. *Naxalism at a Glance*. Delhi: Kalpaz Publications.

Kalha, Ranjit Singh. 2014. *India–China Boundary Issues: Quest for Settlement*. New Delhi: Indian Council of World Affairs and Pentagon Press.

Kampen, Thomas. 2000. *Mao Zedong, Zhou Enlai and the Evolution of the Chinese Communist Leadership*. Copenhagen: Nordic Institute of Asian Studies.

Kandell, Alice. 1971. *Sikkim: The Hidden Kingdom*. New York: Doubleday & Company Inc.

Kao, Ting Tsz. 1980. *The Chinese Frontiers*. Aurora, Ill: Chinese Scholarly Publishing Company.

Karki, Arjun, and David Seddon (eds.). 2003. *The People's War in Nepal: Left Perspectives*. Delhi: Adroit Publishers.

Karnik, V.B. (ed.). *China Invades India*. Bombay, New Delhi, Calcutta, Madras, London, New York: Allied Publishers.

Kazi, Jigme N. 2013. *The Lone Warrior: Exiled in My Homeland*. Gangtok: Hill Media Publications.

Khan, Sulmaan Wasif. 2015. *Muslim, Trader, Nomad, Spy: China's Cold War and the People of the Tibetan Borderlands*. Chapel Hill: The University of North Carolina Press.

Khetsun, Tubten (trans. from Tibetan by Matthew Akester). 2008. *Memories of Life in Lhasa under Chinese Rule*. New York: Columbia University Press.

Kimura, Hisao, and Scott Berry. 1990. *Japanese Agent in Tibet: My Ten Years of Travel in Disguise*. London: Serindia Publications.

Kissinger, Henry. 2012. *On China*. London: Penguin Books.

Kohli, M.S., and Kenneth Conboy. 2002. *Spies in the Himalayas: Secret Missions and Perilous Climbs*. Lawrence: University Press of Kansas.

Kohli, Manorama. 1993. *From Dependency to Interdependence: A Study of Indo-Bhutan Relations*. New Delhi: Vikas Publishing House.

Kumar, Niraj, George van Driem, and Phunchok Stobdan (eds.). 2016. *Himalayan Bridge*. New Delhi: KW Publishers.

Kunnath, George J. 2012. *Rebels from Mud Houses: Dalits and the Making of the Maoist Revolution in Bihar*. New Delhi: Social Science Press.

Laird, Thomas. 2002. *Into Tibet: The CIA's First Atomic Spy and His Secret Expedition to Lhasa*. New York: Grove Press.

Lal, Dinesh. 2008. *Indo-Tibet-China Conflict*. Delhi: Kalpaz Publications.

Lamb, Alastair. 1966. *The McMahon Line: A Study in the Relations Between India, China and Tibet, 1904 to 1914. Volume I: Morley, Minto and Non-Interference in Tibet*. London: Routledge and Kegan Paul; Toronto: University of Toronto Press.

Lamb, Alastair. 1966. *The McMahon Line: A Study in the Relations between India, China and Tibet, 1904 to 1914. Volume II: Hardinge, McMahon and the Simla Conference*. London: Routledge and Kegan Paul; Toronto: University of Toronto Press.

Lamb, Alastair. 1968. *Asian Frontiers: Studies in a Continuing Problem*. London: Pall Mall Press.

Lamb, Alastair. 1973. *The Sino-Indian Border in Ladakh*. Canberra: Australian National University Press.

Lamb, Alastair. 1991. *Kashmir: A Disputed Legacy 1846–1990*. Hertingfordbury, Hertfordshire: Roxford Books.

Lecomte-Tilouine, Marie (ed.). 2013. *Revolution in Nepal: An Anthropological and Historical Approach to the People's War.* New Delhi: Oxford University Press.

Levenson, Claude B. 1988. *Dalai Lama: A Biography.* London, Sydney, Wellington: Unwin Hyman.

Lintner, Bertil. 1990. *The Rise and Fall of the Communist Party of Burma.* Ithaca: Cornell University Southeast Asia Program.

Lintner, Bertil. 2011. *Land of Jade: a Journey from India through Northern Burma to China.* Bangkok: Orchid Press.

Liu, Melinda. 1999. 'Tibet: China's Kosovo? The Inside Story of How the CIA Helped the Dalai Lama', *Newsweek* (cover story, Asian edition), 19 April.

Lohia, Rammanohar. 2002. *India, China and Northern Frontiers.* Delhi: B.R. Publishing Corporation.

Luthra, P.N. 1971. *Constitutional and Administrative Growth of the North-East Frontier Agency.* Shillong: North-East Frontier Agency.

Macaulay, Colman. 1977 [1885]. *Report on a Mission to Sikkim and the Tibetan Frontier 1884.* Kathmandu: Ratna Pustak Bhandar.

MacFarquhar, Roderick, and Michael Schoenhals. 2006. *Mao's Last Revolution.* Cambridge, Massachusetts and London, England: The Belknap Press of Harvard University Press.

MacFarquhar, Roderick. 1974. *The Origins of the Cultural Revolution, Volume 1: Contradictions among the People, 1956–1957.* New York: Columbia University Press.

MacFarquhar, Roderick. 1983. *The Origins of the Cultural Revolution, Volume 2: The Great Leap Forward, 1958–1960.* New York: Columbia University Press.

Maitra, Ramtanu. 2004. 'Pakistan's Bhutan gambit worries India', *Asia Times Online,* November 25. Available at http://www.atimes.com/atimes/South_Asia/FK25Df03.html (accessed on 18 August 2017).

Malik, Mohan. 2011. *China and India: Great Power Rivals.* Boulder and London: First Forum Press, Lynne Reiner Publishers.

Mansingh, Surjit. (ed.). 1998. *Indian and Chinese Foreign Policies in Comparative Perspective.* New Delhi: Radiant Publishers.

Marks, Thomas A. 2007. *Maoist People's War in Post-Vietnam Asia.* Bangkok: White Lotus Press.

Mathema, Kalyan Bhakta. 2011. *Madheshi Uprising: The Resurgence of Ethnicity.* Kathmandu: Mandala Book Point.

Maxwell, Neville. 1981. 'The Deadlocked Deadlock, Sino-Indian Boundary Dispute', *Economic and Political Weekly,* 16(38) (19 September):1545–8.

Maxwell, Neville. 2014. *China's Borders: Settlements and Conflicts*. Newcastle: Cambridge Scholars Publishing.

McGranahan, Carole. 2010. *Arrested Histories: Tibet, the CIA, and Memories of a Forgotten War*. Durham, NC: Duke University Press.

McGregor, Richard. 2010. *The Party: The Secret World of China's Communist Rulers*. London: Allen Lane.

McKay, Alex. 1997. *Tibet and the British Raj: The Frontier Cadre, 1904–1947*. Surrey: Curzon Press.

McKay, Alex. 2003. *Tibet and Her Neighbours: A History*. London: Edition Hansjörg Mayer.

Mehrotra, L.L. 1998. *India's Tibet Policy*. New Delhi: Tibetan Parliamentary and Policy Research Centre.

Ministry of External Affairs. 1960. *Atlas of the Northern Frontier of India*. New Delhi: Ministry of External Affairs.

Ministry of Information and Broadcasting. 1963. *The Chinese Threat*. Delhi: Publications Division, Ministry of Information and Broadcasting.

Mishra, Trinath. 2007. *Barrel of the Gun: The Maoist Challenge and Indian Democracy*. New Delhi: Sheriden Book Company.

Misra, Tilottama (ed.). 2011. *Writings from North-East India: Fiction*. New Delhi: Oxford University Press.

Misra, Tilottama (ed.). 2011. *Writings from North-East India: Poetry and Essays*. New Delhi: Oxford University Press.

Moraes, Frank. 1960. *The Revolt in Tibet*. New York: The Macmillan Company.

Mukherji, Nirmalangshu. 2013. *The Maoists in India: Tribals under Siege*. New Delhi: Amaryllis.

Myrdal, Jan. 2012. *Red Star over India: As the Wretched of the Earth are Rising. Impressions, Reflexions and Preliminary Interferences*. Kolkata: Setu Prakashani.

Nair, P. Thankappan. 1985. *Tribes of Arunachal Pradesh*. Guwahati: Spectrum Publications.

Nanda, B.R. (ed.). 1990. *Indian Foreign Policy: The Nehru Years*. New Delhi: Radiant Publishers and the Nehru Memorial Museum and Library.

Navlakha, Gautam. 2012. *Days and Nights in the Heartland of Rebellion*. New Delhi: Penguin Books.

Nayak, Nihar R. 2014. *Strategic Himalayas: Republican Nepal and External Powers*. New Delhi: Pentagon Press and the Institute for Defence Studies and Analyses.

Noorani, A.G. 2011. *India–China Boundary Problem 1846–1947: History and Diplomacy*. New Delhi: Oxford University Press.

Norbu, Jamyang. 1986. *Warriors of Tibet: The Story of Aten and the Khampas' Fight for the Freedom of their Country*. London: Wisdom Publications.

Onesto, Li. 2005. *Dispatches from the People's War in Nepal*. London and Ann Arbor: Pluto Press; Chicago: Insight Press Inc.

Orton, Anna. 2010. *India's Borderland Disputes: China, Pakistan, Bangladesh and Nepal*. New Delhi: Epitome Books.

Osik, N.N. 1999. *Modern History of Arunachal Pradesh (1825–1997)*. Itanagar, New Delhi: Himalayan Publishers.

Palit, D.K. 1991. *War in High Himalaya: The Indian Army in Crisis, 1962*. New Delhi: Lancer International.

Pandita, Rahul. 2011. *Hello Bastar: The Untold Story of India's Maoist Movement*. Chennai: Tranquebar Press.

Parmanand. 1992. *The Politics of Bhutan: Retrospect and Prospect*. Delhi: Pragati Publications.

Peissel, Michel. 1972. *The Secret War in Tibet*. Boston, Toronto: Little Brown and Company.

Peissel, Michel. 1992. *Mustang: A Lost Tibetan Kingdom*. Delhi: Book Faith India.

Pommaret, Françoise. 1991. *Introduction to Bhutan*. Hong Kong: Odyssey.

Prasad, Ambika. 2011. *Nehru in Parliament: On Social, Economic and Foreign Policy*. New Delhi: Cyber Tech Publications.

Raeper, William, and Martin Hoftun. 1992. *Spring Awakening: An Account of the 1990 Revolution in Nepal*. New Delhi: Viking.

Raghavan, V.R. 2013. *Nepal as a Federal State: Lessons from the Indian Experience*. New Delhi: Vij Books India.

Raizada, Shefali. 2012. *Merger of Sikkim: A New Perspective*. Delhi: Swati Publications.

Raj, Prakash A. 2001. *"Kay Gardeko?": The Royal Massacre in Nepal*. New Delhi: Rupa & Co.

Rajagopalan, Rajeswari Pillai. 2012. *Clashing Titans: Military Strategy and Insecurity among Asian Great Powers*. New Delhi: KW Publishers and the Observer Research Foundation.

Ram, Mohan. 1971. *Maoism in India*. Delhi, Bombay, Bangalore, Kanpur, London: Vikas Publications; New York: Barnes & Noble Inc.

Raman, B. 2007. *The Kaoboys of R&AW: Down Memory Lane*. New Delhi, Olympia Fields IL: Lancer Publishers.

Ramana, P.V. 2014. *Understanding India's Maoists: Select Documents*. New Delhi: Institute of Defence Studies and Analyses and Pentagon Press.

Rao, Gondker Narayana. 1968. *The India–China Border: A Reappraisal.* Bombay, Calcutta, New Delhi, Madras, Lucknow, Bangalore, London, New York: Asia Publishing House.

Rasgotra, M. (ed.). 2012. *China and South Asia: Developments and Trends.* New Delhi: Academic Foundation.

Rehman, Iskander. 2007. 'A Himalayan Challenge: India's Conventional Deterrent and the Role of Special Operations Forces along the Sino-Indian border', *Naval War College Review*, 70 (1) (Winter): 104–42.

Riencourt, Amaury de. 1950. *Lost World: Tibet, Key to Asia.* London: Victor Gollancz.

Rittenberg, Sidney, Amanda Bennett. 2001. *The Man Who Stayed Behind.* Durham and London: Duke University Press.

Ronaldshay, Earl of. 2005 [1923]. *Lands of the Thunderbolt: Sikhim, Chumbi & Bhutan.* Varanasi: Pilgrims Publishing.

Roy, Anirban. '2009. Return of the Dalai Lama', *The Northeast Today* (cover story), November.

Roy, Asish Kumar. 2008. *Unfinished Revolution: The Spring Thunder and Beyond.* Kolkata: Minerva Associates.

Rustomji, Nari. 1983. *Imperilled Frontiers: India's North-Eastern Borderlands.* Delhi, Oxford, New York: Oxford University Press.

Ryan, Mark A., David M. Finkelstein, and Michael A. McDevitt (eds.). 2003. *Chinese Warfighting: The PLA Experience since 1949.* Armonk, NY: Sharpe.

Ryavec, Karl E. 2015. *A Historical Atlas of Tibet.* Chicago and London: The University of Chicago Press.

Saikia, Yasmin. 2004. *Fragmented Histories: Struggling to be Tai-Ahom in India.* Durham and London: Duke University Press.

Sali, M.L. 1998. *India–China Border Dispute: A Case Study of the Eastern Sector.* New Delhi: A.P.H. Publishing Corporation.

Sarma, Amulya Chandra. 1986. *Tai Ahom System of Government.* Delhi: B.R. Publishing Corporation.

Satnam (trans. from Punjabi by Vishav Bharti). 2010. *Jangalnama: Travels into a Maoist Guerilla Zone.* New Delhi: Penguin Books India.

Schendel, Willem van. 2005. *The Bengal Borderland: Beyond State and Nation in South Asia.* London: Anthem Press.

Sebastian, Sarish. 2015. *Bhutan: A Journey from Tradition to Modernity.* New Delhi: Adroit Publishers.

Senanayake, Ratne Deshapriya. 1967. *Inside Story of Tibet*. Colombo: The Afro-Asian Writers' Bureau.

Shah, Alpa, and Judith Pettigrew (eds.). 2012. *Windows into a Revolution: Ethnographies of Maoism in India and Nepal*. New Delhi: Social Science Press and Orient Black Swan.

Shakaba, Tsepon W.D. 1967. *Tibet: A Political History*. New Haven and London: Yale University Press.

Shakespear. L.W. 2004. *History of Upper Assam, Upper Burmah and North-Eastern Frontier*. Guwahati, Delhi: Spectrum Publications.

Shakya, Tsering. 1999. *The Dragon in the Land of Snows: A History of Modern Tibet since 1947*. London: Pimlico.

Sharma, Jan. 1998. *Democracy without Roots*. Delhi: Book Faith India.

Sharma, Khemraj. 2013. *Gorkhas in the Wilderness: A Study in North East India*. New Delhi: Concept Publishing Company.

Sharma, Shri Ram. 2003. *India–China Relations 1972–1991*. New Delhi: Discovery Publishing House.

Sheikh, A.G. 2010. *Reflections on Ladakh, Tibet and Central Asia*. New Delhi: Skyline Publications.

Short, Philip. 1999. *Mao: A Life*. London: Hodder and Stoughton.

Shrivastava, Manoj. 2013. *Re-Energising Indian Intelligence*. New Delhi: Vij Books India.

Siddika, Shamima. 1993. *Muslims of Nepal*. Kathmandu: Gazala Siddika.

Sidhu, Waheguru Pal Singh, and Jing-dong Yuan. 2003. *China and India: Cooperation or Conflict?* New Delhi: India Research Press.

Singh, Jasjit (ed.). *China's India War 1962: Looking Back to See the Future*. New Delhi: KW Publishers.

Singh, K. Natwar. 2009. *My China Diary 1956M1988*. New Delhi: Rupa & Company.

Singh, K.S. 1995. *People of India Volume XIV: Arunachal Pradesh*. Calcutta: Seagull Books and Anthropological Survey of India.

Singh, M.K. (ed.) 2012. *Indian Intelligence: Missing in Action*. Delhi: Prashant Publishing House.

Singh, Mithilesh Kumar. 2014. *Increasing Diplomatic Relation Between Bhutan and China: A Great Concern for India*. Delhi: Prashant Publishing House.

Singh, Mukesh Kumar. 2011. *Nepal Foreign Policy*. New Delhi: Sumit Enterprises.

Singh, Mukesh Kumar. 2014. *Nepal in China's Foreign Policy*. Delhi: Prashant Publishing House.

Singh, Prakash. 2011. *The Naxalite Movement in India*. New Delhi: Rupa Publications.

Singh, Sunjoy K. 2015. *Major Operations of R&AW*. New Delhi: Lenin Media.

Singh, V.K. 2007. *India's External Intelligence: Secrets of Research and Analysis Wing (RAW)*. New Delhi: Manas Publications.

Sinha, A.C. 2008. *Sikkim: Feudal and Democratic*. New Delhi: Indus Publishing Company.

Sinha, Chandan. 2013. *Kindling of an Insurrection: Notes from Junglemahals*. London, New York, New Delhi: Routledge.

Sinha, V.B. 1968. *The Red Rebel in India: A Study of Communist Strategy and Tactics*. New Delhi: Associated Publishing House.

Smith, Warren W. 1996. *Tibetan Nation: A History of Tibetan Nationalism and Sino-Tibetan Relations*. Boulder, Colorado: Westview Press.

Smith, Warren W. 2008. *China's Tibet? Autonomy or Assimilation*. Lanham, Boulder, New York, Toronto, Plymouth, UK: Rowman & Littlefield Publishers.

Stewart, Jules. 2006. *Spying For the Raj: The Pundits and the Mapping of the Himalaya*. Phoenix Mill: Sutton Publishing.

Strong, Anna Louise. 2003. *When Serfs Stood Up in Tibet*. Beijing: Foreign Languages Press.

Syed, Anwar H. 1974. *China and Pakistan: Diplomacy of an Entente Cordiale*. London, Karachi, Delhi: Oxford University Press.

Syiemlieh, David R. (ed.). 2014. *On the Edge of Empire: Four British Plans for North East India, 1941–1947*. New Delhi: Sage Publications.

Talukdar, Mrinal (trans. from Assamese by Deepika Phukan). 2014. *1962: Sino-Indian Conflict*. Guwahati: Kaziranga Books.

Teiwes, Frederick C. 1993. *Politics and Purges in China*. Armonk, New York, London, England: M.E. Sharpe.

Teiwes, Frederick C. 2007. *The End of the Maoist Era*. Armonk, New York, London, England: M.E. Sharpe.

Teltscher, Kate. 2006. *The High Road to China: George Bogle, the Panchen Lama and the First British Expedition to Tibet*. London: Bloomsbury.

Tendhon Culture Preservation Society. 2014. *A Short Account of His Holiness' visit to Mon Tawang on his way to India in 1959*. Tawang: Tendhon Culture Preservation Society

Thant Myint-U, 2011. *Where China Meets India: Burma and the New Crossroads of Asia*. New York: Farrar, Straus and Giroux.

Thapa, Deepak, and Bandita Sijapati. 2004. *A Kingdom under Siege: Nepal's Maoist Insurgency, 1996 to 2004*. London and New York: Zed Books.

Thapa, Manjushree. 2005. *Forget Kathmandu: An Elegy for Democracy*. New Delhi: Penguin Books.

Thapa, Manjushree. 2013. *Forget Kathmandu: An Elegy for Democracy*. New Delhi: Aleph Books.

Thapar, Romila, Nandita Haksar, and Anand Teltumbde (eds.). 2013. *Are We Sure About India?* Kathmandu: Himal Books.

Thondup, Gyalo, and Anne F. Thurston. 2015. *The Noodle Maker of Kalimpong: The Untold Story of My Struggle for Tibet*. London, Sydney, Auckland, Johannesburg: Rider. By Dalai Lama's brother who served as a go-between for the CIA and Tibetan freedom fighters in the 1950s and 1960s.

Tsai Wei-ping (ed.). 1978. *Classified Chinese Communist Documents: A Selection*. Taipei: Institute of International Relations, National Chengchi University, Republic of China. Tripathi, D.P. and Deepak B.R. (eds.) *India and Taiwan: From Benign Neglect to Pragmatism*. 2016. New Delhi: Vij Books India.

Umpherston, Charles Aitchison. 2016 [1929]. *A Collection of Treaties, Engagements and Sanads Relating to India and Neighbouring Countries*. Delhi: Facsimile Publisher.

Upreti, Bishnu Raj. 2004. *The Price of Neglect: From Resource Conflict to Maoist Insurgency in the Himalayan Kingdom*. Kathmandu: Bhrikuti Academic Publications.

Van Walt van Praag, Michael C. 1987. *The Status of Tibet: History, Rights, and Prospects in International Law*. Boulder, Colorado: Westview Press. A history of Tibet with the emphasis on its legal status.

Verma, Anand Swaroop (trans. from Hindi by Akhilanand, Dalip Upadhyay, and Ish Mishra). 2001. *Maoist Movement in Nepal*. New Delhi: Samkalin Teesari Duniya.

Wang Lixiong, and Shakya, Tsering. 2009. *The Struggle for Tibet*. London and New York: Verso.

Wangchuck, Ashi Dorji Wangmo. 2012. *Treasures of the Thunder Dragon: A Portrait of Bhutan*. New Delhi: Penguin/Viking.

White, J. Claude. 2005 [1909]. *Sikhim and Bhutan: Twenty-One Years of the North-East Frontier*. New Delhi, Chennai: Asian Educational Services.

Wignall, Sydney. 1996. *Spy on the Roof of the World: A True Story of Espionage and Survival in the Himalayas*. New York: Lyons & Burford Publishers.

Wijer, Birgit Van De. 2010. *Tibet's Forgotten Heroes: The Story of Tibet's Armed Resistance Against China*. Stroud, Gloustershire: Amberley.

Woodcock, George. 1971. *Into Tibet: The Early British Explorers*. London: Faber and Faber.

Woodman, Dorothy. 1969. *Himalayan Frontiers: A Political Review of British, Chinese, Indian and Russian Rivalries.* New York, Washington: Frederick A. Praeger Publishers.

Xun, Zhou (ed.). 2012. *The Great Famine in China, 1958–1962: A Documentary History.* New Haven and London: Yale University Press.

Younghusband, Francis. 1998 [1910]. *India and Tibet: A History of the Relations which have Subsisted Between the Two Countries from the Time of Warren Hastings to 1910; With Particular Account of the Mission to Lhasa of 1904.* Delhi: Book Faith India.

1920. *Military Report on the Bhareli River Area and Tawang. General Staff, India* Calcutta: Superintendent Government Printing, India.

1960. *Documents on the Sino-Indian Boundary Question.* Peking: Foreign Languages Press.

1962. *The Sino-Indian Boundary Question* (Enlarged Edition). Peking: Foreign Languages Press.

1984. *Report on the Administration of Assam For the Year 1921–22* Reprint 1984. Delhi: Mittal Publications.

Index

About the Author

Bertil Lintner is a former correspondent with the *Far Eastern Economic Review*, Hong Kong, the Swedish daily *Svenska Dagbladet*, and Jane's Information Group in the UK. He is currently with *Asia Times Online* and Asia Pacific Media Services.

Lintner has written 17 books on Asian politics and history, including *Outrage: Burma's Struggle for Democracy; Land of Jade: A Journey From India through Northern Burma to China; Bloodbrothers: Crime, Business and Politics in Asia; Great Leader, Dear Leader: Demystifying North Korea Under the Kim Clan; Aung San Suu Kyi and Burma's Struggle for Democracy;* and *World.Wide.Web: Chinese Migration in the 21st Century.* His most recent book, *Great Game East: India, China and the Struggle for Asia's Most Volatile Frontier* describes and analyses the rivalry between India and China, including the struggle for control and influence over northern Myanmar.

In 1985, the Swedish-born Lintner and his wife went on an 18-month, 2,275-kilometre overland journey from northeastern India across Burma's northern rebel-held areas to China. Travelling mostly by foot, but also jeep, bicycle, and elephant, they became the first outsiders in over four decades to cross that isolated area, then controlled by various ethnic insurgents.

Lintner lives in Chiang Mai, northern Thailand, and most of his recent work can be viewed at www.asiapacificms.com.